CORE LINGUISTI

Core Syntax

A Minimalist Approach

Johan Alberto
Oe La Rosa Yacomelo
jmd6493@psu.edu

OXFORD CORE LINGUISTICS

General Editor
David Adger

Published

Core Syntax
A Minimalist Approach
David Adger

I-Language
An Introduction to Linguistics as Cognitive Science
Daniela Isac and Charles Reiss

In preparation

Linguistic Theory
Peter Svenonius

Core Syntax

A Minimalist Approach

David Adger

OXFORD

UNIVERSITY PRESS

OXFORD
UNIVERSITY PRESS

Great Clarendon Street, Oxford OX2 6DP
United Kingdom

Oxford University Press is a department of the University of Oxford.
It furthers the University's objective of excellence in research, scholarship,
and education by publishing worldwide. Oxford is a registered trade mark of
Oxford University Press in the UK and in certain other countries

© Oxford University Press, 2003

The moral rights of the author have been asserted

First published 2003
Reprinted 2012

British Library Cataloguing in Publication Data
Data available

Library of Congress Cataloging in Publication Data
Data available

ISBN 978-0-19-924370-9

Contents

Preface

Core syntax is a somewhat cheeky name for a textbook. There are many 'core' aspects of syntax, depending on the viewpoint you take. In this book, I have tried to highlight three aspects. Many working syntacticians will disagree that these are *the* core areas, but I hope that everyone will agree that they at least provide a consistent perspective.

First, I have tried to emphasize that an important part of doing syntax is constructing a consistent theoretical system within a broad research agenda. The research framework that I have adopted is that of the Minimalist Program, a perspective that has emerged from the work of Noam Chomsky. In the book, I develop certain theoretical ideas which stem from the concerns articulated by Chomsky, and I use these ideas to build a system. I have tried to make the system as consistent (both conceptually and notationally) as I can, and I have tried to emphasize the interactions between theory, analysis, and data, and how developments in any one of these areas affect the others.

The second way in which the material of the book could be considered 'core' is that I have tried to cover a broad range of phenomena which form a (somewhat nebulous) area of empirical importance as far as the recent history of the subject is concerned. These phenomena have also been chosen because they can be used to motivate or to challenge the theoretical ideas that are being developed. I hope that by doing this, students will acquire both an overview of some important areas of empirical concern, and an appreciation of how syntactic arguments are developed.

The third aspect on which I have concentrated is methodological, and it has to do with the importance of rigour in helping to clarify ideas, and the concomitant importance of formalization as a skill which will help students to think through syntactic questions. The strictly derivational approach I have adopted, and the explicit presentation of how derivations are constructed, should help students to learn to be comfortable with some of the formal aspects of syntactic theory.

I hope that the book's emphasis on these three aims will mean that it will outlive the details of current theoretical fashion. The particulars of the theory will certainly change, but the kinds of syntactic argumentation deployed in the field and the importance of rigour and consistency will surely remain, as will, I think, the kinds of questions raised by the research agenda adopted here.

Aside from these three aims, I have also tried to tease out how a theory based on invariant syntactic principles, interacting with the parameterization of featural properties of functional heads, really does provide at least one answer to the Poverty of the Stimulus questions raised by Chomsky. The sections in the chapters which concentrate on this aspect of syntax also try to raise the further question about how parameterization itself can be restricted. This highlights a number of open questions, as does the approach to island phenomena sketched in the final chapters. I hope that at least some students will be encouraged to try to find out answers to these and related questions themselves.

Because the Minimalist Program is a research agenda rather than a particular theory, and because one of my main aims in this book is to introduce students to how internally consistent syntactic systems are constructed, I have melded argumentation and analyses from the literature with ideas that have developed from the particular theoretical choices I have made. For example, the checking theory I have adopted allows variation in the strength of the values of features, rather than in the features themselves, with effects on numerous analyses and on the encoding of parametric variation; the approach to verbal inflection I propose is different from others in the literature (although I do discuss the alternatives); the analyses I sketch for passivization, for subject wh-questions, and for verb-second, for example, are not derived directly from the primary literature, but rather arise from the particular implementation of Minimalism developed here. This was the best way I could see of achieving my three aims of theoretical consistency, a reasonable coverage of core phenomena, and a fair amount of analytical rigour. I hope that readers knowledgeable about the current Minimalist literature will forgive any liberties I have taken.

Finally, some thank-yous: first, to three anonymous OUP reviewers, two of whom later became onymous as Bob Borsley and Liliane Haegeman. All three reviewers went well beyond the call of duty, and provided the book with much needed direction, and I'm hugely grateful to them, as I am to my editor at OUP, John Davey, for advice and encouragement. I'd also like to thank Bob Friedin, Jason Merchant, and Andrew Radford for comments on an earlier draft and Bernadette Plunkett and Gillian Ramchand, both of whom used earlier versions of the book in their teaching, and who provided me with detailed comments about how it was structured. Many thanks too to all the students who have been subjected to earlier versions of this material, and whose patience and forbearance was, at times, amazing. I also need to acknowledge a debt to Donna Jo Napoli's book *Syntax*, from which I have adapted many of my exercises. Bernadette and Gillian join a band of trusty linguistic old faithfuls who have been on call for me whenever I needed to check out that an idea wasn't completely insane. Others in this band are Daniel Harbour, Ian Roberts, George Tsoulas, and the Tequila Cabal. Final thanks are to Anson, *sine quo nihil*.

1

Core Concepts

1.1 What is a sentence?

1.1.1 Utterances, propositions, and sentences

Certain utterances of human languages seem to have a special status, in that they express what you might call 'complete thoughts'. So if I were to say, "It's rather hot, today", any native English speaker will interpret me as conveying a message which is somehow complete. Note that *you* could say exactly the same thing, "It's rather hot, today", which will also convey a complete message. However, if I do this on Sunday, and you do it on Monday, the message communicated is different. Linguists say that the **proposition** expressed is different.

A proposition is that aspect of the meaning of a sentence which allows us to say, "Yes, that's true" or "No, that's false". It describes a state of affairs that holds in the world, and its correspondence with that state of affairs allows us to attribute truth or falsity to the proposition. There are other aspects of sentence meaning which we will address later in the book, but propositional meaning will be the most relevant for us here.

Note that, even though we have expressed different propositions, we have both used exactly the same linguistic form. We have both said the same **sentence**. This little scenario gives us some grasp of a core idea in syntax, the idea of a sentence as an abstraction over **utterances** which have the same form. Linguistic form is not important to a proposition. The same proposition is conveyed by the English sentence (1), the French sentence (2), and the Scottish Gaelic sentence (3), even though these sentences are in different languages:

(1)   John saw Stephan.

(2)   Jean a vu Stephan.

(3)   Chunnaic Iain Stephan.

So a proposition is that aspect of the meaning of a sentence which says something about a state of affairs, and an utterance is an actual use of a sentence. How do we define sentence itself then?

Take any act of linguistic communication, an utterance of (1) by me to you, for example. Somehow you glean a proposition from my utterance of (1). How do you do this? The common-sense answer is that it's because we both know the same language. Focusing in more precisely on the question of how we define sentences, it appears that there is something about my knowledge of English which is shared with your knowledge of English, and that this includes how to form sentences of English, and how the proposition expressed by a sentence depends on its form. Clearly the form is important, since if you were to utter some sequence of sounds that did not form a sentence of English, then I'd have a much more difficult task in understanding what proposition you were trying to convey.

Part of our shared knowledge of language, then, allows us to construct sentences, which we can then utter. Again, the idea of a sentence is more abstract than the idea of an utterance (which is something that you can hear, record, feed into a computer as sound waves, etc.). A sentence itself is something which can't be recorded, heard, or electronically manipulated, only **uses** of sentences can. These stretches of words that you are now reading, delimited by capital letters and full stops, and interspersed with other markings, are uses of sentences. The sentences themselves are defined by the knowledge of English that I put to use in writing them, and that you use in comprehending them. Although it sounds counter-intuitive, what you see on this page are technically utterances, in that they have an external, physical manifestation. Sentences, on the other hand, are internal, mental entities, which have an abstract form.

1.1.2 Acceptability, grammaticality, and stars

The form of sentences is what will mainly concern us in this book. The example I went through above showed that the same sentence form can be used to express different propositions on different occasions of utterance. We can also express the same proposition using different sentence forms. So most people would agree that essentially the same message is conveyed by both the sentences below:

(4)   That monkey is eating the banana.

(5)   The banana is being eaten by that monkey.

And most people would find it difficult to say what message is conveyed by (6) and would reject it as a sentence of English:

(6)   By is eaten monkey banana that the being

Why is (6) not an **acceptable** sentence of English? Well obviously the **order** of the words matters. (6) uses exactly the same words as (5) but the order in which the words come in (6) is somehow not an order which English allows. Acceptability, however, doesn't just depend upon the order of words. (7) is just as unacceptable as (6), but the order of the words seems to be fine (it's just like the order in (4)), it's the *form* of the words that makes the sentence unacceptable, the word after *is* should have the form *eating*, not *ate*:

(7)   That monkey is ate the banana

As well as clearly unacceptable sentences like (7) and (6), we also find sentences which seem odd in some way.

(8)   The amoeba coughed

The acceptability of this sentence depends upon the context in which it is uttered. (8) is unacceptable to most speakers if someone just says it out of the blue. However, one can easily imagine contexts where (8) is quite fine: in a fantasy novel for example, or as a description about what's going on in a children's cartoon. The form of (8) does not appear to be a determining factor in our judgements of its acceptability, it is rather the proposition that is expressed which we baulk at. The acceptability of (8), then, appears to be dependent on our view of the world. In most people's view of the world, amoebas don't cough or faint, and so we judge (8) as unacceptable because it conflicts with our expectations about what words can mean, and about how the world works.

There are also cases of unacceptable sentences which appear to be semantically plausible, but which seem to be awkward. An example of such a sentence is (9):

(9)   I looked the number which you picked out at random by using a needle and a phonebook up.

This sentence becomes more acceptable if the word *up* is placed immediately after the word *look*:

(10)   I looked up the number which you picked out at random by using a needle and a phonebook.

Another way of making this kind of sentence more acceptable is by making the distance between *look* and *up* shorter:

(11)   I looked the number up.

The unacceptability of (9) might have an explanation in terms of how we process the sentence. In an intuitive sense, the words *look* and *up* are closely associated with each other. In (10), they are pronounced together, while in (11) they are separated by a small number of words. In (9), however, there are fifteen words between *look* and *up*. One hypothesis to pursue would be that, on processing the sentence, the hearer accesses the word *look* and expects the word *up* to appear next. However, the hearer has to wait quite some time for the expected word to appear, and presumably process a fairly complex structure in the meantime. We might, therefore, put the unacceptability of (9) down to the fact that the connection between *look* and *up* is difficult to make because there is too much other processing going on.

This kind of explanation for unacceptability is known as a **parsing** explanation. It assumes that the problem with the sentence is not that it does not conform to the rules of the language, but rather that human beings processing (or parsing) the sentence have a hard time assigning the right structure to it. In the most extreme cases we might conclude that the sentence can't be parsed at all—it is **unparsable**.

Notice that this kind of explanation does not appear to be available for examples like (7). We cannot make the sentence any better by reducing the distance between the relevant words. The problem appears to be that the language simply requires a particular relationship to hold between these words, and in (7) it simply doesn't hold. This kind of explanation for the unacceptability of (7) is known as a **grammaticality** explanation, and sentences like (7) are termed **ungrammatical**.

Syntacticians express the claim that a particular sequence of words is not a grammatical sentence of the language under discussion, by marking that sequence with a star, like this:

(12)   *By is eaten monkey banana that the being

(13)   *The monkey is ate the banana

Sometimes a sequence of words is called a **string**. Putting a star at the start of a string is a claim that it isn't a grammatical sentence of the language in question.

Acceptability concerns making a judgement about the status of a string as part of a language, and as such it's an intuition that speakers of the language have. The claim that a sentence is difficult to parse, or that it is ungrammatical, is an attempt to explain its (un)acceptability. As linguists, we cannot know in advance whether a string of words is unacceptable because it is difficult to parse, because it is ungrammatical, or because of some other factor.

The acceptability of a sentence will also often depend upon whether the sentence expresses the intended meaning. Here the judgement doesn't state whether the string is acceptable or not, but rather whether the string is assigned the meaning that is specified. So sometimes you might see the claim that a sequence of words is 'starred (*) under the intended interpretation'. What this means is that the sentence is unacceptable as an expression of a particular proposition. This use of the star is most common when contrasting the meanings of sentences. For example, (14) has the meaning that there are some people in the garden, and not the meaning that it's generally a property of people that they're in the garden, while (15) works in the opposite way, it means that, as a rule, people are stupid. It cannot mean that there exist some stupid people. It is therefore said to be starred under this interpretation.

(14)   People are in the garden.

(15)   People are stupid.

What we have here is a case where the form of the sentence is fine, and the sentence is perfectly grammatical, but the interpretation of the sentence is not the one that one might expect, given the interpretation of other similar sentences.

Here is another example of the same kind of thing:

(16)   How did Julie ask if Jenny left?

This sentence can be a question about the way that Julie asked something (loudly, rudely, etc.), and it is perfectly fine under this interpretation. However, the discussion of this example might make it clear that the intended interpretation is a question about the way that Jenny left (angrily, jauntily, etc.). This kind of interpretation is perfectly possible for a sentence like (17):

(17)   How did Julie say that Jenny left?

However, this is *not* a possible meaning of (16). In that case, we would say that (16) is ungrammatical under this interpretation.

Why do linguists use the star to express the idea that a sentence doesn't have the meaning that might be expected, as well as the idea that a string isn't actually a sentence at all? The reason is that the propositions expressed by sentences are not just dependent on the words in a sentence, but also on the ways that those words are put together. It's our knowledge of language that allows us to put together words into sentences, and something about that knowledge simply stops us from putting the words in (17) together in the same way as those in (16). So speakers of English can't assign a structure to (16) that will give us the same interpretation as the structure for (17).

Remember that we assign a star to a sentence if we think that the explanation for its unacceptability is that it does not conform to the requirements of the **grammar** of the language under discussion (see Section 1.1.3). Put more directly, we assume that speakers can't legitimately assign a structure to the particular string in question at all. In the example we have just discussed, exactly the same situation obtains: speakers can assign two structures to (17) but only one to (16). The absence of one of the structures can be marked with a star, as long as we refer in the surrounding text to the intended interpretation, so that we know which structure is relevant.

1.1.3 Form and order

Let's go back to more obvious facts about the form of a sentence. We can see that the order of words is also relevant to the message (proposition) conveyed by the sentence, so (18) does not mean the same as (4), even though it consists of exactly the same words:

(18)   That banana is eating the monkey.

As was mentioned above, there also appear to be certain relationships between the forms of the words in sentences. So in (18), the first and third words have the form they do because of the form of the second word. If we change the form of the second word, then the forms of the first and third words have to change too:

(19)   Those monkeys are eating the banana.

The same relationship holds in (19), and we can't, for example, swap *are* for *is*, or vice versa:

(20)   *Those monkey are eating the banana

(21)   *That monkeys is eating the banana

Native speakers of English generally judge such sentences not to be part of their language, and therefore as ungrammatical. The relationship between the second word in these sentences, and the other words which seem to take their lead from it, is known as **agreement**, and we will come back to it later on in the book.

Word order and agreement are fairly obvious properties of sentences. When the right word order, or the right agreement relationships are not expressed in a sentence, native speakers know this, and judge the sentence as unacceptable. These phenomena are not obviously susceptible to an explanation in terms of parsing, and we hypothesize that the problem is a purely structural one.

The meanings of sentences are also things which native speakers have strong intuitions about, as we saw above. Most obviously, native speakers of English intuitively know that (4) and (18) differ in meaning, and that (22) has two meanings (i.e. it is **ambiguous**):

(22)   The monkey wrote a poem on its favourite banana.

One meaning of (22) involves the banana being written about, while the other meaning has the surface of the banana actually being written on.

All of these phenomena, and this is only a tiny taster, arise because sentences of English, and all other languages, are not just built out of words strung one after the other in an utterance or on a page, but rather, as mentioned already, because they have a **structure** which specifies certain relationships as holding between the fragments of language that the sentence is made out of. One of the major tasks of linguists who are interested in syntax is to discover what the basic building blocks of language are and what relationships hold between them. The general term that is used to refer to these relationships is the **syntactic structure** of the sentence.

1.2 Tacit knowledge

When I used the word **knowledge** in the last section, I meant knowledge in the particular technical sense that's used in linguistics: knowledge of language isn't like knowledge of history. My knowledge of history is extremely **partial**, **forgettable**, **explicit**, and **learned**. I know that William Wallace was a Scottish Highlander who fought against the English some centuries ago. I'm not sure when he was born, or when he met his (rather grizzly) death—so my knowledge about him is partial. My knowledge of English structures is at the other end of the spectrum. Although you might introduce a new word to me, it's unlikely that you'll be able to introduce to me a new way of building up a sentence of English (unless that structure is special because of the dialect you speak, or because it used to be a structure of English but is no longer). Similarly, I am sure that, at some time, I knew the date of William Wallace's death, but I've forgotten it. There's no sense in which I can be said to forget how to construct sentences of English, unless I suffer a serious brain trauma—something which certainly isn't necessary to make me forget historical dates.

Perhaps the most important difference between knowledge of language and other types of knowledge is that the latter are easily made explicit: I can tell you that Scotland merged its Parliament with that of England in 1707, and then opened a new devolved Parliament in 1999. However, trying to explain how sentences are constructed is something which isn't accessible to my conscious mind: all I can do is use various types of scientific method to try to uncover how it works. Even simple statements like 'a sentence is constructed from an initial subject followed by a predicate' immediately throws us into the realm of technical notions. What's a subject? What's a predicate? Is this the only way to build up a sentence, and if not, then what are the other things involved?

Yet we all possess a highly intricate system that allows us to determine whether certain utterances correspond to sentences of our native language. You know, for example, if you are a native English speaker, that I can utter (23), and that this corresponds to a sentence of English, whereas if I utter (24), although you might be able to glean some message from it, it simply doesn't correspond to any sentence of English:

(23)   Anson is incredibly difficult to please.

(24)   *Anson is incredibly difficult to be pleased

How do you know this? Are you able to articulate why (24) is unacceptable? In fact, it's just not obvious why (24) should be so bad. The kind of knowledge of language which allows you to make this judgement is not accessible to you—the term for this is **tacit knowledge**.

Finally, knowledge of language is acquired in a different way from other types of knowledge. Most children have a command over the core structures of their language by the time they are three. The following sentences were produced by a child at the age of three years and two months (see Pinker 1994, ch. 7):

(25)   Can I put my head in the mailbox so the mailman can know where I are and put me in the mailbox?

(26)   Can I keep the screwdriver just like a carpenter keep the screwdriver?

These sentences contain errors in agreement ((25) contains *I are* rather than *I am* and (26) contains *a carpenter keep* rather than *a carpenter keeps*), but display a complex structure involving combining sentences and operating on their parts. (You will meet many of the syntactic operations that are involved in constructing these sentences later on in the book.) Even more remarkable are experimental studies which show that children at this young age seem to have flawless access to aspects of the structure of sentences which do not seem to come from the data to which they are exposed.

One classic example comes from the syntactic rule which forms yes/no questions in English. Yes/no questions look as follows:

(27)   Has Jenny eaten a cake?

(28)   Will Anson come to the party?

Certainly, such questions appear in the data to which young children are exposed. It might seem a simple task to work out the rules for forming such a question. The examples above are clearly related to the following sentences:

(29)   Jenny has eaten a cake.

(30)   Anson will come to the party.

But notice that when a child hears a yes/no question like those above, that child might be able to dream up any number of rules to construct them from the related sentences:

(31)   1. Swap the first two words around.

2. Swap the first verbal element with the first noun phrase.

3. Put the verbal element that follows the subject in front of it.

It turns out that the right rule is the third one. If the child were to adopt the first rule, then he/she should produce sentences like the following, where the (a) examples give the plain sentence types and the (b) examples give the result of applying the rules:

(32)   a.   The man has eaten the cake.

b.   *Man the has eaten the cake

(33)   a.   The woman who is singing is happy.

b.   *Woman the who is singing is happy

If the child were to adopt the second rule, then we would expect the following results. Don't worry about the notion of **noun phrase** for the moment. It simply means that the first two words are grouped together:

(34) a. The man has eaten the cake.
      b. Has the man eaten the cake?

(35) a. The woman who is singing is happy.
      b. *Is the woman who singing is happy

However, Crain and Nakayama (1987) conducted a series of experiments and showed that the errors expected under these hypotheses never occurred. This was true for children as young as three years and two months. All the children appear to use the third, and apparently most complicated rule, and produce the correct results:

(36) a. The man has eaten the cake.
      b. Has the man eaten the cake?

(37) a. The woman who is singing is happy.
      b. Is the woman who is singing happy?

This kind of argument is known as a **Poverty of the Stimulus** argument: the idea is that the linguistic stimulus that a child is exposed to is not rich enough to provide the information the child needs to acquire the language. It attempts to show that children are in possession of kinds of knowledge about their language which simply isn't plausibly in the input data that they hear.

Even more thought provoking is that fact that, at this point in their development, children are immensely ignorant of the kinds of knowledge that become so important in later life for passing exams, earning money, and preparing food. Yet they can put together highly complicated sentences, with only small deviations from what adults do. The system of knowledge they have is developed to such an extent that it far outstrips any other aspect of their cognitive development which is not obviously instinctual (vision, locomotion, eye-contact, using emotional responses to control their environment). But this knowledge hasn't been taught to them by anyone. In fact, the idea of teaching one-year-old children that sentences are constructed out of subjects and predicates, or that they involve putting together nouns, verbs, and other things in particular ways, is absurd. In many senses, this tacit knowledge is far more like instinct than it is like other kinds of knowledge.

So why, you might ask, do we call it knowledge at all? The answer really has to do with a philosophical discussion that goes back to Plato in the fourth century BCE, who asked the question of how we can know so much with so little input (Plato's main area of discussion was geometry rather than language), a problem which Chomsky has christened **Plato's Problem**. Plato proposed, as a solution, that there are certain abstract forms which we grasp because we are human beings, and therefore our souls exist in the realm of these abstract forms. Knowing something corresponds to our souls grasping these abstract forms. Because the problem is so similar to the problem of how human beings grasp the abstract forms associated with language, we still talk about this as a **problem of knowledge**.

Philosophers often find linguists' use of the term knowledge for the relationship we bear to our language problematic because of the common-sense use of the word knowledge as 'being in possession of true facts', or 'true justified belief'. The linguists' response to this is that knowledge is as reasonable a word as any, but if philosophers want to maintain some special status for the word knowledge, then we'll use something else (for example, **cognize** has been suggested). The linguists' use of the term knowledge (and more especially tacit knowledge) should be taken as a technical term in linguistics.

Another common term for tacit knowledge of language is **grammar**. This is a word to be careful of because it is used in two technical ways: (i) a grammar is a speaker's tacit knowledge of their language; (ii) a grammar is a linguist's explicit theory of a speaker's tacit knowledge of their language. I will be careful in this book to distinguish the two, but it is as well to be sensitive to this distinction, since the two uses of 'grammar' are widespread. Chomsky tends to refer to grammar in the first sense as **I-language**, where I stands for Internal/Individual. So a speaker's I-language is his or her tacit knowledge of their native language and a linguist constructs a theory of this I-language.

We don't know a great deal about how I-language itself is manifested physically or biologically, although it's clear that at least some aspects of it are localized in particular positions in the brain. There are two areas of the brain's left hemisphere which appear to be particularly implicated in our linguistic abilities: **Broca's area** and **Wernicke's area**. We know that these areas are important because sometimes they are affected by some pathology or trauma, and particular linguistic deficits arise. For example, people with a trauma to Broca's area have selective problems in dealing with complex grammatical constructions, although their pronounciation may be fairly normal.

Some aspects of I-language are apparently determined by genetic factors. Researchers have studied families which appear to have a predisposition to **Specific Language Impairment** (SLI). SLI is a term for linguistic

impairments which cannot be easily tied down to more general cognitive difficulties. Myrna Gopnik and her colleagues have argued over a number of years
that the SLIs of one particular family can only be properly explained by genetic
factors, and moreover that these genetic factors affect language specifically.
Studies of identical and non-identical twins appear to back up this idea, and
recently, researchers in genetics have identified the mutation of a particular
gene in affected individuals (see the Further reading section at the end of this
chapter for details).

   Other aspects of I-language are clearly determined by environmental factors.
A child brought up in a linguistic community will acquire the language or languages of that community, no matter what that child's genetic inheritance. The
environment provided by the community provides the linguistic data which the
child needs and which she/he uses, in conjunction with what is provided innately,
to acquire her/his I-language.

   I-language, then, is the component of the mind of members of the human
species which allows us to link together meanings (which are in part propositional
in nature) with forms (sequences of sounds, strings of letters, collocations of
body signs in sign languages). The nature of I-language seems to be that it
is highly creative, in the sense that it can link an infinite array of meanings
to an infinite number of sequences of signs. Because of this, human beings can
communicate with each other in ways that no other species seems able to do, and
our ability to communicate is at least partially responsible for the astonishing
evolutionary success of our species. Without I-language, that is, without an
internalized syntax, we would be unable to communicate fluently, because we
would be unable to externalize our messages except in the crudest ways. Syntax
is, then, key to human achievement at a fundamental level. The project of modern
linguistics is to investigate and try to understand this crucial phenomenon within
the human mind, both as a goal in itself, and as part of a broader attempt to map
our cognitive abilities.

1.3 Syntactic theories

We have so far come to two conclusions: (i) that a sentence is an abstract mental
object, and (ii) that whether a sentence is part of a particular speaker's native
language or not is something which that speaker tacitly knows. We are now in
a position to make a first stab at saying what *syntactic* knowledge is: syntactic
knowledge (or just syntax) is that part of an I-language that is concerned with the

ways that sentences are put together out of basic parts. This is what we construct a theory of.

What is a theory? In the broadest terms, a theory is a statement of **general principles** or laws which can be used to explain some phenomena. We can have theories which apply in many different domains: theories of poetics, of social interactions and structures, of biology, of the physical world. There is no a priori way of deciding what constitutes an appropriate domain for a theory; that is, we do not know in advance of investigation whether a theory developed to explain big things (like the motion of planets) will also explain very small things (like the motion of sub-atomic particles). We do not even really know, in advance of study, whether there is a difference between, say, energy and matter—these concepts, which seem so different from a common-sense perspective, may turn out, after theoretical investigation, to be better understood as the same.

Apart from the domain of a theory (that is, the phenomena which it purports to explain), we have to consider what kinds of statements we can make as part of the theory. What are the statements about, and what possible relations do we allow to hold in these statements? In economic theory, the statements might be about goods and services and the values attached to them; in social theory, the statements might be about the categories that group individuals together or force them apart; in Newtonian physical theory, the statements might be about mass, force, acceleration, and other properties of physical bodies. Notice, once again, that we don't know what the statements are about in advance of investigation. What we do is develop a body of theoretical knowledge, and then explore this theory to determine what its consequences are. A successful theory engenders new and interesting questions, and provides accounts of phenomena in general terms. Part of providing an account of a theoretical domain is giving explanations of phenomena which have already been observed. If the theory is to be really successful, though, it should extend beyond the observed phenomena and make predictions about novel situations. These predictions should be able to be tested, and it should be possible to challenge the theory as it stands if the prediction is wrong.

Some of the most successful theories we have are theories of the natural world: of physics and chemistry and biology. As human beings we have what you might call a **folk understanding** of the natural world, given to us by our biology and by our experience. We know that when it gets dark, it tends to get colder, that someone pushed off a cliff will generally fall, and that if you step on to some water you will generally not float on it. We have also developed scientific understanding of these phenomena involving concepts such as energy, gravitation, and surface tension. Over the years, the theories of these concepts have become more and more remote from our folk understanding, requiring the development of highly abstract mathematical systems. Yet at the same time, these theories have become more successful: they make accurate predictions about what will happen in certain situations; they allow us to develop technologies to interact with the natural world in ways that our ancestors would have marvelled at; and they bring to light phenomena which were previously unobserved and help us to ask new and interesting questions about these.

One of the characteristics of theories of physics, genetics, biochemistry, etc. is that they have a formal aspect to them. By formal, we mean that they are developed as systems which are explicit and contain well-defined concepts. The importance of defining concepts explicitly is that it is then harder to misuse them. For example, if we have a definition of, say, a particular gene type which we use to explain some phenomenon, and then we try to use the same gene type to explain another phenomenon, we can check whether we really mean to use the same thing by investigating what the consequences of applying the same definition is in both cases. A formal approach is extremely useful, then, as a means of ensuring that our theory is really doing what we want it to do.

The approach to syntax that we will take in this book, and which is taken more generally in generative grammar, assumes that certain aspects of human psychology are similar to phenomena of the natural world, and that linguistic structure is one of those aspects. This approach is motivated by some of the phenomena we discussed in the last section: the physical structure of the brain and the genetic structure of human beings both appear to be implicated in linguistic structure. Given this, it might be possible to isolate those aspects of linguistic structure which depend on genetic and neural bases. Since those aspects of structure will have a physical base, it would be unsurprising if the kinds of theoretical approach which have been so successful in dealing with the natural world were helpful in understanding language.

Related to this perspective is a broader issue: one of the most interesting and successful endeavours in the field of human knowledge in general has been the general search for "mathematical patterns in nature" (Freidin and Vergnaud 2001, p. 647 refer to this research agenda as the Galilean approach after the famous Italian scientist (1564–1642)). On the assumption, motivated above, that at least some structural aspects of human language are part of nature, we can ask the question: what are the mathematical patterns in language?

Theoretical linguistics, as we will tackle it here, attempts to build theories of linguistic structure which posit various abstract concepts and determine the relations that hold between them. The consequences of these theories are then explored, and the concepts and relations in the theory thereby undergo development. Part of the general idea of developing theories is to keep them as simple as possible. We try to posit as few concepts and relations as we can get away with (an idea that goes back to the mediaeval English philosopher William of Ockham (1280–1347) and which is sometimes dubbed **Ockham's Razor**). Of course the effects of the theory might be extremely complex, but the base of the theory is kept as simple as possible. This injunction is, in part, a methodological one: it is easier to work with fewer concepts than with more.

Syntacticians, then, are interested in positing general, explicit, falsifiable, and simple theories about syntactic structure. Part of these theories is a statement of what the basic units of syntax are (technically these are known as syntactic **primes**, or syntactic **formatives**), and in what ways these units can be related to each other (that is, the **syntactic relations**). With a theory in place, a syntactician will develop an **analysis** of some set of data. The analysis relates various aspects of the data to concepts in the theory: it states what constitute the syntactic primes within the body of data, and investigates how the syntactic relations between those primes are established. Many different analyses may be possible of a particular set of data within a theory, although the theory will constrain the space of possible analyses. A good analysis may have consequences for the theory: it may show that this theory successfully extends to a new domain of data or it may show that the theory has to be modified in some way.

Syntacticians usually want their theories and the related analyses to be as **descriptively adequate** as possible: this means that the theory should contain sufficient means to adequately describe all of the different structures found in the language under investigation, as well as capturing the myriad interactions between these, thereby providing analyses of the structures of all of the possible sentences of the language. Descriptive adequacy applied to linguistic theory in general requires that this be done for all possible human languages. Descriptive adequacy is a much more stringent condition on the theory than mere **observational adequacy**, which simply says, 'get the right words in the right order'. Descriptive adequacy requires the theory to assign the right structures to the sentences in question.

There is another level of adequacy, **explanatory adequacy**, which is concerned with capturing the commonalities that all languages share but, at the same time, allowing only those languages which are actually possible human languages. An explanatorily adequate theory will be able to explain how, given a particular set of input data, a child fixes on the I-language that they do, rather than on some other I-language which is compatible with the data but makes the wrong predictions.

The aspects of I-language which are common to all of us are known as **Universal Grammar** (**UG**), and a theory of Universal Grammar will state the commonalities that hold across all possible languages (often called **Principles** of UG) and in what ways individual I-languages may diverge from these commonalities (known as the Parameters of Variation of UG—or just **Parameters**). For example, UG may require that all languages have agreement relations between a verb and its subject, but some languages may not pronounce this relationship, or it may obtain also between a verb and its object.

Now, although there are only a few parameters, the interaction of these with each other may lead to fairly divergent structures in the sentences which particular I-languages allow. However, if you think of a child who is born with UG, she or he does not need much exposure to particular sentence types in order to be able to infer just how the parameters for the language they are acquiring need to be specified, because there are only a few parameters, so there are only a few possible analyses. This means that a theory structured in this way will stand a chance of explaining exactly why children acquire language so quickly, and on the basis of data which does not seem to contain enough information to develop the grammar *sui generis* (see Further reading for Section 1.2).

1.4 Back to sentences

One of the core properties of I-language is that it characterizes a potentially infinite number of sentences, and it is this that leads to language having such an amazing capacity to express abstract thoughts and concepts. Many of the sentences we use in our everyday life we've never spoken before, and we seem to have no trouble creating new sentences to describe new situations. We appear to be able to use our I-language to relate an infinite variety of thoughts to an infinite number of sentences. How can this be?

Perhaps human beings simply have this huge number of sentences stored in their brains, and I-languages are just lists of these. This is impossible. Imagine you were to start with a sentence like:

(38)   Paul had an affair

and then add to it:

(39)   Paul had two affairs

(40)   Paul had three affairs . . .

(41)   Paul had eighty eight billion sixty three million forty-four thousand nine hundred and twenty three affairs . . .

(42)   Paul had eighty eight billion sixty three million forty-four thousand nine hundred and twenty four affairs . . .

As you can readily see, Paul's promiscuity is no match for the number of sentences we can have to describe it!

There are many ways to show that the human brain just isn't big enough to store all of the potential sentences. Consider (43):

(43)   Anson thought Julie had fainted.

Notice that we can take this sentence, and **embed** it inside another sentence, to give:

(44)   You said that Anson thought that Julie had fainted.

This process does not end here. We can now embed (44) inside another sentence:

(45)   David wrote that you said that Anson thought that Julie had fainted.

Of course we can keep this going, in principle, forever. In practice, we will keel over from exhaustion, boredom, or death. But the point remains that there isn't an upper limit to the number of sentences that we can in principle produce or understand. Each time we perform the embedding operation, we have a new sentence. Since we can continue the embedding operation indefinitely (at least in principle), there are an infinite number of such sentences.

Our ability to do these things *in principle* comes from our I-language. This is distinguished from our actual performance, which is what happens every time we use our knowledge of language on a particular occasion to produce an utterance, a written form, or a series of physical signs, if the language we are using is a sign language. This distinction between **competence** (which is just another term for I-language) and **performance** (i.e. putting the I-language to use) is important, in that it allows us to focus on what our language allows in principle, rather than in practice. We have already met this distinction when we discussed the difference between grammaticality and parsability. Parsing is a matter of performance, while grammaticality is a matter of competence.

It is possible to study actual uses of language by constructing large corpora of the things people say when they are telling stories, or having discussions, but if we are actually interested in the properties of I-language, this usually won't be necessary (although for some types of linguistics it is crucial: historical linguistics, because we can't ask the speakers, and sociological linguistics, because we're actually interested in the particular use of linguistic forms by different members of speech communities). Moreover, a corpus is of restricted use in another way, since the crucial cases to test our theory may not be available in the corpus. Finally, corpora have no information in them about the ungrammaticality of sentences, and such information is often crucial in theory development.

The property that I-languages have that allows them to be so creative is absolutely dependent upon the fact that sentences of I-languages have structure. If you look again at the examples above, you'll see that what we were doing is constructing a sentence, and then putting that sentence inside another sentence. A general, explicit, and fairly minimal way that we could state this would be something along the lines of (46):

(46)   S → *Paul had an affair.*

(47)   S → *You said that* S

(47) and (46) are known as **Phrase Structure Rules** (PS-rules). They are a kind of theoretical system that was used in early generative grammar, but have since been superseded. You can think of a PS-rule as an instruction to start with the symbol on the left of the arrow and then rewrite it as whatever is on the right of the arrow. This gives us a **derivation** of a sentence using the rules.

A simple derivation giving one sentence goes as follows:

(48)   a.   S (apply rule (46))
           b.   Paul had an affair.

Now let us try another derivation:

(49)   a.   S (apply rule (47))
           b.   You said that S (apply rule (47))
           c.   You said that you said that S (apply rule (46))
           d.   You said that you said that Paul had an affair.

You can see that the output of applying (47) actually provides a new input to which (47) can apply. The rules in (46) and (47) give rise to (or technically

generate), an infinite number of sentences. Now if we have a number of rules like these in our theory of language, and these rules introduce a range of different structures rather than just this very simple one, you can immediately see how the huge variety and infinite number of sentences found in human languages can arise on the basis of an extremely limited range of rules.

Sets of rules which refer back to themselves in this way (that is, where the same symbol occurs on both sides of the arrow) are called **recursive**, and languages which are generated by such rules are also called recursive languages. It is partly the fact that human languages are recursive that allows them to be creative in the specific sense mentioned above. And recursiveness is a simple, explicit property of certain kinds of rules. It seems that we have found a mathematical pattern in language.

Are there non-recursive languages?

Although this example is really just for exposition, it's easily seen that the recursiveness of human languages is a fundamental property that we want to be able to account for using as minimal a theory as possible. We will return to these issues more seriously in Chapter 3.

1.5 Summary

In this chapter we started off with the question: what's a sentence? We first distinguished semantic and physical properties of a sentence from its structural properties via the notions of proposition and utterance. We then came to the conclusion that human beings had the ability to assign a structure to a string of words via tacit knowledge of language. This conclusion was motivated by the different kinds of judgements we can make about strings of words: their parsability, their semantic well-formedness, and their structural well-formedness. We argued that tacit knowledge of language was unconscious, and partially innate, and we termed it I-language.

The next task was to work out how to build an understanding of I-language, and we proposed that one good way is to build a theory, which is formal, general, and maximally simple in its underlying concepts. This theory should provide us with the tools to develop analyses of particular sets of linguistic data, which will account for structural properties of sentences (form and order), and also, we hope, for how those structural properties interface with other language-related phenomena. One condition we would like our theory to meet is that it should provide an explanation for Poverty of the Stimulus facts, and for both linguistic universals and language variation. One candidate, we suggested, was a theory which assumed some very basic syntactic principles, which interacted with limited possibilities of variation (parameters).

Another important requirement on our theory is that it should be able to account for the fact that human languages are recursive in nature, allowing linkage between an infinite array of meanings and an infinite array of structures. It is this linkage which allows human communication to exist at all, and it is human communication which is the basis of the success of our species.

Further reading

Section 1.1.1

For the distinction between utterance, sentence, and proposition, see Cruse (2000), ch. 2; Saeed (1997), ch. 1; Kempson (1977), §3.4.1; and Lyons (1977), §6.2. For a more detailed philosophical discussion, see Lemmon (1966).

Section 1.1.2

Chapter 1 of Chomsky (1965) has an excellent discussion of the difference between acceptability and grammaticality. Pinker (1994), ch. 7 provides a very accessible overview of the idea of parsing and how memory limitations affect it. A more detailed overview can be found in Frazier (1987).

Section 1.2

See Pinker (1994), ch. 9, for a brief introduction to some of the issues in language acquisition. Brown (1973) gives a good range of examples of the kinds of structures that children use early on in their development, as do de Villiers and de Villiers (1985). See Crain and Lillo-Martin (1999), ch. 17 for an accessible discussion of the Crain–Nakayama experiment. Legate and Yang (2002) show that the kind of data that would be needed to rule out the first two rules discussed in the text is either non-existent, or statistically negligible. See also Marcus (1993). See Geschwind (1974) for evidence for localization of linguistic abilities in the brain and Grodzinsky (1990) for a discussion of different types of aphasia and their implications for linguistic theory. Gopnik and Crago (1991) and Gopnik, Dalalakis, Fukuda, and Fukuda (1997) provide some of the basic argumentation for a genetic basis for SLI, and Tomblin and Buckwalter (1998) discuss implications from studies of twins. Lai, Fisher, Hurst, Vargha-Khadem, and Monaco (2001) have identified a particular gene whose mutation seems to be responsible for familial SLI. See Jenkins (2000) for a more general discussion of the biological aspects of language.

Section 1.3

An excellent introduction to the nature of theories in the physical sciences is Feynman (1965). Chomsky (1965), ch. 1, is a classic reference for levels of adequacy for syntactic theory, although Chomsky (1986*b*) updates the discussion. See the introduction to Hornstein and Lightfoot (1981) for a general discussion of questions of explanation in linguistics. For a justification of the idea that language can be treated in the same way as other objects of the natural world, see Chomsky (1995*a*). We will address the question of principles and parameters througout the book.

Section 1.4

See Chomsky (1957), especially ch. 4, for a discussion of phrase structure rules, and Bach (1964), ch. 3 for further detail. A modern take on some of these issues including a good discussion of recursion is provided in ch. 1 of Lasnik (2000), which is worth a read.

2

Morphosyntactic Features

2.1 Introduction

In this chapter we will try to get an answer to the question of what it is that syntax regulates, such that the various facts about form and order that we saw in the previous chapter arise. We will introduce the notion of **morphosyntactic feature**, and tease out the ways that syntacticians motivate the existence of such features. Features play a role in syntax which is a little analogous to the role that atoms play in classical physical theories: they are the basic building blocks of syntax, and the ways that they may be combined, and the ways in which they may relate to each other, are what give rise to the observed phenomena.

2.2 Introducing features

The first task, now that we've outlined our basic assumptions, is to work out what the 'bits and pieces' of syntax are. That is, what is the nature of syntactic **formatives**?

The most obvious answer to this question is that syntactic formatives are simply words. However, this doesn't seem to be quite right. Recall that we looked at agreement in the first chapter, and saw patterns like the following:

(1)   The pig grunts.

(2)   The pigs grunt.

(3)   *The pig grunt

(4)   *The pigs grunts

We find exactly that same pattern with completely different words:

(5)   The bear snuffles.

(6)   The bears snuffle.

(7)   *The bear snuffle

(8)   *The bears snuffles

So clearly it is not the actual word that is relevant here. What seem to be relevant are rather **properties** of words. In the examples above, when the second word ends in an -s, then the third word cannot. Maybe then, what the agreement relation relates is **word shapes**. The shape of a word is called its **morphological form,** and we might hypothesize that the agreement relation relates purely morphological properties, such as whether the word ends in an -s or not.

However, this can't be right. Consider:

(9)   The man chuckles.

(10)   The men chuckle.

(11)   *The man chuckle

(12)   *The men chuckles

In these examples, the second word never ends in an -s, rather the middle vowel of the word changes shape. But the *pattern* we see is exactly the same. Likewise, in the next set of examples, the second word changes shape by adding -*ren*, and the pronunciation of the first vowel also alters:

(13)   The child wails.

(14)   The children wail.

(15)   *The child wail

(16)   *The children wails

The term for when a word form is changed by adding something to the end (or the start) is **affixation**, and the -s, or the -*ren*, in the examples above, are called **affixes**. Affixes that come at the start of a word are called **prefixes**, and those that come at the end are called **suffixes**. In the case of the alternation between *man* and *men* we have a **vowel change**. Other examples of words which pluralize via a vowel change are *foot* ~ *feet* and *mouse* ~ *mice*. When the whole word changes, so that you can't tell by the form of the words that they are related, then this is called suppletion. English does not have a clear case of a suppletive plural, but other languages provide examples: In Scottish Gaelic, the word for "wife", *bean*, has the plural *mnaoi*, and Tlapanec (a Mesomerican native language) has the contrast a^2da^3, "child" with e^3he^3 "children" (the superscripted numbers represent different tones of the vowels).

Now note that in the three sets of examples given above, the actual morphological forms are rather different, but the general pattern is the same. So the kind of property of words that we are looking for can't simply be stated in terms of morphological properties directly. This becomes actually even more obvious if we stop to think about other languages. Many languages have a relation of agreement like the one we have just seen in English, but the morphological resources that languages bring to bear in exhibiting agreement differ vastly. Some languages use suffixation, some use prefixation (such as Kiowa, a Kiowa-Tanoan language of Oklahoma), some use both (Georgian, a Kartvelian language of the Caucasus). But if the agreement relation is the same, then it can't relate word shapes directly. We need something more abstract, which is related by agreement, and which results in all these different word shapes. This more abstract thing is called a **morphosyntactic feature**, or just a **feature** for short.

A morphosyntactic feature is a property of words that the syntax is sensitive to and which may determine the particular shape that a word has. Features seem to be the core elements of languages that relate sound and meaning. To deal with the pattern above, we can say that the second and third word have to agree in their specification for a particular feature. In traditional terms, both must be either singular or plural. The singular form of the word *man*, is, simply, *man*; its plural is *men*. The plural of *child* is *children*, and of *cat* is *cats*. Some words have the same form for their singular and plural forms: *sheep* is an example. This word has no special form for its plural, but it triggers an agreement relation on the verb, just like the other words we have seen:

(17)   The sheep bleat.

(18)   The sheep bleats.

The plural feature clearly has an effect not just on the morphology of the word, but also on its meaning: in this case it affects whether we are talking about one child or more than one; one man or more than one, and so on. Features that have an effect on semantic interpretation in this way are called **interpretable** features. We shall see that the notion of interpretable features, and its opposite,

uninterpretable features, will play a significant role when we come to build up our theory of syntax (see Section 2.4.3 for examples).

Other languages also display the agreement relation. For example, in Arabic, the verb and the subject agree in gender as well as in number. Look at the following example:

(19) Al-'awlaaduu   qadim-uu
      The-boy-[MASC.PLURAL] came-[MASC.PLURAL]
      "The boys came."

This is an example of a sentence from Standard Arabic. The first word in the sentence includes a formative *al*, which corresponds to the English word "the", and a word *'awlaaduu*, which is a plural form of the word for "boy". This word is masculine. You can see all this information in an abbreviated form immediately under the word in the second line of the example. The second line of the example which specifies all this information is called a gloss. The second word in the Arabic corresponds to the word for "came" in English, but has some special marking on it to signify that it agrees with the first word. Essentially this is the *-uu* in the Arabic, which corresponds to the [MASC.PLURAL] specification in the gloss. Putting all this information together, we get the translation in the third line. This way of laying out examples from languages other than English is standard in syntax, and you'll soon get used to reading it if you are not already (see the helpful discussion in Tallerman (1999), ch. 1). The important thing to remember just now is that the first line is always the example, the second the gloss, and the third the translation.

Now compare this example with the following one:

(20) Al-bint-aani   qadim-ataa
      The-girl-[FEM.DUAL] came-[FEM.DUAL]
      "The two girls came."

Here we see the word for girl (which is feminine), with the same *al* prefix we met above. Classical Arabic, as well as having a way of distinguishing between singular and plural, also has a dual, where words which have a dual form are interpreted as being in some kind of a pair. So the dual marking on the first word of the example signifies that there are two girls, as you can see by looking at the translation. Notice that the second word also takes on a special form signifying that it too is feminine, and, moreover that it is dual. If we try to put the Arabic word for "the boys", which has a masculine plural form together with the word for "came" in its feminine dual form, the result is not a sentence of Arabic:

(21)   *Al-'awlaaduu   qadim-ataa
       The-boy-[MASC.PLURAL] came-[FEM.DUAL]
       "The boys came."

This shows us that the first and second words here are in an agreement relation. Given this, we can also predict that putting the Arabic word for "the two girls" together with the word for "came" in its masculine plural form will be ungrammatical, as, indeed, it is:

(22)   *Al-bint-aani   qadim-uu
       The-girl-[FEM.DUAL] came-[MASC.PLURAL]
       "The two girls came."

We can see, then, that the syntactic relation of agreement regulates dependencies between words in a systematic way in very different languages.

One of the tasks we will set ourselves in this chapter, then, is working out what features of words are relevant to syntax.

2.3 What are features?

A morphosyntactic feature, as we said above, is a property of a word. We just saw that in English there is a distinction between singular and plural words, and that this distinction usually (although not always) has an effect on the morphology of the word. We looked at singular and plural **nouns** and at **verbs** that agree with them (we'll use the terms 'noun' and 'verb' intuitively for the moment, and return to how these relate to features in Section 2.4.1). In an intuitive sense, the features responsible for the morphological difference are also responsible for a semantic difference. Usually a plural noun is associated semantically with a group of entities in the world, rather than with a single entity. However, once again the link between syntax and semantics is not strict: the word *scissors* is plural in form, but refers to an entity which is usually conceived of as a single thing.

As well as (usually) having an effect on the morphology and semantics of a word, a feature may also have an effect on the word's syntax. We saw in the previous section that an agreement relation might hold between nouns and verbs in sentences, and we will see in Section 2.4.3 that the featural content of a word also restricts the positions in which it can appear in a sentence.

2.3.1 Feature systems

How should we think of a feature? The simplest approach is to assume that a feature is just a property of a word in the same way as being hard is a property of glass and being bipedal is a property of human beings. Because we are developing a theory of syntax, we try to posit as small a set of features as we can which will allow us to explain the morphological, syntactic, and semantic behaviour of words in sentences.

Let us take the case of English first: we saw that English has a distinction between singular and plural nouns. We can capture this distinction with two features [singular] and [plural]. We can now give a (partial) feature specification for some English words:

(23) a. men [plural]
      b. man [singular]
      c. cat [singular]
      d. cats [plural]
      e. sheep [singular]
      f. sheep [plural]

There are two problems with this approach to English: first, it is not as simple as it could be, and secondly, we might wonder why we cannot have words which are simultaneously [singular] and [plural]:

(24) *blurg [plural, singular]

The reason that this analysis is not as simple as it could be is that we can get away with just a single feature: its presence would signify plurality, and its absence, singularity. This would give us an alternative analysis, as follows:

(25) a. men [plural]
      b. man [ ]
      c. cat [ ]
      d. cats [plural]
      e. sheep [ ]
      f. sheep [plural]

This second approach will work well fine for English, but what about Arabic, which appears to have a three-way distinction, between singular, dual, and plural. It is impossible to capture a three-way distinction with just one feature. With two features, however, it is possible to make a three-way distinction: [singular], [plural], [singular, plural]. Each of these **feature bundles** has its own morphological form and semantic interpretation. Words which are specified just as [singular] are singular morphologically and are interpreted semantically as single entities. Words which are syntactically [plural] have a plural morphological form and are interpreted as referring to a group of entities. Words which have the feature specification [singular, plural] are dual in form and are interpreted as referring to pairs of entities.

Evidence that this might be an interesting direction to pursue comes from Hopi, an Uto-Aztecan language of Arizona. Like Arabic, Hopi has three distinct numbers: singular, dual, and plural. The dual seems to be made up, at least morphologically, of the singular and the plural. This can be seen from the following examples:

(26)   Pam taaqa wari   (singular)
       that man ran-[SG]
       "That man ran."

(27)   Puma ta?   taq-t   yu?ti (plural)
       those man-[PL] ran-[PL]
       "Those men ran."

(28)   Puma ta?taq-t wari   (dual)
       those man-[PL] ran-[SG]
       "Those two men ran."

In the first example, we see a singular noun *taaqa*, "man" agreeing with the verb *wari*, "ran". In (27), we see a plural noun *ta?taq-t*, "men" occurring with the agreeing verb *yu?ti*, which is a suppletive plural of *wari*. To make the dual, we take the plural *ta?taqt* and the singular *wari*, put them together, and we get an interpretation that two men were running. This suggests that dual interpretations are constructed by having both [singular] and [plural] features in the same structure.

So, we could capture the difference between English and Arabic by assuming that English lacks the [singular] feature, while Arabic and Hopi both have it.

However, this explanation isn't really satisfying, since, with two features we would expect four possibilities, rather than three, and languages of the world don't seem to work like this: we simply don't find languages which distinguish four varieties of number feature, and treat them all on an equal basis. It is an interesting research question as to why this is.

One way of solving the problem is to say that languages always have a **default** feature that they fill in when there is no number feature specified. In English, we could say that the feature that is specified on the noun is [plural], so that words like *men* come specified with [plural] but words like *man* are specified as just [ ]. The idea would be that the default feature [singular] is always added to a noun which is unspecified for a number feature by a general mechanism, rather than by special stipulation for each word. The relevant rule could look something like the following:

(29) Add [singular] to a noun which has no other number feature.

This will have the result that we don't get dual in English, because default number features are never added to a word if that word already has a number feature. So a word which is specified as [plural] will never have the default feature [singular] added to it.

This approach has the advantage that it predicts the appearance of three number categories rather than four in languages like Arabic and Hopi. This is because, if a word were to be unspecified for number, a default [singular] feature would always be added. It follows that, although there are four possibilities given by the two number features, only three surface in the languages of the world.

There are other alternatives which seek to deal with the same problem. Some linguists have argued that features are more complex than the simple properties we have assumed here, and they have tried to explain the fact that systems with dual numbers are cross-linguistically rarer than systems which just make a singular $\sim$ plural distinction by proposing that the presence of certain features in a language depends on the presence of others (see Further reading at the end of this chapter for sources).

A closely related alternative to the view we have just been examining is to adopt the idea that features always have **values**, and that these values are **binary**. This means that a feature like [singular] will have the value [+] for a singular noun, and [−] for a plural noun:

(30) man [+singular, −plural]

(31) men [−singular, +plural]

A language with dual forms will allow [+singular, +plural] as a possible feature bundle, and will have a general constraint ruling out [−singular, −plural] bundles cross-linguistically.

In this kind of system, we need an extra constraint to force all the binary-valued features to appear in a bundle, and to always have a value. When this is the case, we say that the word is **fully valued** in its feature specification. This constraint will rule out a case like the following:

(32)   [+singular]

The reason we have to do this is to constrain the system so that it doesn't give us too many possibilities. If we allowed binary-valued features, and we also allowed these features to vary in whether they appear on a noun or not, then we immediately have nine possibilities:

(33)   a.   [+singular, +plural]
       b.   [+singular, −plural]
       c.   [−singular, −plural]
       d.   [−singular, +plural]
       e.   [+singular]
       f.   [−singular]
       g.   [+plural]
       h.   [−plural]
       i.   []

Natural languages don't appear to have nine morphologically or semantically distinguished numbers, so this is obviously not a good result.

A final approach to features is to assume that features may have other values than just [−] or [+]. Under this approach, we could treat [number] as the feature, and [singular] or [plural] as values of this feature. We might write this as follows:

(34)   a.   [number: singular]
       b.   [number: plural]

This system makes it more difficult to deal with dual forms by decomposing them into the interaction of singular and plural, but, it does give us a notation which makes it possible to refer to the natural class of number features. We will see, later in this chapter, that other features form natural classes as well.

The choice about which feature system is right is purely an **empirical** one; as far as number features go, the simplest system seems to be the one where a feature has no value, and may be present or not (such features are said to be **privative**). This system needs a single extra rule to add default features. The binary feature system gives rise to too many possibilities, and needs two extra constraints to rule out the non-occuring ones: the constraint against [−singular, −plural] bundles, and the constraint which forces words to be fully valued. The approach which assumes that there is a feature [number] which itself has the values [singular], [plural], and [dual], is simple, but has the disadvantage that, as it stands, it cannot express the idea that dual number is actually composed out of singular and plural.

On theoretical grounds, we should prefer the simplest system. However, there may be phenomena which force us to adopt a more complex approach. For now, we will adopt the privative feature system where possible. However, as we develop our theory of syntactic relations, we will have cause to treat some features privatively, but others as having values, as described above.

2.3.2 Interface rules

Once we've decided which features are necessary (and this can only be done by looking carefully at the facts of a language), we can use them to determine various things about the way that certain words are pronounced, or interpreted. That is, we can write **interface rules** which map from a syntactic structure consisting of features to a morphological (and eventually phonological) structure on the one hand, and to a semantic interpretation on the other. Take, for example, the following interface rule:

(35)   Pronounce a noun specified with [plural] by pronouncing the noun stem and then *s*.

(35) is a morphological interface rule that relates a syntactic specification (i.e. a collection of features) to a particular morphological form (stem + *s*). A **stem**, for the purposes of this rule, is just a basic form of the word with no affixes attached. It uses the syntactic features to build a morphological form. We could also have a semantic interface rule of the following sort:

(36)   Interpret a noun specified with [plural] as referring to a group of entities.

Neither of these two rules is correct as stated. The morphological rule ignores the fact, discussed above, that some nouns form their plurals in other ways than by addition of -*s*. It will therefore predict non-occurring forms like *mans*. Similarly, the semantic rule given here does not capture what it really means for something to be semantically plural, and it needs to be much more carefully worked out (so that the semantics of dual forms is correct, for example). However, the idea that the morphological and semantic components of the grammar **interpret** morphosyntactic features is a powerful one, and the examples given here just show that neither the morphology nor the semantics is trivial.

A syntactic feature like [plural], then, serves as a way of mediating sound and meaning: a particular feature gives rise to a particular morphological form which is pronounced, and a particular interpretation, thus acting as the link between how the sentence gets pronounced, and what it means. The syntax regulates how words with certain features relate to words with other features.

Before closing this section, we should address one further question. What is the set of features that human languages use? Unfortunately, no one has a definitive answer to this question. There is no linguistic equivalent to the periodic table. Human languages seem to make use of a wide variety of features, which relate to all sorts of aspects of our perceptions of the world: there are features which seem to relate to our core mental capacities such as location, time, measure, and counting; there are features that relate to core aspects of our use of language such as who is speaking, who is being addressed, what the topic of the conversation is, what has been mentioned already; there are also features which appear to relate to social and cultural factors such as who is considered to be in a position of authority in a verbal exchange. Finally, there are many features which seem to have no such provenance, and are internal to the linguistic system, signalling a particular syntactic position, or a particular kind of syntactic relation. We shall meet some of these features in this chapter, and others later in the book.

It may be the case that the set of features to which human beings' syntax is sensitive is universally available at the point of language acquisition and that the child's task is to pick out which particular ones are at play in his/her language. Alternatively, the set of features used in a particular language could be constructed on the fly, by the children learning it, or perhaps a mixture of these two positions it tenable, with notions like 'noun' and 'verb' being universal, but notions like 'subordinate in social standing' being constructed.

The question is hard to answer, but it is important to note that there are certain features that might be plausible, but that don't seem to occur in human languages: features whose semantic interpretation is "uttered on the day of a full moon", for example, or "to the left of the speaker's mother"; or features which have the morphological effect of reversing the word, or deleting every syllable which falls a prime number of syllables from the start of the word. Because of this, the more restrictive approach (and therefore the more explanatorily adequate) seems to be to assume that there is a set of universal features, and that the child's task is to select the features that are at play in the language he or she is acquiring.

The question, then, that can be asked, given our current stage of knowledge, is not "what is the set of features that we use?", but rather "what is the set of features that can be motivated in any particular analysis of a language?".

2.4 Motivating features

The way that we motivated the features discussed above ([singular], [plural]) was on the basis of the fact that: (i) there were relations between the shapes of words (recall that these are termed **morphological forms**), and (ii) there was an effect on semantic interpretation. This is the soundest basis on which to motivate a feature. There are weaker ways to do it too: we can motivate a feature if there is a variation in morphological form that makes no difference to semantic interpretation (form without meaning); or if there is an effect on semantic interpretation, but none on morphological form (meaning without form); or even if there is an effect on neither semantic interpretation nor morphological form, but the feature must be posited because a syntactic relation must be established or the wrong prediction about grammaticality will result. (We shall see that some **case** features fall into the latter category.)

2.4.1 Major category features

The most important set of features that is relevant to syntax is the set of **category features**. These are the features that are responsible for separating words into the traditional **word classes** of noun, verb, adjective, preposition, plus a few others. These features certainly seem to have some semantic basis: nouns, by and large, tend to pick out objects in the world, while verbs tend to pick out events, or actions. Of course, as is well known, this semantic criterion is by no means foolproof. A noun like *race*, for example, seems to pick out something that is clearly an event, and it's difficult to think of a verb like *exist* as denoting an event or action. However, there are also good morphological reasons to separate these two classes. In many languages, nouns and verbs have different morphological forms, and this can be seen to some extent in English:

(37)

Words ending in -tion, -al, -ment, . . . (all nouns)	Words ending in -ise, ize, -ate, -en, . . . (all verbs)
destruction, elevation, elation, station, eruption, removal, arrival, rebuttal, improvement, enlargement, involvement, replacement	improvise, despise, realize, compartmentalize, computerize, enervate, elevate, deflate, relegate, widen, shorten, blacken

Of course, appeal to these particular endings is not infallible. There are verbs that end in -*ment* (*ferment*), *station* can be used as a verb, and there are many words of all classes that end in -*ate*, and -*en* (*prelate*, *late*, *chicken*, *flaxen*). Moreover, there is a vast class of words in English which give no morphological signal as to their word class (*book*, *paper*, *clear*, ...). However, there are enough words that can be categorized by these endings to make appeal to morphological properties reasonable for setting up word classes, and hence the features that distinguish word classes.

In addition to these considerations, it turns out that the morphological form of certain features will depend upon their word class. So, if you take words like: *emotion*, *kindness*, *removal*, *protest*, then they may all add an -*(e)s*:

(38)   emotions, kindnesses, removals, protests

Compare this to words like: *listen*, *destroy*, *knead*, *predict*. These can all take the ending -*ed*:

(39)   listened, destroyed, kneaded, predicted

If we try to put -*ed* endings on the words in (38), only one of these (*protested*) is any good:

(40)   *emotioned, *kindnessed, *removaled, protested

If we try to put an -*s* ending on the words in (39), then all are fine, but they are certainly not interpreted in the same way as the words in (38):

(41)   listens, destroys, kneads, predicts

If we ignore meaning for a moment, we can see that we can separate the two groups of words (with the exception of *protest*) into two different classes purely on morphological grounds. Some of these words allow us to express a [past] feature, which is usually signalled by -*ed* (we will discuss the feature [past] in Section 2.4.3). If we bring in meaning, we see immediately that *protest* can have a radically different meaning in (38) (where it can refer to an event) and (40) (where it describes an action). We can also see that the words in (41), with an -*s* ending, have a different kind of meaning from the words in (38). *Protest* behaves as though it can fall into either class morphologically, and it is semantically ambiguous. But even with *protest*, the word changes its stress pattern depending on what its interpretation is: as a noun it is stressed on the first syllable, and as a verb it is stressed on the second. The lesson we can draw from this is that we can split words in English into at least these two traditional classes on the basis of morphological and interpretative evidence.

So it seems as if we want to make the generalization that whole classes of words (nouns vs verbs) are restricted as to the features that may occur on them ([past] cannot occur on nouns). Moreover, at least some of the words in these classes show distinctive morphological endings that reflect the class they are in. Finally, the two classes broadly seem to have different interpretations. These considerations would be enough evidence to allow our language learner to determine that there are features in English that distinguish these classes. We therefore posit the feature [N] which is part of the featural specification of nouns and [V] which serves in the same capacity for verbs. A plural noun like *men* will then have the partial feature specification in (42).

(42)   men [N, plural]

There is also morphological evidence that adjectives and prepositions constitute further separate classes. Many adjectives in English take on special morphological forms when used to compare things:

(43)   She is shorter; happier; cooler; older than he is.

These **comparative** forms cannot be added to nouns:

(44)   *emotioner, *kindnesser, *removaler

And when added to verbs, they give rise to a different interpretation, as can be seen from *protester*, which means "one who protests" and not "more full of protest" or some such.

As well as comparative forms, there are also **superlative** forms of adjectives, which involve the addition of -*est*. Again, these cannot be added to words in other classes:

(45)   She is the shortest; happiest; coolest; oldest of the lot!

(46)   *emotionest, *kindnessest, *removalest, *protestest

(47)   *listenest, *destroyest, *kneadest, *predictest

The last major class, prepositions, do not, in English, change their form at all. So we cannot add any of the morphological endings we have seen so far:

(48)   at: *atter, through: *throughs, on: *onned, by: *byest

In summary, then, we have four major word classes, which we usually abbreviate as just N, V, A, and P and which we could distinguish using the four features [N], [V], [A], and [P]. Another term for these features is **major category features**. We can refer to [N] as the N-feature of a word and [V] as the V-feature and so on. Note that since we have four categories, it is once again possible to define these by using two features. Here is one possibility:

(49)   a.   noun [N]
       b.   verb [V]
       c.   adjective [N, V]
       d.   preposition [ ]

This more minimal theory would predict that certain syntactic processes would class nouns and adjectives together and other processes would class adjectives and verbs together. It is difficult to show that this is correct before we know more about syntactic processes, so we will leave open the question of whether there is an empirical advantage to adopting the more minimal feature system.

This feature system also has the curious result that prepositions do not have category features. This is almost certainly not correct. An alternative, here, would be to adopt the binary system, giving the following feature specifications:

(50)   a.   noun [+N, −V]
       b.   verb [−N, +V]
       c.   adjective [+N, +V]
       d.   preposition [−N, −V]

In general, we will abstract away from the right choice of the particular feature system here, and simply adopt the idea that there are four category features. See the Further reading section for pointers to further discussion.

2.4.2 More on the content of words

So far we have been investigating what properties of words are relevant to the syntax. We haven't explicitly said what we mean by *word*. This is actually not an easy question at all. In literate societies, we can usually define a word by conventions as to how sentences are represented on the page; but this is not true of all literate cultures, and many linguistic communities are not literate and never have been. Moreover, the conventions for what words are may vary over time, with essentially the same forms being written with word boundaries or not.

For example, Classical Sanskrit texts were written without word boundaries at all and English prevaricates between using *can not* and *cannot*.

The approach that we will take is that it is syntactic features that are crucial, and that languages make different choices as to how they collocate syntactic features into more complex structures, for which the usual term is **lexical items**. These lexical items and the features that they are composed of enter into various syntactic relations. Different languages have different lexical items, not only in terms of pronunciation, but also in terms of the basic featural groupings in the languages. This goes as much for the meanings of lexical items as for their syntactic or phonological specification. So there is absolutely no necessity that different languages should have words that cover the same set of semantic concepts, or have the same set of syntactic features. On this view, it should come as no surprise that a language might have, say, colour terms that do not match the colour terms of other languages. The basic underlying semantic atoms are the same, but the lexical items, that is the molecules that they build up, vary across languages.

As an example, compare English with a language like Scottish Gaelic, where the same colour term is used for the sky and for grass (the term is *gorm*). Scottish Gaelic speakers (most of whom are bilingual in English) are perfectly aware that there is a spectral difference between the colour of the sky and the colour of grass, but their colour vocabulary is not sensitive to the same spectral differences as is the colour vocabulary of English. This is true throughout the colour system of Gaelic: the words *ruadh* and *dearg* are both used to refer to red things, but something which is *ruadh* cannot be shiny, whereas something which is *dearg* cannot be dull. *Glas* can roughly be translated as "grey", as in the colour of stones used to build a house, but it can also refer to what an English speaker would usually categorize as light green. Either *gorm* or *glas* can be used for green things, but only if they are natural, rather than man-made. The term for something which is green because someone has dyed it that colour is *uaine*. What is relevant, then, for many colour terms in Scottish Gaelic, rather than just the particular part of the spectrum, is whether the object is shiny or dull, whether it is man-made or natural, whether it is dark or light, and so on. These properties are as much part of the specification of these lexical items as the fact that they are adjectives, and the features that encode these distinctions are termed **semantic features**.

It seems likely that semantic features are universal, common to us all, but that different languages group semantic features in different ways so as to reflect the artefacts and concepts that are important to the culture in which the language is spoken. Of course, this cultural variation should not be over-emphasized: an enormous amount of what we think, perceive, taste, hear, etc. is common to all human beings as a result of our shared cognitive and physical limitations, and similar or identical collocations of semantic features will be involved in all languages for the lexical items that correspond to these concepts. It may even be the case that it is the universal aspects of our mental capacities that give rise to the basic semantic features. These are then combined in various ways to give rise to more complex concepts, which are then **lexicalized** (i.e. associated with a lexical item, including pronunciation and syntactic features) in particular languages.

Up to now, we have met number features ([singular], [plural]) and major category features ([N], [V], and possibly [A] and [P]). We have just seen that there are also semantic features. In addition, words have a pronunciation, which, if we are to be consistent, must be specified featurally as well. The features responsible for a word's pronunciation are termed **phonological features**, so a lexical item turns out to be a collection of phonological features, semantic features, and morphosyntactic features. It also appears to be the case that phonological features are universal in the sense of there being a universal set, some portion of which is selected in particular languages. Each language, then, specifies what its lexicon (i.e. its set of lexical items) is, constructing its lexical items from putatively universal featural domains. The child learning a language is faced with the task of internalizing this lexicon on the basis of the evidence that he/she hears and sees.

We will assume then, that for words which contain phonological and semantic features, these features are accessed by the interface rules in determining the actual pronunciation or interpretation. Note that nothing that we have said actually forces a word to have all three kinds of feature. In fact, we will encounter a number of syntactic formatives for which there is no good reason to assume a phonological feature specification, and whose pronunciation is determined wholly by the interface rules spelling out syntactic features.

If syntax relates features of words, then the question arises of whether phonological and semantic features of words are accessible to syntax. The standard view is that they are not. So the syntax only has access to the morphosyntactic features.

This is really a methodological restriction, but one with good support, at least on the phonological side. We haven't yet discovered any syntactic relations that hold between words with high vowels, or words that have nasalized first syllables. There are, of course, phonological effects of syntactic relations. So, for example, Welsh nasalizes the first consonant after the preposition *yn*, "in", and the word *fy*, "my":

(51)   Dolgellau ~ yn Nolgellau
             Dolgellau ~ in Dolgellau
             "In Dolgellau (a place name)"

(52)   pen ~ fy mhen
             head ~ my head

However, what we don't find are cases where some syntactic relation becomes established just because two words have, say, nasalized penultimate syllables. In this sense, syntax doesn't, in general, pay attention to what the phonology is doing, although it may dictate what the phonology must do. It makes sense then, to simply say that the syntax can't see the phonological features.

The argument is harder to make for semantic features. There do, in fact, seem to be syntactic processes that are sensitive to whether words denote males or females, singular entities or collections of them, and so on. We have seen examples of the latter already. The agreement phenomenon in English, which we have analysed as being sensitive to the feature [plural], could be thought of as a rule which is sensitive to the semantic category into which syntactically plural things fall. If this were the case, then we would have a syntactic relation (agreement) sensitive to a semantic feature (whether the object referred to is a single entity or a group of entities).

However, it actually seems to be the case that the syntactic rule does not care about whether the object referred to is semantically singular or plural, but rather it refers to whether the object is specified with the syntactic feature, [plural]. We can see this by taking a noun which is semantically singular, such as *scissors* and noting that it triggers plural agreement in a verb:

(53)   The scissors are/*is lost.

A similar example comes from Classical Greek. In this language, neuter nouns, whether they are themselves morphologically singular or plural, always trigger singular agreement on a verb, but plural agreement on an adjective:

(54)   kala   en   ta sphagia
             good-[NEUT.PL] be-[PAST.SING] the sacrifice-[NEUT.PL]
             "The sacrifices were good."

One might argue, in the face of this kind of evidence, that somehow scissors are conceived of as being semantically plural (perhaps because they are a pair), and that in Classical Greek, agreement with verbs is waived when the subject is neuter. However, there is further evidence that agreement must refer to syntactic relations; this evidence comes from the behaviour of gender features.

Many languages have what is called **grammatical gender**, where words are assigned a gender category (masculine, feminine, neuter) which bears no obvious semantic relation to what the word refers to. A good example comes, again, from Scottish Gaelic, where the word for "woman", *boireannach* is grammatically masculine. We can see this from the behaviour of adjectives. When an adjective follows a noun in Gaelic, it agrees with that noun's gender: feminine nouns cause a change in the initial consonant of the adjective, while masculine nouns do not. This change (termed **lenition**) alters *m* to *mh* and *b* to *bh* (as well as affecting other consonants in other ways). The agreement effect can be seen in the following examples

(55)   an duine mòr brèagha
       the man big handsome
       "the big handsome man"

(56)   a' chaileag mhòr bhrèagha
       the girl   big   handsome
       "the big handsome girl"

Here we see that the initial consonant of both adjectives changes to signify agreement with the gender of the noun. However, the noun *boireannach*, "woman" patterns with masculine, rather than feminine nouns:

(57)   am boireannach mòr brèagha
       the woman   big handsome
       "the big handsome woman"

(58)   *am boireannach mhòr bhrèagha
       the woman   big   handsome
       "the big handsome woman"

If one were to assume that somehow women are conceived of as masculine entities by speakers of this language, and hold to the idea that the agreement effect is sensitive to semantic features, then the following data become problematic:

(59)   Thànig   am boireannach mòr agus shuidhe i   sios.
       Arrive-[PAST] the woman   big and sat   she down.
       "The woman arrived and she sat down."

Here we have the pronoun *i*, "she" clearly signifying gender features (it contrasts with the pronoun *e*, "he", which is unacceptable in this context). The pronoun is semantically referring to some entity, and that entity is, in the present case, the woman. Since the pronoun is feminine, it makes sense that the pronoun's features are the ones which are picking out something semantic, which means that there must be syntactic features on the noun to ensure the appropriate agreement with the adjective *mòr*. This means that the noun must have a syntactic feature [masculine] and a semantic feature [feminine]. Agreement accesses the syntactic feature, and pronominal reference the semantic feature. Agreement is, then, a syntactic process accessing syntactic (not semantic) features; it contrasts with pronominal reference, which is essentially semantic.

A similar example can be constructed in modern spoken Dutch. In this language the word *meisje*, "girl" is neuter. It occurs with the neuter **article** and triggers neuter agreement on **relative pronouns**. Consider the following contrast:

(60) <u>De</u> man *die*   het boek leest
      the man that-[MASC] the book read-[PRES]
      "The man who reads the book"

(61) <u>Het</u> meisje *dat/*die*   het boek leest
      the girl   that-[NEUT]/*that-[MASC] the book read-[PRES]
      "The girl who reads the book"

Here we can see that there is agreement of the article (underlined) and the relative pronoun (italicized) with the noun. We will look at articles and relative pronouns in more depth later in the book. What is important here is that there is a clear agreement relationship showing up.

Once again, if we refer to the girl in question with a pronoun, we must use the feminine pronoun rather than the neuter one:

(62) Het meisje zei   dat   ze   het boek leest
      the girl   say-[PRES] that-[NEUT] she-[FEM] the book read-[PRES]
      "The girl says that she reads the book."

(63) *Het meisje zei   dat   het   het boek leest
      the girl   say-[PRES] that-[NEUT] it-[NEUT] the book read-[PRES]
      "The girl says that she reads the book."

On the assumption that the pronoun's function is the semantic one of picking out a referent, these examples show that the neuter agreement that the word *meisje* triggers on a relative pronoun is sensitive to a syntactic rather than a semantic feature.

In general, then, we assume that syntactic relations like agreement access syntactic features, and not phonological or purely semantic features. Some syntactic features have a transparent effect on interpretation (so, by and large, nouns with a [plural] feature in English are interpreted as referring to more than one entity), but some do not. We will assume, then, that syntactic relations hold between purely syntactic features.

2.4.3 Some more minor features

Phi-features

Armed with these ideas, let's return to other features that are relevant to the syntax of English.

Consider the verb *be*. It varies its form in the following way:

(64)

	Present	
I am		we are
	you are	
he/she/it is		they are
	Past	
I was		we were
	you were	
he/she/it was		they were
	Imperative	
	be	

If we look at the past and present forms in the table, we can see that in both sets (a set of forms is called a **paradigm**), the verb has the same form for *we*, *you*, *they*, and plural nouns. Let us assume that the feature that distinguishes these is [plural], which we have met before. Notice that even though *you* will have the feature [plural], it does not necessarily pick out more than one entity, so we see that the morphosyntactic feature does not always have a predictable semantic interpretation, something which reinforces the idea that the semantic interpretation of a feature is not accessible to syntactic processes.

There is also a distinction in the present between *I*, and the other non-plural forms. The traditional way to distinguish between these forms is to appeal to a feature which is related to who is speaking. This type of feature is termed **person**, and there are usually assumed to be three such features: [first], [second], and [third] (these are often just written as 1, 2, and 3). The pronouns *I* and *we* are specified as [1]; the pronoun *you* as [2]; and all other forms as [3]. Intuitively, the interpretation of [1] is related to the person speaking, or a group of people identified with that person; [2] is related to the person or persons addressed by the utterer; and [3] is related to anyone else.

(65)

I [1, singular]	We [1, plural]
you [2, singular]	you [2, plural]
He/she/it [3, singular]	they [3, plural]

Note that this analysis of the pronominal system seems to be rather unconstrained, since we have three-person features. If we were to allow the features to co-occur, in the same way as the feature bundle [singular, plural] co-occurs in our analysis of dual agreement, then we would expect languages to allow the following possibilities: [1], [2], [3], [1,2], [1,3], [2,3], [1,2,3], [ ]. Even if we exclude the empty bundle on the assumption that pronouns must have a person feature, we still have seven possible distinctions, whereas in English, we see only three.

We can rethink this system so that it is more minimal (and hence satisfies Ockham's Razor better) by assuming that we have only the features [1] and [2]. Third person would then simply be [ ], that is, someone who is not speaking, nor being talked to. Note that this analysis differentiates the person system from the number system: The former allows a pronoun to be unspecified for person, while the latter requires that nouns are specified for number (and imposes this requirement via a rule which adds a default [singular] feature):

(66)

I [1, singular]	We [1, plural]
you [2, singular]	you [2, plural]
He/she/it [singular]	they [plural]

Now in this system we predict four possibilities, rather than three. This, it's true, is better than eight, and so the system is more constrained, but this system still allows the possibility of a feature bundle which has both person features specified: [1, 2]. Is there any evidence for this feature bundle in natural languages?

In fact, many languages from all over the world have a so-called 'Fourth Person': Dakota (a Siouan language of North America), Marghi (a Chadic language of Africa), Ngandi (a Gunwingguan language of Australia), and Fijian (a Malayo-Polynesian language). In these languages, there is a plural pronoun (the **inclusive pronoun**) which refers to the speaker, people who count as part of the speaker's group, and the addressee. It's used like the English pronoun "we" in an utterance like "Shall we all go to the cinema". There is also a distinct pronoun which refers to the speaker and people who count as part of the speaker's group, but, crucially, not the addressee (the **exclusive pronoun**). This would be like a use of "we" in "We're all going to the cinema, but you're not". Clearly, this extra pronoun can be simply dealt with by specifying the exclusive pronoun as [1, plural] and the inclusive one as [1, 2, plural].

One example of a language which makes distinctions between inclusive and exclusive pronouns as well as a singular $\sim$ dual $\sim$ plural contrast is Chinook, described by Boas (1911). The full person/number paradigm of Chinook pronouns is as follows. I have excluded gender from this table:

(67)

	[singular]	[singular, plural]	[plural]
[1]	naika	ntaika	ntshaika
[1, 2]		tchaika	lchaika
[2]	maika	mtaika	mshaika
[]	áchka	shtáchka	táska

In terms of person and number distinctions, this seems to be about as complicated as languages get (although Bouma Fijian has an extra number category paucal which is used to refer to small numbers of entities).

The existence of inclusive/exclusive distinctions seems like strong empirical backing for the more minimal system. Further evidence that this is the right way to think about things comes from the fact that we have not discovered any languages which display any more than four distinctions in the person system of their pronouns. So the analysis which assumes three-person features ([1], [2], [3]) **overgenerates**, that is, it predicts phenomena which do not occur. The more minimal system is observationally more adequate.

Note we haven't mentioned the difference between *she*, *he*, and *it*. These all, as we can see above, trigger the same agreement forms, but are clearly differentiated in other ways (by their **gender**). We saw examples above which showed that in some languages gender was a syntactic feature. In English, there do not seem to be any syntactic rules which refer to gender distinctions explicitly, and we will assume that gender in English is only a semantic feature.

These types of features, person, number, and gender, go under the general name of **Phi-features** (often written ϕ-features). Φ-features appear to be interpretable, and are motivated by both semantic and morphological facts. The agreement relation we saw above ensures that some subset of the ϕ-features on subjects agrees with those on verbs.

Case features

Pronouns also change form depending on syntactic relationships other than agreement. So the pronoun *him*, in (68), appears to have exactly the same kind of interpretation as the pronoun *he* in (69):

(68) We all thought **him** to be unhappy.

(69) We all thought **he** was unhappy.

This variation between *him* and *he* is usually described as a variation in **case**. Note that particular case forms are restricted to particular positions in sentences. For example, we cannot switch the two forms of the pronoun around:

(70) *We all thought **he** to be unhappy

(71) *We all thought **him** was unhappy

English is particularly impoverished with respect to case forms, which are only fully differentiated for pronouns, and there are really only three (at most) case forms.

Many other languages mark all nouns for case. One example is Classical Latin:

(72) Puer   hominem vidit
boy-[NOM] man-[ACC] saw
"The boy saw the man."

(73) Puerum homo   vidit
boy-[ACC] man-[NOM] saw
"The man saw the boy."

in (72), the word *puer*, "boy" appears in **nominative** case, while the word *hominem*, "man" is **accusative**. As you can see, (73) swaps the cases around, but leaves the word order intact. Changing the case in this way changes the semantic interpretation of the sentence and you might think that this is because case features are interpretable, and give rise to a specification of the semantic *role* of the words in the sentence (basically, who does what to whom).

This appears to conflict with the examples from English that we saw above. In the English cases the semantic role of the pronoun whose case is being varied does not seem to change. In both cases, whoever the pronoun refers to is being unhappy. We will see in a later chapter that the semantic role of a word depends on aspects of its syntax other than case, and we shall assume, for the present, that the function of case is purely syntactic, and that it is an **uninterpretable** feature.

One example of how the syntactic structure of a sentence may affect the case of nouns comes from Russian. In this language, six cases are distinguished (nominative, accusative, genitive, dative, locative, and instrumental). Certain verbs force particular cases on nouns which appear in the same sentence. For example, the verb which translates English 'read' requires that its **object** be accusative:

(74)   Ivan čital   ètu   knigu
Ivan read-[PAST] this-[ACC] book-[ACC]
"Ivan read this book."

However, when the sentence is negated, the object appears in the genitive case, rather than accusative:

(75)   Ivan ne čital   ètoj   knigi
Ivan not read-[PAST] this-[GEN] book-[GEN]
"Ivan didn't read this book."

The names that linguists use for the various case forms are derived from traditional grammar, and are best just learned as labels. The three that we find in English are **nominative** (the form seen in 46), **accusative** (45), and **genitive** (to which we'll return later).

Here are the nominative and accusative case forms for the pronouns in English:

(76)

Singular		Plural	
Nominative	Accusative	Nominative	Accusative
I	me	we	us
you	you	you	you
he	him	they	them
she	her	they	them
it	it	they	them

Within the system we are developing here, we can posit two features [nom] and [acc], for nominative and accusative respectively. *I* would then be [1, singular, nom], and *me* [1, singular, acc], etc.

In fact, since we are assuming that there are special morphological interface rules which serve to pronounce feature bundles, it is more accurate to say that [1, singular, nom] is pronounced as *I* (or rather, as the phonology associated with the orthographic string *I*), and that [1, singular, acc] is realized as *me*, etc. Given that there is little phonological uniformity in the pronouns, we'll assume that they lack phonological features of their own, and that their pronunciation is determined entirely by the interface rules.

Note that some distinctions are simply not marked: the second person pronoun, for example, is invariant in its form. This means that we have a morphological rule which looks something like the following:

(77) Pronounce a pronoun bearing [2] as *you*, irrespective of any other (number or case) features.

The third case used in English is the genitive case. This is found on pronouns when they signify possession:

(78)

my book		our book
	your book	
his/her/its book		their book

The genitive case also appears to be marked on non-pronominal possessors:

(79) The girl's book

(80) The girls' book

In (80) the *s* sound signifies that the girl referred to is the possessor of the book, with a singular plural distinction being marked in writing, but not in speech, for nouns which pluralize in *s*. We will discuss genitive case in more detail when we come to look at the structure of nouns in Chapter 7.

Verbal features

We have already briefly met one of the main types of feature that are associated with verbs: the tense feature [past]. This feature is associated morphologically with the addition of an affix usually written *-(e)d* or sometimes as just *-t* to the verb stem, giving alternations such as *kick* ~ *kicked* and *push* ~ *pushed*. In addition, many verbs in English have a vowel change associated with the [past] feature: *sing* ~ *sang* and *run* ~ *ran*. Other verbs appear to do both (*sleep* ~ *slept*) and we also find suppletion (*am* ~ *was*) and suppletion of the stem plus affixation of *-t* (*go* ~ *went*).

Semantically, the [past] feature is interpreted, very roughly, as signalling that the time at which the event took place is temporally before the time at which the utterance of the sentence takes place.

We also saw that agreement between the noun and the verb in a simple sentence occur in the present tense. There is no morphological signal of agreement in the past tense in English, so we do not get the following kind of contrast:

(81)   a.   The bears snuffled.
       b.   *The bear snuffleds

In English, it appears that there is no special morphology which can be used to motivate a future tense feature. The future is always signalled by the use of a modal auxiliary as in (82) or an expression using the verb *go*, as in (83):

(82)   Milena will make carbonara.

(83)   Richard is going to chop some wood.

If we take this observation seriously, then we have only a binary opposition in the tense system of English, and this might lead us to propose that there is actually no need for two tense features: there is just the feature [past] and this feature is absent in present tense verbs. Expressions which seem to semantically pick out present or future times are simply special non-past forms. The fact that (82) and (83) are morphologically present tense, and contrast with cases which contain *would* and *was going to* which are morphologically past, seems to back this up.

English contrasts with a language like Scottish Gaelic, in which verbs have a simple morphological past, and a form which is used to express future time, but which lacks present tense forms for all verbs except the auxiliary verb *bidh*, "be". In Gaelic we find the following kinds of example:

(84)   Dh'fhàg   mi e
       [PAST]-leave I   him
       "I left him."

(85)   Fàgaidh   mi e
       leave-[FUT] I   him
       "I will leave him."

Gaelic signals the [past] feature by prefixing the verb and altering its initial consonant, while it signals non-past by adding a suffix. Both of these languages express just a two-way contrast. English distinguishes morphologically between past and non-past, as does Gaelic. The difference seems to be in how the semantic rules interpret the lack of a past feature. In Gaelic we have the possibility of a future interpretation, while in English this is generally signalled periphrastically.

Interestingly, the Gaelic non-past and the English non-past are both able to be used to make generic statements of habit. Compare the use of the non-past Gaelic form with the non-past form used in the translation in (86).

(86)   Leughaidh mi dàin
       read-[FUT] I   poems
       "I read poetry."

This kind of situation, where there is only a past ~ non-past distinction, contrasts with a language like the closely related Modern Irish. The latter is a language which marks past ~ present ~ future distinctions via morphology on the verb. So we find:

(87)   tógann   sé
       leave-[PRES.3] he
       "He lifts."

(88)   thóg   sé
       leave-[PAST.3] he
       "He lifted."

(89)   tógfaidh   sé
       leave-[FUT.3] he
       "He will lift."

This language will require the use of at least two tense features: [past], [future]. The present tense will be unspecified for both of these features. Interestingly, Irish actually has a fourth morphologically simple tense, traditionally termed the **imperfect**, which is used for generic, habitual, or iterated actions in the past. Just as in Gaelic, the future in Irish may be used for generic statements about someone's present habits. Given this, it is tempting to make the tentative suggestion that the imperfect in Irish might be profitably analysed as involving the feature bundle [future, past]:

(90)   thógadh   sé
       leave-[IMP.3] he
       "He used to lift."

Aside from tense and agreement features, verbs in English also appear in a number of other morphological forms. The most important ones are the forms traditionally known as **participles**. Participles come in two broad classes in English: one class can be distinguished morphologically by the fact that it suffixes -*ing* to the verb, while the other is morphologically more heterogeneous and may suffix -*en* or -*ed* or may employ a vowel change.

If we take a verb like *be*, which has the richest set of morphological forms in English, we find that, in addition to the present and past forms of the verb discussed above, there are three other forms that it takes:

(91)   be, being, been

The latter two of these are participles. These verb forms appear when the tense feature is not marked directly on the verb. This can happen because there is no tense specification in the sentence, or because the tense marking is carried by something else (another verb—traditionally called the **auxiliary verb**. We take up the syntax of these constructions in Chapter 5):

(92)   He has been happy.

(93)   I am being whipped.

The form marked by the suffix -*ing* is traditionally called the **present participle**. The present participle can occur after the verb *be* to signify that an action is conceived of as ongoing, or continuous. This contrasts with the **past participle**, marked by -*en*, -*ed*, or a vowel change which occurs mainly after the verb *have*, to signify that an action has been completed. The semantic distinction between ongoing and completed action is one of **aspect**. Participial morphology, in conjunction with particular auxiliaries, is used in English to make certain aspectual distinctions.

We can distinguish participles from non-participles by use of a feature [part], so that a present participle will be [V, part] and a past participle will be [V, past, part]. The syntax of participles and auxiliaries in English is extremely complex, and we will return to it in detail in Chapter 5, where we will propose a featural analysis of tense and participle forms as values of a general inflectional feature, which also encompasses agreement information.

Interestingly, in other languages, participles may show agreement. For example, in Friulian (a dialect of Italian), we find examples like the following:

(94)   Piero el an   mangiâs   i   pirus
       Piero he have-[PRES.3.SING.MASC] eat-[MASC.PL.PART] the pear-[MASC.PL]
       "Piero has eaten the pears."

(95)   Maria e   a   mangiadis   li   caramelis
       Maria she have-[PRES.3.SING.FEM] see-[FEM.PL.PART] the sweet-[FEM.SING]
       "Maria has eaten the sweets."

In these examples the participle agrees in gender and number with the noun which immediately follows it (its object).

One final verbal form which we have not discussed as yet is the bare verb form found in English sentences like (96):

(96)   I am to **eat** macaroni.

(97)   I want to **eat** macaroni.

(98)   I must **eat** macaroni.

Sometimes this bare form of the verb is called the **infinitive.** Infinitives generally do not mark for agreement (although a kind of agreement is found on infinitives in European Portuguese). We will posit a feature [inf] to characterize infinitives.

Other languages mark the infinitive with particular endings. For example, French verbs have different morphological forms for infinitives depending on the particular class of verb:

(99)   a.   Je pars
            I   leave-[1.SING.PRES]
       b.   partir
            leave-[INF]

(100) a.   Je mange
            I   eat-[1.SING.PRES]
       b.   manger
            eat-[INF]

Once again the syntax of infinitives is complex, and we will address it in Chapter 8.

2.5 Summary

We have now covered many (by no means all) of the features that are relevant to the core syntax of English. We have motivated these features on the basis of differences in morphological form, and semantic interpretation. Other languages may have chosen different sets of features from the universal pool of features, and we may need to set up more features when we come to look at these languages. There are other features that will become relevant as we progress through the book, but we shall motivate these as we go along.

The table presents a summary of the most important features we have met so far:

Kind of feature	Features	Comments
tense	[past]	need [future] as well, for Irish
number	[singular][plural]	feature bundle [singular, plural] for dual number
person	[1], [2]	[1, 2] gives 'Fourth' person
gender	[masc], [fem]	need others for different languages
case	[nom], [acc], [gen]	again, may need others
category	[N], [V], [A], [P]	may be reducible to just [N], [V]
others	[part], [inf]	appear on verbs

We have seen that these features are bundled up with other features to make lexical items, so that a word like *trees* is associated with semantic features which are accessed only by the rules of semantic interpretation, (morpho)-phonological features (accessed only by the rules of phonology and morphology), and syntactic features like [N], [plural], [acc]. These syntactic features are accessed by the operations of syntax, and give rise to the particular patternings of words that we recognize as grammar.

Syntactic features may also be accessed by the rules of morphophonology, giving rise to different morphological or phonological forms. We saw examples of this from Welsh nasalization effects.

Syntactic features may also be accessed by the rules of semantic interpretation. Those features which have this effect are called interpretable features. These include features for number, person, and gender. We saw that the features of number and gender could be interpretable or not, depending on the language, in examples from Ancient Greek, Scottish Gaelic, and Dutch. In Scottish Gaelic, we saw that some words could refer to persons of a particular semantic gender (male or female), and we could see this clearly by looking at pronominal reference; however, the grammatical phenomena showed us that the syntactic gender feature of some of these words was different from its semantic gender: that is, the syntactic gender feature on these words was **uninterpretable**. Another clear example of a feature which is uninterpretable is nominative or accusative case. We saw that this feature appeared to simply regulate the syntactic position of words, while telling us nothing about the semantics of those words.

Before we leave this chapter, I'd like to make a comment on the differences between the information specified in the glosses, and the notion of features. Glosses are intended to be informal grammatical descriptions, which make no pretence of being a theory of any kind. They are just there to help the reader. The features we have been discussing in this chapter, on the other hand, are elements of a theoretical system, and, as such, are subject to the normal constraints on theories: they should be simple, minimal, and consistent. For this reason, you might notice discrepancies between feature specifications, and glosses. These are to be expected, for the reasons just mentioned. A gloss is not a theoretical analysis, and so may contain all sorts of extra information.

Exercises

Exercise 1 **Reflexives and ϕ-features**

This exercise is intended to begin to develop your skills in syntactic argumentation. Follow the instructions exactly. Do not try to do more than is asked for each section.

Part A

There is a class of words in English called **reflexive pronouns**. These words are formed from a pronominal plus the word *self* in its singular or plural form. Examples are:

myself	ourselves
yourself	yourselves
himself	themselves
herself	
itself	

In a simple sentence, these words are restricted in their distribution:

(1)   *I kicked yourself

(2)   *He kicked yourself

(3)   You kicked yourself.

Notice that examples like (3) have a special semantic property. The person doing the action described by the verb, and the person affected by this action, are one and the same. In (3), *you* are the kicker and the kickee. The words *you* and *yourself* are said to be **coreferential**, since they both refer to the same person. Other examples of expressions that can be co-referential are *Anson* and *he* in the following sentences:

(4)   Anson thought that he had bought the paint stripper.

(5)   I asked Anson if he was happy.

In (4) and (5), the pronoun *he* appears to take on its meaning via the expression *Anson*. In these particular sentences, another reading is also possible. *He* can refer to someone else entirely, just as *she* does in (6):

(6)   The boy thought she was happy.

In (6), *she* is not coreferential with *the boy*, since coreferentiality appears to require matching ϕ-features.

Let us state this idea as an explicit hypothesis, the **Coreferentiality Hypothesis**:

(7)   For two expressions to be coreferential, they must bear the same ϕ-features.

We can see the Coreferentiality Hypothesis as a kind of general interface rule which relates syntactic features to semantic interpretation.

In the examples with reflexives we have a case of **obligatory coreference**. In (3), *you* and *yourself* are required to be interpreted as coreferential. The same can be said for the following cases:

(8)   He kicked himself.

(9)   We kicked ourselves.

(10)   They kicked themselves.

Using this notion of coreferentiality, we can state a hypothesis that will differentiate between the good and the bad examples above. We will call this hypothesis the **Reflexive Generalization**, for ease of reference. Parts B–F of this exercise will be devoted to revising this hypothesis, so what we have here is just a first attempt:

(11)   The **Reflexive Generalization** (First attempt):
    A reflexive pronoun must be coreferential with another expression in the sentence.

The Reflexive Generalization has the consequence that a reflexive pronoun will have to be coreferential with another expression, and hence, have the same ϕ-features as that expression.

Task 1 Provide some further examples that support this result for person features.

Part B

Now look at the following data:

(12)   You kicked yourselves.

(13)   *We kicked myself

(14)   *They kicked himself

Task 2 Explain how our generalizations account for these examples.

Task 3 Provide further examples that show the hypothesis working for number features.

Part C

Now look at the following data:

(15)   *He kicked herself

(16)   *She kicked itself

Task 4 Explain how these examples are captured by the hypotheses, and provide more examples which show that gender features are relevant.

Part D

The following examples show that this hypothesis is not enough to explain the distribution of reflexive pronouns:

(17)   *Myself saw me

(18)   *Himself saw him

Task 5 Explain why the Reflexive Generalization is not enough to rule out these examples.

Task 6 How might you alter the hypothesis so that it covers these examples? (Hint: there are two possibilities here: one involves the order of the words, the other involves the case of the pronoun inside the reflexive.)

Part E

Look at the following examples:

(19)   *I thought he liked myself

(20)   *You said she liked yourself

Task 7 Whichever hypothesis you came up with for Task 6, explain whether these data are problematic for it or not.

Part F Summary

These data show that the distribution of reflexives is not just conditioned by their ϕ-features, but that word order, case, and other aspects of syntactic structure may enter into their analysis too. This is a general fact about syntactic problems. They rarely confine their solutions to just one part of the grammar.

Exercise 2 **Imperatives**

This exercise draws upon the (admittedly incomplete) hypothesis developed in the last exercise. It involves structures like the following, known as **imperatives**:

(1)   Close the door!

(2)   Eat dirt!

(3)   Know yourself!

The interesting thing about these examples is that they appear to have something missing. Compare these sentences to the following ones:

(4)   Frieda closed the door.

(5)   Kane ate dirt.

Traditionally, these sentences are said to have missing **subjects** (this is a notion we'll come back to).

There are, on the face of it, two obvious ways to think about these examples:

- **Hypothesis A**: imperatives are just like other sentences, and have a subject but this subject is just not pronounced.

- **Hypothesis B**: imperatives are not full sentences. They really don't have a subject at all.

Part A

Look at the following sentences:

(6)   Keep yourself clean!

(7)   Look after yourself!

Task 1 Assume that the Reflexive Generalization from the preceding exercise is correct (although we know it's not the whole story). How do the data in (6) and (7) suggest the correctness of Hypothesis A?

Task 2 Provide some more examples, along the lines of (6) and (7), which support your answer. This is extremely easy, but will get you into the habit of finding relevant examples, a useful skill in syntactic argumentation.

Part B

Look at the following sentences:

(8)   *Keep myself clean!

(9)   *Look after herself!

Task 3 Do this data back up the conclusion you reached in Task 1, or do they contradict it. Explain your answer.

Task 4 Provide further examples that make the same point.

Task 5 These data not only suggest that there is an unpronounced subject in these imperatives, but also suggest what that unpronounced subject is. Say what you think it is, and why.

Part C

Of course it is possible to maintain Hypothesis B and deal with the data we have seen here. What we need to do is adopt an extra hypothesis:

- **Extra hypothesis**: only second-person reflexives are allowed in an imperative.

What we now have is a choice between two grammars: Grammar A adopts Hypothesis A, while Grammar B adopts Hypothesis B plus the Extra hypothesis. Notice that both grammars get the data right. Grammar A says there is a pronominal subject in imperatives with the right ϕ-features to allow only a second-person reflexive in the imperative. Grammar B says that there is no subject at all in imperatives, and that, independently, only second-person reflexives are allowed in imperatives.

Task 6 Choose between grammars A and B, and say what motivated your choice.

Part D

Task 7 English has a construction known as the **tag-question**. Some examples are given below:

(10)   Frieda closed the door, didn't she?

(11)   I can come, can't I?

(12)   You won't be there, will you?

These structures are called tag-questions, because they involve a simple sentence, with an extra 'tag' on the end. The generalization we can make about these structures is roughly as follows:

Tag Question Generalization: The tag in a tag question is constructed from the auxiliary of the main sentence, which is negated if the main sentence is positive, and which is positive if the main sentence is negative, followed by a pronoun which has the same ϕ-features as the subject.

Given this generalization, construct an argument from the following data for either hypothesis A or hypothesis B:

(13)   Close the door, won't you!

(14)   *Close the door, won't he!

Exercise 3 Pronouns and coreference

Part A

This exercise flows on from the last two, but looks at how pronouns and reflexives are distributed. Consider the following data:

(1)   *I kicked me

(2)   I kicked myself.

(3)   *You kicked you

(4)   You kicked yourself.

(5)   *We kicked us

(6)   We kicked ourselves.

Task 1 We can formulate a hypothesis to cover these data, using the same kinds of concepts. We will term this the **Pronoun Generalization**:

(7)   A pronoun cannot be coreferential with another pronoun.

Task 2 Explain how this hypothesis extends to the following data:

(8)   He kicked him.

(9)   They kicked them.

(10)   She kicked her.

(Hint: think carefully about the coreference possibilities in these sentences.)

Part B

Recall the two grammars that you chose between in the last exercise. Grammar A stated that imperatives had an unpronounced subject, while grammar B stated that imperatives had no subject at all, but that only second-person reflexives could appear in imperatives.

Now consider the following data:

(11)   Kick me!

(12)   Kick them!

(13)   *Kick you!

Task 3 Assume Grammar A is the correct grammar, and that the Pronoun Generalization holds. Explain how the new data given above fall out in this grammar.

Task 4 Assume Grammar B is the correct grammar, and that the Pronoun Generalization holds. Explain how the new data don't immediately follow, and revise Grammar B by adding a new hypothesis to fix it.

Task 5 Now explain which of the two grammars is preferable, and why.

Further reading

Section 2.2
The notion of features in syntax derives from work on features in phonology. See Chomsky and Halle (1968) for discussion and further references. Matthews (1974) gives an overview of many of the kinds of morphological processes that are found in languages. For a more detailed overview of issues in morphology see the papers in Spencer and Zwicky (1998).

Section 2.3
See Dalrymple and Kaplan (2000) for a discussion of some of the issues raised by the text, and Harley and Ritter (2001) for an alternative using a feature geometry. The Hopi data are taken from the latter source. An excellent descriptive discussion of constraints on how languages vary with respect to the features they use is Greenberg (1966). The idea that morphology and semantics are both interpretative components of grammar goes back to early work of Chomsky (see Chomsky, 1970). Theories which adopt an interpretative morphology include

those of Anderson (1992) and Halle and Marantz (1993). For a collection of papers focusing on feature-theory, see Muysken and van Riemsdijk (1986).

Section 2.4.1

The use of morphological oppositions to set up major word classes derives from the American structuralist tradition (Bloomfield, 1933). The idea that categories can be defined as bundles of features is found in Chomsky (1965) and further developed in Chomsky (1970).

Section 2.4.2

For a discussion of semantic and grammatical gender see Corbett (1991) and for a more theoretical discussion (best not tackled until you have reached the end of this book) see Ritter (1993). The autonomy of syntax thesis is first (and best) defended in Chomsky (1957).

Section 2.4.3

Aside from the references mentioned above for Section 2.3, Corbett (2000) gives a good discussion of number. See Comrie (1985) and Comrie (1976) for good descriptive overviews of tense and aspect respectively. The agreeing participle data discussed in this section are from Paoli (1997), and see also the first two papers in Kayne (2000).

3

Constituency and Theta Roles

3.1 Introduction

This chapter introduces the idea that syntactic structures are **hierarchical** in nature, with smaller structures coming together to make larger structures, which, themselves, can be parts of yet larger structures, and so on. We shall motivate a syntactic operation, which we will call **Merge**, whose function is to build up larger structures out of smaller ones, with the smallest elements being lexical items.

This follows on from the ideas we developed in the last chapter: syntax starts off with features, as its basic atoms; these features are then combined into lexical items, which are essentially bundles of features, which we have assumed so far are unstructured. These lexical items then combine into larger and larger structures, in a way which we will motivate and make explicit. We shall see that some of the features of some of the lexical items project through the structures, so that larger structures end up having the properties of smaller structures within them. This phenomenon is known as **headedness**, and we will see how capturing headedness in our system allows us to account for some fairly diverse syntactic phenomena.

3.2 Constituents

Consider a sentence like:

(1)   That bottle of water might have cracked open.

Intuitively, the string *that bottle of water* has a semantic cohesion that *of water might* doesn't, even though both are just sequences of adjacent words in the sentence (one word is **string adjacent**, or just **adjacent**, to another if it is right next to it). The first of these sequences seems to be something that we can form a complete meaning out of, in contrast to the second.

What syntactic evidence is there that sentences are organized in this way? There are a number of syntactic **tests** which back up our semantic intuition. First, we can often **replace** a sequence of words with a single word in a sentence, with no change in acceptability, and only a minimal change in meaning. So, consider:

(2)   It might have cracked open.

In (2), we have replaced the sequence *that bottle of water* with the single lexical item *it*. If *it* is a minimal syntactic object (i.e. just a lexical item), then the fact that we can replace the whole sequence *that bottle of water* with *it* suggests that *that bottle of water* is also a single syntactic object. There is no single word that we can use to replace *of water might*, so we don't have any real reason to assume that this sequence is a single syntactic object. Since this purely syntactic test comes up with the same structure that we wanted to posit for semantic reasons, we are on solid ground in claiming that it has some syntactic reality. This test, where we replace a string of a number of words with a single word, is called the **Replacement Test** (or sometimes the **Substitution Test**).

A group of words which can be picked out in this way is called a **constituent**, and tests like the replacement tests are called **constituency tests**. Essentially, a constituent is a group of words which has a certain internal coherence.

One of the ways that syntacticians represent the idea that something is a constituent is by enclosing it in square brackets, like this:

(3)   [That bottle of water] might have cracked open.

The square brackets here enclose a constituent. Since the whole sentence is also a constituent, we can actually add square brackets around the whole sentence:

(4)   [[That bottle of water] might have cracked open]

In fact, we also have evidence from replacement that the constituent *that bottle of water* itself has further structure, since we can replace *bottle of water* with the single word *one*:

(5)   That one might have cracked open.

In this example, the word *that* is used to pick out an item which bears some relation to the spatial position of the speaker (compare with *this bottle of water*).

What characterizes the entity picked out is that it must be a bottle of water. The string *bottle of water* semantically constrains the relevant property of the real-world object picked out by *that*. Once more, the semantic and syntactic tests give the same result.

Using the square bracket notation, this gives us the following, more complicated structure:

(6)   [[That [bottle of water]] might have cracked open]

What these examples show is that sentences are organized into constituents, and constituents themselves are organized into smaller constituents. The smallest constituent is simply the lexical item. The usual convention is to use the word constituent to talk about syntactic objects which consist of more than one lexical item.

Turning to the remainder of the sentence, we can replace *cracked open* with *done*, again with no real change of meaning:

(7)   That bottle of water might have done

This suggests that *cracked open* is a constituent. We can also replace *have cracked open* with *do*:

(8)   That bottle of water might do.

The meaning of the sentence changes more radically here, since we have removed the verb *have*, which signified that the action described by the sentence is to be viewed as being completed (recall we discussed the contribution of *have* followed by a past participle in the last chapter). However, once we take this into account, the examples in (7) and (8) suggest a fairly intricate structure for this sentence, with constituents embedded inside other constituents. We can display this in square bracket notation, but you can see that this gets rather hard to follow:

(9)   [[That [bottle of water]] might [have [cracked open]]]

One way of representing the constituent structure of a sentence, which is a little easier on the eye (and brain) is to explicitly represent each constituent in a sort of **tree structure**, as in (10).

(10)

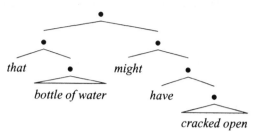

Each bullet point in the tree structure in (10) represents a constituent made up of the two syntactic objects that are just underneath it in the tree, joined to it by the two lines (or, since this is a tree-like structure, **branches**). The leftmost bullet point is a constituent made up of the word *that* and another more complex constituent built up out of the words *bottle of water*. Where you see a triangle in the tree, this just represents structure for which we have decided not to put in a detailed analysis.

What this procedure shows us is that there are good syntactic reasons to say that a string of words which makes up a sentence has the kind of internal structure shown in the tree in (10). Note that the tree structure in (10) and the bracketed string in (9) are two ways of representing exactly the same thing about the constituent structure of the sentence.

A test which is closely related to replacement is the **ellipsis** test. A constituent is said to be **ellipted** if it is deleted from the structure. In the examples we looked at above, we can ellipt *cracked open*, instead of replacing it with the appropriate version of the word *do* (past participle, past tense, etc.):

(11)   That bottle of water might have.

(12)   That bottle of water might.

In addition to Replacement and Ellipsis diagnostics for constituency, there's also the fact that we can **move** certain sequences of words around in a sentence with minimal change of meaning. So if we take a sentence like:

(13)   Anson danced extremely frantically at Trade.

We can also say

(14)   At Trade, Anson danced extremely frantically.

or

(15)   Extremely frantically, Anson danced at Trade.

but not

(16)   *Frantically at, Anson danced extremely Trade

or

(17)   *Danced extremely, Anson frantically at Trade

All of these examples involve taking a string of adjacent words and moving them to the start of the sentence. But (16) and (17) are unacceptable. The simplest thing to say would be that it is constituents which are susceptible to syntactic processes like movement. This means that, when we move something, we are moving a constituent. So, in the examples above, *extremely frantically* is a single constituent, while *frantically at* is not.

So there are two core tests to see whether sequences of words are constituents: **replacement** of the sequence with a single word and **movement** of the sequence to another position in the sentence. It is important to note that when these tests are successful then what you have is an **argument** that a particular sequence forms a constituent, rather than proof that it does. It is even more important to notice that when one of these tests fails, we cannot conclude that the sequence is not a constituent, we can only conclude that there is no evidence that it is.

This last point is something that often confuses people. To see why this is so, consider the following examples:

(18)   The old house collapsed.

(19)   *house the old collapsed

The word *house* is trivially a constituent, because it is a lexical item, and lexical items are the basic minimal constituents. However, we cannot move this constituent to the start of the sentence to form (19). Why is this?

We shall discover in later chapters that movement processes, although they uniformly apply to constituents, are subject to other constraints. One of these constraints forbids movement out of a subject, and this will **independently rule out** the sentence in (19).

This means that the ungrammaticality of (19) is not due to the fact that we have moved a non-constituent, but rather because we have moved a constituent illegitimately. This is a general lesson about movement tests: when they fail, they don't tell us anything for sure about constituency, because there may be independent reasons for their failure.

There are other tests for constituency, which generally are just more complicated forms of the movement test. The most useful is possibly the **clefting** test.

A cleft is a sentence that has the general form:

(20)   It's BLAH that BLAH

or

(21)   It was BLAH that BLAH

For example:

(22)   It's [Anson] that I like.

(23)   It's [under the bed] that's the best place to hide.

(24)   It was [Julie and Jenny] that arrived first.

(25)   It was [over the hill and through the woods] that they came running.

Some of these examples sound a little stilted, but most people agree that they are grammatical.

If we look carefully at the cleft sentences, then we see that they are related to simpler sentences:

(26)   I like Anson.

(27)   Under the bed is the best place to hide.

(28)   Julie and Jenny arrived first.

(29)   They came running over the hill and through the woods.

There's a simple formal relationship. The cleft is formed by taking a string of words from the simple sentence, putting that string after the words *It's* or *It was*, and then glueing on the new sequence to the front of the remainder of the simple sentence with a *that*:

(30)   a.   I like Anson →
       b.   Anson + I like →
       c.   It's Anson + I like →
       d.   It's Anson that I like.

(31)   a.   Julie and Jenny arrived first →
       b.   Julie and Jenny + arrived first →

    c.   It was Julie and Jenny + arrived first →

    d.   It was Julie and Jenny that arrived first.

Now clefting only seems to affect constituents, and can be used as evidence that some sequence of words is a constituent. So the sentence in (31) is good evidence that *Julie and Jenny* is a constituent of this sentence. This argument is backed up by the replacement test, since we can replace *Julie and Jenny* with the single word *they*:

(32)   They arrived first.

When clefting fails, then we have no evidence that the sequence isn't a constituent, but no evidence that it is. Let's try with arbitrary sequences from one of the sentences above:

(33)   a.   Julie and *Jenny arrived* first →

         b.   Jenny arrived + Julie and first →

         c.   It was Jenny arrived + Julie and first →

         d.   *It was Jenny arrived that Julie and first →

We can immediately see that the (d) example in (33) is ill-formed, and so we have no evidence that *Jenny arrived* is a constituent of this sentence.

Sometimes, the results of constituency tests can be apparently contradictory. Let's take the sequence *arrived first* in our sentence above. If we perform the clefting procedure with this sequence we get:

(34)   *It's arrived first that Julie and Jenny

but we can replace our sequence *arrived first* with *did* with perfectly fine results:

(35)   Julie and Jenny did.

It appears that replacement tells us one thing but movement tells us another.

However, these results aren't really contradictory. The example in (34) allows us to draw only the conclusion that there is no evidence from clefting that *arrived first* is a constituent. The example in (35) suggests that there is an argument that can be made from replacement. On balance, then, we'd say that *arrived first* does form a constituent, since there could be independent reasons why (34) is ungrammatical. This is why it's important to try different constituency tests. It could be that there are independent factors leading to why one test or another fails.

We've just seen that the syntactic formatives in sentences seem to be organized into various groupings. Moreover, it looks as if larger constituents contain smaller ones, which, in turn, contain even smaller ones. So our theory of the fundamental syntactic relation will have to ensure that it has these properties.

In the next section, we'll define the operation Merge, which takes two syntactic items and joins them to make a larger one. In effect what we'll be doing is building a system which will give us directly the kinds of constituent structure we've just seen.

3.3 Fundamental notions

Recall that our purpose in this book is not just to describe language, but rather to develop a theory. We have seen, in the previous section, that there is a great deal of motivation for the idea that syntactic structures are hierarchical in nature. What we shall do in this section is begin to develop a theory that will give rise to these hierarchical structures.

To this end, we're about to introduce some new terminology and some very simple formalism. We need the terminology so that we can talk about the ways that structures are built up, and we need the formalism so that we can be sure that we are being as explicit as possible. Remember that we want to build a general, explicit, and minimal picture of what's going on in sentence structures.

What we want our syntactic theory to do is to provide some operation that will build structures out of lexical items, and larger structures out of smaller ones. Let us, then, posit an operation, which we call **Merge**, which has the property of joining two syntactic objects together. This operation is motivated by the facts that we saw in the previous section, which showed that words in sentences group into constituents. Merge is essentially a constituent building operation.

The way that this operation is usually notated is by first giving the objects that are being joined **labels**. Usually, the label that is used is some subset of the features of the object, most commonly the major category feature, but other features may also be relevant. We then join both the merged objects to a point placed higher up on the page, to form a new object, the label of which is written on the higher point. So in the example in (36), the labels of the two objects we are merging are X and Y. We merge them to form a new object whose label is Z.

(36)

$$
\begin{array}{c}
\text{Z} \\
\diagup\diagdown \\
\text{X} \quad \text{Y}
\end{array}
$$

It's important to note that the new object is the whole structure, and not just the letter Z itself. Z is just the label of this whole structure. The lines joining the labels are called **branches**, and the whole structure is called a **tree**, just as we saw above. The new object created by Merge is said to **immediately contain** the original objects.

The tree in (36) is a representation of the syntactic object Z, which reflects the idea that Z is built up out of two other objects, X and Y. This is just the kind of thing we need to capture the constituency relations between elements of the sentences we saw above.

Trees are by far the most common way of representing complex syntactic objects, but it is easy to come up with other kinds of representation. We've already seen the bracket notation, and it is trivial to add labels to the brackets, giving a **labelled bracketing notation**:

(37)   [$_Z$X Y]

In (37), I've used X and Y and Z to stand for arbitrary labels. Z is the label of the whole syntactic object, which consists of two other syntactic objects labelled X and Y. Z is said to immediately contain X, and also to immediately contain Y. Another way of saying this is to say that Z is the **mother** of X and Y, or that X and Y are the **daughters** of Z, and that X and Y are consequently **sisters**.

One final piece of tree terminology for now: the sections of the tree connected by the branches are called **nodes**, with the lowest nodes (i.e. the representations of the lexical items) called **terminal nodes**, and the topmost node of a tree called the **root node**. So the tree is upside down.

We have just stipulated that Merge joins *two* syntactic objects together. Of course it would be possible to define Merge so as to put three objects together, or seventeen, or to put no specific limit on how many elements a single application of Merge can join into a single object. We will adopt the idea that Merge joins two elements together as a **working hypothesis**. This will mean that all of the syntactic structures that we propose will be **binary branching**. We'll see some evidence which supports this hypothesis in the next chapter.

The Binary Branching hypothesis means that the following structures cannot be formed by Merge:

(38)

(39)

A second point to note about Merge is that it doesn't distinguish between (40) and (41):

(40)

(41)

That is, Merge does not specify the **linear order** of the elements that it merges. Of course, we have to write down the structures somehow, so we either write (40) or (41), but from the point of view of Merge these are exactly the same syntactic object. They are both composed out of the same two syntactic objects.

However, we know that order is crucial to natural languages. It is the order of the words that makes (42) acceptable, while (43) is ungrammatical:

(42)   Harry collapsed.

(43)   *Collapsed Harry

So we need to impose some ordering on the structures built up from Merge in some other way. The usual term for this is that we need to **linearize** the structures. We will come back to this in Section 4.2.

Since Merge forms syntactic objects out of syntactic objects, it is a recursive operation, in the sense we discussed in Chapter 1. This means that we can build ever larger constituents using just Merge:

(44)

Here, we've taken the object Z and merged it with W to make a new object S.

Finally, Merge only combines objects at their root nodes. So if we have two objects like those in (45) and (46), we can only merge them as in (47):

(45)

(46)

(47)

The example in (48) is not well formed, given this property of Merge:

(48)

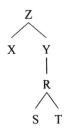

The simplest way to think about this is, again, to keep your mind firmly on the idea that Merge combines whole constituents: it cannot therefore insert one constituent inside another. In (47), we have Merged the constituent labelled by Z with that labelled by R. We can legitimately do this by creating a new constituent labelled by M which immediately contains Z and R. In (48), however, we have taken R and tried to Merge it with Y. The resulting tree is unary branching and therefore ill formed. We could try to create a new node which contains Y and R, and which is contained by Z. This will give us (49):

(49)

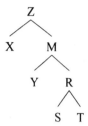

As is fairly obvious, this operation is rather more complicated than simple Merging at the root, since we essentially have to pick apart the object Z and insert a new object inside it. Unless there is a good reason not to, we adopt the simplest operation, and will assume that Merge only applies to root nodes. This condition will rule out the structures discussed above.

We will see in the next chapter that this approach actually makes the right empirical predictions.

Summarizing, we have defined an operation Merge which takes two syntactic objects and creates a new object out of these which immediately contains each of the objects that we started with.

We haven't yet said how the label of the new object is computed. We shall see in the next section that the label of the new object is determined by its **head**.

3.4 Determining the head

There are two ways to think about the notion head. One is practical: how do we determine the head of a constituent? The other is more theoretical: what is it that makes a particular syntactic object a head?

The answer to the first question can be given intuitively as follows: the head of a constituent is the most important element in it. The vague term 'most important' here covers a multitude of sins, but essentially it picks out the element that is most characteristic of the constituent as a whole.

For example, the following two sentences are well formed:

(50)   Pigs love truffles.

(51)   Humans love to eat pigs.

But they contrast with the following example:

(52)   *Peter is pigs

So we can say that *pigs* has a restricted **distribution** in sentences: it can't just turn up anywhere. In fact, all words have a somewhat restricted distribution in English (and in other languages), although some are more restricted than others.

Now, we can show, using constituency tests, that the italicized sequences in the following four sentences are constituents:

(53)   *Those pigs* love truffles.

(54)   *The old pigs* love truffles.

(55)   *Some happy pigs which can fly* love truffles.

(56)   *Some disgruntled old pigs in those ditches* love truffles.

In all of these cases the italicized strings can be replaced with the pronoun *they*.

Notice that all of these constituents appear in the same **sentence frame** as the simple noun *pigs*. That is, immediately before *love truffles*. Furthermore, all of these constituents can appear in the same position as the simple noun in the sentence frame in (57), i.e. after *humans love to eat*:

(57)   Humans love to eat *those pigs*.

(58)   Humans love to eat *the old pigs*.

(59)   Humans love to eat *some happy pigs which can fly*.

(60)   Humans love to eat *some disgruntled old pigs in those ditches*.

In all of these examples the italicized sequences are also constituents. We can see this by the fact that the pronoun *them* can replace any of these strings, and also by the fact that they can be moved to the start of the sentence by clefting.

(61)   Humans love to eat them.

(62)   It is *some disgruntled old pigs in those ditches* that humans love to eat.

However, just like the simple noun *pigs*, these sequences are ungrammatical in a sentence frame like that in (63):

(63)   *Peter is *those pigs*

(64)   *Peter is *the old pigs*

(65) *Peter is *some happy pigs which can fly*

(66) *Peter is *some disgruntled old pigs in those ditches*

So we can conclude that all of these sequences share their distribution with the simple noun *pigs*. In some sense, it is the simple noun here that dictates the syntactic behaviour of the other elements that combine with it to form a larger constituent.

Now, of course, it can't be the case that there's something special just about the word *pigs*. We could have chosen any word to make the point. Somehow, in these particular sequences, *pigs* ends up being the most important word, and our syntactic system must tell us why that is the case. We can say that *pigs* is the head of each of the constituents we have been discussing in the sense that it determines the distribution of the constituent.

Notice that in all of these cases it is also the head that determines agreement with the verb. All of the italicized constituents in the examples given above have plural heads, and the verbs in each case show plural agreement. So the head of a constituent determines both its distribution, and the effect that it has on agreement relations.

There's another sense in which *pigs* is important. If we think of the meanings of the sentences we've been looking at, we can intuitively see that each of the italicized constituents picks out something in the world which we could characterize as a set of pigs, and not, for example, as a set of ditches. The head of this constituent determines an important fact about its **reference**, which is the real-world object that the word is used to pick out in an utterance of the sentence in question.

So we have two important criteria for picking out heads: (i) the head of a constituent conditions the distribution of the constituent of which it is a part, (ii) the head of a constituent is the most important element of the constituent semantically.

We can make the example slightly more complicated. Say we take a constituent like *owners of pigs*. Here we have a constituent made up of two nouns and a preposition between them. Which of these things is the head of the constituent? We can discount the idea that it is the preposition *of*, since *owners of pigs* clearly has a different distribution from a prepositional phrase, like *at the cinema*.

Given this, the head of this constituent must be one of the two nouns. Notice that the constituent more or less has the same distribution as the simple noun *pigs*:

(67)   *Owners of pigs* love truffles.

(68)   Humans love to eat *owners of pigs*

(69)   *Peter is *owners of pigs*

So can we conclude that *pigs* is the head of our phrase? No, because the simple noun *owners* also has the same distribution:

(70)   *Owners* love truffles.

(71)   Humans love to eat *owners*.

(72)   *Peter is *owners*

In fact, it turns out that all simple nouns in the plural share this distribution. The feature [N], then, appears to be one of the features that regulates word order in English.

Since we can't tell on purely distributional grounds which of the nouns in our constituent is the head, we must appeal to something else. It turns out that the two nouns in this construction are not equal when it comes to determining the agreement on the verb. Consider the following contrasts:

(73)   Owners of a pig love to eat truffles.

(74)   *Owners of a pig loves to eat truffles

In both of these examples, we have made the second noun singular. However, the agreement on the verb is plural. This suggests that it is the noun *owners* which is the head.

So the main answer to the practical question of how we identify the head of a constituent is that the head is the semantically most important element in the constituent, and it is the element that determines its distribution and the agreement relations that the constituent establishes with other components of the sentence.

It's very easy to capture the idea that the head determines the distribution and agreement properties of a constituent in the system we have so far. We adopt a new notion **projection**, where features from a daughter node project on to the mother node in a syntactic object.

To capture the idea that the distribution of a constituent is determined by its head, we simply say that it is the features of the head that project in any merged structure. Since the syntax is sensitive to these features, it will be able to treat a head with a feature, and a projection of that head, in the same way. So the fact that *kiss Peter* behaves in the same way as *drink absinthe* can be captured by the claim that the heads of both of these constituents are the verbs that they contain. In a tree structure, we have:

(75)

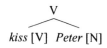

kiss [V]   *Peter* [N]

(76)

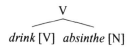

drink [V]   *absinthe* [N]

In each of these cases the new constituent which has been formed by Merge is labelled by the features of its head. I have used the category label as an abbreviation for the features of the head. Sometimes you might see the orthographic form of the head used as the label. I have chosen the former approach as it makes things more transparent when we come to talk of noun phrases and verb phrases in the next chapter.

We've seen that we can determine the head of a constituent, given the constituent, and facts about its reference and distribution. The question is, can we *predict* which element will be the head, were we only to have the syntactic objects out of which the constituent is built up? Put another way, if we Merge two syntactic objects to form a constituent, can we predict which one will be the head, and therefore have the head-like properties we've just discussed? This is the issue addressed in the next section.

3.5 Predicting the head—θ-roles and selectional features

This section introduces a new idea and proposes one particular theoretical implementation of this idea. The idea is that lexical items, as one of their properties, have a need to combine with other syntactic objects. That is, certain lexical items are unable to stand on their own as syntactic objects. Unless they Merge with something else, the structure in which they occur will be ill formed.

The way we will implement this idea is by extending the concepts we already have: in particular we will use the idea of features, and the interpretability property of features.

3.5.1 θ-roles and the θ-criterion

Before developing an argument which will show that certain lexical items need to Merge with other syntactic objects if they are to be well formed, we will introduce some ideas from semantics which will be relevant.

The first idea follows from our discussion of proposition in Chapter 1. When you take a word like *demonize*, on its own it certainly doesn't express a complete proposition. Minimally, *demonize* expresses a relationship between two objects in the world, where one demonizes the other. Compare this with a verb like *disappear*. *Disappear* intuitively involves only one object in the world, the object that disappears. *Demonize* and *disappear* contrast with words like *donate*, which intuitively involves three objects: someone donates something to someone.

Semantically, these words correspond to what you might think of intuitively as **concepts**. Some of these concepts, or combinations of them, are important enough for human communication to be fossilized into meanings of words. Once a concept has been fossilized into a linguistic meaning, it is said to be **lexicalized**. The concepts that are lexicalized in a particular language are called **predicates**. A predicate is something that can be used to characterize a situation in the world, but often the predicate needs more linguistic material to complete the message. This is what we saw above with the predicates *demonize*, *disappear*, and *donate*. On their own, these verbs aren't propositions. They need help.

When a predicate needs one other (possibly complex) concept to combine with it in order to express a proposition (like *disappear*), then it's said to be a **one-place predicate**. When a predicate needs two other constituents (*demonize*), it's a **two-place predicate**, and **three-place predicates** require three. Human languages don't seem to lexicalize predicates which have more than three places, although it is possible to conceive of verbs like *buy* and *sell* as requiring someone to do the selling, something to be sold, someone to receive it, and a sum of money which is exchanged.

There are some predicates that do actually express a proposition on their own. Weather verbs like *rain*, *snow*, etc. are usually thought of like this. These are called **zero-place predicates** and, semantically, need nothing else to express whole propositions. You might be puzzled by this, since, in English, these predicates do appear with other material in sentences:

(77)   It rained.

(78)   It snowed.

However, the *it* that appears with these predicates doesn't really seem to be semantically active. That is, it doesn't contribute anything extra in building up the proposition. Somehow, it is required syntactically, although it is not required semantically. Notice that you can never say the following:

(79)   *The weather rained

(80)   *The day snowed

These sentences are conceptually plausible, but are still unacceptable. Why? Because the constituents *the weather* and *the day* have some real semantic content, unlike the *it* seen in (77) and (78). Semantically, these weather predicates seem to be sufficient to characterize a situation on their own and, in fact, putting in another expression with its own semantic content is impossible.

Now predicates seem to subclassify the kinds of expressions they need into different semantic types. If you consider the verbs in the following examples, you'll see that they are 1-place predicates, and that the expression that they combine with appears to play the role of initiating the action described:

(81)   Alison ran.

(82)   Anson joked.

(83)   The horse galloped.

These verbs are said to combine with an expression which plays the role of the **Agent** of the proposition (or sometimes the **Causer** or **Actor**). This contrasts with the following 1-place predicates, where the expression plays the role of the thing that undergoes some change of state or position:

(84)   Alison collapsed.

(85)   Anson appeared.

(86)   The horse fell.

In these examples, the predicate is said to combine with a **Theme**; a Theme is understood to be something which undergoes physical movement because of the effect of the predicate. One-place predicates which combine with an Agent are called **Unergative** predicates, while one-place predicates which combine with a Theme are called **Unaccusative** predicates. This is a very important distinction which has implications for syntactic structure, and we will come back to it below.

Many two-place expressions combine with both an Agent and a Theme:

(87)   Anson kicked the cat.

(88)   Jenny swallowed the fly.

(89)   Truman punched Johnson.

These two-place predicates are called **Transitive** predicates.

There are various other roles that we will come across (**Goal, Source, Experiencer**), and one way to think about them is to see them as generalizations over parts of the semantics of predicates. Certain predicates share the property of combining with Themes, forming a single semantic sub-class of predicates, that is differentiated from those that combine with Agents.

Linguists usually refer to these properties of predicates as **thematic roles**, and conceptualize of predicates as having thematic roles as part of their lexical semantics. In general, thematic roles only have a limited place in syntactic theory: they are really a concept which is relevant to lexical semantics. For this reason, we will not go into the different roles in any depth here. See the Further reading section for other works that discuss these.

There is a convention in linguistics that, if we are talking about how many thematic roles a predicate assigns, we refer to **theta-roles** (where theta is short for thematic, and itself is often abbreviated to θ). So instead of saying that a predicate needs two expressions with semantic content to make up a proposition, we can say that the predicate has two **θ-roles to assign**. The notion of assignment here is a convenient metaphor; we will return in Section 3.5.2 to the details of the actual mechanism that we need to implement it.

A one-place predicate, then, has one θ-role to assign, a two-place predicate has two and so on. Unaccusatives and Unergatives are alike in having only one θ-role to assign (and this whole class of predicates with only one θ-role to assign is called the class of **Intransitive** predicates). **Transitives**, on the other hand, have two θ-roles to assign. There are also, of course, predicates with three θ-roles, so called **Ditransitives**:

(90)   Arthur gave the tapestry to Lancelot.

(91)   The butler sent the poison to Dinah.

In (91), the butler is acting as the Agent, the poison is the Theme, and Dinah is said to be the **Goal** of the action.

The θ-roles assigned by predicates are of course purely semantic, but they seem to have an effect on the syntax. When a predicate has a θ-role to assign, but there's nothing in the sentence to which the θ-role can be assigned, then the sentence is usually judged as unacceptable:

(92)   *Anson demonized

(93)   *Anson put a book

These data suggest that every θ-role must be assigned to a constituent in the sentence. Moreover, each θ-role can be assigned to only one constituent. So we do not find a situation where a single constituent is assigned two θ-roles:

(94)   *Dantes accused

(94) cannot have the interpretation where Dantes is both the accuser and the person accused. This interpretation is ruled out if a constituent cannot be assigned more than one θ-role, since (94) would involve both the Agent role and the Theme role being assigned to the constituent *Dantes*.

Let us state this as a generalization, which we will come back later to derive from other theoretical principles:

(95)   **The Unique Θ Generalization**

Each θ-role must be assigned but a constituent cannot be assigned more than one θ-role.

Notice that the Unique Θ Generalization does not say that every constituent needs to be assigned a θ-role. There is empirical evidence against making this claim. Take an example like

(96)   Anson demonized David every day.

Here *demonize* is assigning its two θ-roles to *Anson* and *David*. What about the constituent *every day*? We've seen already that *demonize* only has two θ-roles, and they're both assigned here. *Every day* is therefore not assigned a θ-role. So although every θ-role must be assigned to a constituent, not all constituents are assigned θ-roles.

Only some of the constituents of a sentence are assigned θ-roles, and these are known as **arguments**. So, an argument is defined as a constituent in a sentence which is assigned a θ-role by a predicate.

Let's summarize this discussion:

1. A predicate has θ-roles to assign.

2. These θ-roles are assigned to constituents in the sentence.

3. The constituents to which the θ-roles are assigned are called arguments.

4. Every θ-role must be assigned to a constituent.

5. A constituent cannot be assigned more than one θ-role.

3.5.2 Unassigned θ-roles

The situation is a little more complicated than this. There are some predicates that seem to allow their θ-roles to remain unassigned. Examples include the verb *donate*:

(97)   The landlord donated a helicopter.

Donate is a three-place predicate, but only two of its θ-roles have been assigned in (97). There does not appear to be a constituent that is assigned the Goal θ-role. But notice that this sentence has to be contextualized. It isn't acceptable to utter it to someone out of the blue. The person who is being spoken to must know where the helicopter is being donated to. It's almost as though the θ-role is being assigned to the topic of the discussion. The question, then, is whether the topic of a sentence is a constituent, just one which is not overtly expressed in this example. If it is, then we can maintain the generalization that every θ-role is assigned to exactly one constituent.

There are also some predicates that are tricky in that they appear to allow θ-roles to be unassigned in the absence of context.

(98)   The students demonstrated (the technique) this morning.

(99)   I have eaten (my hat) already.

The bracketed phrases in (98) and (99) are optional. Why should this be?

The answer to the question just posed depends on the semantics of the verbs in (98) and (99). It turns out that these verbs are ambiguous between being one-place and two-place predicates. Take *demonstrate* first. In one meaning, this verb implies that the subject shows someone a way to carry out an action; this is the transitive (two-place) predicate. In the other meaning, the predicate also implies that there is a display of some kind going on, but there is no intention that the display is for the purpose of showing someone how an action is carried out, rather it is intended to show someone that the referent of the subject of the sentence is concerned about something. Exactly how to relate these two meanings is again a matter for lexical semantics, rather than for syntax.

Similar remarks can be made about *eat*. In its intransitive incarnation, this verb means to ingest the normal kind of food one requires for nourishment. In the transitive version, however, the verb just means to apply the same kinds of actions one usually applies to food ingested for nourishment to something or other. This is why, when there is no object, it is entailed that whatever was eaten was eaten for nourishment, while, in the presence of an object, this is not entailed, as you can see by the example above. This second example is far more subtle, but shows once again that there is enough in the way of a lexical semantic distinction to motivate two different syntactic specifications in terms of θ-role assignment.

All in all, it looks as if our generalization that every θ-role must be assigned to exactly one syntactic constituent holds quite well (although we have not given any good arguments that the topic of a sentence is a syntactic constituent with no phonological expression). As mentioned above, the Unique Θ Generalization allows us to predict much of syntactic structure from the properties of lexical items, which is theoretically a good move (since we need to specify the semantic properties of lexical items anyway) and which is also a useful practical aid in drawing tree structures for sentences.

3.5.3 Selectional features and lexical representation

The discussion above seems to suggest that syntax is somehow derived from semantic properties of lexical items. However, this is not quite the case. The point is that the Unique Θ Generalization is rather a useful generalization about how the syntactic structures interface with semantic interpretation. We still need to define a number of *syntactic* properties of lexical items, aside from their semantic properties.

Take, for example, a verb like *feel*:

(100)   Julie felt hot.

(101)   Julie felt he was there.

(102)   Julie felt a twinge in her arm.

All three of these sentences have an interpretation where Julie experiences some internal sensation. What θ-role will we assign to the constituent that plays the role of engendering the feeling? A fairly standard analysis would be to say that *Julie* is assigned an **Experiencer** θ-role, while *hot, he was there*, and *a twinge in her arm* are assigned a Theme (or perhaps **Source**) θ-role. But *hot* is an adjective, *a twinge in her arm* is nominal in nature, and *he was there* is a whole sentence. So the Theme θ-role can be realized as any of these syntactic categories. This means that it is not possible to predict the syntactic category from the θ-role. It must be independently specified.

It follows from this that we need to define a mechanism whereby certain syntactic properties are associated with particular θ-roles; the θ-assigning properties of lexical items don't, on their own, allow us to determine the category of a syntactic argument.

The argument goes the other way too. We have seen proper names acting as Agents, Themes, and Experiencers so far. So we can't predict from the category of a constituent (assuming proper names are nouns) what θ-role it will be assigned. This means that, even though there is a tight relationship between semantic roles and syntactic requirements, the latter can't be straightforwardly predicted from the former.

The standard way to express statements about the category of the constituent to which a particular θ-role is assigned is by means of **categorial selectional features** (usually abbreviated **to c-selectional features**), and it is to these that we now turn.

A c-selectional feature is a categorial feature on a lexical item, which does not determine the distribution of the lexical item itself; rather it determines the category of the elements which will be able to Merge with that lexical item.

This sounds complicated, but an example should make it clear. Take a word like *kissed*: this clearly has a V-feature since it is the past tense of a verb, but it also has (at least one) **c-selectional N-feature**. This N-feature signifies that something that Merges with *kiss* must itself have a categorial N-feature. So we can Merge a noun like *pigs* or like *Peter* with *kiss*, but we cannot Merge another verb, or a preposition:

(103)   kissed Peter; kissed pigs; *kissed eat; *kissed by

Another name for c-selectional features is **subcategorization features**.

What are c-selectional features? Recall the distinction we made in Chapter 2 between interpretable and uninterpretable features. Interpretable features are those features which have an effect on the semantic interpretation of a category. Uninterpretable features are features which seem to make no difference to the semantics of a sentence, but which are somehow required if we are to explain the (un)grammaticality of certain sentences. Case features, for example, simply regulate the position of certain nouns in certain structures.

We will now adopt an idea about uninterpretable features which we will use throughout the book: we will assume that the syntactic structure to which the semantic interface rules apply should consist only of interpretable features. If this structure contains uninterpretable features, then the semantic rules will not be able to assign a complete interpretation to everything in the structure. We will call this general constraint **Full Interpretation**:

(104)   **Full Interpretation**: The structure to which the semantic interface rules apply contains no uninterpretable features.

It follows from Full Interpretation that uninterpretable features must be eliminated from the syntax before the semantic interface rules apply. The intuition we will pursue is that this is what the job of syntactic operations is: they apply in order to eliminate uninterpretable features.

There are a number of ways of implementing this idea. The one we will adopt for concreteness is the following: if an uninterpretable feature enters into a syntactic relation with another feature of a particular sort, the uninterpretable feature is marked for elimination. Features which are marked in this way undergo a sort of self-destruction when they appear at the level where the semantic interface rules apply. They all vanish.

Let's now look at how to apply these ideas to c-selectional features: we will say the following:

(105)   The **Checking Requirement**: Uninterpretable (c-selectional) features must be **checked**, and once checked, they can delete.

(106)   **Checking under Sisterhood**: An uninterpretable c-selectional feature F on a syntactic object Y is checked when Y is sister to another syntactic object Z which bears a **matching** feature F.

To see this in action, imagine we have a tree like that in (107):

(107)

$$X$$
$$Y[uF] \quad Z[F]$$

I have notated that the feature F on Y is uninterpretable by prefixing it with u. Now, by the statement in (105), uF on Y must be checked and it gets to be checked by being in a syntactic relation with another F feature somewhere else. Since Z is a sister to Y, the syntactic relation of sisterhood allows feature matching to take place, and uF to be checked. We will notate this by marking uF with a strikethrough. So the tree in (107) will transform into the tree in (108):

(108)

$$
\begin{array}{c}
\text{X} \\
\diagdown \\
\text{Y}[u\text{F}] \quad \text{Z}[\text{F}]
\end{array}
$$

When the derivation stops and the semantic interface rules apply, all the checked uninterpretable features self-destruct, so that the final representation consists only of interpretable features, as required by Full Interpretation.

From this perspective we can now see c-selectional features as simply uninterpretable categorial features on a head. So a word like *kiss* has an interpretable [V] feature (which contributes to its interpretation as involving an event) and an uninterpretable [uN] feature. If *kiss* Merges with a noun bearing an interpretable [N] feature, then this Merge allows the checking of the uninterpretable [N] feature on the verb. As a tree we have:

(109)

$$
\begin{array}{c}
\text{VP} \\
\diagdown \\
\text{kiss } [\text{V},u\text{N}] \quad \text{pigs } [\text{N}]
\end{array}
$$

This tree is generated from the lexical item *kiss*:

(110)   kiss [V, uN]

This featural specification will rule out the starred examples in (103), since in both the bad cases *kissed* is combining with something which is not nominal. This means that its uninterpretable (c-selectional) [uN] feature will not be checked. If, however, *kiss* Merges with *pigs*, then they are in a syntactic relation and the N feature of *pigs* and the [uN] feature of *kiss* match. This checks the [uN] feature on the verb, leading to eventual grammaticality.

This same idea immediately allows us to deal with the examples which we ruled out via the Unique Θ Generalization. The verb *demonize* takes two arguments. Concentrating just on the Theme argument, we need to specify a c-selectional feature on *demonize*. Since this verb needs to combine with a nominal, we'll assume that it has a c-selectional N-feature (the " . . . " here just signifies that the verb has other features, in which we are not interested here):

(111)   demonize [V, *u*N, . . .]

This **lexical specification** will rule out examples where *demonize* combines with an adjective or prepositional constituent:

(112)   *Anson demonized old

(113)   *Anson demonized up the Khyber

However, it will also rule out a case where the verb has no argument of any sort:

(114)   *Anson demonized

This is because the *u*N feature on the verb will not be matched by anything else in the structure, and will therefore not be checked, contrary to what is required by the Checking Requirement.

What we have done here is provide a syntactic implementation of the Unique Θ Generalization: we say that each θ-role is associated with a c-selectional feature of some sort, and therefore a syntactic constituent must Merge with the lexical item bearing this feature. It then follows that each θ-role will be associated with a selected constituent in the sentence.

3.5.4 S-selectional features

Now c-selectional features appear actually to do only part of the job that we need to have done. This is because lexical items constrain more than just the syntactic category of the constituents with which they combine. They also constrain the semantics. In the following examples, you can see that the verb *intone* can be followed either by a nominal, or by something which looks much like a simple sentence:

(115)   Genie intoned the prayer.

(116)   Genie intoned that she was tired.

So, in terms of category, we would want to say that *intoned* can have either of the following c-selectional features: [*u*N] or [*u*Sentence] (we will come back to the real category of a sentence later on). However, not just any nominal will do:

(117)   *Genie intoned the mirror.

In this sentence, there is a semantic mismatch between the requirements of the verb, and the nominal that is merged with it. We can represent this by semantic features: in this case we might say that the sister of the verb *intone* must be [+sayable]. Likewise, we could rule out examples like the following by requiring that the single argument of the predicate be [+animate]. Rather than c-selectional features, the concept that is relevant here is **s(emantic)-selectional features**:

(118)   *The bookcase ran

(119)   *The airport panted

(120)   *The fig chortled

We will not go through all the kinds of s-selectional features that have been proposed, since this, once again, is really a matter for lexical semantics, rather than syntax. However, there are three semantic categories that are very important for an understanding of the interface between semantics and syntax. These are: **proposition, entity**, and **property**. Propositions we have already met. The difference between a predicate like *eat* and a predicate like *intone* is that *intone* can s-select a proposition, while *eat* only s-selects an entity (that is, something which semantically is some kind of object, or thing), giving us the following pattern:

(121)   I intoned that she was happy.

(122)   *I ate that she was happy

(123)   *I intoned fruit

(124)   I ate fruit.

Properties are best thought of as some kind of attribute of an entity. So an entity like an apple might have the property that it is green, or that it is rotten, or that it is poisoned. One good way to think about properties is to think about how propositions are built up. Usually we talk about propositions as describing a situation, or state of affairs. They do this by attributing a property to an entity. So the proposition that the apple is poisoned is built up out of the property of being poisoned and the entity the apple by stating that the property holds of the entity.

Certain verbs need to Merge with syntactic objects which are, semantically, properties, rather than propositions or entities. A good example is a verb like *become*:

(125)   *Anson became that he was happy

(126)   Anson became happy.

(127)   Anson became the Mayor.

Clearly *become* cannot combine with a proposition (125). If you think carefully about the meaning of (126) and (127), you'll see that they involve the entity Anson changing the set of properties that he has by adding a new property (that of being happy, or that of being the Mayor). (127) does not mean that there is some entity that is the Mayor (who has a name, lives in a big house, and runs the city) and Anson becomes him or her, rather it means that Anson takes on the property of being the Mayor (which is really a role of some kind, rather than an object).

Properties, propositions, and entities, then, are our major semantic categories that lexical items s-select for. Each of these categories has a number of sub-categories: so entities might be animate or inanimate, abstract or concrete, etc. (It might seem odd to talk of inanimate abstract entities, because we usually associate the word entity with something animate; however, we are using entity here in a technical sense to mean just something which human beings conceive of as, somehow, a thing.) Propositions might be factual or non-factual, assumed by the speaker to be true or not, and so on. Properties seem to have a wide range of possibilities, such as being audible, coloured, etc. (witness the weirdness of examples like *That bookcase is loud* or *This song is red*). Notice that properties, like entities and propositions, can be fairly complex:

(128)   He became [fond of peanuts].

(129)   He is [unhappy about his contact-lenses].

You might wonder if it isn't somewhat of an overkill to have both c-selectional and s-selectional specifications. In fact, a continuing strand of research over the last twenty-five years or so has attempted to derive c-selectional features from s-selectional features, but no one has been completely successful yet. For our purposes, we'll simply assume that both are required.

However, although s-selectional features are important for capturing our judgements about unacceptability of sentences, we will assume that Merge itself is blind to these properties, following our more general perspective on the idea that semantic properties do not drive syntactic operations:

(130)   Merge does not inspect s-selectional properties.

This means that sentences which violate some s-selectional requirements will be syntactically well formed. Our system will generate such sentences, and the rules of semantic interpretation will construct a semantic representation out of them. However, that representation will be semantically anomalous.

Selectional features of both types are associated with θ-roles. A useful way of thinking about this is to imagine that lexical items have, as part of their specification, a slot for each θ-role that they assign. These slots are arranged into a list, called a θ-**grid**. Each slot has two aspects: one looks at the lexical semantic part of the word, and states what particular thematic role and s-selectional properties are associated with the slot; the other looks at the syntactic aspect of the slot, and states what syntactic category features are associated with it. So a lexical item like *donate* has the following internal structure:

(131)

Donate	Syntax (c-selection	θ-grid (i.e. list of	Semantics (s-selection	Thematic roles
V	features)	θ-roles)	features)	
	N	x	entity	Agent
	N	y	entity	Theme
	P	z	entity	Goal

The table in (131) specifies part of the lexical entry for the verb *donate*. I have represented the θ-grid as a list of letters (x, y, z). The θ-grid just tells us how much of the verb's lexical semantics is syntactically active (in this case the lexical semantics is partitioned into three parts for use by the syntax). The relations between the θ-grid and the lexical semantics of the predicate tell us what thematic roles and s-selectional properties are associated with each element of the θ-grid, while the c-selectional features tell us what categories of the syntactic arguments are assigned those roles.

3.6 Triggering Merge by feature checking

We have now built up the following definition of Merge:

(132)   **Definition of Merge:**
   1. Merge applies to **two** syntactic objects to form a new syntactic object.
   2. The new syntactic object is said to **contain** the original syntactic objects, which are **sisters** but which are not linearized.

3. Merge only applies to the **root** nodes of syntactic objects.

4. Merge allows the checking of an uninterpretable c-selectional feature on a head, since it creates a sisterhood syntactic relation.

Setting up the definition of Merge in this way gives us an independent way of determining the head of a Merged structure:

(133)   **Definition of Head:** The head is the syntactic object which selects in any Merge operation.

Recall that we implemented selection by assuming that c-selectional features were uninterpretable, and we stated the following requirement:

(134)   The **Checking Requirement:** Uninterpretable features must be checked, and once checked they delete.

We've seen how this works schematically already (in Section 3.5.3). I repeat the basic structure here for ease of reference:

(135)

$$kiss \ [\text{V} \dots]$$

$$kiss \ [\text{V}, \cancel{u\text{N}} \dots] \quad pigs \ [\text{N}, \dots]$$

The verb *kiss* has a c-selectional feature [*u*N] and the noun *pigs* has the categorial feature N. This means that Merge can take place between the V and the N and that the [*u*N] feature of the verb is checked by the categorial feature of the noun.

As already mentioned, this idea now gives us a handle on the facts that we earlier captured by appealing to the Unique Θ Generalization. Recall that the Unique Θ Generalization required that each θ-role be assigned to a constituent. Now, if a head bears a number of c-selectional features, each associated with a θ-role via a θ-grid, and if c-selectional features are uninterpretable and must be eliminated, then it follows that each c-selectional feature will have to be checked, leading to the assignment of each θ-role. Examples like (136) will be ungrammatical because a c-selectional feature of *put* has not been checked:

(136)   *Anson put a book

Given our definition of head, this system of feature checking also ensures that the verb is the head of the new constituent in a structure like (135). This follows since the verb selects, and hence, is the head. The defining property of heads is that they project their features. Let us state this as follows:

(137)   **Headedness**: The item that projects is the item that selects.

We predict, then, that the constituent *kiss Peter* should have the same distribution as other verbs, rather than as other nouns. This seems to be exactly right:

(138)   I want to [kiss pigs].

(139)   I want to [sing].

(140)   That I should [kiss pigs] is my fondest dream.

(141)   That I should [dematerialize] is my fondest dream.

(142)   *[Kiss pigs] is my happiest memory

(143)   *[Computerize] is my happiest memory

We can now return to a question about how Merge works that we raised in Section 3.3. In that section, we proposed that Merge always applies to the root nodes of two trees. Putting this together with our approach to heads, we now predict that it is impossible for a syntactic object A to Merge with object B, checking B's selectional features, if A still has selectional features which are unchecked.

Why is this? Well, if we were to Merge with an element with unchecked selectional features, then these features could never be satisfied by an application of Merge, because they would be 'stuck inside' the structure. Schematically, we rule out structures like (144):

(144)

$$
\begin{array}{c}
\text{X} \\
\diagdown \\
\text{Y } [u\!\!\!/\!Z] \quad \text{Z } [u\text{W}]
\end{array}
$$

In the tree in (144), Z checks the c-selectional feature of Y (which is [uZ]), and Merge forms the syntactic object X out of Y and Z (where Y is the head of X, by our definition). However, there is nothing around to check the c-selectional feature of Z itself (that is, [uW]). Even if we merge some W later on, it will never be a sister to Z, and so never be able to check the c-selectional feature of Z, since c-selectional features are only checked under sisterhood.

(145)

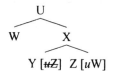

This means that we will be left with an unchecked uninterpretable feature, and this will violate Full Interpretation.

This all sounds rather abstract, but it has immediate desirable consequences. Take an example like the verb *become*, which we looked at earlier. *Become* s-selects for a property, and c-selects for an Adjective, so we have examples like:

(146) Anson became [$_A$ muscle-bound].

(147) Daniel became [$_A$ blond].

But if we have an adjective like *fond*, which itself has selectional requirements, we find that we have to satisfy these:

(148) *Julie became [$_A$ fond]

(149) Julie became [$_A$ fond of Lloyd].

Now, the system we have set up forces us to generate a structure for (149) where *fond of Lloyd* is a constituent, rather than one where *became fond* is a constituent, that is, we have (150) rather than (151):

(150)

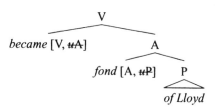

(151)

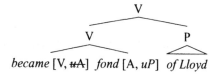

Why is this? If you look at the tree in (151), you can see that the adjective *fond* has a c-selectional feature [*u*P], but this feature has not been checked, and never can be. This problem does not occur in the topmost tree (150).

This turns out to be the right result. Pseudoclefting tests show us that while there is evidence for *fond of Lloyd* being a constituent, there is no evidence that *became fond* is a constituent (see exercise 1 of this chapter for pseudoclefts):

(152)   What Julie became was [fond of Lloyd].

(153)   *What Julie did of Lloyd was [become fond]

We can conclude then, that a fairly abstract property of our system gives the right results for particular facts about English syntax. This is obviously the kind of result we want.

A good example of this whole system in action comes from nouns that have θ-roles to assign. We can deal with an example like *letters to Peter* by adopting the idea that *letters* has a θ-grid with a single argument on it. This argument is associated with: (i) an optional c-selectional feature [*u*P] which allows a prepositional element to merge; (ii) the semantic specification that this entity has the thematic role of Goal. Concentrating on the c-selectional requirement, it seems, at first glance, that we incorrectly predict that an example like the following should be grammatical:

(154)   *letters to

(155)

N
———————
letters [N, pl, ~~*u*P~~] P

Here the c-selectional feature of *letters* has been checked by the P-feature of the preposition. To ensure that (154) isn't generated, we assume that *to* itself has a c-selectional feature. Let's assume that *to* has a selectional N-feature, [*u*N]. Given that selectional features must be checked, we now rule out structures like (156) and hence examples like (154):

(156)

N
———————
letters [N, pl, ~~*u*P~~] P [*u*N]

The structure in (156) will always have the unchecked N feature of the preposition, because, no matter what else is Merged, it will be merged higher up in the tree. This entails that the c-selectional feature of *to* will never be checked. The only way out of this dilemma, as in the case that we saw above, is to satisfy the selectional feature of *to* before merging with the noun.

(157)

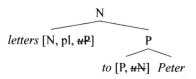

The proposal that Merge always applies to root nodes, then, receives strong empirical back-up. We can derive this requirement from a more general fact about the way that syntactic derivations work, if we say that syntactic operations in general always apply to the root projection of a tree. In the examples we have seen above, Merge applies between two syntactic objects, one of which bears a c-selectional feature. The checking of this feature is also a syntactic operation, which applies to the head of the root of the tree, matching this with another feature. Checking and Merge, then, always apply at the root, so that syntactic derivations are **extended** by the application of operations to the root projection of the tree. Let us state this as a general constraint:

(158)   The **Extension Condition**: A syntactic derivation can only be continued
         by applying operations to the root projection of the tree.

The Extension Condition effectively prohibits setting up syntactic relations between objects which have already been constructed inside a structure. For example, imagine the following schematic tree:

(159)

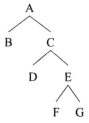

On the assumption that A is the projection of the head B, it will be possible to set up syntactic relations between B and C for checking purposes. In fact, we will see in later chapters that it is also possible to set up syntactic relations which span more distance in the tree: between B and F, for example. However, the

Extension Condition prohibits a syntactic operation applying to, say, D, since it is not the root projection of the tree in (159). Any operation involving D must apply before B is Merged (i.e. it must apply while D is the head of the root). This will disallow Merge of some object with D, and it will also disallow checking between D and, say, F.

Summarizing, the (syntactic) head of a constituent built up by Merge is the lexical item that projects its features to the new constituent. That lexical item will be the one that triggered application of Merge in the first place by being specified with c-selectional features that need to be checked. All c-selectional features must be checked by applications of Merge. Unchecked features on a tree result in the structure being ill formed. Finally, syntactic operations always apply to the root projection of the tree.

3.7 Summary

This chapter has gone from the concrete to the abstract at a fairly fast pace. The important conceptual points are the following:

(160)

- Sentences have a complex hierarchical structure.
- This can be captured by the binary tree-building operation Merge.
- Properties of heads project through this structure.

We proposed a number of principles:

(161)   **Full Interpretation**: The structure to which the semantic interface rules apply contains no uninterpretable features.

Pursuing the intuition behind (161), we suggested that one of the roles of syntactic operations was to eliminate uninterpretable features from syntactic representations. We implemented this intuition by assuming two further ideas:

(162)   The **Checking Requirement**: Uninterpretable (c-selectional) features must be **checked**, and once checked, they can delete.

(163)   **Checking under Sisterhood**: An uninterpretable c-selectional feature F on a syntactic object Y is checked when Y is sister to another syntactic object Z which bears a **matching** feature F.

And we saw that the following generalization followed from the mechanisms we proposed:

(164)   The **Unique** Θ **Generalization**: Each θ-role must be assigned but a constituent cannot be assigned more than one θ-role.

We also imposed a strict condition on how derivations run:

(165)   The **Extension Condition**: A syntactic derivation can only be continued by applying operations to the root projection of the tree.

This condition allows derivations to continue only by application of operations to the outermost layer of the tree.

We also met a number of general phenomena for which we provided theoretical explanations.

Phenomenon	Explanation
constituency	Binary Merge interacting with the checking requirement on c-selectional features
headedness	Unchecked features of the selector project to the mother node
classes of predicates	θ-roles are associated with selectional features via the θ-grid
selectional restrictions	C-selectional features as uninterpretable categorial features which have to be checked under sisterhood

Exercises

Exercise 1 Pseudoclefts

There is another type of sentence which is often used to provide constituency tests: the *pseudocleft*. Pseudoclefts work in a similar way to clefts: they involve removing a constituent from a sentence and then joining it back on with other stuff in the way. Some examples should make this clear:

(1)   I love focaccia and sun dried tomatoes.

(2)   What I love is focaccia and sun dried tomatoes.

(3)   We donated a chopper to the new hospital.

(4)   What we donated a chopper to was the new hospital.

(5)   Alison and David soaked their feet after dinner.

(6)   When Alison and David soaked their feet was after dinner.

(N.B. This last sentence is, again, a little stilted. It sounds better if you put *The time* before *when*. The same applies to the where-pseudocleft in (8): it sounds better if you prefix *The place* before *where*)

(7)   Alison and David soaked their feet in the kitchen.

(8)   Where Alison and David soaked their feet was in the kitchen.

Part A

Task 1 Write down a procedure, as explicitly as you can, which explains how to form a pseudocleft out of a simple sentence.

Part B

Task 2 Does your procedure extend to the following example? If not, alter it so that it covers all the examples so far.

(9)   What Alison and David did was soak their feet in a bucket.

Part C

Task 3 Now apply your procedure to the following sequences from (5):
    their feet after dinner;
    Alison and David;
    soak their feet
Discuss what your results mean for the constituency of this sentence.

Part D

Task 4 Now use all the other constituency tests you can and state what you think are the major constituents of (7).

Exercise 2 Replacement tests

Work out the constituency of the following sentences, using replacement, movement, clefting and pseudoclefting tests.

For replacement, try to use the following single words to replace sequences: pronouns, *one*, *this*, *these*, *that*, *those*, forms of the verb *do* (sometimes these sound better if followed by the words *so* or *that*), *there*, *then*.

(1) Anson shot the pterodactyl with his rifle in the jungle.

(2) Julie and Fraser ate those scrumptious pies in Julie's back garden.

(3) Michael abandoned an old friend at Mardi Gras.

(4) In every club in London, people threw up their hands in the air.

(5) We decided to paint the bathroom a lurid lime green colour.

Exercise 3 **Phrasal verbs**

Part A

The following two sentences look superficially similar:

(1) He looked up the number.

(2) He walked up the hill.

However, it turns out that they have rather different constituent structures. The most striking fact is that in (1) but not (2) the word *up* can appear at the end of the sentence:

(3) He looked the number up.

(4) *He walked the hill up

Traditionally, verbs which behave like *look up* are called **phrasal verbs**.

Task 1 Think up five more examples of phrasal verbs, and five examples of verbs which are not phrasal but can appear in sentences like (1) and (2) with the same superficial structure.

Task 2 Show, using the clefting test, that your phrasal verbs and your non-phrasal ones have a different constituency.

Task 3 Show, using replacement, that your phrasal verbs and your non-phrasal ones have a different constituency. (Hint: use the word *there* as a test for a PP constituent.)

Task 4 Show, using a simple movement test, that your phrasal verbs and your non-phrasal ones have a different constituency.

Part B

Phrasal verbs differ in their syntax from non-phrasal verbs in a number of other ways. For example, phrasal verbs with pronominal object tend towards unacceptability if the prepositional element precedes the pronoun:

(5)   He looked it up.

(6)   *He looked up it

Task 5 Test to see whether this is true for your own examples, and show any contrasts with non-phrasal verbs.

Task 6 Try to think up other ways in which the syntax of phrasal verbs differs from the syntax of non-phrasal ones. (Hint: think about the position of adverbials like *slowly*, *often*, prepositional constituents like *in the town*, and expressions like *as quickly as he could*.)

Exercise 4 Trees

Study the trees below. For each tree state: (i) the root node; (ii) the terminal node(s); (iii) the node(s) that are immediately contained (dominated) by the root node; (iv) the node(s) that immediately dominate a terminal node; (v) the sister(s) of the nodes you picked out in (iii); (vi) the sisters of the nodes you picked out in (iv).

(A)

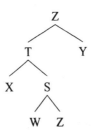

(B)

(C)

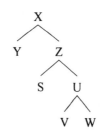

(D)

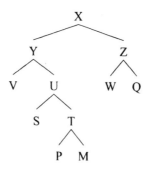

Exercise 5 **Merging trees**

Now draw the trees that result from merging the following. Since Merge does not determine linear order there are two answers for each:

(i) (A) and (B); (ii) (A) and (C); (iii) (C) and (D); (iv) (B) and (D).

Exercise 6 **Distribution and heads**

Make up sentences which show whether the following pairs of constituents have the same distribution. Remember that you are looking for judgements of grammaticality, so you might have to come up with odd contexts to make the sentence acceptable. Once you have done this, hypothesize which word is the head, and give a justification for your hypothesis. I have done the first one for you as an example:

(1)   on the boat; inside an egg

These do share distribution. The following examples suggest this:

(2)   He wrote the book on the boat/inside an egg.

(3)   He put his money on the boat/inside an egg.

(4)   The chicken gestated on the boat/inside an egg.

(5)   I live on a boat/inside an egg.

I hypothesize that the heads are *on* and *inside* respectively, since removing them results in a completely different distribution.

(6)   on the boat; there

(7)   six shot glasses; drinking the absinthe

(8)   coffee-flavoured; very interested in cocktails

(9)   drank tequila; fond of tequila

Further reading

Section 3.2
The basic constituency tests go back to Bloomfield (1933), Wells (1947), and Harris (1951), to name but a few of the practitioners of American Structuralist syntax. More up-to-date discussion can be found in most of the standard textbooks (Haegeman and Guéron 1999, Radford 1981, Ouhalla 1998).

Section 3.3
Terminology for trees can also be found in most standard textbooks. The idea that syntactic structures are binary goes back to work of Richard Kayne (especially Kayne 1984).

Section 3.4
See the papers in Corbett, Fraser, and McGlashan (1993) for discussions of the notion head in grammatical theory, and Lyons (1968) for an early but thorough theoretical discussion.

Section 3.5

The notion of thematic role goes back to Fillmore (1998) and Gruber (1965). Today this notion continues to be a controversial one. See Dowty (1991), Jackendoff (1987) and the papers collected in Wilkins (1988) for discussion. An accessible discussion can be found in Saeed (1997). The difference between c-selection and s-selection was first explored in depth by Grimshaw (1979). See also the discussion in Chomsky (1986*b*). For the idea that intransitive verbs split into two different syntactic classes, see Perlmutter (1978) and Burzio (1986).

Section 3.6

The main ideas from this section (feature checking) come from Chomsky (1995*b*), ch. 4 and Chomsky (2000), although Chomsky does not implement c-selection in the way that I have done here. For the precise definition that Chomsky gives for Full Interpretation (adapted slightly in the chapter) see these works.

4

Representing Phrase Structure

4.1 Introduction

The previous chapter introduced the idea that the syntactic operation Merge combines lexical items into larger syntactic objects, and then combines these into larger objects still, giving rise to complex hierarchical structure. In the current chapter, we will see that the hierarchical structures we met in the last chapter are organized into **phrases**, and that this organization derives from their selectional properties.

We will concentrate on one of the most important aspects of sentence structure, the structure built up around the verb. We will see that verb phrases arise from the interaction between the selectional properties of the verb, and the way that phrase structure is built up through syntactic operations.

We will also introduce a new syntactic relation: **c-command**. We will see how c-command can be used as a diagnostic tool to probe into the internal workings of the verb phrase, and we will use it to motivate various aspects of the internal structure of the verb phrase.

Finally, we will round off with an overview of the general architecture of the theoretical system we are engaged in developing.

4.2 The structure of phrases

In the previous chapter, we saw that sentences have a complex hierarchical structure, and we captured this by proposing that sentences are built up using the binary operation Merge, which combines syntactic objects together. The idea that it is the properties of the selecting head that project into the higher structure allows us to capture the fact that the most important element inside a structure determines its distribution. In this section we will focus on how far the properties of a head project up through the structure.

4.2.1 First Merge—Complements

Recall that one of the important predictions made by our system was that all the c-selectional features of an element have to be checked before that element is Merged with a c-selecting head. This was what ruled out examples like (1):

(1) *letters to

This is ruled out because *to* has a c-selectional [*u*N] feature which has not been checked. Since c-selectional features are checked under Merge, and Merge always takes place at the root node, there is no way for this feature of the preposition *to* ever to be checked. It is 'trapped' inside the structure.

On the other hand, if we check the [*u*N] feature of *to* by first Merging a noun with the preposition, then we get grammaticality:

(2) letters to Peter

Syntactic objects which have no c-selectional features to be checked (such as the constituent *to Peter* in (2)) are called **maximal**, since they project no further. A maximal syntactic object of category X is abbreviated XP, and is said to be a **phrase** of category X. So a maximal object which is nominal is NP, a maximal object which is prepositional is PP, and so on. This means that we can annotate a tree for (2) above in the following way:

(3)

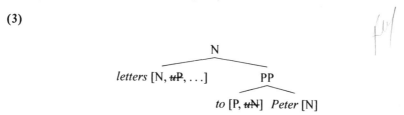

I have not put a phrasal annotation on the root node of the tree, as we don't yet know whether it will be the head of some further Merged structure (i.e. I have not specified whether there are further selectional features that need to be satisfied, hence the ' . . . ' in the feature specification of *letters*).

I have also not marked the teminal node *Peter* as a phrase although, technically, it is one. It has no selectional features to be checked, and so, given our definition, it is a maximal projection. It is also a **minimal projection**, since it is just a lexical item (but see Chapter 7 for further discussion).

The preposition *to* on its own is minimal (since it is a lexical item) and not maximal (since it has a feature to check). The syntactic object containing *to* and *Peter* is maximal (since it contains no selectional features), and not minimal (since it is not a lexical item). The following table summarizes this, and adds comments on the other nodes in the tree:

(4)

Node	Minimal	Maximal	Comments
Peter	yes	yes	A lexical item with no c-selectional features
to	yes	no	A lexical item with a c-selectional feature
to Peter	no	yes	Neither a lexical item nor has c-selectional features
letters	yes	no	A lexical item with a c-selectional feature
letters to Peter	no	??	Not a lexical item; may still have features to be checked

It is very important to note that the phrasal status of a node is derived from its featural composition: if a node has no c-selectional features to be checked then it is maximal. This means that if a lexical item like *to* checks its c-selectional features by Merging with a noun like *Peter*, the new object constructed by Merge does not have any c-selectional features to be checked, and hence is phrasal.

It follows from this discussion that only maximal projections can be sisters of c-selecting heads. If a non-maximal projection is Merged, its unchecked c-selectional features will be 'trapped', leading to ungrammaticality (since all uninterpretable features must be checked).

As an example of how the phrasal status of a node changes when Merge applies, take a verb like *burn*. *Burn* has two θ-roles, both associated with c-selectional N-features. Concentrating on the theme role, we can Merge the tree in (3) with the projection of *burn*, to give:

(5)

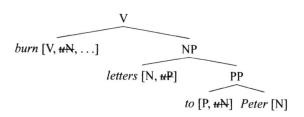

Notice how the projection of *letters* which is merged with the verb is now phrasal, since all of its selectional features have been checked. It turns out that there were no further c-selectional features hidden inside the [...] of its feature bundle as specified in (3) (this is not always the case for nominals as you will see in Chapter 7). This NP itself satisfies the c-selectional feature of *burn*. Again, I have not marked the projection of the verb as phrasal, since its phrasal status is not determined until it has Merged with yet further material.

Notice also how the constituent structure we have derived gives the right results. If (6) is an order or a command, then we can have the three following sentences (recall the imperative structures introduced in Exercise 2, Chapter 2):

(6) Burn letters to Peter!

(7) Burn letters to him!

(8) Burn them!

We can see from the replacement test in (8) that we have the right constituency here.

The kind of structure we are building up here, where a possibly complex phrasal element merges with a lexical item which projects, is called a **head-complement structure.** Head-complement structures arise from the first application of Merge to satisfy a selectional feature of a head.

The NP *letters to Peter* is said to be the **complement** of *burn* in (5). The PP *to Peter* is the complement of *letters*, and the NP *Peter* is the complement of *to*. In English, complements come to the right of the head that selects them. This is also true for languages like French, Gaelic, and Arabic. Other languages, like Japanese, Korean, and Turkish, have complements which precede their selecting heads, as you can see from the following example from Japanese:

(9)   Hanako ga   **Taro o**   tataku
      Hanako subj Taro   obj hit
      "Hanako is hitting Taro."

Whereas *Taro*, the complement of the verb *tataku*, "hit", follows its verb in English, it precedes it in Japanese (marked bold in the example).

Nominals in Japanese also take their complement to the left rather than to the right:

(10) **buturigaku no**   gakusei
      physics   genitive student
      "The student of physics"

A traditional name for nominal complements of verbs is objects. So in an example like (11), *Meg* is the object of *met*, and also its complement. Languages where the object comes after the verb are usually termed Verb-Object languages (abbreviated to VO). Languages where the object comes before the verb are Object-Verb languages (OV).

(11)   Michael left Meg.

In general then, when a head X combines with only a single complement (i.e. it has just one selectional feature to satisfy) then we find the following two **linearizations** of the basic head-complement structure:

(12)

(13)

In this book we will assume that the different orders arise because of different linearization properties of head-complement structures, as outlined here. However, see the Further reading section for pointers to alternative analyses of this sort of linguistic variation.

4.2.2 Second Merge—Specifiers

In our example above, we assumed that *burn* has two elements on its θ-grid. One of these was associated with a Theme θ-role and selectional N-features. The other is associated with an Agent θ-role, as in:

(14)   Paul burns letters to Peter.

Here *Paul* is assigned the Agent θ-role, and *letters to Peter* is assigned Theme. We said above that checked c-selectional features delete and therefore they cannot project any further. However, there is still an unsatisfied selectional feature associated with the verb which remains after the complement has been Merged. In order for this selectional feature to be satisfied, another nominal must be Merged, and this nominal will then be assigned the Agent θ-role. Let us see how this might work:

(15)

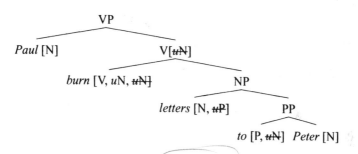

In this tree, we can mark the root node as phrasal, since we now know there are no more selectional features of V to be checked. I have explicitly shown two selectional N-features on the verb: one is checked by the merged complement, but the other, because it is not satisfied by the first application of Merge, is checked by the NP *Paul*. This happens in this way because one of the c-selectional features of the verb is unchecked, and projects to the next node up in the tree. At this point, it can be checked when an NP Merges as its sister.

Notice that we now have three levels of projection for the verb: we have the lexical item itself (the **minimal projection**, written as X^{min}—in this particular case we have V^{min}). A minimal projection isn't really a projection of anything; it is simply the lexical item. The second level is the **maximal projection**, which results when all selectional features have been checked (written as XP (VP), or sometimes as X^{max} (V^{max})). Finally, we have an **intermediate projection**, sometimes called the **bar-level projection**, and written as X' (V') or $\bar{X}$ ($\bar{V}$). The intermediate projection is not a lexical item, but there are still selectional features left to check. It is extremely important to note that the different levels of projection are **derived** from feature checking, rather than being extra primitives that we have introduced into the theory.

Recall that we defined 'complement' above as the sister of a lexical item or, equivalently, as the product of the first Merge operation with a head. The sister of an $\bar{X}$ projection (*Paul* in the tree above) is termed a **specifier**. Specifiers are the outcome of the second Merge operation. In contrast to complements, specifiers in English are linearized to the left of their head.

Once again, we find languages with apparently different linearizations of Specifier-Head structures. For example, whereas in English the Agent precedes the remainder of the VP, in Malagasy, it appears to follow it:

(16)   Manasa   lamba ho an' ny ankizy **ny lehilahy**
       PRES-wash clothes for ACC the children the man
       "The man is washing clothes for the children."

However, the idea that what we have here is a rightwardly linearized specifier is once again controversial. The actual structure of these sentences is far more complex (again, see the Further reading section).

One point about abbreviations: the abbreviation for 'maximal projection' is X^{max}, or more usually, XP; the abbreviation for 'minimal projection' is X^{min} or just X. In the example above *burn* is a V^{min}, but this is equivalent to just saying that it is a V. *Peter* is also a minimal category (an N^{min} or just N), but at the same time it is a maximal category (N^{max} or NP).

4.2.3 Adjunction

We now return to some data that we introduced when discussing θ-roles. Recall that some of the constituents in sentences are assigned θ-roles by heads. We gave the following example:

(17)   Anson demonized David every day.

Here the two θ-roles that are associated with the θ-grid of *demonize* are assigned to *Anson* and *David*. We can capture this by saying that *demonize* has two c-selectional N-features associated with its two θ-roles, and that, since these features have to be checked, both θ-roles are assigned.

The other major constituent in the sentence (*every day*) does not receive a θ-role from *demonize*, or from anything else in the sentence. Semantically it seems to have the function of placing in time the situation described by the rest of the sentence. Here are some other examples of constituents which also have a **modificational** rather than an argumental role:

(18)   Anson demonized David **at the club**.

(19)   Anson demonized David **almost constantly**.

(20)   Anson **very happily** demonized David.

These constituents are known as **adjuncts**. Adjuncts are elements that are somehow incorporated into a sentence, but not via the checking of selectional features.

Note that the term adjunct is not a term for categories, but rather a term for syntactic objects which occupy a particular position in the tree, much like the terms complement and specifier. Adjuncts may be of all sorts of categories. We will see that Adjectives and their AP projections may function as adjuncts in nominal phrases (Chapter 7), and that PPs may function as adjuncts in both NPs and VPs (you can see a PP adjunct in (18)). The category for the adjuncts in (19) and (20) (*constantly* and *happily*) is **Adverb** (abbreviated **Adv**). Adverbs are usually related to adjectives in terms of their morphological form. Both the adverbs in (19) and (20) are formed from related adjectives by adding the affix *-ly*. You can see that the adverbs in these examples combine with other elements to form **adverbial phrases** (AdvPs), in the same way as all other categories may project.

The mechanism by which adjuncts are incorporated into phrase structure is still a major research topic. In this book we'll adopt a fairly conservative position: adjuncts are sisters of phrasal nodes. This approach ensures that there is parallelism between adjuncts and specifiers and complements. Complements are sisters of lexical items; specifiers are sisters of $\bar{\text{X}}$ nodes, and adjuncts are sisters of XP nodes:

(21)

Notice that the phrasal level of XP does not change, since there is no satisfaction of a selectional feature.

The question here, then, is what triggers the integration of an Adjunct into the tree. When we discussed Merge above, we suggested that it only applied when triggered by a selectional feature. But no selectional feature appears to be satisfied here. Moreover, we cannot put a selectional feature on the adjunct, since then the adjunct would be the head of the construction. However, the evidence is that adjuncts are never the heads of their constructions: a constituent which has an adjunct **adjoined** to it behaves distributionally just as though the adjunct wasn't there.

We can see this by taking an adverb like *quickly*. If we adjoin this to a verb phrase, then the verb phrase's distribution is exactly the same, as you can see from the following examples:

(22)   a.   Burn the letters (quickly)!
       b.   I burnt the letters (quickly).
       c.   I plan to burn the letters (quickly).
       d.   *Burn the letters (quickly) is the best thing to do.
       e.   Burning the letters (quickly) is the best thing to do.

We don't need to know about these different structures to tell that whether we have the adjunct or not makes no difference to the distribution of the verb phrase: it is (un)acceptable in exactly the same sentence frames, whether the adverb is present or not.

So adjuncts are not incorporated into the sentence by Merge. We will assume, instead, that there is another basic operation, which we will call **Adjoin**, and which, unlike Merge, does not need to be triggered. Adjoin is somewhat like the version of Merge that we rejected above, which inserted one syntactic object into another, although it is far more restricted. Adjoin inserts a phrasal object into another phrasal object at its outermost level. It does not create a new object, it expands one of the old ones by stretching its outermost layer into two parts and inserting the adjoined object between them:

(23)

Any phrase can be adjoined to another phrase, and adjunction in English is assumed not to be linearized, so that an adjunct can usually appear on either side of a phrase.

The properties of adjoined elements that follow from this approach are that they are always hierarchically outside complements and specifiers; that they may appear on either side of the phrase they are adjoined to; that they don't receive θ-roles, and, via a stipulation, that they are phrasal.

If we go back to our previous examples, we can deal with a case where the VP is modified by the adverbial adjunct *quickly* in the following way:

(24)   Kiss Anson quickly!

Recall that imperatives have an unpronounced Agent. For the moment we will just assume that this Agent is in the specifier of VP, and we will notate it as *e* for 'empty element'. This gives us the following tree:

(25)

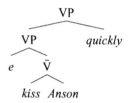

Since adjuncts can adjoin on either side, we can also have:

(26)   Quickly kiss Anson!

(27)

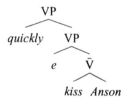

We will return to the syntax of adjuncts in more detail in the next couple of chapters. The crucial points to remember are that adjuncts freely target phrasal categories, and that they adjoin to these creating an adjoined structure.

Before leaving Adjuncts, we should note a problem which we will deal with in the next chapter: if adjuncts target phrasal nodes, and the subject of a verb is in the specifier of that verb's VP, then how are sentences like (28) possible?

(28)   Julie quickly answered the question.

Here we have a case where the adverb comes between the subject and the verb, but we've just said that our system predicts that adjuncts will always be hierarchically external to specifiers (and complements). In this example, at first blush anyway, it looks as though the adjunct gets Merged before the specifier, so that when we pronounce the sentence, the specifier *Julie* is pronounced first. Let us leave this problem for the moment, and address it in the next chapter.

4.2.4 The structure of the verb phrase

We have now built up a picture of the phrasal projection of the verb: the VP. We have seen that the verb Merges with a complement to give a $\bar{V}$, and then with a specifier, satisfying all its c-selectional features and giving a VP. We have also seen that adjuncts may adjoin to this VP. This means we have the following schematic structure for a transitive verb phrase:

(29)

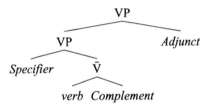

We have also seen that Specifiers and Complements have to be phrasal (that is, they must have no c-selectional features).

The system we have been developing seems to allow more than one selectional feature to appear on a lexical item (this was the analysis of verb phrases we discussed above). This raises the question of the **order** of checking of features; how does the system determine which one gets checked first?

The reason that this question is important, even for the simple examples that we have looked at so far, has to do with the semantics we want to give our syntax. In an example like (30), there is no ambiguity as to which noun phrase is interpreted as the agent, and which as the theme:

(30)   Jenny poked Jonathan.

However, under the system we have so far set up, c-selectional features are matched with θ-roles via the θ-grid. If we check the wrong feature first, then we would predict that the θ-roles would be assigned the other way around (with Jonathan being the poker, and Jenny the pokee). This is, of course, a matter for how we configure the interface between the syntax and the semantics, and we will address it in Section 4.5.

The structure that we have built up is only preliminary, and will need some modification. Specifically, we need to address the question of the structure of intransitives and ditransitives. We also need to address the question of how the verb phrase is integrated into the rest of the sentence (a task which we will postpone until the next chapter).

4.2.5 X̄–Theory

We have now developed a system which gives us much of what is traditionally known as **X̄–Theory** (pronounced X-bar theory). X̄–Theory was originally conceived of as a set of constraints on phrase structure (recall the phrase structure rules introduced in Chapter 1), which stipulated that all phrases have to have heads, and that the two crucial types of phrase are the head-complement structure, and the specifier-X̄ structure. X̄–Theory was commonly stated as a set of general constraints that require all phrase structure rules to have the following general format:

(31)   XP → ZP X̄

(32)   X̄→ X WP

Trees generated by such rules will always have the general form in (33), where I have used the variables X, Z, and W to stand for arbitrary labels.

(33)

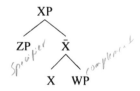

ZP here is the specifier of X, while WP is its complement.

Often you will see trees which are drawn along these lines. There are two major differences between these trees and the tree structures we have developed above. The first is that many proponents of X̄–Theory assume that lexical items are dominated by or contained within the minimal projection level rather than actually *being* that minimal level. The second is that X̄–Theory enforces projection through *all* the levels. These two properties taken together mean that every phrase immediately dominates a bar-level projection which immediately dominates a minimal level projection which immediately dominates the lexical item. This is true, in X̄–Theory, whether there is a specifier or complement or not. The tree in (15) would look as follows under the X̄ system:

(34)

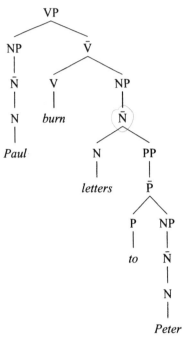

As you can see, the only real difference is that, when a head has no complement or specifier, in the X̄ system, each level of projection is nevertheless filled in. The X̄ system leads to trees that are more uniform, but, on the other hand, there are many extra layers of structure in this tree.

In contrast, because the phrasal status of a node is derived from its lexical properties in the system we have been developing, bar-level projections only appear when there is a specifier. If the head combines with just a complement, and all of its features are satisfied at that point, then the complement is automatically phrasal. Likewise, if a head has neither complement nor specifier, then it is automatically phrasal. So, as we have seen already, proper names and pronouns (under the analysis we have so far given them, which may be too simple—see Chapter 7) are automatically phrasal, and at the same time automatically minimal, since they are lexical items.

4.3 C-command

We are now going to introduce a new syntactic relation aside from sisterhood. We shall see that this syntactic relation is implicated in the analysis of reflexives, and that it gives us an extremely useful tool for diagnosing structure. Once we have developed a theory of this relation, we will use it to choose between a number of different structural hypotheses which are available for the analysis of ditransitives.

4.3.1 Defining the relation

As we have seen, the operation Merge builds up tree-like structures. In any tree, the most important syntactic relation that holds between two nodes is that of sisterhood, which is built up by the fundamental operation, Merge. In addition to sisterhood, there is another important syntactic relation which holds between nodes in a tree: this is the relation of **c-command** (an abbreviation of constituent-command).

We shall define c-command in the following way:

(35)   A node A **c-commands** a node B if, and only if A's sister either:

    a.   is B, or

    b.   contains B.

Let's look more carefully at this definition. The 'if, and only if' part (sometimes abbreviated to 'iff') means that whenever either of the two conditions hold, then A will c-command B, and whenever A c-commands B, one of those two conditions has to hold. This is a common way of writing definitions in syntax.

The first condition is straightforward enough. The second condition is best thought of as an instruction: if you want to see whether one node c-commands another, see whether its sister contains that other node.

An example:

(36)

Here, X c-commands Y, but nothing else. This is because Y is X's sister. Since Y doesn't contain any other nodes, it turns out that X c-commands only Y in this tree. Z, however, c-commands S (because S is Z's sister) and also W and R (since W and R are contained in S).

Note that S c-commands Z, X, and Y (nothing in the definition refers to precedence, so a node can c-command preceding as well as following nodes).

The node T doesn't c-command anything, nor is it c-commanded by anything, since it contains all the other nodes and hence has no sister.

Before we go on, it will be useful to see examples of c-command in action. Remember from Exercise 1 in Chapter 2 that there is a class of words called reflexives in English which have to have the same ϕ-feature specification as another word in the sentence in which they occur. We saw in that exercise that certain relationships had to hold between the reflexive and the word with which it had to share features (known as the **antecedent** of the reflexive). It turns out that one of these relationships is c-command. The next section goes through an argument to this effect, and in the following section, we will explore another argument that c-command is a crucial syntactic relation.

4.3.2 Reflexive binding

The following contrast is a stark one:

(37)   I shaved myself.

(38)   *Myself shaved me

If we take the Reflexive Generalization we started with in Exercise 1 in Chapter 2, then we can see that nothing in this generalization helps us explain this contrast. The generalization looked as follows:

(39)   **The Reflexive Generalization**
A reflexive pronoun must be coreferential with another expression in the sentence.

We also assumed the following:

(40)   For two expressions to be coreferential, they must bear the same ϕ-features.

Now, in both of our examples we have two expressions which share ϕ-features, one of which is a reflexive. The generalizations we have here, then, don't seem to be able to capture the contrast between the two examples.

We can improve on this situation by revising the Reflexive Generalization:

(41)   **The Reflexive Generalization (revised)**
A reflexive must be coreferential with a c-commanding expression.

Now, since an object is c-commanded by a subject (since the object is contained in the subject's sister ($\bar{V}$, under our current assumptions), but not vice versa, the contrast follows. In (38), the reflexive is not coreferential with a c-commanding expression, because, even though it is coreferential with *me*, it is not c-commanded by *me* as you can see from the following tree:

(42)

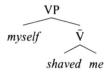

The new Reflexive Generalization, making reference to c-command, gives us the theoretical power to explain the contrast we are interested in.

You might think that the Reflexive Generalization should be thought of as involving precedence, rather than c-command. Imagine, for example, we say that a reflexive has to be coreferential with a preceding expression. This will also capture our contrast.

(43)   The Reflexive Generalization (revised)
A reflexive must be coreferential with a preceding expression.

However, this new hypothesis does not extend well to other data. Consider the following examples:

(44)   The man I saw left.

(45)   *The man I saw shaved myself

In this example, the pronoun *I*, which can usually be a perfectly fine antecedent for *myself* (see, for example, (37)), precedes the reflexive, but the sentence is not well formed. However, we can show by constituency tests that *the man I saw* in other grammatical sentences is a constituent:

(46)   The man I saw left.

(47)   He left.

(48)   You wanted to meet the man I saw.

(49)   It was the man I saw that you wanted to meet.

Since *the man I saw* is a constituent, it contains the pronoun *I*. The structure is, roughly:

(50)   *[The man I saw] shaved myself

Now let's look at the relationship between *I* and *myself*. We can see immediately that *I* does not c-command *myself*, since there is a node above it which does not contain the reflexive. In a tree structure, we have the following kind of rough structure:

(51)

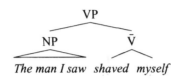

The man I saw shaved myself

We will see in the next chapter that there is further structure for this sentence than what is shown here. However, this is not relevant, since what is crucial for testing our hypothesis is the relationship between *I* and *myself*. We can see immediately that the V̄ which contains *myself* is not the sister of *I*. Nor is this VP contained in a sister of *I*, since any such sister will have to be contained within the NP *The man I saw*. So we can conclude that *I* does not c-command *myself*, although it does precede it. It appears, then, that the notion we need is c-command, rather than precedence, if we are to deal with these kinds of data. We therefore reject the version of the Reflexive Generalization which involves precedence, and maintain, instead, the version which makes reference to c-command.

A similar story will explain the ungrammaticality of (52):

(52)   *[My mother] hated myself

The possessive pronoun *my* here is inside the subject *my mother* and hence does not c-command the reflexive, thus violating the Reflexive Generalization.

4.3.3 Negative polarity items

There are a number of words in English known as Negative Polarity Items (usually abbreviated as NPIs—not to be confused with NPs!). These are words like *any* and *ever*, which appear to require a negative element to appear in the sentences in which they occur:

(53)   *I wanted any cake

(54)   I didn't want any cake.

(55) *I saw him ever

(56) I didn't see him ever.

Let us state this as a basic generalization, which we will then revise when faced with further data:

(57) **The NPI Generalization:** NPIs must occur in a sentence which is negative.

Just as the Reflexive Generalization needed to be revised, so does the NPI Generalization. This can be seen from the following contrast:

(58) No one wanted any cake.

(59) *Any boy saw no one

Assuming that a sentence containing the words *no one* is counted as a negative sentence, then in (58), we have a negative sentence containing the NPI *any*, and our generalization correctly predicts this to be grammatical. However, in (59), we have a negative sentence containing *any*, but the sentence is ungrammatical.

We can revise the NPI Generalization using the notion of c-command to capture these facts:

(60) **The NPI Generalization (revised):** NPIs must be c-commanded by a negative element.

We have already seen that objects are c-commanded by subjects, but not vice versa. Given this, example (59) is ruled out because the *any boy* is in subject position and therefore not c-commanded by *no one*.

This new approach extends to further cases fairly naturally. Take an example like (61):

(61) *The picture of no one/hung upon any wall

In this example, *The picture of no one* is a constituent, as can be seen from replacement tests:

(62) It hung on the wall.

Given this, the negative element *no one* is inside this constituent, and therefore cannot c-command the NPI *any*, thus ruling out the sentence. Once again we see that what is relevant here is a structural notion (c-command), rather than a purely linear one (precedence) or even a semantic one (negativity).

4.3.4 Summary

We have seen that the notion of c-command is relevant to explaining the distribution of reflexives and NPIs. We will see that it is also relevant for explaining the behaviour of pronouns and other NPs in the exercise section of this chapter.

If our explanation for reflexives and NPIs is correct, then what we have is a tool for diagnosing the structure of sentences. If we are careful, we can put reflexives or NPIs in various positions in sentences that interest us, and use the resulting patterns of grammaticality to see whether c-command relationships obtain. This is an important result, since it adds new diagnostic tools, in addition to constituency tests, to our syntactic toolbox. In the next section we will use all of these tools to try to work out the structure of ditransitive verb phrases.

4.4 Ditransitives

The basic structure that we have built up for transitive verbs looks to be in trouble when we come to predicates with three arguments. Under the system we have built up so far, we have seen that verbs have a Complement, which is the first phrase to be Merged with the head, and a Specifier, which is the second. In this section we will look at what happens when we have a third argument.

4.4.1 Three-argument predicates

As we saw in Chapter 3, some predicates have three arguments. The relevant examples contain predicates like *give* and *receive*:

(63)   Benjamin gave the cloak to Nathan.

(64)   Nathan received the cloak from Benjamin.

Clearly in (63) and (64), there are three participants in the event: Benjamin, Nathan, and the cloak. Accordingly, the NPs and PPs in the syntax are assigned θ-roles by the predicates *give* and *receive*. These predicates, like the predicate *donate* that we met in the last chapter, are three-place predicates.

4.4.2 Ternary or binary branching?

The immediate question that arises with three-place predicates is the question of constituency. How is a ditransitive VP structured? In this section we shall look at two analyses, one involving a ternary branching structure, and the other involving a binary structure.

The first analysis is one which involves a **ternary-branching** structure. This looks as follows:

(65)

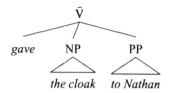

Note that this analysis is not available to us if we maintain just the binary operation Merge. In order to construct a structure like in (65), we would need an operation which builds ternary syntactic structures as well as binary ones.

There is another analysis which is open to us within the theoretical restrictions set by Binary Branching. We simply say that *to Nathan* and *from Benjamin* are merged with the projection of the verb after the object has been Merged. In each case the Merge of the PP checks off a selectional feature on the projection of the verb. This gives us structures like the following:

(66)

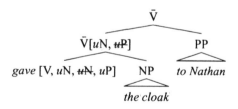

To make this work, we need to say that *give* has three selectional features, and so it is specified as [uN, uN, uP]. One of the N-features is checked by the object and the other by the subject. The selectional P-feature is checked off by the Goal. Notice that this analysis involves the recursion of the V̄ level, which is something we haven't seen as yet. This might be a little worrying, since the only cases where we have seen recursion of a node like this is with adjuncts, and adjuncts, unlike Goals, don't get a θ-role.

This analysis also raises, once again, the question of the ordering of checking. This time, this question is more urgent, since we need to ensure that the P feature is not checked off before one of the N-features. If the system allowed this, then we would expect the PP to be sister to the verb, predicting the following word order:

(67) ??Benjamin gave to Lee the cloak

This sentence is unacceptable, unless it carries a very special intonation (with a pause before *the cloak*) which, we will assume, is associated with a special structure where the object has moved rightwards over the PP. The unacceptability of these examples is increased when we put a pronoun in for the object, backing up the idea that there is something special going on in such structures. We therefore don't use structures where the PP precedes the NP as evidence for determining the basic analysis of ditransitives:

(68)   a.   *Benjamin gave to Lee it
        b.   Benjamin gave it to Lee.

Notice that the ternary branching analysis and the $\bar{\text{V}}$-recursion analysis make different claims about constituency. Under the latter analysis, the verb and its object form a constituent, while this is not the case in the ternary branching approach.

Can we find evidence which will support one constituent analysis over the other?

It seems that movement tests do not support the binary branching analysis. It is not possible to cleft VPs in most dialects of English, but there is a construction, called **VP-Preposing**, where the VP moves to the left of the sentence.

(69)   a.   Benjamin said he would run away and he did [run away].
        b.   Benjamin said he would run away and [run away] he did.

(70)   a.   Madeleine planned to catch the sardines and she did [catch the sardines].
        b.   Madeleine planned to catch the sardines and [catch the sardines] she did.

When we apply this constituency test to our ditransitive examples, we find that it is possible to VP-prepose the verb together with the object and the Goal:

(71)   Benjamin said he would give the cloak to Lee and [give the cloak to Lee] he did.

However, it turns out not to be possible to prepose just the verb and its object:

(72)   *Benjamin said he would give the cloak to Lee and [give the cloak] he did to Lee

The Binary Branching analysis treats *give the cloak* in this sentence as a verbal constituent, and we might, therefore, expect to be able to prepose it. However, this is impossible, so we have no evidence that this is the correct constituency.

What about other constituency tests? Replacement/Ellipsis seems to give the same results:

(73)   a.   Who gave the cloak to Lee?
       b.   *Benjamin (did) to Lee

The (b) example shows that we cannot take the string *give the cloak* and ellipt it or replace it with the simple auxiliary *do*.

One final constituency test we might try is co-ordination. In English, the word *and* can be used to conjoin two phrases:

(74)   [The intrepid pirate] and [the fearful captain's mate] sank the galleon.

(75)   Owly hated [the evil bat] and [the wise eagle].

(76)   Owly [hated the evil bat] and [loved the wise eagle].

(77)   The [very old] and [extremely wise] owl.

In (74), we have co-ordinated two NPs in subject position; in (75) we have co-ordinated two NPs in object position; (76) shows the co-ordination of two verbal projections and (77) the co-ordination of two APs. Co-ordination does not seem to apply to non-constituents, as the following examples show:

(78)   *Owly hated [the evil] and [the wise] eagle

(79)   *Owly [hated the] and [loved the] bat

Co-ordination, however, sometimes gives results which aren't immediately consistent with other constituency tests, and so it's a test to be used carefully. For example, the following examples are possible, even though it is unlikely that the co-ordinated strings are constituents:

(80)   [Lee's youngest] and [Dawn's oldest] son ran away.

Note that this sentence has a particular intonation, with a long pause after the words *youngest*, and a special intonation on the word *son*. Why should this be? One possibility is that this is really a case of constituent co-ordination, but the noun in the first noun phrase has been ellipted, so that (80) is really (81), without the first occurrence of *son* being pronounced. Since the first constituent has an ellipted element in it, the word *son* is pronounced in a special way to signal that this word provides the interpretation for the ellipted element.

(81)   [Lee's youngest 0] and [Dawn's oldest son] ran away.

With this in mind, we can look at our ditransitives. Note that, in this case, we can have the following, which is on the margins of acceptability:

(82)   Benjamin [gave the cloak] and [sent the book] to Lee.

Once again, however, we need to have a substantial pause after *cloak* as well as odd intonation on the PP *to Lee*, suggesting that we have a case of deletion again:

(83)   Benjamin [gave the cloak 0] and [sent the book to Lee].

Given the results of the other tests for constituency of verb plus object in ditransitives, and given the alternative explanation for the grammaticality of (82), it seems that we must once again draw the conclusion that this binary branching analysis is not supported by any evidence from constituency.

We have seen, then, that there is no evidence that the verb and the object form a constituent to the exclusion of the PP. This seems to rule in favour of the ternary structure, even though we have adopted only binary Merge. However, it turns out that there is some evidence for another binary constituency pattern in a ditransitive VP, where the object and the PP form a syntactic unit. We shall explore the consequences of this idea in the next section.

4.4.3 A binary alternative

It is co-ordination, interestingly, that provides some evidence for an alternative view of the constituency of ditransitive VPs. Consider the following example:

(84)   Sam gave [the cloak to Lee] and [the magic chalice to Matthew].

This appears to be evidence for a different constituent analysis, with the object and the Goal in constituency. Given the discussion above, should we analyse this kind of sentence as involving VP co-ordination and deletion of the verb instead?

(85)   Sam [gave the cloak to Lee] and [0 the magic chalice to Matthew].

There doesn't appear to be the same kind of phonological pause that we saw in the examples above. If the intonational evidence is worth taking on board, the grammaticality of (84) with no special intonational pattern would lead us to propose that *the cloak to Lee*, and *the magic chalice to Matthew*, are just plain old constituents.

This is a fairly weak argument so far, but suggestive. Let us take this evidence at face value for the moment and see whether an alternative binary branching analysis, which treats the object and the goal as forming a constituent together, might work.

The rough structure of ditransitives, from this perspective, will look something like the following:

(86)

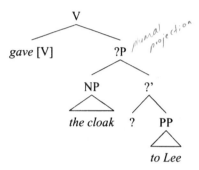

In this structure, the PP is the complement of some other head which has the object in its specifier. The phrasal projection of this head (just marked with a question mark in the tree for the moment) is the complement of the verb. To deal with the co-ordination data, we simply allow co-ordination of whatever ?P is.

Notice that this structure is compatible with the lack of evidence for a verb object constituent that we reviewed above, since, like the ternary structure, it makes no claim that the verb and the object are a constituent in a ditransitive structure.

One point that might cause us concern is that there is no evidence from movement for the existence of the constituent marked '?' above:

(87)   *Benjamin thought he would give the cloak to Lee and [the cloak to Lee] he gave.

However, it is not implausible that there are independent factors ruling (87) out. The VP-preposing operation may be sensitive to the category of the constituent being preposed, and ?P may just not be the right kind of constituent.

We now have three different structural hypotheses on the table: one is a ternary branching hypothesis, and the other two are binary branching. Of the latter two, the first hypothesis assumes that the Goal is essentially right adjoined to V̄, while the second assumes that there is a new constituent so far just labelled '?', which contains both the object and the Goal. The only structure which is consistent with the (admittedly weak) evidence from co-ordination is the third one, with the new '?' constituent.

Is there some other way that we can distinguish between the ternary and binary branching structures? One avenue that has been suggested is a set of asymmetries in c-command relations in some closely related structures called **double object constructions**.

A double object construction is a ditransitive which is lacking a preposition. The following examples illustrate:

(88)   a.   Benjamin gave Lee the cloak.
      b.   Calum sent Nathan the binoculars.
      c.   Lee showed Benjamin the unicorn.

The Goal in a double object construction is usually called the **indirect object**. Each of these examples has a corresponding sentence which contains a preposition (this is true for many, but not all, double object verbs):

(89)   a.   Benjamin gave the cloak to Lee.
      b.   Calum sent the binoculars to Nathan.
      c.   Lee showed the unicorn to Benjamin.

Notice also that the co-ordination data work out in the same way for double object constructions as for ditransitives. It is possible to co-ordinate the direct and indirect objects together, as though they were constituents:

(90)   Benjamin gave [Lee the cloak] and [Nathan the chalice].

The interesting thing about double object constructions is that there is an asymmetry in the way that reflexives can be bound in these constructions. We can see this in examples like the following:

(91)   *Emily showed himself Benjamin in the mirror

(92)   Emily showed Benjamin himself in the mirror.

Now, we have seen that the Reflexive Generalization requires a reflexive to have a c-commanding antecedent. If we adopt the ternary branching structure, then the indirect object and the direct object c-command each other:

(93)

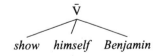

Remember that the Reflexive Generalization, as we formulated it above, does not make reference to linear order (precedence), only to c-command. If this is the correct formulation, then the ternary branching structure would lead us to expect that the reflexive would be well formed in indirect object position, contrary to fact (91). This is because *Benjamin* c-commands *himself* in (93), since these two nodes are sisters.

The Binary Branching structure which assumes that one of the arguments is adjoined to V̄, suffers from the same problem; once again *Benjamin* c-commands the reflexive, yet the sentence is ungrammatical:

(94)

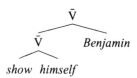

The Binary Branching structure which assumes the ?P, however, turns out to make the right predictions. We have the following structure:

(95)

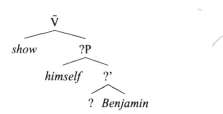

Notice in this structure that *Benjamin* does not c-command *himself*, correctly predicting that the reflexive will not be able to take Benjamin as its antecedent.

We can't make the same argument for the simple ditransitives with a Prepositional Goal, since the preposition will always block c-command from its complement to the object of the verb, whether we adopt a ternary or binary analysis. This means that the ungrammaticality of (96) is consistent with a ternary branching analysis as well as with a binary branching one incorporating ?P:

(96)   *Emily showed himself to Benjamin in the mirror

To see this, look at the following ternary structure:

(97)

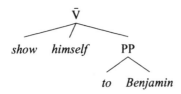

Since *Benjamin* is contained inside the PP, it can't c-command the reflexive. The same point can be made for the Binary Branching analysis with a V̄-adjoined Goal:

(98)

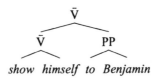

This means that the cases with PP goals don't help us to choose between the possible analyses; only the Double Object constructions can be used in this way. When we look at Double Object constructions, we see that there is an asymmetry in c-command relations between Goal and Object, suggesting a structure with the extra constituent labelled '?'. This is consistent with the argument we made earlier from co-ordination.

We have just seen that we can't make exactly the same argument for simple ditransitives (with PP goals) as for double object constructions. However, this doesn't mean that the analysis for the latter doesn't extend to the former. Since we need a ?P to deal with double object constructions, and since ?P allows us to maintain binary branching, it seems reasonable to adopt the assumption that simple ditransitives also contain a ?P, an assumption which also makes sense of the co-ordination data. We shall therefore assume the following structure for simple ditransitives:

(99)

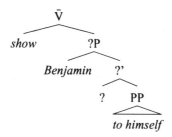

Summarizing, although there is only weak evidence from constituency tests (from co-ordination) that we should adopt the ?P analysis of ditransitives, we can use the behaviour of reflexives to determine the c-command relationships inside the VP, and thereby motivate one structure over another.

4.4.4 Causatives and little *v*

We now need to think about what the featural content of the head marked '?' might be. There have been a number of different answers adopted in the literature (see the Further reading section of this chapter). The approach we will initially adopt here is one which assumes that the syntactic relation between the verb and '?' is one which mimics a semantic relation: that of **causality**.

Many languages have structures, traditionally called **causatives**, which involve the juxtaposition of a verb with a special particle or auxiliary marking causation. Even English has structures a little like this:

(100) a. Emily caused Benjamin to see himself in the mirror.
       b. Benjamin caused Lee to have the cloak.
       c. Benjamin caused the book to go to Ross.

It is immediately obvious that these sentences are rough **paraphrases** of simple ditransitives:

(101) a. Emily showed Benjamin himself in the mirror.
       b. Benjamin gave Lee the cloak.
       c. Benjamin sent the book to Ross.

The intuition is that the paraphrases involving *cause* are actually very much like the basic structure that Merge produces for the examples with simple ditransitives. Notice that we can **transform** the causative examples into the ditransitives by some simple steps:

(102) a. Emily caused Benjamin to see himself in the mirror. → delete *to*
       b. Emily caused Benjamin see himself in the mirror. → move *see* to a position adjacent to *caused*
       c. Emily caused + see Benjamin himself in the mirror. → replace *caused-see* with *showed*
       d. Emily showed Benjamin himself in the mirror.

Other languages display aspects of these operations more clearly than English. French, for example, is a language where the subject usually precedes the verb:

(103) Georges mange.
       Georges eat-[PRES, 3SG]
       "Georges eats."

However, in a causative construction, the verb precedes the subject:

(104) Pascale fait   manger Georges.
       Pascale make-[PRES.3SG] eat-[INF] Georges
       "Pascale makes George eat."

It appears that we have a **Movement** operation, which takes a structure formed by applications of Merge, and then moves one of the elements of that structure into another position in the tree. In this particular case, the verb moves in front of the subject. We will mark the position which has been left behind by enclosing the words that were there in angled brackets:

(105) Pascale fait   manger Georges ⟨manger⟩.
       Pascale make-[PRES.3SG] eat-[INF] Georges
       "Pascale makes George eat."

Another language which seems to show the same syntactic process is Chichewa (a Bantu language). In Chichewa, the position of the causative element may be filled by an auxiliary, or the verb itself may appear in this position. We can see this in the next example:

(106) Mtsikana ana-chit-its-a   kuti mtsuku u-gw-e
       girl   [AGR]-do-cause-[ASP] that waterpot [AGR]-fall-[ASP]
       "The girl made the waterpot fall."

In this example we have two verbs, both of which mark for agreement (as a prefix) and for aspect (a suffix). The verb *-chit-*, "do" is followed by a particle (*-its*) marking that the sentence is a causative sentence. The verb *-gw-*, "fall", assigns its theme role to *kuti mtsuku*, "the waterpot". The word for girl receives an Agent role because it is a causer. We will assume that this role is assigned by the particle *-its*. Now consider the following example:

(107)   Mtsikana anau-**gw**-its-a   kuti mtsuku   ⟨gw⟩
        girl   [AGR]-**fall**-cause-[ASP] that waterpot
        "The girl made the waterpot fall."

Here, the same verb *-gw-*, "fall" has moved into the higher complex, constructing the morphologically complex verb *make-fall*.

Given that this kind of example is found in other languages, we will adopt the hypothesis that the derivation we gave above for *show* from (roughly) *cause to see* actually reflects what is going on, and that the ? is really a projection of the verb which then undergoes movement into a higher position, which encodes causality. We will notate this new causal category *v* (pronounced 'little *v*'). The structure before and after movement looks like this:

(108)

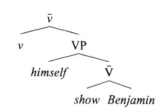

(109)

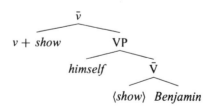

Rather than saying that *show* is literally *cause-see*, we assume that *show* basically has the meaning "see" but must move into a verb with the meaning "cause". As usual, we have labelled the nodes of the tree with just the category feature of the head, so the VP containing the object and indirect object is a projection of the verb *show*. This is true even once *show* moves into a position adjacent to the causal verb. This causal verb is often known as a **light verb** and this kind of analysis is known as a **VP-shell** analysis.

We will return later to the exact structure which is the output of the movement operation of *show* to *v*. For the moment we will just notate it as *v + show*.

Notice that this has the curious consequence that the constituent labelled VP doesn't have an overt verb in it. It has a sort of 'ghost' of the moved category in it, which does not feed the rules of morphology or phonology, in that it is not pronounced. These 'ghosts' of moved elements are usually called **traces**, and we will notate them (as we have already done informally), by enclosing them in angled brackets.

This same causative analysis will extend to cases where we have PP goals:

(110)

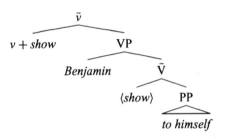

So far in this discussion, we have not addressed the question of how selectional features work. Recall that we originally proposed that the verb contained a number of c-selectional features that were checked off when various arguments were Merged. We will maintain this view here, so that *show*, above, is specified as [V, *u*N, *u*P], and little *v* as [*v*, *u*N]. This will give a representation which looks as follows:

(111)

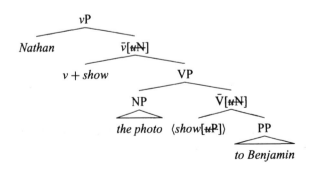

Here we see c-selectional features being checked under sisterhood. V first checks its [*u*P] feature via Merge of a PP. The unchecked [*u*N] feature is projected to V̄ and is checked by Merge of the NP sister to V̄ (i.e. the specifier of V). Little *v* then Merges with the complete VP (see below for the relation between these two categories) and projects its c-selectional [*u*N] feature to *v̄*. Merge of the NP Agent then checks this selectional feature.

When a selectional feature projects to a bar-level category, we will normally just represent it as being on that category. However, it is important to remember that such c-selectional features are actually lexically specified on the head, and only come to be on the bar-level category due to projection.

We also need to have some way of ensuring that little *v* is projected. One approach we might take would be to say that little *v* c-selects VP. However, this would be rather different from what we have said already about selection: up until this point we have assumed a tight relationship between selectional properties and θ-roles. But there is no clear sense in which little *v* is assigning a θ-role to the VP.

In order to keep the relation between little *v* and VP conceptually distinct from selection, we will just assume that there is a special **Hierarchy of Projections**, such that whenever we have a little *v*, it always has a VP complement. In an intuitive sense, little *v*P is an extension of the projection of VP, in that it is still verbal, but it adds further semantic information. We will state the Hierarchy of Projections as follows:

(112)   *v* ⟩ V

If the Hierarchy of Projections is not met, then the structure will be ruled out. This means, for example, that the following structure is not generated by the system:

(113)

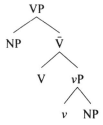

This new analysis, then, allows us to maintain a single version of Merge, which allows only binary branching structures. It also links ditransitive structures in

English to causative structures in general, attempting to explain their properties by tying them down to properties of other structures.

The analysis that we have developed is more complicated than anything else we have seen so far. As well as the syntactic operation Merge, it involves a new operation **Move**. This is a clear theoretical cost at the moment, and it's not clear why it's any better, from a theoretical point of view, to have binary Merge and Move, rather than binary and ternary Merge. We could imagine, for example, allowing ternary Merge and dealing with the reflexive data by refining the Reflexive Generalization, or by assuming a different kind of structure for Goals in Double Object constructions (perhaps they have an unpronounced preposition attached to them).

We will adopt the Merge and Move approach, however, and explore its consequences. We will see in Chapter 5 that there is evidence for movement of certain auxiliaries and in Chapter 6 that the subject in English sentences also moves. When we come to look at the structure of noun phrases in Chapter 7, we will see further evidence for movement processes, and after that point, movement will become fairly ubiquitous in our system and it will bear a heavy explanatory burden. We will not, in general, explore whether a non-movement analysis of these constructions is possible (it often is) or preferable. I will provide references in the Further reading section to non-movement approaches.

We have come to the conclusion in this section that ditransitives are more highly structured than they, at first blush, appear. We have argued (on the basis of co-ordination) that the object and the prepositional phrase are contained in a single constituent, and that the former c-commands the latter (on the basis of the behaviour of reflexives). In the next section, we will explore whether this VP-shell analysis can be extended to simple intransitives and transitives.

4.5 Linking

We now return to a question that we raised in Section 4.2.4, but which we have not dealt with yet: how do we constrain the order of checking so that the syntax semantics interaction works out correctly. Put more concretely, if we take a verb like *show*, then we need to say that it has two selectional features. We proposed above that these features were checked as follows:

(114)

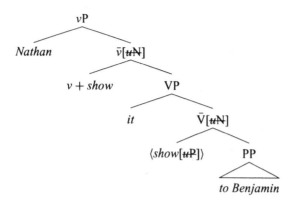

However, the question is why they could not be checked the other way around:

(115)

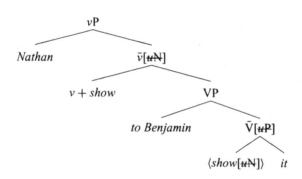

If this were possible, then we would generate the following ungrammatical sentence:

(116)   *Nathan showed to Benjamin it

Recall that we argued that sentences where the PP appeared closer to the verb than the object were only possible because of a separate movement process, and that this movement process was unavailable for pronouns. This means that the only possible parse for a sentence like (116) is one where the object and PP arguments are in their base position. This sentence clearly shows that the base position of the object is the specifier of the verb, rather than its complement.

The question, then, is how to constrain the order of checking for c-selectional features. The answer we will propose comes out of another question: how do we reconcile the analyses we have put forward for transitive and ditransitive predicates?

The VP-shell analysis for three-place predicates puts the Agent of the predicate in the specifier of the little *v*, and the Theme in the specifier of VP. If we compare this to the analysis we gave of transitive verbs, we see that analysis put the Agent in the specifier of VP, and the Theme in the complement of V.

These two analyses are compatible, but they lead to the idea that there is no uniform way that particular θ-roles are represented in the syntax. The Theme appears in either the complement, or the Specifier of VP, depending on which particular predicate you're looking at.

Many linguists have found this state of affairs to be rather unsatisfactory, mainly because it would mean that children acquiring the language would have to learn which particular structures occur with which predicates. This is often referred to as the **Linking Problem**. If, on the other hand, each θ-role had a particular syntactic configuration associated with it, then children acquiring the language can predict the syntactic structures that various predicates project on the basis of the θ-roles assigned by that predicate.

These linguists advocate a very tight relationship between θ-structure and phrase structure which is embodied in a hypothesis called the **Uniformity of θ-Assignment Hypothesis** (UTAH). The UTAH is seen as a solution to the Linking Problem and can be stated as follows:

(117)   **UTAH:** Identical thematic relationships between predicates and their arguments are represented syntactically by identical structural relationships when items are Merged.

The UTAH would rule out cases where the Theme is variously a specifier or a complement, or the Agent can be either the specifier of *v*P or the specifier of VP. You can see that the function of the UTAH is to rule out **classes of analyses**. It is a guiding hypothesis, which may turn out to be wrong, much like the Binary Branching hypothesis. It will be supported if the analyses it rules out turn out to be worse at capturing the empirical facts than the analyses it rules in.

Let us assume the UTAH. How can we make our two previous analyses compatible with each other assuming the UTAH? One way would be to assume that all Agents appear in the specifier of little *v*P, so that a simple transitive verb, like *burn*, would have the following representation:

(118)

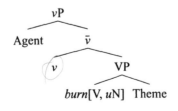

Thinking again about paraphrases, this kind of structure could be roughly paraphrased as follows:

(119)   X causes Y to burn.

If we look at this tree, and compare it to the tree we decided upon for three-place predicates, then we can see that the Agent is the specifier of *v*P. What about the Theme? It looks as if it is a complement here, but a specifier in the case of three-place predicates. However, we can use the fact that in both cases the Theme is the daughter of VP. We can then define Goal as the daughter of V̄. Each of the Thematic roles can then correspond to a unique phrase-structural configuration:

(120)   a.   NP daughter of *v*P → interpreted as Agent
        b.   NP daughter of VP → interpreted as Theme
        c.   PP daughter of V̄→ interpreted as Goal

We will explore some of the consequences of this approach in the exercises at the end of this chapter. Notice that the double object construction discussed in the last section seems to pose immediate problems for this approach. We will address these problems in Exercise 1.

Adopting the UTAH also gives us an answer to the question of the order of checking of selectional features. If the features are checked 'the wrong way round', then the UTAH will be violated. Take, for example, the ill-formed structure in (115), repeated here as (121). It is immediately evident that no interpretation can be given for the PP, since it is not the daughter of V̄:

(121)

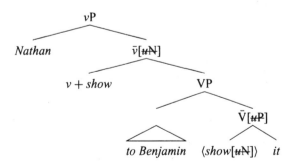

Of course, theories incorporating the UTAH also make very specific predictions about the structures associated with unergative and unaccusative predicates.

Since unergative predicates have a single Agent argument, that argument will have to appear as the daughter of *v*P, and since unaccusative predicates have a single Theme argument, that argument will appear as the NP daughter of VP. We get the following two structures:

(122)   Unergatives like *run, laugh, jump*:

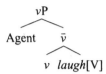

Intuitively, this structure means something like "X is the cause of an event of laughter". This contrasts with the following structure for an unaccusative verb:

(123)   Unaccusatives like *fall, collapse, wilt*:

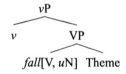

The rough paraphrase for unaccusatives is something like: "X undergoes an uncaused falling event". Note that we are using the notion "cause" here in a very abstract sense, essentially to indicate whether there is an agent involved in the event.

I have assumed here that there is also a *v*P in unaccusatives, but that the head of this *v*P is semantically non-causal, and so does not have an Agent in its specifier. An alternative, also consistent with the UTAH, would be to say that there is no little *v* in this structure. We will adopt the former assumption so that we can maintain the Hierarchy of Projections. This will mean that we always have a syntactic little *v* projection above a VP, but that the semantics of this little *v* may vary depending on the semantics of its VP complement. Once again, this is a controversial assumption, and one that we are adopting for convenience only here (see the Further reading section).

This idea, that Unaccusatives and Unergatives have different structural con-figurations associated with them, as well as different thematic roles to assign, is forced upon us, if we accept the UTAH. It predicts that unaccusatives and unergatives should display syntactic differences, which can be tied down to the distinct positions of the verb's single argument.

There is good evidence that this is the case. Take the two following sentences from Italian:

(124)   Molte ragazze telefonano.
         many girls   phone
         "Many girls are phoning."

(125)   Molte ragazze arrivano.
         many girls   arrive
         "Many girls are arriving."

The verb *telefonare*, "to telephone" is clearly unergative, since its single argument is interpreted as an Agent, in control of and causing an event of telephoning to take place. In contrast, the verb *arrivare*, "to arrive", is usually assumed to have a single theme argument. If you arrive at a destination, you have clearly undergone motion, and there is no necessary implication that you were the cause of this motion (you could have arrived by being driven in someone else's car, for example), or that you acted in any way to ensure that the arrival event happened (compare this to telephoning, where you have to be engaged in the activity of telephoning throughout).

Given this, the UTAH will predict that we have two different structures for these apparently parallel sentences. This seems to be a correct prediction, since these two sentences behave differently with respect to a range of syntactic diagnostics.

The most famous of these is auxiliary selection. When we put these sentences into the perfect tense, different auxiliaries appear with each:

(126)   Molte ragazze hanno telefonato.
         many girls   have phone-[PAST PART.3SG]
         "Many girls have phoned."

(127)   Molte ragazze sono arrivate.
         many girls   are arrive-[PAST PART.3PL]
         "Many girls have arrived."

In addition, we see different patterns of ϕ-feature agreement on the past participles, with the unaccusative verb agreeing with the subject, while the unergative verb does not.

We are not in a position to provide analyses of why we find these differences (see the Further reading section), but the fact that unaccusatives and unergatives display different syntactic characteristics is just what we expect from the UTAH. We will return to cases that further motivate this difference in Chapter 6.

4.6 The architecture of the system

We are now in a position to look at the general properties of the system we have been developing. Recall that we are trying to build up a theory of I-language, which captures the underlying structures of the sentences we use and understand. The approach we have taken relies on what is technically known as a **derivation**. A derivation can be thought of as the result of successively applying syntactic operations (in this case, the movement operation, which we will just call **Move**, plus Merge and Adjoin) to syntactic objects to form successively larger syntactic objects.

In the examples we have seen so far, we start off with a lexical item (say a verb) and merge another one (say a noun) with this. The outcome is a new syntactic object. This new object may then combine with another, and so on. Each application of Merge (or any other syntactic operation) moves the derivation a step forward. At some point, the derivation stops, because no further syntactic operations can be applied. The syntactic object at the final stage of the derivation is interpreted by the conceptual and semantic systems of the mind.

Notice that a derivation of a sentence will involve many smaller sub-derivations that will construct the constituent parts of a sentence. If we are to adjoin a VP to a PP, then smaller derivations must construct the PP and the VP separately.

What kinds of things are inputs to a derivation? The smallest elements in a derivation are lexical items which consist of phonological, semantic, and syntactic features. So a derivation starts off with a collection of lexical items, and provides a route from this collection to a well-formed sentence, if possible. A collection of lexical items is technically known as a **numeration**, although we will not be concerned with the technicalities of this here.

The syntactic system takes a numeration as its input, and gives, as output, a series of syntactic objects. So the first task of a derivation is to **Select** an element from a numeration. Since none of our syntactic operations can apply to a single lexical item and nothing else, the operation Select will apply again, and introduce another item. Now the syntax can merge or adjoin these two items to form a new syntactic object. Once a syntactic operation has applied, we have a **step** in the derivation.

(128)   a.   Step 1: Select A.
        b.   Step 2: Select B.

c.   Step 3: Merge A and B.

We now have a single syntactic object, so Select applies again, furnishing a new element from the numeration. At this point we may Merge/Adjoin this new element with our old syntactic object, or we may apply Select again and Merge/Adjoin the two selected elements to form a new syntactic object. Let us follow this latter possibility:

(129)   a.   Step 4: Select C.
         b.   Step 5: Select D.
         c.   Step 6: Merge C and D.

We could now apply Merge/Adjoin to the two constructed syntactic objects, or we could apply Select once more, and so on. If we take the former route, we have:

(130)   Step 7: Adjoin the output of Steps 3 and 6:

At some point, we will have exhausted the numeration, and we will not be able to apply any more syntactic operations. At this point, the derivation **terminates**. What we have now is a series of syntactic objects, one of which is the terminal object. This can have no further syntactic operations applied to it. When a derivation successfully terminates with all its uninterpretable features checked, it is said to **converge**; if it terminates but there are unchecked uninterpretable features, it is said to **crash**, by analogy with a computer program.

So far we have just seen this applying abstractly. Now let's have a look at a concrete example:

Numeration

{saw, *v*, Sam, Benjamin}

Derivation

Step 1 Select *saw* and *Benjamin*, Merge, satisfying *u*N feature of *saw*.

Output

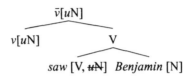

VP

saw [V, *u*N] *Benjamin* [N]

Step 2 Select *v* and Merge with output of Step 1, respecting the Hierarchy of Projections.

Output

$\bar{v}$[*u*N]

v[*u*N]   V

saw [V, u̶N̶] *Benjamin* [N]

Since no selectional feature is checked in Step 2, the c-selectional feature of *v* projects along with its other features to the $\bar{v}$ mother node. The checked c-selectional feature of *saw* does not project.

Step 3 Move *saw* to *v*.

Output

$\bar{v}$ [*u*N]

v + *saw*   V

⟨*saw*⟩ *Benjamin* [N]

We have not yet provided a trigger for the operation that moves the verb to *v*. This operation is obligatory (or else we would predict the wrong order of verb and object in ditransitive constructions). We return to the mechanism that implements movement of this type in the next chapter.

Step 4 Select *Sam* and Merge with output of Step 3, satisfying *u*N feature of $\bar{v}$:

Output

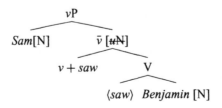

*v*P

Sam[N] $\bar{v}$ [u̶N̶]

v + *saw*   V

⟨*saw*⟩ *Benjamin* [N]

You can see that the derivation itself is fairly simple. When Merge takes place, it simply takes either a lexical item, or the outputs of previous operations, as its inputs.

Move is much more complex: it zooms in on part of a tree which has been constructed as an earlier output (in our case the lexical item *saw*) and makes a copy of that item, which it then Merges with another part of the tree (in this case the little *v*). It leaves behind the trace of the extracted item. In the current derivation, we see an example of movement of a lexical item. As we continue to develop the theory, we will also see the movement of phrases is possible.

All of the outputs of a derivation are, of course, syntactic objects.

One of these syntactic objects will interface with the parts of the mind which are concerned with meaning, sometimes called the **Conceptual-Intentional** (**CI**) system. It will be able to do so because of the way that the syntactic system has arranged the semantic features of lexical items. This is why word order and morphological inflections have an effect on meaning. The syntactic object which has this function is commonly known as **Logical Form** (**LF**), and it is said to be an **Interface Level**, since it is where the interface rules apply. Most usually LF is taken to be the terminal syntactic object.

One might imagine that, in a similar fashion, some syntactic object in the derivation will interface with the parts of the mind which are concerned with the physical realization of the object in terms of sounds, or gestures, sometimes called the **Articulatory-Perceptual** (**AP**) system (another interface level). However, research into phonology and phonetics over the last forty years or so has suggested that the level that interfaces with the AP system isn't a syntactic object, because other processes than purely syntactic processes are involved in constructing it. Instead, the assumption has been that a particular syntactic object in the derivation is the input to these extra processes which are concerned with pronunciation, morphological rules, etc. Such an object is known as the point of **Spellout**. Spellout is assumed to be a set of operations that apply to a syntactic object to give rise to a representation which interfaces with the AP system. This representation is known as **Phonetic Form** (**PF**). It is important to distinguish the Spellout point from PF. The latter is a level that interfaces with language external systems, while the former is just a tree structure to which various non-syntactic operations might still apply.

Because the syntax relates a numeration to both sound and meaning, it allows us to establish a link between them, thus accounting for the communicative power of language. In the rest of this book we will be mainly concerned with the properties of the syntactic derivation, rather than with properties of the interface levels. However, we will see that whether a phenomenon is to be handled by the syntactic component, or by the interface between syntax and either semantics or phonology, is often quite obscure, and requires careful argument.

The general architecture of the system we are assuming, then, looks as follows:

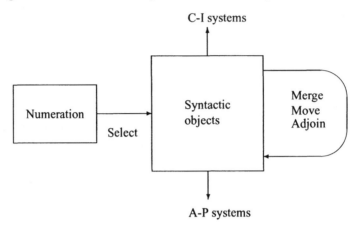

We have a numeration, drawn from the lexicon, to which the Select operation applies. This puts various lexical items on what you might think of as a syntactic tabletop; a workspace for the application of the syntactic operations Merge, Move, and Adjoin. These operations apply recursively, as marked by the arrow, so that after each application the state of the workspace changes. One of the syntactic objects interfaces with the Conceptual-Intentional systems (this object is called LF), and another interfaces with the Articulatory-Perceptual systems (this object is the Point of Spellout). All of these syntactic objects are tree-like in nature.

There are of course many other ways to configure the syntax, and the system outlined here hypothesizes that syntax is highly derivational. Other theories propose that there is no derivation, but rather a set of interacting constraints imposed by syntax-internal rules and language external interface levels. There is a great deal of debate in the field as to which approach is empirically or theoretically better.

4.7 Summary

In this chapter we have seen how the idea that syntactic objects are built up via the operation Merge, together with selectional properties of heads, leads to some fairly complex structures. We developed tools for annotating syntactic structures, developing the ideas of complement, specifier, and adjunct. This gave us the following basic structure for a phrase:

(131)

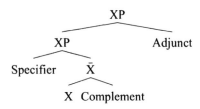

We then explored a new kind of syntactic relation: c-command. C-command is somewhat like an extended version of sisterhood. A node c-commands its sister, and everything contained within its sister. We saw how reflexives and negative polarity items were sensitive to this relation, and then we used it as a tool to probe the structure of ditransitives.

We adopted the following definition of c-command:

(132)   A node A **c-commands** a node B if, and only if A's sister either:

    a.   is B, or

    b.   contains B.

Putting together conclusions from co-ordination and c-command, we proposed that ditransitives, rather than having a ternary structure, were organized into a layered or shell-like verbal phrase, with a little v head taking a VP as its complement. Rather than assuming a selectional relation between v and its VP complement, we adopted the idea that syntactic structures had to conform to a Hierarchy of Projections, and proposed the following as a fragment of this:

(133) $v\rangle$ V

We then extended our analysis of ditransitives by introducing the UTAH. This hypothesis is one way of accounting for how children are able to project syntactic structures on the basis of their input data. It states the following:

(134)   **UTAH:** Identical thematic relationships between predicates and their arguments are represented syntactically by identical structural relationships when items are Merged.

As one specific instantiation of this idea, we proposed the following linkages between thematic and syntactic structure:

(135)   a.   NP daughter of vP → interpreted as Agent

     b.   NP daughter of VP → interpreted as Theme
     c.   PP daughter of V̄→ interpreted as Goal

The idea is that children can associate the semantics they have for certain verbal concepts with situations they see in the world. With this semantics in place, children can then use the UTAH to partially determine the relevant syntactic structures. Using what they know about other syntactic principles, and their possible parameterizations, children can then subconsciously work out what particular kind of grammatical system they are acquiring on the basis of the utterances associated with the situations. Children therefore use a complex array of syntactic and semantic clues to determine the properties of the language they are acquiring.

We noted that the UTAH was a very strong hypothesis, which could well turn out to be wrong either in general, or in the particular version supposed here; the way to test such a hypothesis is to see whether the kinds of analyses it rules out should, indeed, be ruled out on empirical grounds, and vice versa for those analyses that it rules in. We saw a very sketchy example of this with unaccusatives and unergatives.

Taking the UTAH at face value, we then were forced to reappraise our earlier analysis of transitive and intransitive verb phrases. We proposed that all verb phrases had the same basic skeletal structure, with a little v taking a VP complement. We assumed essentially two versions of little v: one which had a specifier and which was roughly interpreted as having causal (or, more loosely, agentive) semantics, and one which had no specifier, and was semantically vacuous. The latter version of v appears with unaccusative verbs to maintain the Hierarchy of Projections.

Finally, we took a look at the general structure of the whole system: it is derivational, and essentially rules sentences as grammatical or not depending on whether a well-formed derivation can be constructed for them. When a well-formed derivation can be constructed from an input of a set of words, and the final syntactic object that is built up contains no unchecked uninterpretable features, then we have a grammatical sentence. Otherwise the sentence is ungrammatical. Of course, the sentence can be perfectly grammatical, but still unacceptable, for semantic reasons, or because of parsing problems.

In summary, here are the most important phenomena we met, and the basic components of the explanations we provided for them.

Phenomenon	Explanation
Variation in word order	Linearization of head complement and head-specifier structures
Distribution of reflexives	C-command and the Reflexive Generalization
Distribution of NPIs	C-command and the Reflexive Generalization
Co-ordination and reflexives in ditransitives	VP-shell structures
Word order in ditransitives	Movement of V to little v and the Hierarchy of Projections
Different behaviour of unaccusatives and unergatives	UTAH

Exercises

Exercise 1 **UTAH**

Task 1 Give derivations, along the lines of that given in the text, for the vPs in the following two sentences:

(1)   Romeo sent letters to Juliet.

(2)   Romeo sent Juliet letters.

Task 2 Explain whether the UTAH correctly predicts the interpretation for these sentences. Make reference to (120) in the chapter.

There have been a number of proposals in the literature about how to reconcile the UTAH and these two constructions. See the Further reading section.

Exercise 2 **Pronouns and c-command**

This exercise and the next give you some practice with incorporating the notion of c-command into syntactic arguments. You are already familiar with the Pronoun Generalization, from Chapter 2.

(1)   The Pronoun Generalization

A pronoun cannot be coreferential with another pronoun.

Part A

Task 1 For each of the following sentences, say whether the grammaticality judgement given is predicted by the Pronoun Generalization, on the assumption that the words in bold are coreferential, and explain why you think the judgement is predicted or not:

(2)   *Anson kissed him.

(3)   *Moya played football with her

(4)   *She intended Jenny to be there

Part B

Task 2 Now assume the following revised generalization, and explain how it is empirically superior:

(5)   The Pronoun Generalization (revised)

A pronoun cannot be coreferential with another NP.

Part C

Task 3 The revised generalization, however, does not predict the following cases. Briefly explain why.

(6)   Moya's football team loved her.

(7)   That picture of Jenny in a rubber dress doesn't flatter her.

(8)   Anson's hen nibbled his ear.

The sentences which are not predicted by the Pronoun Generalization are, of course, reminiscent in their structure to those sentences which caused us to revise the Reflexive Generalization. If we revise the Pronoun Generalization in the same way, we can capture these data:

(9)   The Pronoun Generalization (revised)

A pronoun cannot be coreferential with a c-commanding NP.

Task 4 Show, using replacement and movement tests, that this revised generalization makes the correct predictions for the problematic sentences.

Exercise 3 R-expressions and c-command

Part A

Task 1 The new Pronoun Generalization does not predict the correct judgements for example (4) above or for the following sentences. Explain why.

(1)   *He liked **Anson**

(2)   *They shaved **David and Anson**

Part B

Examples like these have prompted linguists to propose another generalization for referring expressions, like proper names. Referring expressions (often abbreviated as R-expressions) have their own reference and appear to be unable to be coreferential with any c-commanding antecedent. Here is a simplified version of that third generalization:

(3)   The **R-Expression Generalization**
       An R-expression cannot be coreferential with a c-commanding NP.

Task 2 Explain how the full set of judgements from this and the previous exercise is now explained by the three generalizations.

Part C

We will now rephrase these three generalizations in terms of another concept: binding. We shall define binding as follows:

(4)   A binds B iff A c-commands B and A and B are coreferential.

We can now state our three generalizations as follows:

(5)   a.   A reflexive must be bound.
       b.   A pronoun cannot be bound.
       c.   An R-expression cannot be bound.

Task 3 Using the terms binding, reflexive, pronoun, and R-expression, explain how the following sentences fall under the Binding Generalizations or not.

(6)   **His** hen loves **Anson**.

(7)   ?**Anson** saw **Anson**. (Assume that this is basically OK)

(8)   That picture of **her** flatters **Jenny**.

(9)   *She liked **Moya**'s football

(10)   **Moya** said **she** liked football.

(11)   *****She** said **Moya** liked football

We will return to the contrast between (10) and (11) in later chapters.

Exercise 4 NPIs

Part A

Task 1 Explain why (2) is problematic for the NPI Generalization given in this chapter and repeated here:

(1)   The **NPI Generalization (revised)**
NPIs must be c-commanded by a negative element.

(2)   No one's mother had baked anything.

Part B

Task 2 Using NPIs, make up examples with three-place predicates, along the lines of the examples with reflexives in the text, which construct an argument for or against the VP-shell hypothesis.

Make sure you check the judgements on your examples with at least four native speakers of English.

Exercise 5 **Derivations**

In the text, we saw a full example derivation for a *v*P. You should use this as a model to construct similar derivations for the *v*Ps in the following sentences:

(1)   Anson gave Flutter to Jenny.

(2)   Julie filed letters to herself.

(3)   Mary fell. (Remember that *fell* is unaccusative.)

(4)   Mary ran. (Remember that *ran* is unergative.)

Further reading

Section 4.2
The system developed in this chapter relies mainly on Chomsky (1995*b*), ch. 4, although the notion of checking was introduced in Chomsky (1993) and some of

these ideas go back further still. The $\bar{X}$ system grew out of Chomsky (1970), and later work by Jackendoff (1977) and Stowell (1981). The question of linearization has been of major theoretical importance lately, starting with the proposals of Kayne (1994), who argued against the earlier idea that there were different linearizations of head complement and head specifier structures across languages (this earlier idea is due to Travis (1984)). Kayne proposed that different linearizations arose from movement. For arguments that leftward complements arise from movement see especially Zwart (1993), and see Guilfoyle, Hung, and Travis (1992) and Rackowski and Travis (2000) for contrasting views of apparent rightward specifiers. Cinque (1996) is a good overview of the movement approach to deriving linearization. Chomsky (1995*b*) does not propose a separate operation for Adjoin, but incorporates it into Merge. The question of how adjunction works is a fraught one. See Kayne (1994) and Cinque (1999) for theories which have no adjunction operation at all.

Section 4.3

The first careful discussion of c-command is Reinhart (1976) although the notion of some kind of extended sisterhood relation goes back to very early generative grammar. Chomsky (1980) discusses issues in the syntax of reflexives, pronouns, and c-command. The notion of c-command is pervasive in syntactic theory; the definition we have used is adapted from Chomsky (1995*b*). The use of co-ordination as a constituency test is discussed by Radford (1981), ch. 2, and see Dougherty (1970) for an early but detailed discussion. The definition adopted here follows a suggestion of Jason Merchant's.

Section 4.4

The binary branching approach to ditransitives adopted in the text derives from Larson (1987). See Pesetsky (1995) for further discussion, Jackendoff (1990) for an alternative view, and Larson (1990) for a reply. Barss and Lasnik (1986) provide a discussion of a range of c-command effects in double object constructions.

Sections 4.4.4 and 4.5

Baker (1988) is a defence of the UTAH which discusses causatives and a range of other constructions that appear to require the kind of movement process adopted in the text and develops a theory of this kind of movement (**incorporation**). Baker (1996) is a good discussion of double object constructions, ditransitives, and the UTAH. Pinker (1984), developing insights of Grimshaw (1981), argues that children make use of linking principles in language acquisition. See also

Atkinson (1992), ch. 7. See Kratzer (1996) for the viewpoint that there are different types of little v with different semantic properties.

Section 4.6

The architecture outlined here is that of Chomsky (1995b) with some updating. This is the best place to look for a discussion of the concepts discussed in the text, although it is difficult reading.

5

Functional Categories I—TP

5.1 Introduction

One of our initial primary aims was to characterize the notion of sentence in I-language terms. We are now in a position to do this: we know that sentences consist of constituents, which may be embedded within each other, and which bear θ-relations, selectional relations, and modification relations to each other; we know that these constituents are characterized by features that are projected from the lexical items which head them, and we have developed in some detail a view of the particular elements that go into making up vP.

In this chapter, we shall see that sentences have a core consisting of the projections of a lexical category (the verbal cluster) surmounted by a series of other categories, which project, but do not assign θ-roles. The most important of these categories is T: the category that hosts the tense features for the whole sentence. We shall see that there is evidence that sentences are really projections of T, with the subject in the specifier of TP, and the vP being the complement of T, giving the following schematic structure:

(1)

We have already developed an analysis of the structure of the lexical category at the core of TP: the verb phrase. We argued for the idea that the verb phrase consists of two parts: a 'little' v, which is responsible for assigning the Agent θ-role, and a 'big' V, which assigns Theme and Goal roles. We assumed that 'big' V raises and adjoins to 'little' v, an assumption which was necessary to reconcile the

UTAH and the surface word order. This type of movement is called **head movement**, and we shall motivate further instances of head movement in this chapter.

We will also go back to the question of the position of the subject. In Chapter 4, we assumed that the subject was assigned its θ-role in the specifier of little v. In this chapter, we shall see that the subject moves into a higher specifier, that of TP. We will, however, leave a detailed discussion of the evidence for this type of movement, and an analysis of its mechanics for Chapter 6.

First, though, let us consider some of the evidence that sentences are projections of the category T.

5.2 Sentences are headed

In this section we will examine the question of whether, just like verb phrases and noun phrases, sentences have syntactic heads. We will argue that they do, and we will motivate the idea that the most important contribution of the head of the sentence has to do with tense.

5.2.1 Theoretical considerations

One traditional idea of the structure of sentences is that they are formed by taking a subject, and saying something about that subject by means of a predicate (usually the VP). Under this approach, a sentence is built up out of a subject and a VP, as follows:

(2)

This idea looks sensible in many ways, but it means that the sentence doesn't have a head. The properties of the category Sentence aren't projected from any lexical item. If (2) were the right structure, we would have to have a new kind of rule in our grammar saying how the category of Sentence is introduced, and what its properties are. If (2) is incorrect, and the sentence is headed by T, as in the structure in (1) above, then we have no need to extend our grammar; we simply have T in the lexicon, and the properties of sentences are essentially projections from the properties specified on T, just as PPs are projections of P, and NPs are projections of N. In short, there's nothing special about the category Sentence; it works like every other category in our syntax.

We have, then, theoretical motivation for adopting the idea that sentences are headed. In the next section we will look at some of the empirical arguments that support this idea.

5.2.2 Empirical evidence

Modals

Many sentences in English have, in addition to a main verb, one or more **auxiliary** verbs. These auxiliaries are a small set of specialized verbs which perform restricted semantic functions.

Let us first look at sentences with only one auxiliary:

(3)   Gilgamesh may seek Ishtar.

Here, the subject *Gilgamesh* is assigned its θ-role by the verb *seek*, which is semantically a two-place predicate. The subject and its θ-role assigner are separated by the auxiliary verb *may*. *May* is one of a small class of verbs, the **modal** verbs, which occur in a position preceding the lexical verb, and which semantically signify notions such as obligation, possibility, permission, futurity, and so on. Other examples of modals are:

(4)   Gilgamesh must seek Ishtar.

(5)   Gilgamesh can seek Ishtar.

(6)   Gilgamesh should seek Ishtar.

(7)   Gilgamesh will seek Ishtar.

Notice that modals occur before, and not after, the lexical verb:

(8)   *Gilgamesh seek may Ishtar

We can see that modals are outside the constituent formed by the verb and its object, since this constituent can be pseudoclefted (9) and may be moved away from the modal (10):

(9)   What Gilgamesh may do is [seek Ishtar].

(10)   ...and [seek Ishtar], Gilgamesh may

This tells us that the modal is in constituency not just with the verb, but rather with the whole *v*P, so (11) is the correct structure, rather than (12):

(11)

(12)

Modals are in complementary distribution with each other in most (but not all) dialects of English (we shall look at some of the dialectal differences in the exercises):

(13) *Gilgamesh must should seek Ishtar

(14) *Gilgamesh might can seek Ishtar

Our discussion so far suggests that there is a single position in the structure in which modals appear, and that this position is outside the VP but after the subject. Schematically, we have something like the following structure:

(15)

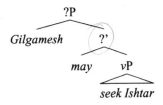

Modals also appear to inflect for the morphological feature of tense, although past tense modals seem to have a different semantics from that which you might expect. Traditional grammars (see, for example, the *Oxford English Grammar*)

treat the modals as inflecting for tense as follows:

(16)

Present	Past
may	might
can	could
shall	should
will	would
must	

Must is assumed to have no past form.

This categorization is supported by an interesting phenomenon in English called **Sequence of Tense**. Sequence of Tense is a generalization about the relationships between the verb forms in sentences like the following:

(17)   I believe [she is pregnant].

(18)   I think [she is pregnant].

(19)   I believed [she was pregnant].

(20)   I thought [she was pregnant].

(21)   *I believed [she is pregnant]

(22)   *I thought [she is pregnant]

In each of these sentences the first verb assigns two θ-roles: the Agent role is assigned to the subject of the whole sentence, while the Theme role is assigned to the whole proposition that is believed or thought. This proposition is picked out by the embedded sentence, which comes after the first verb. I have bracketed these sentences. We will discuss cases where sentences are embedded within other sentences in more detail in Chapter 8. The examples in (21) and (22) are unacceptable to most speakers of English. These are odd examples, since they look as though they should be perfectly well formed, but it is impossible to assign them a normal interpretation.

When the first verb (the **matrix** verb) is in the past tense, then the verb in the embedded clause is also in the past tense. This is the case even if the proposition that the embedded clause picks out is thought to be true at the moment of speech time rather than before it. This means that in (19), it doesn't have to be the case that the referent of *she* has had her baby and is therefore no longer pregnant.

Sentences where the embedded verb is in the present tense, but the matrix verb is in the past tense ((21)–(22)), are ungrammatical.

We can extract a generalization from these cases: past tense on the matrix verb forces past tense on the embedded verb, irrespective of the semantic interpretation of the embedded verb. Note that this generalization is a purely syntactic one which relates the forms of the verbs in the matrix and embedded sentences. As we saw, the verb in the embedded sentence may be interpreted as present (i.e. the pregnancy might still be going on) even though the form of the verb is morphologically past.

Now consider what happens when we look at sentences with modals:

(23)   I believe [she may be pregnant]/[she can do that]/[she will go].

(24)   I think [she may be pregnant]/[she can do that]/[she will go].

(25)   I believed [she might be pregnant]/[she could do that]/[she would go].

(26)   I thought [she might be pregnant]/[she could do that]/[she would go].

(27)   *I believed [she may be pregnant]/[she can do that]/[she will go]

(28)   *I thought [she may be pregnant]/[she can do that]/[she will go]

As you can see, the modal verbs that are in the right-hand column of the table in (16) behave like past forms, as far as the Sequence of Tense generalization goes. This argument supports the traditional classification of modals into past tense and present tense forms, even though one cannot argue that a sentence like (29) denotes a proposition that described some situation as holding before the speech time:

(29)   She might be pregnant.

This set of facts suggests strongly that modals split **syntactically** into present and past forms, and that this is a process which is independent of their interpretation.

From this discussion, we know that modals are in a position to the left of the main verb, and that their tense features are subject to the syntactic dependency of Sequence of Tense. We can make theoretical sense of these properties by assuming that modals bear a category feature T (mnemonic for a category that bears Tense features) and Merge with vP in the following way:

(30)

$\bar{\text{T}}$

modal vP

Note that when there is a modal to bear the tense features of the sentence, the main verb remains uninflected for tense:

(31)   *Gilgamesh might loved Ishtar

Do

English sentences also display other auxiliaries which mark for tense. In the following examples, we see the **emphatic** auxiliary *do*:

(32)   Enkidu did free animals.

(33)   Enkidu does free animals.

In these sentences, the tense features are again marked on the auxiliary, and not on the verb.

This is in contrast to sentences with very similar meanings (that is, with exactly the same θ-roles and lexical semantics) where tense is marked directly on the verb:

(34)   Enkidu freed animals.

(35)   Enkidu frees animals.

These facts tell us once again that the tense features of the sentence *can* be syntactically marked on a position outside the *v*P, the position that the emphatic auxiliary appears in. Tense can also be marked directly on the verb; we return to how this happens in Section 5.3.1.

Just as we saw with modals, if there is an emphatic *do*, the tense features are pronounced on this, rather than on the verb:

(36)   *Enkidu do freed animals

In general, then, the tense features may be marked on a position outside the *v*P, as well as on the verb itself.

The idea that tense features reside in a position outside *v*P is backed up by the following examples:

(37)   Enkidu said he would free the animals and [free the animals] he will.

(38)   *Enkidu said he freed the animals and [freed the animals] he

(39)   Enkidu said he freed the animals and [free the animals] he did.

We met this construction in Chapter 4 and termed it VP-fronting (although, given the analysis we proposed, *v*P-fronting would be more accurate).

In VP-fronting the lexical verb complex (consisting of little *v* and big V together) and its complements are moved to a position in front of the subject. If the *v*P is preceded by a modal, then no more need be said. However, if there is no modal, and the sentence is just a simple tensed sentence, then the tensed *v*P cannot be fronted, as you can see from (38). Instead, an untensed verb form is used in the fronted *v*P, and tense marking appears on the verb *do*, which is stranded in the same position that a modal would be. Notice that this occurrence of *do* does not seem to signal any special emphasis. The basic structure of VP fronting is as follows:

(40)

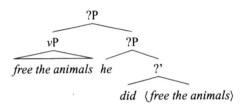

Assuming that *do* in these examples really just marks tense, then we can identify the question mark category here as T.

Another argument to the same effect can be made on the basis of a construction called **VP-ellipsis**. In this construction, the verb phrase is simply omitted. The sentence can be interpreted because the preceding linguistic context is rich enough to fill in the missing material. Normally, special linguistic markers are used to signal that ellipsis has occurred, words like *too*, *also*, and phrases like *as well*, although this is not necessary:

(41)   Gilgamesh loved Ishtar and Enkidu did [ ] too.

(42)   Gilgamesh fears death and Shamash does [ ] as well.

The square brackets signal the **elided** material (i.e. material which is missing). This material can be filled in from the immediately preceeding context. However, what is filled in is just the bare VP, with no tense marking. The tense is again carried by the auxiliary *do*. In VP ellipsis, the auxiliary just seems to be carrying tense information, and nothing else.

To

A final element in English that supports the idea that there is a position outside the *v*P associated with syntactic tense is the word *to*, which looks very similar to a preposition, but which appears in a certain type of sentence: **infinitival** sentences. Infinitival sentences usually occur as embedded sentences in English, and they do not appear to mark tense at all:

(43)   She tried [to leave].

(44)   We wanted [to eat cake].

The verbs *try* and *want* assign two θ-roles: one to their subject, another to the bracketed clause. Note that the verb in the bracketed clause must be in its untensed form:

(45)   *She tried [to left]

(46)   *We wanted [to ate cake]

Notice also that the marker *to* is in complementary distribution with the modals:

(47)   *She tried [to may leave]

(48)   *She wanted [to can leave]

And that emphatic *do* is impossible in infinitivals:

(49)   *She tried to do go

These two facts suggest that *to* is somehow replacing tense features. Notice also that in VP ellipsis, it is not possible to insert the *do* that usually carries tense features.

(50)   Enkidu wanted to live and Ishtar tried to.

(51)   *Enkidu wanted to live and Ishtar tried to do

Such data further back up the conclusion we have been edging towards in this section: there is a head which merges with *v*P, and which contains certain kinds of features which are tense related.

Putting all this together, we have argued that:

1. Modals are in a position in the sentence associated with tense features.
2. Emphatic *do* is in this same position, as is non-finite *to*.
3. This position is outside the *v*P, but follows the surface position of the subject.
4. Morphological tense marking may appear in this position.

These conclusions, within the general framework of assumptions we have been developing, support the following kind of structure:

(52)

```
              TP
            /    \
      Subject     T̄
                 /  \
                T    vP
```

Modals, *do*, and *to* are all heads. Within the theory we are developing here, heads project. If each of these heads is categorized as a T head (where T is a mnemonic for Tense), then they can Merge with *v*P, projecting T̄, and, once they have the subject as their specifier, TP.

The position we have just reached seems a little paradoxical. In the last chapter, we concluded that the subject of a sentence was Merged in the specifier of little *v*P. The evidence we have just reviewed, however, suggests that the subject of the sentence is actually in the specifier of TP. The way we shall reconcile these two analyses is to suppose that the subject has undergone a movement process, which raises it up out of the specifier of *v*P, and Merges it back into the structure in the specifier of TP. We will return to the motivation for this movement operation in Chapter 6. For the moment, we will simply assume that this movement takes place, and we will draw tree structures accordingly.

This means that a simple transitive clause actually has the following schematic structure:

(53)

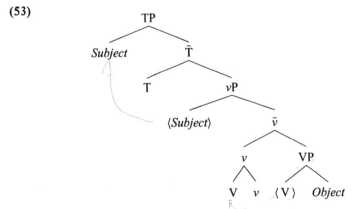

In this tree, two movements have taken place: the verb has moved and **adjoined** to little *v*, and the subject has moved and become the specifier of TP. The position from which the movement took place is marked by enclosing a copy of the moved element in angled brackets. We have assumed that V adjoins to little *v* for concreteness here.

Functional categories

Categories like T, which head a projection, but which do not assign θ-roles, are usually called **functional categories**. Functional categories clearly have a semantics, but their semantics is quite different from the θ-related semantics of items which bear the category features V, N, A, and P. Sometimes these four categories are (a little confusingly) called the **lexical categories**.

The split between lexical and functional categories has grown in importance in the theory of Generative Grammar, and now functional categories serve not only to add non-thematic semantics on to lexical categories, but also to provide positions in the structure of clauses and phrases which relate to lexical categories in various ways. In the remainder of this chapter, we will focus on the relationships between the head T and elements lower in the structure, while in the next chapter we will focus on the way in which the specifier of T works as a landing site for movement. In later chapters we will also meet functional categories above nominals, and yet more functional categories in the clause. One intuitive way to think about functional categories is that they erect a syntactic skeleton above lexical categories which serves to hold together the various syntactic relations that take place in the phrase.

In fact, we have already met a category which is akin to other functional categories: little v. Although little v does bear a θ-relation to its specifier, its relation to its complement is non-θ-theoretic. As we have seen, the relationship between little v and the lexical category V is determined by the Hierarchy of Projections. This same Hierarchy of Projections determines the position of T, so that we have:

(54)   Hierarchy of Projections
    T $\rangle$ v $\rangle$ V

5.2.3 Cross-linguistic evidence

Given that we have proposed a structure where tense is not necessarily associated with the verb, but is rather marked higher up in the structure, we might expect to see languages which display tense marking outside the VP.

Certain creole languages appear to have this property. In Mauritian Creole, for example, verbs themselves do not mark for tense. Tense (and aspect) distinctions are instead marked by the use of particles placed before the verb and after the subject:

(55)   mo mahze
       I   eat
       "I eat."

(56)   mo ti   mahze
       I   [PAST] eat
       "I ate."

A similar case can be found in Sranan, an English-based creole spoken in Surinam. Sranan also has a simple past tense marker *ben*:

(57)   mi waka
       I   walk
       "I walk (habitually)."

(58)   mi ben   waka
       I   [PAST] walk
       "I walked."

The past tense marker can be separated from the verb by aspectual heads signifying progressive aspect, or futurity:

(59)   mi ben   e   waka
       I   [PAST] [PROG] walk
       "I was walking."

(60)   mi ben   o   waka
       I   [PAST] [FUT] walk
       "I was about to walk."

These last cases suggest that there is the possibility that further heads are Merged with *v*P before T is Merged. We will see that this is true of English when we come to look at English auxiliary structures in more detail.

5.3 Tense marking

5.3.1 Tense on main verbs

We have assumed that Modals, emphatic *do*, and *to* are all T heads, and that sentences in general are projections of Ts. However, we have not addressed how tense is pronounced on elements which are not T heads: on verbs and on other auxiliaries.

   The first question we might ask is whether verbs have the category feature T. We can dismiss this idea immediately, since we know that we need to posit the category feature V for verbs, and we have argued for a view of their syntax which involves a little *v* as well. Moreover, verbs are clearly not in complementary distribution with modals, emphatic *do*, or *to*, since they co-occur with them in the same sentence.

However, we have seen that verbs can be morphologically marked with tense distinctions:

(61)   Gilgamesh misses Enkidu.

(62)   Gilgamesh missed Enkidu.

Somehow, we need to establish a relationship between the tense feature on T (past, or present) and the verbal complex.

Checking and valuing features

The approach to this that we will pursue treats this relationship like an agreement relationship. We assume that there is a tense feature on the verbal complex, and that this tense feature has to be the same as the tense feature on T. This gives us the following basic configurations:

(63)   a.   T[past] . . . V + *v*[past]
        b.   T[present] . . . V + *v*[present]
        c.   *T[past] . . . V + *v*[present]
        d.   *T[present] . . . V + *v*[past]

This is somewhat like the Matching requirement that we met in Chapter 3 when we talked about selectional features. Recall that, there, we specified that an uninterpretable categorial feature on a head (that is, a c-selectional feature) was checked by a matching categorial feature, and that when this happened, the uninterpretable feature deleted. We stated this as the Checking requirement, which is repeated here:

(64)   **The Checking requirement**
        Uninterpretable features must be checked, and once checked, they can delete.

As far as selectional features go, we assumed that they are checked under the syntactic relation of sisterhood. We now draw a distinction between categorial features and non-categorial features, and we allow the latter to be checked under c-command. We will call the operation that checks features under c-command **Agree** (note the capital letter, to distinguish it from the traditional grammatical phenomenon of agreement).

(65)   **Agree**

An uninterpretable feature F on a syntactic object Y is checked when Y is in a c-command relation with another syntactic object Z which bears a **matching** feature F.

If we look at the various configurations we just saw above, we can see that we can rule out the ill-formed ones by assuming that whatever tense feature is on the verbal complex is uninterpretable. Tense features, as one might expect, are interpretable when they are on T:

(66)   a.   T[past] . . . V + v[~~upast~~]
       b.   T[present] . . . V + v[~~upresent~~]
       c.   *T[past] . . .V + v[$u$present]
       d.   *T[present] . . . V + v[$u$past]

The last two examples are ruled out because the uninterpretable tense feature on the verbal complex has not been checked.

We now ask the question of how we ensure that the 'right' uninterpretable feature appears on the little v in the first place. We could, of course, just say that it depends on the choice that is made in the initial set of words (the numeration). If you choose a little v with a [$u$past] feature, and end up Merging in a T with a [present] feature, then the features won't match, and the uninterpretable [$u$past] feature won't be checked. This **pure checking** approach is conceptually rather neat, since it would mean that we could use exactly the same technology as we have already developed.

However, there is an alternative which we will explore here, which is to say that little v is simply specified as having an uninterpretable tense feature, and what happens when this feature is checked is that it gets a **value** from the tense feature on T. Recall that features were classed into types, in Chapter 2: [past] and [present] were tense features; [nom] and [acc] were case features; [1], [2], and [plural] were ϕ-features, and so on. With this in mind, we can say that T bears a tense feature which has, for example, the value [past] and that v bears an uninterpretable tense feature which is **unvalued**. What the checking operation does is **value** the tense feature of little v, as well as check it (since it is an uninterpretable tense feature).

Schematically we have the following:

(67)   T[tense : past] . . . v[$u$tense :] → T[tense : past] . . . v[~~utense~~ : past]

In this structure, [past] on T is a tense feature, and so it matches the unvalued tense feature on *v*. The tense features match and the unvalued tense feature on little *v* receives a value from the tense feature [past] on T.

It immediately follows from this that the mismatched structures in (66) are impossible, since the value of the tense feature on little *v* is just *determined* by the tense feature on T.

We can make this more general, and incorporate it into our definition of Agree as follows:

(68)   **Agree**

In a configuration

$$X[F:val]\ldots Y[uF:\ ]$$

where . . . represents c-command, then F checks and values *u*F, resulting in:

$$X[F:val]\ldots Y[uF:val]$$

The advantage of this second approach (**checking by valuing**), is that instead of generating an ill-formed structure with non-matching features and then ruling it out because of the presence of an unchecked feature, we simply never generate the ill-formed structure in the first place.

The syntactic relation of Agreement is, then, one way of checking uninterpretable features. These features will get a value from a matching interpretable feature. If there is no matching feature with a value, then the unvalued feature will remain unvalued, and, we will assume, unchecked. This means that, in a configuration like (69), checking can't take place.

(69) $[uF:\ ]\ldots[uF:\ ]$

However, if the features are privative and require no value, then they simply check in the way that we have already seen:

(70)   a. $[G]\ldots[uG] \rightarrow [G]\ldots[uG]$

      b. $[uG]\ldots[uG] \rightarrow [uG]\ldots[uG]$

We now have two syntactic relations which check features: Agreement and Sisterhood. In fact, the latter reduces to a more local version of the former, since sisterhood is just one subtype of c-command.

Applying the system

Let us see in more detail how this system might work for the problem at hand: how to ensure that tense features are pronounced on the verb, when there are no auxiliaries. The core of the analysis will be that it is *v* that hosts an uninterpretable feature which can take a tense feature as its value. We will call this feature Infl (for inflection):

(71)   Little *v* contains an uninterpretable inflectional feature [*u*Infl :].

First, we will build a *v*P, where V has raised to *v*. We assume, for concreteness, that V **adjoins** to *v*, giving the following structure:

(72)

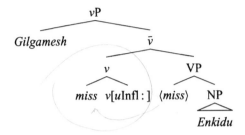

This structure then Merges with T, which is a null head containing just a categorial feature T and the interpretable feature [past]. The tense feature on T Agrees with that on *v*, and the latter is thereby valued:

(73)

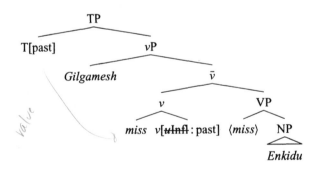

When this structure is spelled out, the little *v* and the verb itself are pronounced as the past tense of the verb.

In a morphologically simple case like the present one, this amounts to simply spelling out *v* with the checked uninterpretable Infl feature valued as [past] as *ed*. This feature is visible to the rules of Spellout. Let us state the relevant rule explicitly:

(74)   Pronounce *v*[*u*Infl : past] as *ed*.

As we saw in Chapter 2, morphology can be considerably more complex than this. For example, certain verbs, like *eat*, change their vowel in the past tense. In this case we need a special rule which looks something like the following (as usual, I'm using orthographic rather than properly phonological representations—this is for convenience only):

(75)   Pronounce *eat* as *ate* when it is adjacent to *v*[*u*Infl : past], and in this case, do not pronounce *v*[*u*Infl : past].

Notice that the same system can be used to deal with the pronunciation of agreeing present tense marking, as in (76):

(76)   Enkidu misses Gilgamesh.

Recall that verbal agreement in English is restricted to the present tense. An elegant way of capturing this in our system is to say that in this situation T bears only a number feature, and it is this number feature that values Infl on *v*. For example, a [singular] number feature on T will match with [*u*Infl :] on *v*, valuing it as [*u*Infl : singular]. This will eventually lead to a pronunciation of little *v* as *(e)s*, as in *misses*. The semantic rules will interpret T lacking a tense feature as present tense.

Summarizing this section, we have proposed that for English main verbs an Agree relationship is established between the featural content of T and little *v*. This Agree relationship ensures that the semantics imposed on the sentence by the interpretable tense feature of T is compatible with the morphological form of the tense inflection in the sentence. The result is that a morphologically past tense sentence is also interpreted as past tense.

From a theoretical perspective, the Agree relationship is a simple extension of the techniques we used in previous chapters to ensure selectional relationships were established. Instead of the syntactic dependency which results in feature checking operating under sisterhood, it operates under the extended version of sisterhood: c-command. Selectional feature checking, under this view, is just a more local version of Agree.

5.3.2 Tense on auxiliaries

We now turn to progressive and perfect auxiliaries, and investigate how their tense features are checked.

Again, the first question we need to ask is whether these auxiliaries are just T heads. If this were the case, we need establish no special syntactic structure for them, since they will just be specified with interpretable tense features which are pronounced. The answer to this question, however, has to be no, since these auxiliaries can co-occur with modals and non-finite *to* (although, interestingly, not with emphatic *do*—see Section 5.5):

(77) I might have eaten some seaweed.

(78) I'd planned to have finished by now.

Recall that we proposed that modals and non-finite *to* are T heads, and that there is only one T in a sentence (since T is the head of the sentence). We can also have more than one auxiliary co-occurring, suggesting that they bear different category features from T, and from each other:

(79) I could have been flying helicopters by now.

(80) I have been flying helicopters for years.

The auxiliaries always come in a particular order, Modal-Perfect-Progressive, and any of the three can be left out:

(81) *I have might be flying helicopters

(82) *I am having eaten seaweed

(83) I might be leaving soon.

The tense marking is always on the first auxiliary, but furthermore each auxiliary has a particular morphological effect on the next verbal element: the perfect *have* auxiliary is always followed by the past participle, the progressive *be* is always followed by the present participle (ending in *-ing*) and the modal is always followed by the bare verb stem.

The perfect auxiliary

The perfect auxiliary is Merged outside of *v*P, as we can see from VP-preposing:

(84) I'd planned to have finished, and [finished] I have.

It forces the main verb to be in the past participle form:

(85) I have eaten/*eat/*ate/*eating.

Let's assume that the perfect auxiliary *have* has the interpretable categorial feature [Perf].

Recall that we said that *v* had to be instantiated with an uninterpretable inflectional feature. Let us suppose that Perf is a possible value of such a feature. This will mean that [Perf] on *have* and [*u*Infl :] on *v* will Agree, and that [*u*Infl :] on *v* will be valued as [Perf]:

(86)   *have*[Perf] . . . *v*[*u*Infl :] → *have*[Perf] . . . *v*[*u̶I̶n̶f̶l̶* : Perf]

The derivation will then go as follows: once *v*P has been built up, Perf merges with it. Perf Agrees with *u*Infl, valuing it. In the Spellout component, the checked [*u̶I̶n̶f̶l̶* : Perf] feature on little *v* is spelled out as a participle affix. We have then the following structure (note that I have specified an [*u*Infl :] feature on Perf too, since it will end up being the tensed element in the clause):

(87)

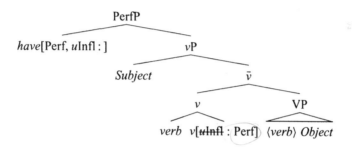

At this point in the derivation, the same null head T that we met above merges and checks an *u*Infl feature on *have*, valuing it as (for example) [past]:

(88)

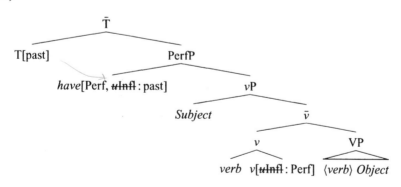

When *have* comes to be spelled out, it will be spelled out in its past form, *had*, via the appropriate morphological interface rule.

So far, the treatment of tense marking on a perfect auxiliary is just the same as that on a main verb. However, there is good evidence that the Perfect auxiliary actually raises to T, in the same way that a main verb raises to *v*. This means that we have the following structure, rather than (88):

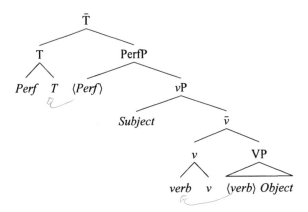

We will address this evidence in the next section. Before we do so, notice that we can apply exactly the same analysis we have just developed for the Perfect auxiliary to the Progressive one.

The Progressive auxiliary

Assume that the auxiliary *be* has an uninterpretable categorial feature Prog, and that it therefore projects ProgP. This feature values the [*u*Infl] feature of little *v*, so that little *v* ends up being pronounced as -*ing*. A sentence like (89) will have the structure in (90), at a point in the derivation before subject raising takes place:

(89)   Gilgamesh is fighting Humbaba.

(90)

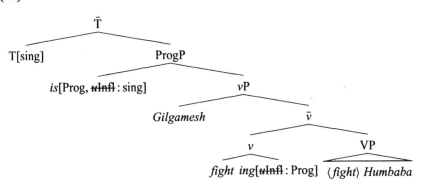

Once again, as we will see in the next section, the auxiliary moves to T:

(91)

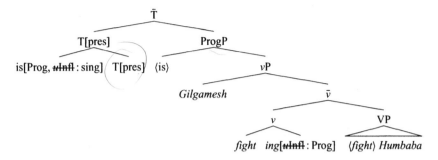

Notice that the Progressive and Perfect auxiliaries come in a strict order:

(92)   Gilgamesh has been fighting Humbaba.

(93)   *Gilgamesh is having fought Humbaba

We will not account for this ordering effect here. It is currently a major research question as to what orders functional projections in the clausal domain, and there is no clear consensus at the moment. We will simply incorporate these ordering facts into our Hierarchy of Projections:

(94)   Hierarchy of Projections
      T ⟩ (Perf) ⟩ (Prog) ⟩ v ⟩ V

The bracketed heads are those whose appearance is optional.

   Summarizing, we have seen that English, in addition to Modals, *do*, and *to*, has a null T head which checks tense features on the head of the projection to which it is sister. We claimed above that, if this projection was an auxiliary, then this auxiliary moved and adjoined to T. We will review the evidence for this in the next section.

5.4 Head movement

We have seen that we need to propose movement of V to *v* in order to derive the correct word order for English verbal phrases. This kind of movement is known as **head movement**, since it obviously moves heads. In this section we will see that there is striking evidence for head movement of auxiliaries into T. This evidence is based on the interaction of auxiliary placement with negation.

5.4.1 The position of negation

In English, negation is marked by a particle *not* or its reduced form *n 't*. Negation comes in two forms: **sentential negation**, which simply denies the truth of the non-negated version of the sentence, and **constituent negation**. A simple example of sentential negation is (95), which has the paraphrase in (96):

(95)   I haven't left yet.

(96)   It is not true that I have left yet.

Constituent negation, on the other hand, does not deny the truth of the whole sentence, but rather states that the sentence is true of something which is not the negated constituent. The following examples show this:

(97)   I was sitting not under the tree (but under the bush).

(98)   I was eating not a peach (but an apple).

(97) shows an example of constituent negation of a PP, and (98) shows constituent negation of a NP. We also find constituent negation of VPs:

(99)   I might be not going to the party (but washing my hair).

That this is constituent negation is a little more difficult to see. Note that it has the meaning in (100), rather than that in (101):

(100)   It is true that I might be doing something other than going to the party.

(101)   It is not true that I might be going to the party.

We will concentrate here on readings which involve sentential negation, so that we will mark as ungrammatical sentences which have only a constituent negation reading.

In a sentence with a full selection of auxiliaries, sentential negation follows the modal:

(102)   Gilgamesh might not have been reading the cuneiform tablets.

(103)   *Gilgamesh might have not been reading the cuneiform tablets

(104)   *Gilgamesh might have been not reading the cuneiform tablets

(103) and (104) are grammatical only on a constituent negation reading, for most speakers. There is a fair amount of dialectal variation in these constructions, but we will be concentrating on the fairly standard dialect which requires the sentential negation marker to follow the modal in these examples.

When there is no modal, then sentential negation follows the Perfect auxiliary, if there is one:

(105)   Gilgamesh has not been reading the cuneiform tablets.

(106)   *Gilgamesh has been not reading the cuneiform tablets

If there is no Perfect, then negation follows the Progressive auxiliary:

(107)   Gilgamesh is not reading the cuneiform tablets.

The lesson to be drawn from this paradigm of data is that sentential negation always follows the first auxiliary. The analytical question is what this means structurally.

5.4.2 Movement of Auxiliaries to T

If we take a sentence with the full complement of auxiliaries, then we see that negation follows the modal. Since we have assumed that the modal is a T head, it follows that negation is to the right of T and that it therefore Merges before T. Given that it is to the left of Perf, it Merges after Perf. On the assumption that Negation is a head, this gives us the following kind of structure:

(108)

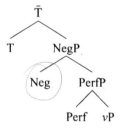

We can incorporate this observation into our Hierarchy of Projection:

(109)   Hierarchy of Projections

T ⟩ (Neg) ⟩ (Perf) ⟩ (Prog) ⟩ *v* ⟩ V

But if Negation is Merged higher up than Perf, how can we ever generate sentences where it follows Perf, like those sentences discussed above? That is:

(110)   Gilgamesh has not read the cuneiform tablets.

The simple answer is that, in English, the highest auxiliary verb moves to T, in the same way that V moves to *v*:

(111)

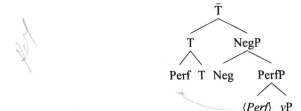

The same analysis holds when there is only a progressive auxiliary: it too moves and adjoins to T:

(112)   Gilgamesh is not reading the cuneiform tablets.

In order to maintain uniformity for our structures, we also assume that this kind of movement of heads takes place even when there is no negation in the structure, so that a sentence like (113) has the structure in (114):

(113)   Gilgamesh has eaten the honey.

(114)

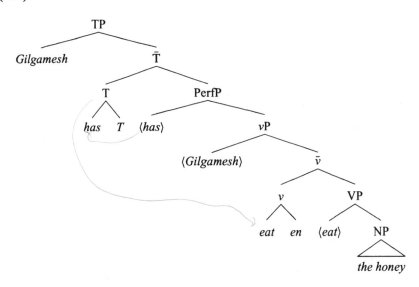

We now have two situations: T either checks tense on an auxiliary, in which case the auxiliary raises to T, or checks tense on little *v*, in which case no raising takes place.

The reason we know that when T checks tense on little *v* no raising takes place is that, in English, main verbs come after negation, rather than before it:

(115)   *Gilgamesh flew not the broomstick

If the verb raised to T, then we would expect sentences like (115) to be grammatical in modern-day English. They are not: the way to express a negated main verb is to use the auxiliary *do*:

(116)   Gilgamesh didn't fly the broomstick.

We will return to the syntax of these sentences in Section 5.5. For the moment it is enough to see that the main verb stays low in the structure, in contrast to auxiliary verbs.

We now have a theoretical question to deal with: why does a tensed auxiliary raise to T, but a tensed verb stay *in situ* (i.e. in its unmoved position)? The reason that this is a theoretical question is that it concerns the kinds of properties that motivate movement to take place. Since we are building a theoretical system, we need to have a mechanism which will ensure that the derivation will produce the right results.

One way of doing this is to say that, in addition to having the property of interpretability, features also have a second property, usually known as **strength**. The most obvious property of strength is that it triggers movement operations to take place. If we represent strength by an asterisk after the relevant feature, then we have the following schematic derivation:

(117) $X[u\overset{\frown}{F}*] \ldots Y[F] \rightarrow X[\cancel{u}F*] \: Y[F] \ldots \langle Y[F] \rangle$

Here, X and Y are heads with matching features F. Agree between the F features takes place, since the feature on X is uninterpretable and needs to be checked. Moreover, F on X is strong, which means that the checking has to take place locally, rather than at a distance. This then **triggers** the operation Move, which then places X and Y in a local (sisterhood) relation, leaving behind a trace of Y. The generalization about strength is therefore the following:

(118)   A strong feature must be local to the feature it checks/is checked by.

In (117), it is the higher feature that is strong. However, we have given no reason to suppose that it could not be the lower feature that is strong:

(119) $X[F] \ldots Y[uF*] \rightarrow X[F] \: Y[\cancel{u}F*] \ldots \langle Y[uF*] \rangle$

We have also assumed that the movement operation moves constituents *up* the tree, rather than moving them downwards. Again, this is a theoretical option that's open to us. We'll discuss whether there's evidence for downwards movement in Section 5.5; for the case at hand, the movement is clearly in an upwards direction, since we want to ensure that an auxiliary which is Merged lower than negation raises to a position higher than it.

Many more conceptual questions about this property of strength immediately arise: is it a purely formal property of features, or, like interpretability, is it related to one of the interfaces? One suggestion has been that strength relates to morphology in a parallel way to the way that interpretability relates to semantics. Under this view, strength is really morphological interpretability. Unfortunately, this question is still far from settled, so we will simply use the notion of strength as a mechanism to drive movement in a purely formal way.

With this much in place, we can now at least provide feature specifications which will derive the correct results. Let us say that the tense value of the uninterpretable Infl feature on Perf (or Prog) is strong. This will mean that when [*u*Infl] on an auxiliary is checked by the tense feature of T, the auxiliary needs to get into a local relationship with T. This need for locality then triggers movement of Perf to adjoin to T.

This is a two-step process: first, the inflectional features on T and Perf Agree, and the uninterpretable inflectional feature on Perf is valued. Secondly, Perf must raise to adjoin to T, so that the checker and checkee are local (sisters).

(120)

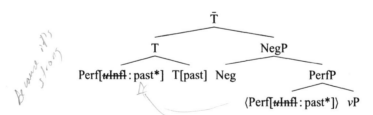

Notice that this solution allows us to capture the behaviour of main verbs. We can say that the inflectional feature on little *v* is **weak**, and that, as a consequence, no locality is required between T and *v*. This is why main verbs in English never precede negation.

(121)

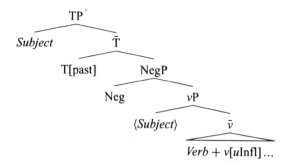

The complex behaviour of auxiliaries and main verbs in English can then be captured as follows:

(122)   When [*u*Infl :] on Aux is valued by T, the value is strong; when [*u*Infl :] on *v* is valued by T, the value is weak.

We can adopt the same mechanism to capture the obligatory movement of the verb to little *v*: we say that little *v* bears a strong uninterpretable V feature which is formally much like a selectional feature. However, since the relationship between little *v* and VP is determined by the Hierarchy of Projections, this feature is satisfied by movement of V to *v*, rather than by merge of *v* and VP:

(123)

$$vP$$

$$v \qquad VP$$

$$V \quad v[\cancel{u}\cancel{V^*}] \quad ... \langle V \rangle ...$$

5.4.3 V to T movement

Unlike English main verbs, French main verbs do appear before negation, in just the same positions as auxiliaries do:

(124)   Jean n'a pas aimé Marie.
John has not loved Mary
"John didn't love Mary."

(125)   Jean n'aime pas Marie.
John loves   not Mary
"John doesn't love Mary."

These two sentences show that the perfect auxiliary in French (*avoir*), and the main verb in a sentence with no auxiliaries (*aime* in (125)) both come to the left of the negative particle *pas*. Note that formal French also requires an extra negative element *ne/n'*, which precedes the verb. This particle may be omitted in colloquial French, and also appears in certain non-negative sentences:

(126)   Avant que je ne sois   arrivé,...
        Before that I NE be-[SUBJ] arrived,...
        "Before I arrived,..."

Because of facts like these, it is usual to treat the true marker of negation in French (that is, the equivalent of English *not*), as *pas*. We will ignore the syntax of *ne* here, but see the Further reading section for more on this.

Given this, it is clear that main verbs move to a position preceding negation in French, in contrast to English.

We can deal with the parametric difference between English and French by simply saying that in English the valued tense feature of auxiliaries is strong, but that of little v is weak, while in French, when uninterpretable Infl features are valued as tense, they are always strong. This gives us the following distinctions:

(127)

	Tense valued on Aux	Tense valued on v
English	strong	weak
French	strong	strong

This approach will correctly rule out examples such as the following, since the tense features on little v have not got into an appropriately local configuration with the tense features on T:

(128)   *Jean (ne) pas   aime Marie
        John not loves Mary

Let us just go through a rough derivation of a simple French sentence to drive the point home:

(129)   Jean n'aime pas Marie

Step 1 Merge *aime*, 'love' with the object *Marie*.

Step 2 Merge the result with little *v*[*u*Infl : , *u*V*], raise *aime* to adjoin to *v* (satisfying the *u*V* feature on *v*), and then Merge in the subject *Jean*:

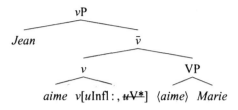

Step 3 Merge the negation *pas* with the output of Step 2.

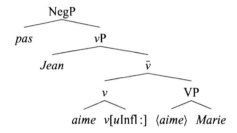

Step 4 Merge T[pres] with the output of Step 3. The tense feature on T matches the inflectional feature on *v*, and the inflectional feature on *v* which is valued as a tense feature is strong, so the whole little *v* complex raises to T. To save space, we represent the trace of the moved complex just as a string in angled brackets, rather than as a structure:

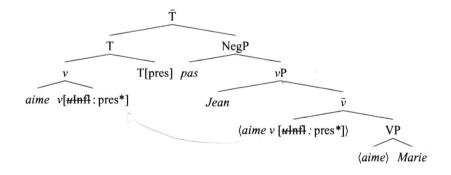

Step 5 Still at the same node, the subject moves into the specifier of TP. For the motivation behind this movement, see the next chapter.

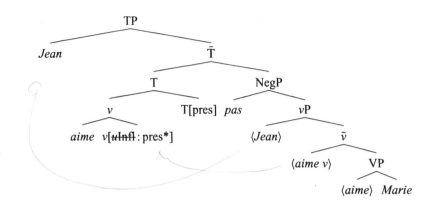

5.4.4 Aux *in situ*

Swedish contrasts with both English and French in that neither auxiliaries nor main verbs appear to the left of Negation. Because of other facts about the syntax of Swedish, I have presented here data from subordinate clauses, rather than from simple sentences. Note that both the main verb and the auxiliary appear to the right of negation (which is marked in bold).

(130)   om   hon **inte** har köpt   boken
whether she not has bought book-the
"whether she hasn't bought the book"

(131)   om   hon **inte** köpte boken
whether she not   bought book-the
"whether she didn't buy the book"

This kind of language fits into our parametric pattern: we can say that in Swedish, the uninterpretable tense feature is always weak. This gives us the following typology:

(132)

		Tense on Aux	Tense on *v*
English		strong	weak
French		strong	strong
Swedish		weak	weak

You might notice that there is one possibility in our table which is not attested: a case where main verbs raise to T, but auxiliaries do not. I do not know of such a case, which would have the tense value of *u*Infl on *v* strong, but that on auxiliaries weak. If this turns out to be truly a gap in the possible set of languages, then our theory should rule out this possibility in principle. As things stand, however, we predict the existence of such a language.

5.5 *Do*-support

5.5.1 Basic properties of *do*-support

One final property of the English auxiliary system that we have not addressed is the interaction between main verbs and negation. We noted above that auxiliary verbs raise to T across negation in English, but that main verbs do not. We implemented this in our theory by assuming that the tense feature of little *v* is weak, and that the verb + *v* complex therefore does not move. But this incorrectly predicts the following sentences:

(133)   *Gilgamesh not flew the dragon

(134)   *Tiamat not destroyed the world

These sentences are, of course, ungrammatical. Their grammatical counterparts in modern English are the following:

(135)   Gilgamesh did not fly the dragon.

(136)   Tiamat did not destroy the world.

The insertion of *do* here is called **do-support**. *Do*-support applies in negative sentences like (135) and (136), and, as we saw earlier, it also applies in VP ellipsis and VP-fronting sentences which have only a main verb:

(137)   Tiamat did not defeat the gods but Gilgamesh did [ ].

(138)   Gilgamesh wanted to seduce Ishtar, and seduce Ishtar he did [ ].

The question of why *do*-support applies in modern English is one which has perplexed linguists working within generative grammar since Chomsky's early analysis of auxiliaries in *Syntactic Structures*. Chomsky proposed a specialized rule which would insert *do* if other rules failed to apply. The application of this rule would generate a well-formed structure, thereby 'rescuing' the sentence. *Do*-support, in Chomsky's system, is a kind of **last-resort** strategy which kicks in when the rule which attaches tense to main verbs fails to apply for some reason.

In the remainder of this section we will go through outlines of a few different analyses of *do*-support, so that you can see that they all have problems. Each analysis requires a certain set of stipulations to make it go through, and none of these analyses seems particularly minimal. This is a clear case where the data that we have radically underdetermine the analysis.

Before we do this, let's look more closely at the contexts that trigger *do*-support. They are of two types: T is separated from the verb by negation, or T does not c-command a verb at all (in VP-fronting and VP-ellipsis constructions). Note that T can be separated from the verb by other material, such as an adverb. In (139), we can see that the adverb *never* attaches below T:

(139)   Gilgamesh has never flown a dragon.

(140)   *?Gilgamesh never has flown a dragon

In (139), the auxiliary *has* has moved to T, and is followed by the adverb *never*. This means that *never* is attached lower down than T, giving the rough structure in (141):

(141)

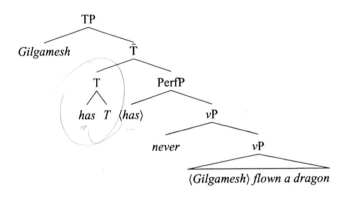

Now, assuming that *never* also adjoins somewhere below T in a sentence with no auxiliary, we can see that it intervenes between T and the verb in a simple sentence:

(142)   Gilgamesh never flies dragons.

(143)

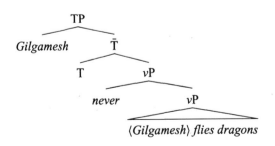

However, *do*-support does not apply here; the only possibility is emphatic *do*. Somehow, for *do*-support to apply, it is crucial that *not* itself intervenes between T and little *v*.

5.5.2 Affixal negation

The first proposal we will go through is one which proposes that *not* is actually an affix which is adjoined to T. This would be like saying that English T comes in two forms: a positive form and a negative form. The negative form has a special morphological requirement, that it suffixes to an overt head. If no overt head appears in T, then a special morphological operation inserts *do*.

Let us see how this might work. The numeration would contain a lexical item, T[neg]. Part of the morphological specification of this item is that it suffixes to auxiliaries. If T[neg] is spelled out and there is no attached auxiliary, the sentence is syntactically well formed but morphologically bad. In such cases, a special morphological rule attaches *do* to the left of T[neg].

More concretely, take a sentence which contains a Perfect auxiliary:

(144)   Gilgamesh hasn't left.

Here we can see that when T comes to be spelled out, there is an attached auxiliary, which has moved to T in order to satisfy its strong tense features. No special *do*-support rule need kick in, since T[neg] is already suffixed to an auxiliary. This contrasts with (145):

(145)   *Gilgamesh not left

In this sentence, the inflectional features of little *v* are weak, and so no movement takes place. When T[neg] comes to be spelled out, its suffixal nature requires an attached head to its left, but there isn't one. The sentence is then syntactically well formed, but ruled out by a morphological requirement of T[neg]. The only way to 'save' the sentence is to insert a default auxiliary to the left of T[neg], giving (146):

(146)   Gilgamesh didn't leave.

However, there are (at least) two problems with this proposal:

1. Why is it that the tense features appear on the auxiliary, rather than on the verb?

2. How do we explain the fact that *do*-support also applies in VP-ellipsis and VP-fronting contexts?

The first problem arises from the following kinds of examples:

(147) *Gilgamesh didn't ate the honey

(148) *Gilgamesh doesn't ate the honey

In these sentences, T has valued past features on little *v*, giving rise to past morphology on the main verb. Then *do*-support has applied, since T[neg] is affixal. Whether we have a past or present version of *do* is irrelevant: our system incorrectly generates one or the other of (147) or (148).

The second problem is one of omission, rather than overgeneration. By saying the *do*-support is triggered by affixal negation, we don't explain why it applies in VP-ellipsis or VP-fronting contexts, neither of which need be negative.

5.5.3 Affixal tense

An alternative that has often been suggested is that Neg is simply a head, as we proposed in Section 5.4, and that it is T *in general* that is a suffix. If there is nothing for T to suffix on to, it attaches to the head of its sister. In a sentence with an auxiliary, the suffixal nature of tense is always satisfied, since head movement has created the right structure:

(149)

$$
\begin{array}{c}
\text{T} \\
\diagup \diagdown \\
\textit{aux} \quad \textit{T}[\textit{suffix}]
\end{array}
$$

However, if there is no auxiliary, T suffixes to the head of its sister, which is little *v*. This will *morphologically* transform a tree like (150) into one like (151):

(150)

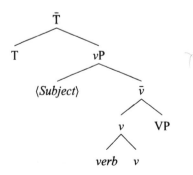

(151)

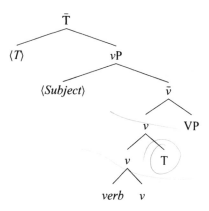

In a negative sentence, the head of the sister of T is Neg, which is not a verbal category, and therefore not something that T can suffix to: *do*-support then kicks in as a last resort.

(152)

Similarly, in VP-ellipsis and VP-fronting, there is no overt sister to T, and so T cannot suffix to anything, giving rise to *do*-support once again.

(153)

However, this approach also has its problems. If we meld this analysis with our analysis of the checking relation between T and the tense features on little *v*, then the same puzzle arises as appeared in the affixal negation analysis. Why is it impossible to have both *do*-support and an inflected verb? That is:

(154)   a. *Gilgamesh didn't ate the honey
     b. *Gilgamesh don't ate the honey

These sentences would be wrongly predicted to be grammatical, since T has valued past features on little *v*, but in the morphological component, when T is spelled out, it should trigger *do*-support in the presence of negation. We therefore predict (154), on the assumption that the morphology is sensitive to the actual features of T.

We could stipulate a solution to this problem by saying that when T checks the tense features on little *v*, somehow the suffixal property of T is deleted. This isn't a particularly elegant solution, however.

A more compelling argument against following this approach, at least given the theory as we have developed it so far, is that it assumes that we have a syntactic movement operation which applies after the point of Spellout, rather than in the syntax proper. This may well be the correct way to go, but our Spellout rules so far are simply pronunciation rules. In the interests of keeping these rules simple, and keeping the movement operation in the syntax component, we will reject this analysis.

An alternative idea, which still maintains that T is affixal, would be to say that the suffixing operation is *syntactic* rather than morphological. If we assume that it is this operation which is responsible for attaching the tense morphology to the verb, then we have a way out of the problem just mentioned.

First, we would abandon the approach we took to the checking relation between T and tense features on little *v*. We would say instead that there is no such checking relation, but that the tense feature on the verb arises because of a syntactic operation which moves T down the tree and attaches it to *v*. This makes use of the movement operation but moves something *downwards* into a lower position in the tree. This will give us exactly the same tree as we saw above, but this time it would be a syntactic structure, rather than a morphological one. I repeat the tree here:

(155)

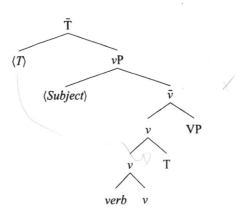

This will immediately explain why we don't get *do*-support plus tense marking on little *v*, since tense marking on a verb is derived in this system not by spelling out little *v*, but rather by suffixing T to *v*. However, this analysis has problems of its own.

First, it does not throw any light on why it is that in a VP-fronting operation, the fronted VP is not inflected.

(156)   … and [eat the honey] he did.

(157)   …* and [ate the honey] he

To see this, consider a point in a derivation where the *v*P has been constructed, and then T is Merged. Since, by assumption, T-suffixation is a syntactic rule, it should be able to apply, suffixing tense marking on to the verb, just as in the tree in (155). After raising of the subject, the *v*P should then be able to front, incorrectly deriving (157), with the structure in (158):

(158)

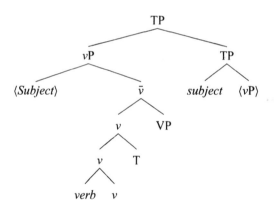

Again, we could stipulate our way out of this problem by ensuring that the T-suffixation rule only applies after VP-fronting, or VP-ellipsis. However, we have no way in our theory of ensuring that this happens: we only have properties of lexical items, Merge, Move, and Adjoin. There just isn't any way to impose an **extrinsic** (that is externally defined) ordering over syntactic movements. In our theory, these movements take place when triggered by the properties of lexical items, rather than at the behest of some external device.

We conclude, then, that solving the problem of English verb inflection via a lowering operation is the wrong approach. In fact, many syntacticians have ruled out lowering operations altogether, making a general claim that movement always has to be to a position in the tree which is higher than the base position of the moved element. We will not discuss this further here. See the Further reading section.

5.5.4 Tense chains

One final approach we will look at introduces a new object into our syntactic theory: the **chain**.

A chain is an object which is formed by an Agree operation. Whenever one feature checks against another, we say that the two syntactic objects entering into the checking relation are in a chain. So, for example, when T checks tense features with little v, T and v are in a chain. We write this chain as follows:

(159)   (T, v)

One crucial fact about chains is that each **link** in the chain (that is, each syntactic object in the chain), must c-command the next one. If c-command does not hold, then the chain is **broken**.

The idea we will appeal to is that the spellout component is sensitive to chains and that the spellout rule for a chain formed by checking tense features is as follows:

(160)   **Pronouncing Tense Rule (PTR)**
          In a chain (T[tense], v[uInfl : tense]), pronounce the tense features on v only if v is the head of T's sister.

This rule will have the following effect. In a simple sentence with just a main verb, T will check tense with little v. Little v is the head of T's sister, and so the tense feature on little v is pronounced.

If there is a negation intervening between T and vP, then the negative element *not* will be the head of T's sister.

(161)

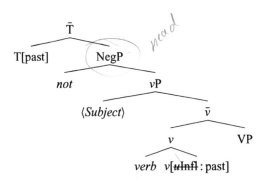

Not is not part of the tense chain, so the PTR will fail to apply, and a last-resort rule of *do*-support will apply instead, correctly predicting *do*-support in negatives:

(162)   I did not understand.

Note that here we have a valued [*u*Infl : past] feature on little *v*; however, the PTR prohibits this being pronounced, since *v* is not the head of T's sister.

In a VP-fronting context, the *v*P has been moved and adjoined to TP. This means that T no longer c-commands *v*, and so the chain is broken. The PTR cannot apply, and *do*-support kicks in, correctly predicting *do*-support in VP-fronting environments.

(163)

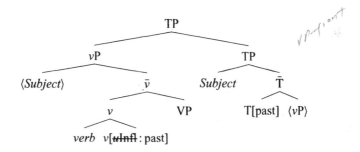

(164)   . . . and [love Ishtar] Gilgamesh did.

Since PTR is a pronunciation rule, it clearly cannot apply to something which has undergone ellipsis. It is impossible to pronounce tense features on little *v*, if little *v* is not being pronounced at all. Since the PTR cannot apply, *do*-support does instead.

(165)   Enkidu didn't love Ishtar but Gilgamesh did [*vP*].

Finally, in sentences with an auxiliary, the auxiliary has raised across negation and adjoined to T. This means that the auxiliary is T's sister, so PTR applies, and tense is pronounced on the auxiliary:

(166)   Gilgamesh hasn't kissed Ishtar.

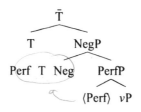

The PTR approach overcomes the empirical difficulties faced by the other approaches, but it has theoretical problems. First, we have introduced a new notion into our theory: the idea of a chain. Ideally, we would like to do without such objects. We have also stipulated a language-specific pronunciation rule, and again, it would be preferable to avoid this. Nevertheless, we will adopt the PTR approach to *do*-support in what follows.

5.6 Summary

In this chapter we have seen that sentences are headed by a functional (non-θ-assigning) category T, which hosts the tense features of the sentence. Evidence for T as the head of the sentence came from the appearance of lexical items which bore tense features, such as modals and emphatic *do*. To account for the position of the subject with respect to these elements, we assumed that it moved to the specifier of TP, an assumption we will motivate in the next chapter.

We proposed that tense features are checked in a configuration where one tense feature c-commands a matching one, which we made explicit via the operation Agree:

(167)   **Agree**
        In a configuration

$$X[F : val] \dots Y[uF :]$$

        where ... represents c-command, then F checks and values uF, resulting in:

$$X[F : val] \dots Y[uF : val]$$

We dealt with the morphological expression of tense by assuming that a checked tense feature formed part of the input to a morphological interface rule. This had the effect that morphological tense marking appears attached to the verb.

We proposed that tensed auxiliaries in English are Merged lower than T but raise there in order to satisfy the strength of particular features:

(168)   A **strong** feature must be local to the feature it checks/is checked by.

Strength, then, is a property of features or feature values which usually causes movement to take place in order to achieve locality between the two features in the checking relation. We assumed that sisterhood is the local configuration required.

This approach to strength allows us to capture the behaviour of selectional features by saying that they are always strong, and therefore always checked under sisterhood. Other uninterpretable syntactic features may be weak, in which case they can be checked via Agree. When we have a strong feature on a head, and the head does not select its complement, then that feature will, in general, trigger a movement operation so that the required sisterhood configuration will obtain.

This general approach gives us an analysis of the distribution of tensed auxiliaries and negation. We saw that there were parametric differences between English, French, and Swedish which could be captured by different strength specifications of features.

We also refined our Hierarchy of Projections, so that it now looks as follows:

(169)   **Hierarchy of Projections**
         T ⟩ (Neg) ⟩ (Perf) ⟩ (Prog) ⟩ *v* ⟩ V.

The projections in brackets are assumed to be optional, while the other projections are obligatory. This Hierarchy is assumed to universally dictate clause structure, with differences between languages being confined to the strength and interpretability of features of heads and specifiers in the hierarchy.

Finally, we looked at the phenomenon of *do*-support, and argued that one way to capture it in a uniform fashion is to adopt the idea that morphological interface rules are sensitive to the notion of chains, where chains are formed in the derivation whenever Agree takes place. However, if a chain is broken by a subsequent operation in the derivation, then this may be reflected in the eventual morphological form.

Once again, here are the most important phenomena we have met, and the basics of their explanations:

Phenomenon	Explanation
Positioning of modals, *do*, and *to*	Sentences are TPs with these elements bearing a category feature T
Position of the subject to the left of these elements	Subject moves from *v*P to the specifier of TP
Where the tense features are pronounced and how they are interpreted	Feature checking under Agree
Distribution of auxiliaries with respect to Negation	Hierarchy of Projection coupled with Aux to T movement and feature strength

Phenomenon	Explanation
Variation in order of verbs, auxiliaries, and negation across languages	Different specifications of strength on features
Do-support	Breaking of tense chain affecting pronunciation rules

Exercises

Exercise 1 **Negation in infinitivals**

Task 1 Non-finite clauses are headed by *to*, as we have seen. What problems does (1) raise for carrying over the analysis developed in the text to non-finite clauses?

(1)   Gilgamesh decided [not to kill Ishtar].

Task 2 Hypothesize a way to solve this problem, and draw a tree for your analysis. What strengths and weaknesses can you see with your approach?

Exercise 2 **Copular constructions**

In most varieties of English the verb *be* also has the function of relating a subject to a non-verbal predicate, as follows:

(1)   Gilgamesh is [in the dungeon].

(2)   Shamash is [a dangerous sorcerer].

(3)   Tiamat is [extremely evil].

In each case we have a [3, sing, pres] version of the verb *be*. It is preceded by a subject, and followed by a PP, an NP, and an AP respectively.

Part A

Task 1 Assume that *be* is a version of little *v*, with the subject in its specifier and the PP, NP or AP as its complement.

(4)

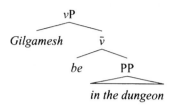

Provide a derivation for (1), on the basis of this structure, showing all movements.

Part B

Task 2 Construct the negative versions of these sentences. What do your examples tell you about the position of *be* here? Revise your derivation if you need to.

Part C

Task 3 Explain why (5) is ungrammatical (in Standard English)

(5)   *Gilgamesh doesn't be in the dungeon

Exercise 3 **Ellipsis and auxiliaries**

As we saw earlier, it is possible in certain circumstances to get away without pronouncing a verb phrase. This is the VP-ellipsis construction we discussed in the text.

One of the constraints on VP ellipsis is that the elided VP must be similar to a VP which has just been mentioned, and is recoverable from the context of the utterance. For example, (3) is an acceptable continuation of (1) but not of (2):

(1)   Lloyd's car fell over a cliff last year...

(2)   Computer viruses increased in virulence last year...

(3)   and Julie's truck did [ ] too.

(3) is an odd continuation of (2) because the elided VP is naturally interpreted in the same way as the VP in (2). This gives an interpretation for (3) along the lines of (4), which is an odd sentence, to say the least:

(4)   !Julie's truck increased in virulence last year.

One way we can account for this is by assuming an identity condition on the process of VP-ellipsis:

(5)   **Identity Condition on VP-Ellipsis (ICVE)**

A *v*P can only be elided if its content can be recovered from an *identical v*P in the preceding discourse.

Assume ICVE in the exercise which follows.

Part A

Task 1 Say, for each of the following sentences, what the elided material is. Does this support the ICVE or not?

(6)   I will eat a mango, and Gillian will [ ] too.

(7)   Raffi has made pasta, and David has [ ] too.

(8)   Brita is making scones, and Gillian is [ ] too.

Part B

Task 2 Now look at the following sentences. If you fill in the blanks using literal identity of form with the preceding VP, what is the result?

(9)   I ate a mango and Gillian did [ ] too.

(10)   Raffi makes pesto pasta, and David does [ ] too.

Do these data support or threaten the PRT approach to English auxiliaries? (Hint: draw the tree structures and assume ICVE applies to the *syntactic* structure.)

Part C

Task 3 Now look at the following sentences:

(11)   Raffi slept well, and Gillian will [ ] too.

(12)   David ate mangoes and Raffi should [ ] too.

Explain whether these structures are expected or unexpected under the PTR analysis given in the text.

Part D

Task 4 The following examples are degraded for most speakers. Explain why.

(13)   *Gillian has made pasta and David is too

(14)   *I am eating a mango and Gillian has too

In some dialects these sentences can be dramatically improved by the addition of a version of the verb *do*. Why do you think this is?

(15)   ?Gillian has made pasta and David is doing.

(16)   ?I am eating a mango and Gillian has done.

Exercise 4 **French verbs and auxiliaries**

In French, we find data like the following:

(1)   Jean aime bien Marie
John loves well Mary
"John loves Mary a lot."

(2)   *Jean bien aime Marie
John well loves Mary

(3)   Jean a   bien aimé Pierre
John has well loved Peter

Task 1 Use these data to argue for the spellout positions of the main verb and the perfect auxiliary in French.

    Can you incorporate the following data into your approach?

(4)   Jean a   aimé bien Pierre
John has loved well Pierre

Exercise 5 **English *have***

The verb *have* has a number of functions in present-day English. One of these is the perfective auxiliary we have already met, exemplified in (1). Another is its use to signify possession, as in (2):

(1)   I have eaten the muffin.

(2)   I have a book.

There are a number of syntactic characteristics that separate these two *haves*.

Part A

Task 1 Provide negative versions of (1) and (2). If you are not a native English speaker, you should find one who will act as a consultant for you. It is important you don't just look this up in an English grammar. For most dialects of English there is a syntactic difference between the negative versions of these examples.

If you find such a difference, hypothesize what might be going on, using the concepts developed in the analysis of auxiliaries in the text. You should make use of what we already know about the surface position of the perfect auxiliary in (1).

Part B

Now provide yes/no versions of our examples. Do these data back up your hypothesis, or do they make you revise it?

Part C

Now construct tag-questions for the examples, and evaluate your (revised) hypothesis against these data.

Part D

Adverbs can often be used as a partial diagnostic of structure. In the following set of sentences, the adverb *often* has been placed in different parts of the clause structure. I have not given any judgements for these sentences, you should supply them yourself. Once you have done so, see whether your hypothesis accounts for the pattern you have found.

(3)   I have often eaten muffins.

(4)   I often have eaten muffins.

(5)   I have often a cold.

(6)   I often have a cold.

Exercise 6 Double modals

Certain dialects of English allow the appearance of more than one modal in the same sentence. The following data are from Hawick (pronounced "hoik") in Scotland:

(1)   He will can go.

(2)   He might could go.

In this dialect *can/could* is always the second of the two modals:

(3)   *He can will go

(4)   *He could might go

(5)   *He can can go

The modals seem to have to agree in Tense:

(6) *He will could go

(7) *He would can go

Can/could can appear after *to* in an infinitival clause:

(8) I would like to could swim.

(9) I want to can do it.

(10) He's bound to could do it.

(11) *I would like to might do it

(12) *He's bound to should do it

There are a number of possible analyses of this construction. Here are two competing hypotheses:

- **Hypothesis 1**: the double modal is a single word.

- **Hypothesis 2**: one of the modals is really an adverb.

Using the following data sets, evaluate these two hypotheses. If you end up deciding that they are both wrong, formulate your own hypothesis:

Data set 1

(13) He will can do it.

(14) Will he can do it?

(15) *Can he will do it?

(16) *Will can he do it?

(17) *Can will he do it?

Data set 2

(18) He might no could have done it.

Data set 3

(19) He'll no can do it, will he?

(20) He'll no can do it, can he?

(21) He might maybe do that, mightn't he?

(22) *He might maybe do that, mayben't he?

(23)   He can't possibly do that, can he?

(24)   *He can't possibly do that, possibly he?

Data set 4

(25)   All the boys should could go.

(26)   The boys all should could go.

(27)   The boys should all could go.

(28)   The boys should could all go.

Further reading

Section 5.2

The idea that there is a separate functional category T which bears syntactic tense properties and heads the sentence came to the fore with Chomsky (1986*a*), and was further developed in Pollock (1989). See Haegeman (1997) for an overview of how this idea developed in syntactic theory in the 1990s. For a discussion of the syntax of English modals in a framework of assumptions related to ours, see Roberts (1985).

Section 5.3

The problem of how to relate tense and the main verb in English stretches back to the earliest days of Generative Grammar, and was one of the major analyses in Chomsky (1957). The proposal advanced here, that feature checking between T and *v* takes place under an Agree operation, capitalizes on the introduction of Agree by Chomsky (2001*b*). I have taken this approach because it seems to follow naturally from the operations we have developed so far in the theory. The idea that features can receive values via Agree is developed in Chomsky (2001*b*), and bears affinities to the idea of **unification** found in grammatical frameworks such as HPSG (Pollard and Sag 1994) and LFG (Bresnan 2001) and used extensively in computational linguistics (Shieber (1986)).

Section 5.4

The idea that auxiliaries raise to T in English and French, but that there is a difference in the behaviour of verbs across the two languages, is argued for by Pollock (1989), based on an earlier analysis expressed in Emonds (1978) (these authors also discuss the syntax of French *ne*). Pollock's proposals went further than what we consider here: see also Iatridou (1990) for a critical response.

The idea of head movement was first defended in an extended way by Koopman (1984). For an excellent overview of head movement in general, but one which should only really be tackled once you've finished this book, see Roberts (2001). The idea of strength of a feature as the driving force behind movement is introduced in Chomsky (1993), and developed in different ways in Chomsky (1995b). The * notation we have adopted is borrowed from Roberts and Roussou (2002), although they have a slightly different notion of strength.

Section 5.5

The phenomenon of *do*-support was dealt with by Chomsky in Chomsky (1957). Since then, a number of different analyses have been put forward: Lasnik (1995) tries to relate Chomsky's earliest ideas about auxiliaries and *do*-support to his later ones. The idea developed here, that the notion of Chain is involved, adopts the idea of Chain from Chomsky (1981) but puts it to rather different use.

6

Subjects and Objects

6.1 Introduction

In this chapter we address the question of the position of the subject in clause structure and we look at the syntactic dependencies that both subjects and objects enter into.

We proposed, in Chapter 4, that subjects of transitive verbs are Merged in the specifier of a little *v*.

(1)

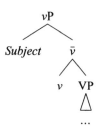

We also proposed, in the last chapter, that sentences were headed by T, which hosts finite auxiliaries:

(2)

This leads to an apparent contradiction, when we look at the position of subjects with respect to auxiliaries: the position of the subject is to the left of the auxiliary, rather than being to the right, as would be expected if we just put the two structures above together:

(3)   Cassandra has foretold disaster again.

In (3), *Cassandra* is the Agent of the verb *foretold*. As such, it is Merged in the specifier of the little *v* projected immediately above the VP. However, it appears **linearly** to the left of the finite auxiliary, rather than to the right of this auxiliary.

The way that we solved this problem in the last chapter was to say that there are really two subject positions, related by a movement operation. The subject of a transitive verb Merges in the specifier of little *v*P (the **base** subject position), and then Moves to the specifier of TP (the **surface** subject position):

(4)

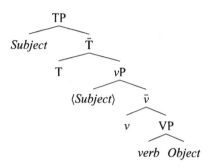

Since the finite perfect auxiliary in (3) is in T, the phrase *Cassandra* is correctly predicted to precede it (recall that specifiers precede their heads in English).

In this chapter we will look carefully at this proposal, which we have so far only motivated as a way to achieve the correct word order. We will show that there is good evidence for two subject positions related by movement, and we shall propose a mechanism which will drive the movement operation. Once this much is in place, we will look at other cases of movement of a nominal phrase into the specifier of TP, and the implications that this general approach to subjects has for parametric variation.

6.2 Subject movement

6.2.1 Quantifier stranding

The first piece of evidence that the subject has moved to its surface position, from some lower position, comes from the behaviour of so-called **floating quantifiers**. These are determiner-like elements which usually attach to NPs:

(5)   **All** the dragons had escaped.

(6)   **Both** the twins might have been at the party.

The reason that these quantifiers are called floating quantifiers is that they may also appear to be 'floated' some distance away from the NP with which they are associated:

(7)   The dragons had **all** eaten the pigs.

(8)   The twins might have **both** been at the party.

Not all quantifiers behave like this. Take *most*, or *many*, for example:

(9)   a.   Most dragons have been neutered.
      b.   *Dragons have most been neutered.

(10) a.   Many vampires have become vegetarian.
      b.   *Vampires have many become vegetarian.

There are a number of ways in which one might analyse quantifier float. Early approaches proposed a specific transformational rule, which moved the quantifer out of the subject to some position further to the right in the sentence. Roughly, such a rule would take a structure like (11), and perform an operation on it to derive (12):

(11) $Q + NP \ldots VP \rightarrow$

(12) $NP \ldots Q + VP$

More recently, analyses have been proposed which turn this idea on its head, and argue that the quantifier has been **stranded** by the movement of its associated NP. Roughly, we have the reverse of the operation outlined above:

(13) $\ldots Q + NP \ VP \rightarrow$

(14) $NP \ldots Q + \langle NP \rangle VP$

Of course, for this latter analysis to be correct, it has to be the case that the NP starts off in a low position and raises to a higher one. This is exactly the structure proposed for the word order reasons we discussed above.

Let us make this analysis a little more specific. We will assume that floating quantifiers are heads. The difference between these quantifiers and non-floating ones is that they take an NP complement, rather than an N complement:

(15)   [$_{NP}$ All [$_{NP}$ the dragons]]

(16)   [_NP_ Both [_NP_ the twins]]

(17)   [_NP_ Most [_N_ dragons]]

At the moment, this analysis is at odds with the idea that heads always project, unless we categorize quantifiers as nouns, thereby allowing them to project NPs. We will resolve this problem in the next chapter, when we will look closely at the internal structure of nominal phrase constituents.

With this in mind, let's see how a derivation of a sentence like (18) will proceed:

(18)   The dragons had all eaten the pigs.

Our theory Merges subjects in the specifier of little _v_P:

(19)

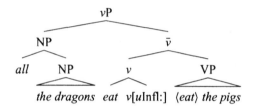

We then Merge Perf, checking a [_u_Infl] feature on little _v_, followed by T, checking the strong tense feature on Perf, and triggering raising of Perf to T:

(20)

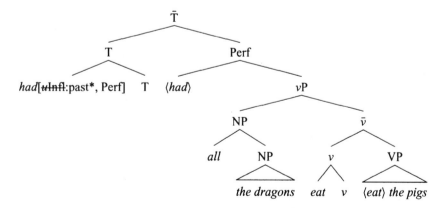

Now, on the assumption that an NP moves to the specifier of TP, we are faced with a choice: do we move the NP _all the dragons_ giving (21), or just the subpart of it which constitutes the NP *the dragons*? Taking the latter option will give (22):

(21)

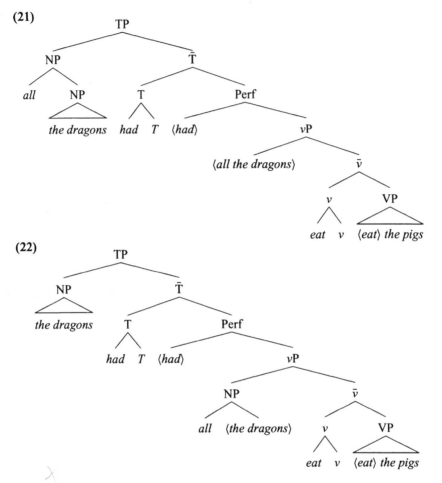

(22)

It is precisely the possibility of this choice that allows us to explain the phenomenon of floating quantifiers. In essence, the quantifiers don't float anywhere; rather they are stranded when their complement undergoes movement.

What we see here is that the phenomenon of quantifier float receives a rather elegant analysis under the assumption that there are two subject positions related by a movement operation. No such analysis is possible on the assumption that there is a single subject position (say, the specifier of TP).

The important point to note about this kind of argument is that it takes a problem which had been previously dealt with by using an idiosyncratic rule, and solves it in a principled fashion, which involves the theoretically elegant assumptions that θ-roles are assigned locally, and that movement may apply to subparts of an NP. This kind of argument, where a phenomenon which can be described by a construction-specific rule can actually be explained as a consequence of general principles interacting together, is a classic example of the way that syntacticians try to provide deeper explanations by using theoretical principles, rather than just descriptive devices.

This approach to quantifier float also makes the correct empirical predictions when we look at the positions of quantifiers with respect to adverbs. Notice that quantifiers may appear to the right of *v*P adjoined adverbs:

(23)   The dragons simply all died out.

Again, this is explained in the same way. The *all* has been stranded in the specifier of *v*P, which is why it appears below, and to the right of, the adverb.

6.2.2 Expletive constructions

There is a second set of constructions which seem to support the idea that the subject is Merged low in the tree and raises to its surface position: **expletive constructions**.

An expletive is an element that may fill the surface subject position but does not receive a θ-role from the predicate. English has two types of expletive: *there* and *it*:

(24)   There are many fish in the sea.

(25)   There were people playing on the beach.

(26)   It's quarter past four.

(27)   It's extremely windy today.

The *it*-expletive structures will not concern us here, since they appear to involve zero-place predicates which have no subject, and we are concerned here precisely with the position of the thematic subject of verbs which take arguments.

The *there*-sentences involve an **unstressed** *there*, which does not behave like the normal locative proform *there* found in examples like the following:

(28)   I saw people playing there on the beach.

It is important to be sure when you have a true expletive *there*, and when you have a locative one. The true expletive is always unstressed, and provides no semantics of actual location.

Notice that *there* expletive sentences have counterparts which have the same thematic structure, although they differ in terms of emphasis or the precise interpretation of the subject.

(29)   Many fish are in the sea.

(30)   People were playing on the beach.

We can show that the expletive is truly a structural subject by employing the tag-question operation.

Recall from the exercises in Chapter 2 that tag-questions involve taking the subject of a sentence and prefixing it with a negative auxiliary, and then adding the whole complex to the end of the sentence:

(31)   Ron's likely to be on the Web, isn't he?

(32)   Jenny hasn't eaten all her Clinique make-up again, has she?

If we apply the tag-formation operation to a *there*-sentence, we find that *there* behaves as the structural subject:

(33)   There's going to be a party, isn't there?

(34)   There were people eating fire at the fair, weren't there?

While it is possible to have both *there* and a thematic subject in the sentence, the latter must appear to the right of *there* (note that this sentence is well formed when *there* is taken to be a locative):

(35)   *[Many people were [there playing on the beach]]

Expletive constructions, then, have the schematic form in (36):

(36)   *there* T ... *Subject v*P.

Moreover, there are thematically identical sentences which look just like (36), but where the expletive has been replaced by the thematic subject:

(37)   *Subject* T ... ⟨*Subject*⟩ *v*P

Clearly the existence of these structures supports the idea that there are two subject positions related by movement.

Now that we have established this, a theoretical question is once more raised: what mechanism ensures that this movement takes place? This question, and some possible answers to it, will be the subject of the next section.

6.3 Case and EPP

As a way into the theoretical question posed at the end of the last section, we will revisit a phenomenon we noted in Chapter 2: the distribution of cased pronouns.

Recall that English pronouns may bear case features, which regulate their distribution:

(38)   She has kissed her.

(39)   *Her has kissed her

Here we see that only the nominative ([nom]) pronoun can appear in the surface subject (specifier of TP) position, immediately to the left of the tensed auxiliary. Similarly, only the accusative pronoun can appear in the object position, immediately to the right of the main verb:

(40)   *She has kissed she

The pattern we see here is the following: cased forms of the pronoun are tied to particular positions in the structure. Since, in the theory we have been developing, positions in structures are essentially related to heads (complement or specifier), we can assume that the case of nominals is driven by properties of particular heads.

6.3.1 Subjects and EPP features

Let us focus first on nominative case, which appears to be associated with finite T. Can we use the mechanisms we have already developed to ensure that the specifier of TP will be marked with nominative case?

In fact, we don't need to introduce any new mechanisms to do this. The operation Agree already applies to ensure that particular features match between heads and other syntactic elements that they c-command. We can therefore simply say the following:

(41)   T bears an uninterpretable case feature [$u$case:nom], which values a case feature on an NP under Agree.

Since the function of case features is to regulate the syntactic distribution of nominal phrases, rather than to mark any special semantic properties, we will assume that they are uniformly uninterpretable. Case features have the usual properties of uninterpretable features: they must be checked and they are not related to any special semantics.

Before we look at how this proposal works in practice, notice that the uninterpretability property of the **valuer** of a case feature is different from what we have seen before. Up to this point, we have always seen features matching in pairs: one member of the pair is interpretable and one uninterpretable. More specifically, the interpretable member of the pair has always been the one with the value. With case features, however, we want both of the members of the checking relationship to be uninterpretable. Various linguists have found this idea unintuitive, and it also leads to some technical problems that we will pick up on in Chapter 8, section 8.2.6. However, we will adopt it here for the meantime.

Let's see how this type of system will work in practice:

(42)   **numeration** =   {pronoun[3, sing, case], pronoun[3, sing, case], know,
        v[uInfl:, uN], T [pres, nom]}

In this numeration, I've adopted some abbreviations, since we're focusing on case features here. I've notated an unvalued uninterpretable case feature as just [case] rather than the 'official' [$u$case:]. When a case feature is checked and valued, rather than writing [$u$case:nom], for example, I'll just write [nom]. Finally, if a case feature is already valued, but hasn't been checked, I'll write [nom], rather than [$u$case:nom].

Step 1 Merge *know* and one of the pronouns, satisfying c-selectional feature of *know*. Pending a better analysis of pronouns (see Chapter 7), we will just assume that they are nouns.

VP
_____
know [V, u̶N̶]   pronoun[N, 3, sing, case]

Step 2 Merge v with the output of Step 1, satisfying the Hierarchy of Projections. V raises to v.

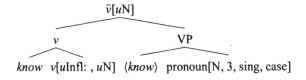

$\bar{v}$[uN]

v VP

know v[uInfl: , uN]   ⟨*know*⟩   pronoun[N, 3, sing, case]

Step 3 Merge the other pronoun with the output of Step 2, satisfying the selectional N feature of v which has been projected to $\bar{v}$.

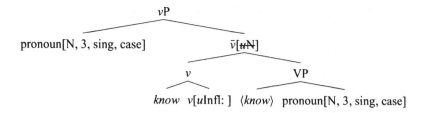

Step 4 Merge T[pres, nom] with the output of Step 3.

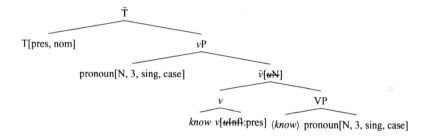

Step 5 T and little *v* Agree and T values the Infl feature on *v*. T and the pronoun in the specifier of *v*P also Agree for case, and the pronoun's case feature is valued as [nom]. The uninterpretable features in an Agree relation are now checked:

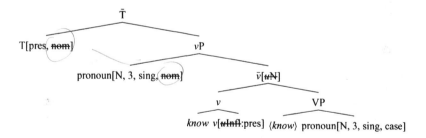

At this point in the derivation, all the uninterpretable features are checked (except [case] on the pronoun complement to V, which we will come back to in the next section), and we have forced the appearance of a nominative nominal in the structure. The spellout rules for English will ensure that this pronoun is pronounced as *he*:

(43) Pronounce pronoun[N, 3, sing, ~~nom~~] as *he*.

The forcing of a nominative nominal to appear in the structure follows from the assumption that finite T always bears a [nom] feature. This means that, were there no nominative in the remainder of the sentence, then the [nom] feature on T would never be checked, and the derivation would crash. This is the right result, and rules out (44):

(44)   *Him knows him

However, we haven't yet ensured that the nominal in the specifier of vP moves to the specifier of TP. How do we do this?

Once again, we already have the mechanism. Recall that movement is forced by feature strength: it is this that triggers auxiliaries to raise to T. In order to capture the idea that the base subject moves to the surface subject position, we simply need to specify that one of the features in the Agree relationship holding between T and the pronoun is strong.

The most obvious feature here is [nom]. If we say that [nom] on T is strong, then this will force locality between the two case features in the Agree relation, which will mean that the base subject has to move, giving the following final step in the derivation:

Step 6

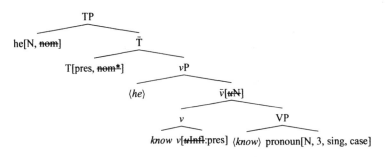

However, there are a number of problems with this approach. The most important one is that it raises an empirical problem for expletive constructions. In English, it is difficult to tell how case assignment is working in these constructions, because pronouns are independently ruled out in the base subject position:

(45)   *There was he/him in the garden.

However, other languages mark case on full nominal phrases which can appear in expletive constructions, and it turns out that these phrases are nominative. The following examples from Icelandic illustrate this pattern:

(46)   það   hefur maþur   dansað i garðinum
       There has   man-[NOM] danced in garden-the
       "A man has danced in the garden."

(47) það   hefur einhver   borðað epli
          There has   someone-[NOM] eaten   apple-[ACC]
          "Someone has eaten an apple."

Here we see the expletive það in the surface subject position with the lower subject position being occupied by a nominative nominal. If it is strength of the nominative feature on T that forces the subject to move to the specifier of TP, then we would predict that the nominative phrase would move to the specifier of TP. However, as these examples show, the specifier of TP may be filled by an expletive, and the nominative nominal may stay *in situ*. It follows that it cannot be strength of the [nom] feature on T that is responsible for the fact that the specifier of TP is filled.

Moreover, the specifier of TP must be filled, so examples like (48) are ungrammatical as simple declarative statements in Icelandic:

(48) *hefur einhver   borðað epli
          has   someone-[NOM] eaten   apple-[ACC]
          "Someone has eaten an apple."

So something forces the specifier of TP to be filled, but it can't be strength of nominative case on T (or on the NP).

For this reason, we adopt the idea that T checks nominative case, but that it is strength of another feature which forces something nominal to appear in the specifier of TP. This feature will essentially be just like a c-selectional feature on T, requiring the presence of a nominal in the specifier of T. Using the notation we have developed so far it is just [uN*]. However, this selectional feature, unlike selectional features of lexical categories, is not associated with a thematic role (recall that T, being functional, has no θ-roles to assign). It is a purely **formal** uN feature. This means that the featural specification of finite present T will be as follows:

(49) T[pres, nom, uN*]

T bears an interpretable tense feature, an uninterpretable nominative feature (remember, by convention, we abbreviate [$u$case:nom] as just [nom]), and a strong uninterpretable N feature. Because of a historical accident, this uN* feature on T is called the **EPP feature** (see the Further reading section).

Let's now go back to Step 6 in our derivation. Instead of [nom] being strong, we assume that finite T bears an EPP feature, which projects in the normal way to T̄:

Step 6 T has Merged, and Agreed with *v* for tense, and with the pronoun in the specifier of *v* for case. T's EPP feature Agrees with this pronoun for category, and, once projected to T̄, is satisfied locally (under sisterhood), via movement of the pronoun into the specifier of TP:

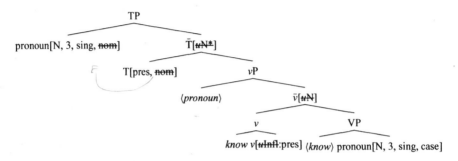

This new approach extends to expletive constructions on the assumption that expletives have no case to check. In the numeration for an expletive sentence, we have just the same elements as for the non-expletive counterpart, except for the appearance of the expletive itself. At the point after the derivation where T has Merged, and Agreed with the base subject, instead of raising the subject, we Merge in the expletive, thereby satisfying the EPP feature. Our previous Icelandic example would look as follows (I have used English, rather than Icelandic, words for ease of comprehension):

(50)

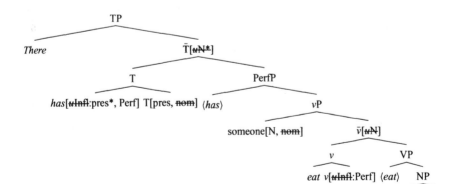

Icelandic actually also gives us some further evidence that the EPP property should be divorced from nominative case checking. In Icelandic, it is possible to have **dative subjects**. These are NPs bearing dative case, which, however, appear in the structural subject position.

(51)   Jóni   líkaði bókin   ekki
       John-[DAT] liked book–[NOM]-the not
       "John didn't like the book."

While we will not give an analysis of these structures here, they clearly show the need for distinguishing between nominative case checking, and the requirement that the structural subject position (the specifier of TP) be filled. Examples like (51) show that we cannot collapse these two constraints into one.

6.3.2 Objects and locality of feature matching

We have now achieved two things: we have ensured that nominative case correctly correlates with the presence of finite T, and we have ensured that some element, either the base subject or an expletive, appears in the specifier of TP. However, we have not yet dealt with the question of accusative case. Nothing we have said so far will rule out the following example:

(52)   *He knows he.

Clearly, we need to make a parallel set of assumptions to deal with accusative case: that is, we need to say that some head associated with the vP bears an [acc] feature which enters into an Agree relationship with the object.

Obviously there are two possibilities: v and V. At this stage in our theory development, there seems to be no knock-down argument for either one, although, in the next section, we will see a suggestive argument that it is little v that bears accusative case. Let us suppose that this is so, then we have a derivation which schematically looks as follows:

(53)

1. Merge V and Object, then Merge little v[acc].
2. Object bears an unvalued [case] feature and Agree takes place, valuing this as [acc].
3. Merge in Subject, and then T.
4. Agree takes place between tense on T and v; [nom] on T and Subject; and [N] on T and Subject.
5. Subject raises to the specifier of TP to satisfy strength of EPP on T.

This will rule out the example in (52), since the pronoun in object position has its case feature valued as [acc] rather than [nom].

However, we now have a new question: what would rule out a derivation where Agree takes place between the EPP feature of T and the N feature of the object, rather than the subject? Such a derivation would have the object raising to the specifier of TP, with the subject staying in its base position:

(54)   [*TP* Him has [*vP* he known ⟨him⟩]]

This is clearly ungrammatical, but nothing we have said rules it out so far.

What has gone wrong in (54) seems to be that Agree has 'skipped' a syntactic element: it has overlooked the subject, which is the closest [N] element to T, and matched with the N-feature of the object. Let us make the strongest claim, and rule out such cases in principle by a constraint on the locality of feature matching:

(55)   **Locality of Matching**: Agree holds between a feature F on X and a matching feature F on Y if and only if there is no intervening Z[F].

We define 'intervening' in the following way:

(56)   **Intervention**: In a structure [X ... Z ... Y], Z intervenes between X and Y iff X c-commands Z and Z c-commands Y.

Let's see how this way of constraining Agree works in our example. Take a structure which looks as follows:

(57)

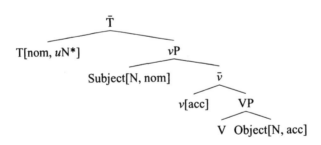

T bears [nom] which values case on the subject as [nom]. Little *v* bears [acc], which values case on the object as [acc]. What about the EPP feature *u*N* on T? Given Locality of Matching, N on T can only enter into an Agree relation with the Subject. This is because the subject c-commands the object, and T c-commands the subject, so the subject intervenes between T and the object.

Given this intervention, we cannot set up an Agree relation between N on T and N on the object, because there is an intervening element, the subject, which also bears N. This will rule out the derivation of the ungrammatical sentence. The object can never raise to satisfy the EPP of T simply because the object never enters into an Agree relation with T when there is a 'closer' (that is, intervening) subject.

(58) *Him has he known ⟨him⟩

Before we leave the question of locality, notice that it has implications for the treatment of floated quantifiers. Take a structure like the following:

(59)

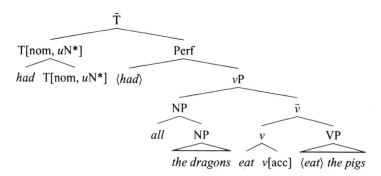

Now, the EPP feature of T needs to be satisfied by moving an NP to T's specifier. First, EPP on T must Agree with some NP that T c-commands. Since *had* has adjoined to T, the T node is 'stretched', so that the features are shared between the two Ts in the tree. For this reason, I have represented the features on both nodes. This allows the feature [nom] and the EPP feature to c-command PerfP and everything contained inside it.

By Locality of Matching, the object is too far away for feature matching to apply between it and either [nom] or [uN*], just as we saw above. However, the subject is structurally complex in such a way that there are two NP nodes: the NP *the dragons* and the NP *all the dragons*. We have not yet dealt with the details of the internal structure of nominals (see Chapter 7), and once we do so we will revise many of our assumptions about features driving movement of nominals. However, our definitions actually give the right kind of result here.

Let's assume, just as we did informally above, that *all*, and other quantifiers which allow themselves to be stranded, take NP complements. This means we have the following rough structure:

(60)

In this structure there are two NP nodes, but notice that neither c-commands the other. This means that the higher NP node does not intervene for feature matching between T[*u*N*] and the lower NP node, thus allowing the latter to raise:

(61)   [*NP* the dragons] have [*vP* [*NP* all ⟨[*NP* the dragons]⟩] died.]

6.3.3 Subject-verb agreement

Our approach to case checking extends naturally to a related phenomenon: subject-verb agreement. We discussed this phenomenon in some depth in Chapter 1. Recall that, in English, plural and singular subjects give rise to different agreement patterns on present tense verbs:

(62)   a.   The librarian likes books.
        b.   *The librarian like books

(63)   a.   *The librarians likes books
        b.   The librarians like books.

Now, since T sets up an Agree relation with the subject in the specifier of *v*P for case, and with little *v* itself for tense and *φ*-feature agreement, we have both relationships required to give the observed patterns.

To see how this works, take a plural noun phrase like *The librarians*. The noun here bears an interpretable feature [pl] and an unvalued case feature.

Turning now to the specification of T, present tense T bears an EPP feature, a case feature, and the present tense feature, but it also carries uninterpretable *φ*-features, which need to be cheecked.

Putting all this together, we get the following structure:

(64)

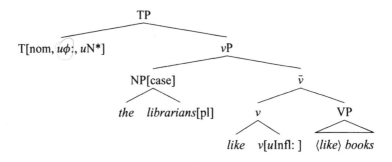

I have not yet marked any feature checking in this structure, and I have assumed a very simple binary branching analysis for *the librarians* (see Chapter 7

for a more sophisticated analysis). Let's see how checking between T, *v*, and the subject would work.

First, the case feature on T values the case feature on NP. I have represented the case feature as being on the whole NP. We will look in more detail in the next chapter at this assumption, but it will serve for our present purposes. As well as Agree holding between the tense features, it also holds between the EPP feature and the categorial feature of the subject, and between the ϕ-features of the NP (the relevant one in this case being plural) and the $u\phi$ features on T. This last Agree relationship values the $u\phi$ features on T.

(65)

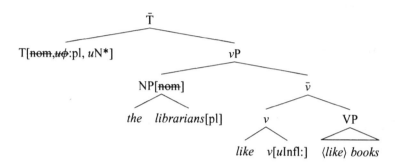

Now we can turn to the valuing of the *u*Infl feature on little *v*. The value of Infl on *v* derives from whatever relevant features are on T. The only one relevant is the ϕ feature which has itself received its value from the subject. Agree then holds between the ϕ feature on T and the [*u*Infl:] feature of *v*. This gives us the following representation:

(66)

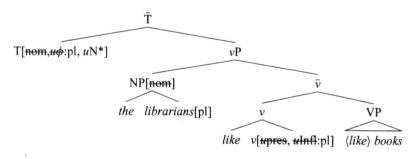

The various Agree relationships that have been set up conspire to essentially transmit the agreement information on the subject NP, via T, to where it is eventually pronounced, on little *v*. Finally, the subject moves to the specifier of TP to satisfy EPP.

(67)

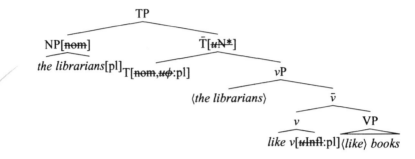

Of course, when little *v* is spelled out, the spellout rules are sensitive to its featural content, giving -*s* or zero as appropriate.

6.3.4 Interim summary

Let's summarize where we've got to, in terms of the theory:

(68)

1. Finite T bears [nom] and *v* bears [acc].
2. Finite T bears [*u*N*], the EPP feature, which causes something to Merge into the specifier of TP (either an expletive, or a nominal phrase).
3. Agree is constrained so that feature matching only takes place between a feature F and the closest matching feature F c-commands.

This theory provides an account of the distribution of subjects and objects in sentences, as well as of the case patterns that we find. In addition it extends to capture expletive constructions and is consistent with our approach to floating quantifiers.

We also make a further prediction: if there is no intervening subject, then Agree should be able to take place between the object and the EPP feature of T, and the object should then raise to the specifier of TP. The next two sections explore some of the ramifications of this prediction.

6.4 Unaccusative subjects

In Chapter 4 we saw that one result of the UTAH was that verbs which took only a Theme argument should realize that argument essentially as an object:

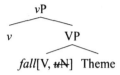

fall[V, *u*N]   Theme

We proposed that these unaccusative verbs were therefore syntactically distinct from verbs which took just a base subject in that they were associated with a little *v* projection which lacked a specifier.

This analysis immediately makes a prediction, once we put it together with the theory we developed in the last section: since there is no intervening subject between the EPP feature of T, and the N feature of the Theme, the Theme should be able to undergo movement to the specifier of TP to satisfy EPP on T. Moreover, since finite T has [nom] case, the single argument of unaccusatives should be able to agree with T in case features too. Finally, if T and the object match case features, the unaccusative version of little *v* must lack a case specification, or else there would be an unchecked case feature in the sentence.

This line of reasoning forces us to assume that the little *v* which occurs with an unaccusative predicate lacks both case features and a selectional *u*N-feature (and hence, a specifier). In fact, it is the lack of accusative case with these predicates which gives them their name: unaccusatives.

Let's take an unaccusative verb like *arrive* and see how a derivation will go:

(69)   Gilgamesh arrives.

Step 1 *Arrive* takes a single Theme argument, and therefore Merges with it projecting VP, in accordance with the UTAH.

VP

arrive [V, *u*N]   *Gilgamesh* [N, case]

Step 2 The output of Step 1 then combines with the version of little *v* which lacks a specifier and [acc]; *arrive* raises to this *v*.

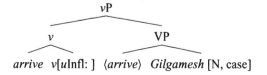

arrive *v*[*u*Infl:]   ⟨*arrive*⟩   *Gilgamesh* [N, case]

Step 3 Merge T[*u*N*, nom, *u*ϕ:] with the output of Step 2; [nom] on T values case on *Gilgamesh*, so even though this NP is Merged in object position, it receives nominative case from T. The uninterpretable ϕ-features on T are valued by the ϕ-features on the NP as singular; [*u*N*] (the EPP feature) on T also checks with the N feature of *Gilgamesh*. Since [*u*N*] is strong, it triggers movement of this NP into its specifier; the newly valued [sing] on T checks with [*u*Infl:] on little *v*, valuing it:

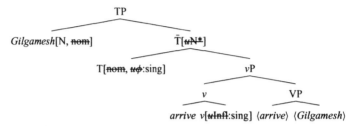

The result of this derivation is a structure which, on the surface, looks identical to the structure of an unergative verb like *run*. However, the derivation itself is different. Instead of moving an underlying subject to a surface subject position, we have moved an underlying object to a surface subject position.

This now makes a prediction: we should be able to find syntactic phenomena which treat the subjects of unaccusatives in the same way as they treat objects of transitives, since they are both Merged in the same position. There are many such phenomena (see the Further reading section for details) but here we will focus on a celebrated example from Italian.

6.4.1 *Ne*-cliticization

Italian and many other languages have a special syntax for certain pronominal elements, traditionally called **clitics**. In Italian, a clitic object pronoun cannot remain in its base position, but, instead, has to be positioned immediately to the left of the finite verb or auxiliary. This means that a simple SVO sentence is impossible when the object is a pronoun:

(70) Maria ha visto Gianni
      Maria has seen Gianni
      "Maria has seen Gianni."

(71) *Maria ha visto lo
      Maria has seen him
      "Maria has seen him."

Instead, we find the following order:

(72)   Maria lo   ha visto
        Maria him has seen
        "Maria has seen him."

This process applies to simple object pronominals, and also to pronominals which follow numerals. In this case, a special form of the clitic is found, *ne.* The clitic *ne* is often termed the **partitive** clitic:

(73)   Gianni trascorrerà   tre   settimane a Milano
        John   spend-[FUT.3PL] three weeks   in Milan
        "John will spend three weeks in Milan."

(74)   *Gianni trascorrerà   tre ne   a Milano
        John   spend-[FUT.3PL] three of-them in Milan
        "John will spend three of them in Milan."

(75)   Gianni ne   trascorrerà   tre a Milano
        John   of-them spend-[FUT.3PL] three in Milan
        "John will spend three of them in Milan."

There seems to be a syntactic restriction on this process of *ne*-cliticization, such that it is impossible from a subject position:

(76)   Alcuni persone trascorreranno tre   settimane a Milano
        Some   people spend-[FUT.3PL] three weeks   in Milan
        "Some people will spend three weeks in Milan."

(77)   *Alcuni ne   trascorreranno tre   settimane a Milano
        Some   of-them spend-[FUT.3PL] three weeks   in Milan
        "Some of them will spend three weeks in Milan."

The generalization about *ne*-cliticization we will use in the following argument, derived from these observations, is as follows:

(78)   *Ne*-cliticization is only possible from a phrase in object position.

If we now turn our attention to intransitive verbs, we find that Italian, like French, raises the verb to T, and like Icelandic expletive constructions, allows subjects to remain in their base position:

(79)   Telefoneranno   tre persone domani
        Telephone-[FUT.3PL] three people tomorrow
        "Three people will telephone tomorrow."

Here the verb *telefoneranno* has raised to T, and the subject *tre persone* has remained in the specifier of *v*P:

(80)

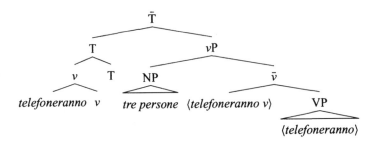

We will abstract away from the EPP feature of T here: we could say that, in Italian, T lacks EPP, or that it is satisfied by a phonologically null expletive. The important fact here is that *ne*-cliticization is impossible in such structures with an unergative verb:

(81)   *Ne   telefoneranno   tre   domani
    Of-them telephone-[FUT.3PL] three tomorrow
    "Three of them will telephone tomorrow."

However, with an unaccusative verb, *ne*-cliticization is well formed:

(82)   Ne   arriveranno   tre   domani
    Of-them arrive-[FUT. 3PL] three tomorrow
    "Three of them will arrive tomorrow."

To the extent that our generalization about *ne*-cliticization is correct (that the 'source' of the clitic must be in object position), this is a good argument that the subjects of unaccusatives are generated in object positions, rather than as the subjects of *v*P.

Notice that this argument does not really provide a deep analysis of why *ne*-cliticization only takes place from object positions, and to that extent, it is vulnerable to criticism. For example, an alternative approach might say that *ne*-cliticization can only apply to elements contained in Themes, rather than in Objects. Such a semantic analysis of the phenomenon would allow us to deny the UTAH and hence to deny that the single argument of an unaccusative predicate is Merged as an object. We could then provide a coherent account of the data above which does not assume a different syntactic structure for unaccusatives and unergatives (see the Further reading section for details). To make the argument watertight, we would have to provide a proper analysis of *ne*-cliticization which shows that it is syntactically restricted. We will not do this here, but, again, see the Further reading section for details.

6.4.2 Possessor datives in Hebrew

Before leaving unaccusatives, we will look at one more argument that their single argument is Merged in a different position from the argument of an unergative. The relevant data come from Modern Hebrew. Once again, we will not provide a fully fledged analysis of the facts, but rather establish a generalization, and use it to provide an argument.

In Hebrew, one way of signifying possession is to use a special prepositional element *le*. For example, in (83), the flowers are understood to be possessed by Rani:

(83)   ha-praxim navlu le-rani
       the-flowers wilted to-Rani
       "Rani's flowers wilted."

It turns out that this **possessor dative**, as it is usually termed, is systematically incapable of signifying possession of the subject of a transitive verb:

(84)   Le-mi   ha-yeladim xatxu 'et ha-gader
       To-who the-boys   cut   ACC the-fence
       "Whose fence did the boys cut?"
       "*Whose boys cut the fence."

In this example the possessor dative is used as a question word. The entity which is understood to be possessed can only be the referent of the phrase in object position (the fence), rather than the referent of the subject (the boys). The same facts hold across sentences of this type:

(85)   Le-mi   ha-yalda nigna ba-psanter
       To-who the-girls played in-the-piano
       "Whose piano did the girls play?"
       "*Whose girls played the piano."

For one class of intransitive verbs, possessive datives are ruled out:

(86)   *Le-mi ha-xatulim yilelu
        To-who the-cats   whined
        "Whose cats whined?"

The example in (86) is ungrammatical on the interpretation where the prepositional element *le-mi* is interpreted as a possessor. (Other, non-possessive, interpretations, however, are possible.)

We might try to capture this behaviour with the following generalization:

(87)   Possessor datives are unable to associate with subjects.

However, this will immediately get us into trouble with examples like (88):

(88)   Le-mi   ha-mitriya   nafla
To-who the-umbrella fell
"Whose umbrella fell."

It seems that we need to differentiate between one-argument verbs which take a true subject, and those which do not—this is once again the unergative/unaccusative divide. Only if we assume this distinction can we capture the behaviour of possessor datives:

(89)   Possessor datives are unable to associate with arguments (that originate) in the specifier of vP.

Sentence (89) will rule out the ungrammatical case in (86), on the assumption that whiners are agents and therefore Merged in the specifier of little vP. It will also correctly rule in (88), since things that fall are treated as Themes rather than as agents. By the UTAH, the single argument in (88) is the sister of V, rather than the specifier of little vP, so the example is predicted to be grammatical by the combination of our generalization and the UTAH.

Once again, we will not flesh this out into a proper analysis, and so it is vulnerable to the same kind of criticism as the previous argument. However, see the Further reading section for sources of more detailed arguments that the syntactic solution is the only viable one.

We have seen in this section that the surface syntax of unaccusative verbs, in English at least, is driven by the same mechanisms as affect other verb classes: in each case the featural properties of T trigger movement of an argument from inside vP to the specifier of TP. When there is only a single argument, then this argument raises, obscuring the structural differences between unaccusatives and unergatives. When there is more than a single argument inside vP, the closest one raises.

6.5 Passives

The final case of movement to subject position that we will look at in this chapter is the **passive** construction. Passives are alternants of simple sentences (their **active** counterparts), where the subject is somehow **demoted** in importance and where the object comes to be in the structural subject position.

(90)   a.   Medea killed Jason.
        b.   Jason was killed.

In each of these sentences, the NP *Jason* receives the Theme or Patient θ-role and is therefore, by the UTAH, Merged as sister to the verb. However, in the (b) example, this phrase has moved to the surface subject position (the specifier of TP): it precedes the finite auxiliary and is picked out by tag-questions as the structural subject.

Given what we have said so far, the direction of our analysis of passives is fairly clear. Passives are akin to unaccusatives, in that they do not assign accusative case to their object, and they do not appear to have a thematic subject. Because of these traits, the object checks [nom] case with [nom] on T and raises to the specifier of TP so as to satisfy T's EPP feature:

(91)

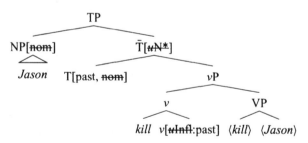

This derivation seems to capture the basic properties of passive, but leaves much unexplained. As it stands, it predicts that the following sentence is the passive of the (a) example in (90):

(92)   *Jason killed

This sentence is grammatical, but on the wrong reading. It cannot mean "Jason was killed". Our analysis, so far, does not explain the obligatory presence of the auxiliary *be* in English passives.

A second point to notice is that, under this analysis, the inflection on the main verb is checked by T. However, the main verb in a passive construction is actually not a finite form at all: rather it is a past participle:

(93)   The poisoned garments were stolen/*were stole

We will solve these two problems in the same way, by positing a Passive functional head, part of the Hierarchy of Projections, that is realized in English via the auxiliary *be*. This head bears the categorial feature Pass and immediately selects *v*P. Like all the other auxiliaries in English, it bears an [*u*Infl:] feature. The particular semantic contribution of Pass is to select only an unaccusative little *v*P. This will give the following representation, at the point where T is Merged:

(94)

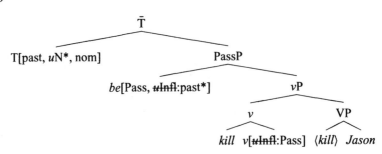

Notice that Pass values the *u*Infl feature on little *v*. The spellout rule for this feature complex is exactly the same as the spellout rule for *v* bearing checked [*u*Infl:Perf], so passive *be* will be followed by a past participle.

Since Pass is a functional head with a realization as an auxiliary, it bears a strong Infl feature, and raises to T, just like other auxiliaries. This will give an intermediate structure something like (95):

(95)   was killed Jason

T's [nom] feature checks against that of the object, and its EPP feature checks against the categorial feature of the object and triggers raising:

(96)

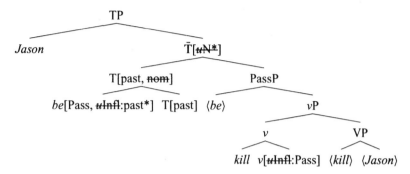

The morphological interface rules apply to this representation, to produce:

(97)   Jason was killed.

This analysis makes use of precisely the tools we already have at our disposal: the extra functional head is motivated by the morphological presence of the auxiliary, and the syntax of this new auxiliary is the same as the syntax of all the other auxiliaries we have seen. Moreover, the idea that the function of this auxiliary is to select an unaccusative little *v*P simultaneously explains the lack of accusative case and the lack of a thematic subject. Finally, the mechanisms we have used to trigger movement of the object into the surface subject position are precisely those that were previously motivated by the behaviour of thematic subjects and single arguments of unaccusatives. In a sense then, we have 'deconstructed' the passive; it is not a special construction, but rather just another functional head in the Hierarchy of Projections: when this functional head is present, it brings into play a range of independent syntactic behaviours. This means that there is no special passive construction, but rather just a single head with its featural specification.

Of course, we have barely scratched the surface of the passive in our analysis. We have not, for example, explained why it is possible to 'add' an agent using a prepositional *by*-phrase in English, whereas this is impossible with an unaccusative:

(98)   Jason was killed by Medea.

(99)   *Jason arrived by Medea

(100)   *There arrived by Medea

We have also not looked at the interesting range of variation across languages in the passive, with some languages allowing expletive constructions with passives which are impossible in English. For example, in French, it is possible to fill the surface subject position of a passive with an expletive, allowing the object to remain in its base position:

(101)   Il a été tué   trois hommes (par l'assassin)
            It has been killed three men   (by the-assassin)
            "Three men were killed (by the assassin)."

(102)   *There were killed three men (by the assassin).

Some languages allow unergative predicates to passivize, such as the German example in (103):

(103)   Es wurde getantzed
            It was   danced
            "There was dancing."

However, few, if any, languages seem to allow passivization of an unaccusative, a fact which is a mystery on our current analysis. See the Further reading section for alternative approaches which address some of these problems.

6.6 Adverbs

In this section, we leave the question of movement of elements to the structural subject position, and take a brief look at adverbs, to examine what implications the idea that sentences are headed by TP has for the syntax of these elements.

Once we make the move of assuming that sentences are headed by T, we find that there are positive consequences for other parts of the grammar. Recall that adverbs are adjunct elements which adjoin to phrases. In a sentence like (104), the adverb intervenes between the subject and the rest of the sentence:

(104)   Enkidu quickly freed the animals.

Since the adverb must be adjoined to *v*P, but comes in between the subject and the verb, the subject must be outside *v*P. The TP hypothesis captures this with no further stipulations, since the subject will be in the specifier of the TP:

(105)

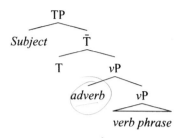

In addition to this, we predict that an adverb like *quickly* will not be able to precede a modal verb:

(106)   *Enkidu quickly may free the animals

(107)   Enkidu may quickly free the animals.

This is because the subject is in the specifier of the T which the modal has raised to. Since adverbs have to adjoin to phrases, there is no room for the adverb in (106).

The picture outlined here also allows us to analyse sentences where the adverb adjoins to PerfP and ProgP:

(108)   Gilgamesh may quickly have cast the spell.

(109)   Gilgamesh should slowly be tickling the mandrake.

These examples appear to be better than (106), but not as good as cases where the adverb is closer to the main verb:

(110)   Gilgamesh may have quickly cast the spell.

(111)   Gilgamesh should be slowly tickling the mandrake.

Note that the ungrammaticality of the following sentences is predicted if we assume that adverbs adjoin to vP projections, or higher projections, rather than to VP:

(112)   *Gilgamesh failed often Herbology

(113)   *Ron captured quickly a gryphon

Interestingly, under this same assumption, we also predict that if the verb could move to T, as we claimed that it did in French, then these sentences should be well formed, since the verb would cross a *v*P-adjoined adverb:

(114)

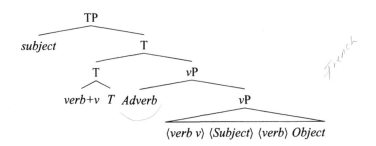

This appears to be the right prediction. The earlier stages of English, which allowed examples where the verb has raised higher than negation, also allowed an adverb to intervene between a verb and its object. These two observations can be tied together by the idea that earlier stages of English raised V + *v* to T, while later stages barred this operation:

(115)   Satan their chief undertakes alone the voyage (Milton, *Paradise Lost*, Book II, The Argument, 1668).

(116)   Adam consents not (Milton, *Paradise Lost*, Book IX, The Argument, 1668).

Both of these sentences are taken from the prose summaries of the various books of *Paradise Lost*. In (115) we see the verb *undertakes* separated from its object *the voyage* by the adverb *alone*, while in (116) we see the verb *consents* preceding, rather than following, *not*. Neither structure is well formed today. It appears that, in 1668, it was possible to raise main verbs to T.

VP adverbs like *quickly, slowly, messily, weirdly*, which tell us something about the **manner** in which the action described by the verb takes place contrast with adverbs like *probably, unfortunately, perhaps, surely*. These adverbs tell us something about the certainty of the speaker as to the truth of the whole proposition. Interestingly(!), they are best placed at the start of the whole sentence:

(117)   Perhaps Gilgamesh should be leaving.

(118)   Fortunately Hermione passed Herbology.

(119)   Ron failed Demonology, unfortunately.

These structures are easily accommodated if these **propositional** adverbs adjoin to TP:

(120)

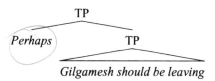

However, these adverbs also appear to be able to intervene between the subject and an auxiliary verb:

(121)   Gilgamesh perhaps should be leaving.

(122)   Hermione fortunately has passed Herbology.

We shall leave the structure of these sentences aside, and simply note that they require a particular intonational pattern, which may reflect the fact that they have a more complex derivation than one simply involving an adjunction operation.

6.7 Word order and movement

We have now reached a point where we can return to the question of parametric variation across languages. Recall that in Chapter 5 we proposed that the differences between English, French, and Swedish could be accounted for by specifying different strength properties of features on the heads given by the Hierarchy of Projections. We said that the tense value of Infl on little v was strong in French, but weak in English and Swedish. Conversely, we proposed that the uninterpretable tense features on auxiliaries were strong in English and French, and weak in Swedish. This allowed us to capture the differences between these languages in a very minimal way.

This system proposes that the distribution of features in the clause is set by universal syntactic principles (The Hierarchy of Projections, the projection properties of heads under Merge) and that the cross-linguistic variation arises because of the parameterization of properties of these features (notably, strength). Parameterization, here, simply refers to the particular option that a language takes of having a feature being either strong or weak.

We can apply the same reasoning to the strength of the features which drive subject movement. We have supposed in what we have seen already that the EPP feature in English is strong. Now, imagine that the EPP feature in a language is weak, then this would mean that nothing would move into the specifier of TP, and so the subject should be found in its base position.

This kind of analysis has been proposed to handle so-called VSO languages, which have a Verb-Subject-Object order. Take, for example, the following sentence from Scottish Gaelic:

(123)   Chunnaic Iain Màiri
         see-[PAST] Iain Màiri
         "Iain saw Màiri."

In this sentence we see the verb coming before its subject. One way to analyse this structure is to say that the subject remains in its base position, and the verbal complex in little *v* raises to T:

(124)

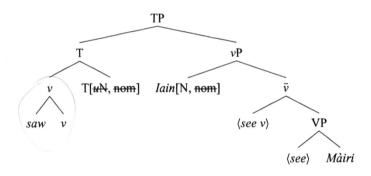

Here Agree applies between T and the subject, but the EPP feature of T is weak, and so does not have to be satisfied locally.

Some evidence for this kind of analysis comes from VP ellipsis constructions in the language. Recall that in English, the process traditionally called VP ellipsis actually applies to *v*P (here I have used strikethrough to express that the constituent has undergone ellipsis, rather than for feature checking):

(125)   Have you seen Mary? I have [*v*P ~~seen Mary~~].

If we adopt the analysis in (124), then we predict that if *v*P is ellipted, then both the subject and the object will be deleted in a VSO language. This is because both of these constituents are inside *v*P. This is in contrast to English, where the subject has raised to the specifier of TP, and so it is the verb and the object that are deleted.

This is exactly the right result. Scottish Gaelic (and Irish) have a specialized way of replying to a yes/no question, like the English example in (126).

(126)   Did you see Mary?

There is no general word for yes or no in these languages; instead, the person answering the question repeats the verb, in either its positive, or negative form (these forms are suppletive in the language, hence the lack of morphological relatedness):

(127)   Am faca   tu   Màiri?
         Q   see-[PAST] you Mary
         "Did you see Mary?"

(128)   Chunnaic
         see-[PAST]
         "Yes."

(129)   Chan fhaca
         Neg see-[PAST]
         "No."

Now this construction looks fairly mysterious, unless we analyse it as a kind of ellipsis. A perfectly reasonable, although somewhat wordy answer to *Did you see Mary?* is *I did see Mary*. In Scottish Gaelic, this is exactly what we are getting, except that we have applied VP ellipsis to make the answer less wordy:

(130)   Chunnaic ~~mi Màiri~~
         see-[PAST] *I Mairi*
         "Yes."

As expected, this operation deletes both subject and object.

To the extent that this is the correct approach, we seem to have some evidence that the EPP is weak in VSO languages (or perhaps, even, the feature is absent in these languages), but the tense features of little v are strong. This gives us the following typology:

(131)

	Tense on aux	Tense on v	EPP on T
English	strong	weak	strong
French	strong	strong	strong
Swedish	weak	weak	strong
Scottish Gaelic	strong	strong	weak

Once again this typology raises the question about the missing possibilities: are there languages with weak EPP and weak features on aux or little *v*? This would essentially be a language where everything stays down inside *v*P. If these languages do not exist, why is this?

6.8 Summary

In this chapter we have seen that there are up to two subject positions in basic clause structure: one associated with θ-role assignment, and one associated with case and EPP checking. We motivated these two subject positions on the basis of evidence from quantifier stranding and expletive constructions.

We proposed that the two positions could be occupied by the same element, in which case they were related by a movement operation. This movement operation is triggered by the EPP feature of T, which we argued to be a strong uninterpretable N feature. This feature is analogous to c-selectional features, and is checked by the specifier of TP in a sisterhood relation with $\bar{T}$. However, the EPP feature, unlike selectional features on lexical categories, is not associated with a θ-role: it is a purely formal feature.

In order to capture the distribution of case features on pronominals, we assumed that T also bears a [nom] feature, and that little *v* bears an [acc] feature. We refined our approach to feature matching, adopting the idea that feature matching was constrained by a Locality Condition:

(132)   **Locality of Matching**: Agree holds between a feature F on X and a matching feature F on Y if and only if there is no intervening Z[F].

Intervention is defined as follows:

(133)   **Intervention**: In a structure [X ... Z ... Y], Z intervenes between X and Y iff X c-commands Z and Z c-commands Y.

We saw that this captures the fact that thematic subjects rather than objects were the elements that usually move to the surface subject position. However, in the absence of a thematic subject, the theory has the consequence that the object can undergo this movement.

We saw that this prediction seems to be correct: objects of unaccusatives and passives move to the surface subject position in English. This approach is further motivated by the behaviour of *ne*-cliticization in Italian, and possessor datives in Modern Hebrew. We developed a sketch of an analysis of passives which involved extending the Hierarchy of Projection with a Pass functional head:

(134)   **Hierarchy of Projections:** T 〉 (Neg) 〉 (Perf) 〉 (Prog) 〉 (Pass) 〉 v 〉 V

Pass has the special property that it selects an unaccusative little vP.

Finally, we showed that this general approach allows us to extend our typology of languages, via that claim that strength of the EPP feature was also parameterized. We saw that this leads to some welcome empirical consequences for at least one subtype of VSO language.

Once again, here are the most important phenomena we met, and the basics of their explanations:

Phenomenon	Explanation
Floating quantifiers	Quantifiers are stranded after movement from the specifier of vP to the specifier of TP
Expletive constructions	EPP checked by expletive, and [nom] by the *in situ* subject
Distribution of cased pronouns and other NPs	[nom] on T, [acc] on V, EPP and Locality of Matching
Unaccusatives and Passives	Special little v lacking a specifier and [acc]; otherwise, same syntactic principles as actives
(At least one type of) VSO order	Weak EPP on T, with V raising
Adverb distribution	Different levels of adjunction interacting with verb movement

Finally, we introduced some abbreviations to make our notation more compact. These look as follows:

(135)   a.   [$u$case:] (an unchecked case feature) is abbreviated to just [case]

b.   [~~$u$case~~:nom] (a checked valued case feature) is abbreviated to [~~nom~~]

c.   [$u$case:nom] (an unchecked case feature with its own value) is abbreviated to [nom].

Exercises

Exercise 1 **Trees**

Using all the structures you have learned so far, draw trees for the following sentences. You should put in all the relevant features, including case features:

(1)   Cassandra has warned Agamemnon again.

(2)   Medea might have given Jason a poisoned robe (just treat *a poisoned robe* as an NP with no internal structure).

(3)   They should have all sent Oedipus to Colonus.

(4)   Perhaps Iphigenia will have murdered Oedipus by tomorrow.

Exercise 2 **Case**

Explain how each of the pronouns in the following examples checks its case feature. Say for each one why the sentence is ungrammatical. You will have to propose your own solution for case assignment by prepositional phrases.

(1)   *Me gave it to him

(2)   *I sent she away

(3)   *I introduced her to he

Exercise 3 **Passives and floating quantifiers**

Draw trees for the following two sentences:

(1)   The dragons have all been slain.

(2)   All the dragons have been slain.

Exercise 4 **Expletives**

We did not provide tree structures for English expletive constructions in the text. Using what you learned about copular *be* in the exercises of the last chapter, give a derivation for the following sentence. You may use a triangle for the PP.

(1)   There was a dragon in the cave.

Exercise 5 **A problem of quantifer float**

Explain why the following data are unexpected, on the analysis developed in the text:

(1)   *The dragons were slain all

(2)   *The Greeks arrived all

Exercise 6 **Ditransitive passives**

Task 1 Give a derivation for the following example:

(1)   The book was donated to the hospital.

Task 2 Now explain why the following example is ungrammatical:

(2)   *The hospital was donated the book to

Exercise 7 **Adverbs again**

Explain what difficulties the following examples pose for the analysis in the text. Try to provide an alternative approach which captures all the data:

(1)   Ron certainly will buy a dog.

(2)   Ron definitely has bought a dog.

Further reading

Section 6.2

The idea that there are really two subject positions related by movement became prominent in the late 1980s. Early proponents of this idea are Koopman and Sportiche (1991), Koizumi (1993), among many others. For a good discussion of the notion of subject in the kind of grammatical approach taken here, see McCloskey (1997), and see Bobaljik and Jonas (1996) for a discussion of the relevant Icelandic facts. For the approach to quantifier float discussed here see Sportiche (1988), but see Bobaljik (1998) for some cautionary remarks. Expletive constructions have received a lot of attention. See Milsark (1974), Safir (1985), Safir (1987), Belletti (1988), Lasnik (1992), Lasnik (1995) and Vikner (1995) for discussion and further references.

Section 6.3

The approach to case checking adopted here derives from Chomsky (1995*b*) and includes ideas from Chomsky (2000) and Chomsky (2001*b*). The idea that the operation Agree is constrained by some kind of locality is also from these works, but derives from much earlier intuitions (most notably from Rizzi 1990). In Chomsky (2001*a*), the checking approach is modified so that heads, rather than checking case features, provide values for unvalued case features.

Section 6.4

The idea that verbs split into unaccusative and unergative classes is originally due to Perlmutter (1978). Other works dealing with this idea include Burzio (1986), Belletti (1988), Baker (1988). The Hebrew data come from Borer (2002) and are based on earlier work by Borer and Grodzinsky (1986). A comprehensive recent study is Levin and Rappaport-Hovav (1995).

Section 6.5

Passives received attention from the earliest days of Generative Grammar (see, for example, Chomsky 1957, Chomsky 1965, Freidin 1975). For a good cross-linguistic discussion, see Postal (1986). Influential theoretical approaches include Jaeggli (1986) and Baker, Johnson, and Roberts (1989) and see Zaenen, Maling, and Thráinsson (1985) for a discussion of some pertinent Icelandic facts. The passive has not received so much attention within Minimalist theorizing, and the approach sketched in the text is basically an attempt to apply independently needed mechanisms to this phenomenon.

Section 6.6

Adverbial syntax was a neglected area of study within Generative Grammar until recently. See Baker (1981), Costa (1996), Rivero (1992), Stroik (1990), Travis (1988), and more recently Cinque (1999) and Alexiadou (1997).

Section 6.7

The argument that some VSO languages involve the subject remaining in the verb phrase is from McCloskey (1991), but see McCloskey (1997) for evidence that the syntax of these languages may be more complicated than is suggested here.

7

Functional
Categories II—the DP

So far in this book we have paid most attention to the structure of the clause, and the way that the requirements of lexical items are met via Merge and Move. In this chapter, we will focus instead on the structure of the phrase which has, as its lexical core, a nominal element, rather than a verb. We will argue that, just as the verb in a clause is surmounted by a series of functional projections, so is the noun. These functional projections in both cases add non-θ-related semantics and have the syntactic effect of providing positions for movement of both heads and phrases. The theory we will develop, then, implies that the true head of a nominal phrase is a functional category, which is the topmost of a series of functional categories, just as T is the topmost of a series of functional categories in the clause.

More specifically, we will see that the topmost functional category in the nominal phrase is that which is usually, in English, filled by a determiner. This means that we will be arguing for the idea that noun phrases are really **determiner phrases** and that they have the following kind of structure:

(1)

Here DP stands for a phrase headed by an element of category D.

We shall see that, just as TPs contain other functional elements than just T, DPs also have a richer functional structure. We will also see that this functional structure is responsible for checking case features, and for providing 'landing sites' for phrasal and head movement processes.

7.1 The category D

In this first section we will concentrate on the syntactic behaviour of determiners, as a preliminary to our argument that these constitute the head of nominal phrases.

7.1.1 Types of D

Take a simple phrase like:

(2)   The letter

The word *the* has a set of **distributional equivalents**, that is, words which can slot into the same position in the phrase. The following example shows just some of these:

(3)   The/a/this/that/some/every/each letter

All of these words are required to come before the noun in English:

(4)   *Letter the/a/this/that/some/every/each

If we pluralize the noun, then we find the following as some of the possibilities:

(5)   The/these/those/some letters

The words which are distributional equivalents with *the* are traditionally called **determiners**, and are assumed to have a new category feature—a **D-feature**. In addition to these examples, we also find plural nominals which appear without an overt determiner (**bare plurals**).

(6)   letters (are on the table)

Sentence (6) shows that a plural noun in English can stand on its own. Notice that this isn't true with a singular noun:

(7)   *letter (is on the table)

The contrast between the last two examples suggests that the well formedness of bare plural is due to the existence of a **null determiner**. We can capture the contrast by saying that English possesses a null plural determiner, there is no null singular determiner. Sentence (7) is then ruled out if determiners are obligatory in nominal phrases, a proposal we will return to in Section 7.2.6.

The different Ds are traditionally split into subcategories. The determiner *the* is called the **definite article**, while the determiner *a* is traditionally called the **indefinite article**.

The definite article can be used with both singular and plural nouns, as we saw above. The indefinite article *a*, can only be used with singular nouns:

(8)   a.   the letter/ the letters
      b.   a letter/ *a letters

What we see here is an apparent agreement relation between the D and the number feature of the noun.

The plural equivalent of *a* seems to be *some*, when it is used with a plural noun:

(9)   some letters

However, here things get complicated, since *some* can also be used with a singular (10), and the bare plural noun is also used like a plural form of the indefinite (11).

(10)   We need some technician to help us.

(11)   Show me letters!

As well as the articles *the* and *a*, we also have the **demonstratives**, *this* and *that*, and their plural forms *these* and *those*. These words serve to pick out things in the world via their proximity to the speaker, giving the **proximal** demonstrative *this/these* and the **distal** one *that/those*:

(12)   this chair; that chair

(13)   these chairs; those chairs

The feature that distinguishes proximal from distal determiners is related to person features. Recall that person features are interpreted as picking out the speaker or the addressee. Proximal demonstratives similarly pick out an element which is considered to be near the speaker or not. Just as we have third person pronouns, which are pronouns used for neither the speaker nor the addressee, some languages have demonstratives for items which are neither close to the speaker, nor close to the addressee. For example, Scottish Gaelic distinguishes the following three demonstratives:

(14)   an duine seo
       the man   this
       "This man"

(15)   an duine sin
        the man   that
        "That man"

(16)   an duine siud
        the man   yonder
        "That man over there"

Unlike the articles, demonstratives can occur without a following noun, in which
case they are traditionally called **demonstrative pronouns**:

(17)   I ate **that**.

Finally, we have words like *all*, *each*, and *every*, which are traditionally
called **quantifiers** (we discussed some aspects of the syntax of DPs containing
quantifiers in Chapter 6). The latter two only occur with singular nouns:

(18)   every chair; *every chairs

(19)   each chair; *each chairs

The semantic function of **quantification** is to pick out the whole set of chairs,
either as a lump sum (*every*), or as a set of distinct individuals (*each*). Other
quantifiers include words like *all*, *both*, *most*, and *many*.

   Before we look at determiners from a more theoretical perspective, it's worth
pointing out that determiners combine with a (potentially complex) phrasal
constituent. We can see this using simple replacement tests:

(20)   These expensive and illegal bottles of absinthe are to be smuggled from
        Hungary.

(21)   These ones are to be smuggled from Hungary.

Here the single word *ones* replaces the string *expensive and illegal bottles of
absinthe* suggesting that it is a constituent, and giving the following schematic
structure (I have marked the maximal projections here with question marks,
since we will return to what their exact category is later):

(22)

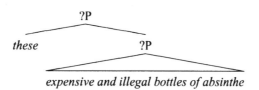

It is also worth pointing out that, although determiners come before the noun in English, this is not true for all languages. For example, in Madi (a Sudanic language) determiners follow the noun:

(23)   ebi re/di
        fish the/this
        "The/this fish"

This latter fact is reminiscent of the variation we saw between head-initial and head-final structures in the VP (that is, between VO and OV languages).

Summarizing, we have seen that there is a class of words which appears prenominally, and which can be subclassified into articles, demonstratives, and quantifiers. We expressed the commonality between these words by assuming that they had a shared category feature D. In the next section, we will look at the semantic relation that determiners bear to the rest of the phrase in which they occur. We will see that this relation is not one of θ-role assignment, a fact which suggests that determiners, like auxiliaries, are functional categories.

7.1.2 The semantics of Ds

The most important fact for a semantic analysis of these determiners is that they do not have a θ-related semantics. That is, they do not assign θ-roles to arguments, as, say, Ns or Vs do. Rather, their semantics appears to have to do with restricting the range of referents picked out by the nominal with which they (may) occur.

Take, for example, the definite article. Definiteness is a complicated phenomenon, but one useful way to think about it is that it links the nominal phrase to the context of the utterance in a particular way. More specifically, it has to do with whether the phrase in which the article appears describes, or picks out, something which the speaker can assume the hearer is **familiar** with, or not. In English, if the speaker can assume that the person he or she is talking to has already come across the thing referred to, then a definite determiner is used, otherwise an indefinite is used.

For example, in the first of the following two conversations, the use of the definite article in the italicized phrase seems odd, because the cocktail shaker hasn't already been mentioned, whereas in the second, the definite article seems perfectly appropriate:

(24)   Speaker A: Are you having a party this year?
        Speaker B: Yeah, tonight. I'm just off to buy *the new cocktail shaker*.

(25)   Speaker A: Did you buy a new cocktail shaker and some gin for the party?

   Speaker B: Yeah, *the new cocktail shaker* was really expensive, though.

The oddness of (24) here doesn't have to do with grammaticality. Speaker B's sentence is perfectly well formed, and if the indefinite determiner *a* was used in place of *the*, the sentence would be acceptable in this context. The sentence is odd in this conversation because the definite determiner adds something to the sentence which has to do with each speaker's knowledge of the background to the conversation. No 'new cocktail shaker' has been mentioned, and so using the definite determiner with this phrase leads to **infelicity** (pragmatic unacceptability). Similarly, the indefinite determiner signifies that the referent of its phrase is to be considered something new in the discourse. This is why, if we swap *a* for *the* in (25), the discourse again becomes disjointed: the use of *a* is infelicitous here, because there is indeed a 'new cocktail shaker' which is familiar to both participants in the conversation.

Notice that you can sometimes get away with using the definite article even if the particular thing hasn't yet been mentioned, but its existence, and therefore its familiarity to the hearer, can be inferred from what's been said. This phenomenon is known as **accommodation**:

(26)   Speaker A: Did you buy stuff for the party?

   Speaker B: Yeah, *the cocktail shaker* was really expensive, though.

Definiteness, then, is something which helps to integrate an utterance into a conversation. It does this by giving clues to the hearer about what the speaker thinks he/she already knows. Linguistic devices that do this kind of work are said to have a **pragmatic effect**.

Demonstratives have a similar semantics to articles, in that they signify how the speaker wants to direct the hearer's attention: demonstratives signify that the speaker assumes that the hearer will be able to identify the referent of the phrase as being close or far away, in either spatial or discourse terms.

Quantification, however, serves a different semantic purpose. Whereas definiteness signifies a discourse property of the referent of its phrase, quantification doesn't pick out a referent at all. To see this, take an example like (27).

(27)   No vampire can survive sunrise.

Clearly the phrase *no vampire* here has no referent. You can't point to the thing that the phrase *no vampire* picks out, because it doesn't pick out anything. The same is true for phrases like *each vampire* or *every vampire*. These phrases don't have a referent in the usual sense of the word.

What, then, is the semantics of these quantifiers? The easiest way to think about this is to look at quantifiers in whole sentences:

(28)   No vampire slept.

(29)   Every vampire slept.

In (28), what we are saying is that the set of entities picked out by the predicate *vampire* and the set picked out by the predicate *died* are disjoint: they do not have even a single element in common. There may be lots of vampires around, and there may be lots of sleeping things, but these sets do not overlap. The same kind of analysis can be developed for *every* in (29). In this case, the set of vampires is asserted to be completely included in the set of sleeping things.

It is interesting, then, that we have two completely different semantic functions (familiarity and quantification) carried out by elements with the same syntactic category (D). However, what is crucial for our purposes here is that the semantics of elements of category D is not θ-related.

We have come across categories which bear a non-θ-related semantics to other categories already: this is the relation between T and *v*P, for example. By analogy, it appears that D, like T, is a functional category.

In the next section we will focus on how to syntactically represent Ds, so as to capture this property.

7.2 Ds as heads

7.2.1 Complementary distribution of Ds

The first important syntactic thing to notice about this set of words is that they are in **complementary distribution**. What this means is that, because they have exactly the same distribution, they compete for the same position in the structure of the phrase.

(30)   *The this man

(31)   *Each a man

(32)   *Some those letters

(33)   *The the man

Early approaches to generative grammar assumed that phrases were structured by having certain slots in them. This was done by using phrase structure rules like those we saw briefly in Chapter 1. A noun phrase would have a single determiner slot, and a single noun slot, and its structure would be specified by a rule like the following:

(34)   NP → Det N.

This rule would generate trees like the following:

(35)

```
        NP
       /  \
     Det    N
```

Likewise, in a prepositional phrase there would be one slot for a preposition and one for the noun phrase.

(36)   PP → P NP.

(37)

Since a single node in a tree can accommodate only one element, it follows that a noun phrase could have only one determiner and only a single noun. Similarly, it would be impossible to have two or more prepositions heading a single PP, or more than one NP complement of the preposition. All of these properties are stipulated in the phrase structure rules. In this way, the notion of complementary distribution, and the particular case of complementary distribution of Ds, is automatically dealt with.

However, the approach to syntax we have been developing here does not make use of these structure-specific rules. Instead, it appeals to general principles, such as the universal Hierarchy of Projections, and to the operations Merge and Move. We would like to develop an analysis of the syntax of Ds in these terms.

Putting our discussion from the last few sections together, we find that the general properties of elements which are of category D and which we want to capture with a syntactic analysis are the following:

1. There seems to be an agreement relationship between D and N in terms of number.
2. Ds may occur on either side of their related Ns in different languages, in a way which is reminiscent of linearization of heads and their complements.
3. Ds combine with a complex constituent.
4. Their semantics is related to notions of familiarity, quantification, and proximity, rather than to notions of θ-role assignment.
5. Ds, in English, occur in complementary distribution.

We will tackle the last of these factors first.

7.2.2 Capturing the complementary distribution

The approach we have been outlining so far deals with complementary distribution of functional categories via the Hierarchy of Projections. The Hierarchy states the category and position of various functional categories in the clause: the reason that modals and non-finite *to*, for example, are in complementary distribution is that they both have the category feature T, and the Hierarchy of Projections only provides one 'slot' for elements of this category in a clause.

We can transfer this idea from the clausal to the nominal domain. We have already motivated the idea that Ds are functional categories, just like T, Neg, Perf, Prog, and Pass: they do not have a θ-related semantics. Just as functional categories in the clausal domain are determined by the Hierarchy of Projections, so we would expect functional categories in nominal expressions to be determined by a nominal version of the hierarchy.

We will explore this idea and state a new Hierarchy of Projections, which appears above nominal rather than verbal lexical categories:

(38)   **Hierarchy of Projections**
    a.   *Clausal*: T ⟩ (Neg) ⟩ (Perf) ⟩ (Prog) ⟩ (Pass) ⟩ *v* ⟩ V.
    b.   *Nominal*: D ⟩ N.

Recall the way we developed the clausal Hierarchy of Projections from a simple to a more elaborate structure. As you might have guessed, the same fate will befall the nominal Hierarchy.

If this idea is on the right track, then we have the following structure for nominal expressions:

(39)

DP
D   NP

This proposal immediately captures the complementary distribution of Ds. Since there is only one D slot, there can be only a single determiner. By its very nature, it also captures the non-θ-related semantics of Ds. Elements of the Hierarchy of Projections do not bear a θ-theoretic selectional relationship to each other.

The new approach to nominals also correctly accounts for the fact, discussed above, that Ds combine with complex constituents. The NP node in (39) is phrasal by the general principles of our system, since it projects no further. Phrasal categories are capable of being complex and it is therefore no surprise that we find a syntactically complex constituent here. The structure of our previous example is then:

(40)

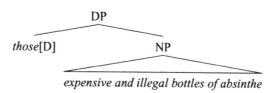

DP

those[D]   NP

expensive and illegal bottles of absinthe

Furthermore, as we have already seen, the linearization of heads and their complements may vary across languages. Since NP is complement to D, under our new analysis, it is expected that the linear order of D and N should vary, with some languages having DN order, and others ND (such as the Madi example discussed above).

7.2.3 Implications of this analysis

However, this approach threatens an idea that we have maintained since Chapter 3: the idea that N is the head of nominal phrases. It will also mean that all of the cases we have been treating as NPs will have to be recategorized as DPs, and that selectional N features (including the EPP feature of T) will have to be recategorized as selectional D features (so that the EPP feature is [uD*] rather than [uN*]).

Similarly, verbs and prepositions, which we said had selectional N features, must rather have selectional D features. A typical tree will then be represented as (42), rather than as (41).

(41)

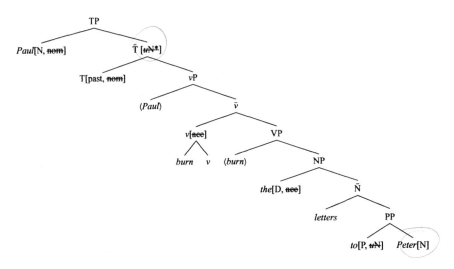

(42)

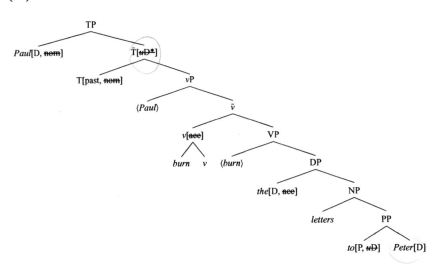

This recategorization does not mean that we lose anything real in the system. The distributional motivation for why phrases of the same type occur in the same position can be easily stated in terms of D features rather than N features. Notice that NPs still exist in our new system, but they are now complements of D; this is as expected since we have morphological motivation for the existence of an N feature, and Ns clearly combine with elements such as PPs to make larger phrases where N projects.

We conclude then that our previous analysis of nominal phrases as NPs is too simplistic. NPs do exist, but they are the complements of a functional category. Ds are the heads of nominal phrases.

change

At this point in the chapter, it would be a good idea to redraw all the trees you constructed in doing the exercises for the last chapter. You should use our new analysis of nominals as DPs, and note carefully how that affects the selectional features and EPP features in the trees.

7.2.4 Further questions

Bare nominal phrases

With this much in place, we can now turn to some further questions raised by the DP analysis. The first that we will consider is how we deal with bare plural nominals like *letters*. If these are simply nouns, then they will not satisfy the selectional requirements of verbs (since these are now stated in terms of c-selectional D features, rather than c-selectional N features). This will predict the ungrammaticality of such obviously grammatical examples as (43):

(43)   a.   I wrote letters.
        b.   We ate jellyfish.

The verb *write* c-selects a DP, under our new approach. We need to say this since we can have the following:

(44)   I wrote the letters.

But if *write* c-selects a DP in (44), then it should be c-selecting a DP in (43). It follows that the bare nouns *letters* and *jellyfish* are DPs, even though they contain no overt D.

Note that in many other languages corresponding examples with bare nouns are indeed ungrammatical, as the following examples from French show.

(45)   *J'ai écrit   lettres
        I-have written letters
        "I have written letters."

(46) J'ai écrit des lettres
      I-have written some letters
      "I have written letters"

In languages that behave like this, we simply say that no null D is available.

Putting this together with our previous argument, it appears that English bare plurals are really DPs, and that they have a null determiner, as required by the Hierarchy. This is the conclusion we also reached in Section 7.1.1:

(47)

0 [D] *letters*[N]

Pronouns

We can incorporate pronouns into our new system by treating them simply as Ds. When a pronoun is merged into the tree, it receives a θ-role and is selected, and so automatically it has phrasal status:

(48)

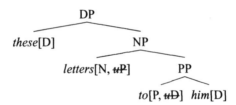

This approach also makes sense of examples like the following:

(49) [We linguists] love to argue.

(50) [You friends of the king] are all the same.

Here we see the pronoun, which is a D, exceptionally taking an NP complement.

7.2.5 Possessors—Specifiers of DP

We have, so far, developed an analysis for nominal phrases which treats them as DPs, rather than as NPs. Since, on this analysis, D is a head, we might expect it to have a specifier, as well as a complement. In this section we will propose that certain possessor phrases in English and other languages appear as the specifier of DP.

Possessor semantics, in English DPs, is syntactically realized in two main ways: via a preposition (51), and via a construction traditionally known as the **Saxon Genitive** (52):

(51)   An idea of Evan's.

(52)   Evan's idea.

We will concentrate here on the latter construction.

The presence of a Saxon genitive is blocked by the appearance of an overt article in English:

(53)   *The Evan's idea

(54)   *Evan's the idea

One interpretation of this might be that articles and Saxon genitives are in complementary distribution, and hence compete for the same position in the DP. However, this would be inconsistent with what we have said already: our approach treats Ds as X^0 elements, but Saxon genitives can clearly be XPs:

(55)   [One of our oldest friend's] idea.

Another approach to this problem, consistent with what we have said already, is to treat the Saxon genitive as the specifier of a null D:

(56)

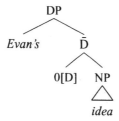

We have already met one null D which is used with plural Ns; here we would say that there is a second null D which occurs with a Saxon genitive specifier.

Is there any evidence that this is the right approach? In fact, there is actually an overt determiner in English which is not in complementary distribution with the Saxon genitive: *every*.

(57)   Evan's every idea was completely insane.

(58)   The Emperor's every wish was immediately carried out.

These examples show that there needs to be enough structural space within the DP to host an overt determiner and a Saxon genitive. The structure is as follows:

(59)

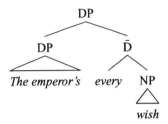

This analysis of *every* naturally extends to the other cases of Saxon genitives in English if we adopt the idea that the latter contain a null D.

The analysis outlined here receives some cross-linguistic back-up from the following examples from Hungarian:

(60)   Peter   minden kalap-ja
        Peter's every   hat-[DEF]
        "All Peter's hats"

(61)   Peter   ezen/azon kalap-ja
        Peter's this/that   hat-[DEF]
        "This/that hat of Peter's"

(62)   Peter   valamannyi kalap-ja
        Peter's each   hat-[DEF]
        "Each hat of Peter's"

An approach which places prenominal possessors in the specifier of DP makes immediate sense of such data. Whereas all Hungarian Ds allow a specifier, only *every* and a null D do in English.

7.2.6 More null Ds

We have now seen many examples of overt (that is, pronounced) determiners, and two possible examples of covert (that is, silent, or null) determiners: one is found with plural nouns, and the other with genitive possessors:

(63)   I have sent 0 letters to Environmental Health

(64)   The microphone-salesman's 0 irritating patter was relentless.

We have also seen that it is impossible to have a null determiner with singular nouns like *letter*:

(65)   *I have sent 0 letter to Environmental Heath

Sentence (65) is accounted for because *send* c-selects a DP, but there is no null D which combines with a singular noun in English.

This is a purely English-specific fact. There are other languages which allow null Ds to appear with singulars, as the following example from Gaelic shows:

(66)   Chuir   mi litir   dha
      send-[PAST] I   letter to-him
      "I sent a letter to him."

In this example the bare singular *litir*, "letter" occurs with a null determiner which means that it projects to a DP. This DP can then satisfy the c-selectional requirements of *chuir*, "sent".

Mass and count

We do, however, find a singular null determiner with a certain class of nouns (italicized here) in English:

(67)   Andrew likes *lard* on his sandwiches.

(68)   *Oil* spread over the sea-shore.

(69)   The wizard turned the beetle into *beer* with a wave of his wand.

These nouns, *lard*, *oil*, *beer*, are so called **mass nouns**, and contrast with **count nouns** like *letter*, *beetle*, *sandwich*. Mass nouns also contrast with count nouns in not pluralizing easily:

(70)   lards; oils; beers

These words mean types of lard, types of oil, and types of beer respectively. It seems impossible to make the actual noun itself semantically plural, because mass nouns denote substances which are inherently uncountable. This means that syntactic marking for the feature plural is interpreted instead in an odd way. The distinction between mass and count nouns appears to be a semantic feature to which the syntax is sensitive.

This allows us to say that we have a null determiner which agrees with its complement in terms of mass status. We can implement this easily by specifying an uninterpretable feature on the null D which will be checked only if the D c-commands an appropriate nominal:

(71)   D [*u*mass]

(72)

$$DP$$
0[D, ~~*u*mass~~] *lard*[N, mass]

We have now met three types of null D: plural, mass, and the null D that appears with a genitive specifier.

Proper nouns

There is an argument for a fourth null determiner in English which occurs with proper names. Notice that proper names may occur with determiners:

(73)   The Peter we all like was at the party.

(74)   The Paris I used to know is no more.

These sentences have slightly odd interpretations: in each case the proper name is assumed to hold of more than one thing in the world, and the determiner is used, together with other modifiers, to clarify which thing is meant.

Distributionally, we can see that the subjects of (73) and (74) can be replaced with just the proper name:

(75)   Peter was at the party.

(76)   Paris is no more.

What this suggests is that *Peter*, and *the Peter I used to know* are both DPs. One easy way of capturing this is to assume that there is a null determiner in (75) and (76) which takes the proper name as its complement:

(77)

$$DP$$
0[D] *Peter*

This analysis receives further support from languages where proper names must occur with a determiner, such as the following example from Greek:

(78)   O   Giorgos ephuge
       The George left
       "George left."

We can implement this by specifying that the featural content of the complement NP of the D is [proper]:

(79)   D [*u*proper]

Spelling out null Ds

When we talk about null Ds, it is important to be aware that what we are really saying is the following: the spellout rules for particular feature bundles result in a null phonology. Null Ds, just like everything else in our system, are just the spelling out of feature bundles; it's just that the spelling out lacks any phonological value.

We can illustrate this by examining those null Ds that occur with only a plural complement:

(80)   a.   *man arrived
           b.   Men arrived.

How do we ensure that the (a) example is not generated?

First, we know that some D must be generated. In (80), both examples involve a subject in the specifier of TP. Since T bears the EPP feature [*u*D*], the specifier of T must be a DP, or else the EPP feature would not be checked.

So what we need to do now is ensure that there is no D with a null pronunciation that occurs with singulars.

This is fairly easy to do, given the Agree mechanism we have already motivated. We can say that the indefinite determiner in English has the following feature specification:

(81)   D[indef, *u*num:]

Now, when this D combines with an N(P), the interpretable number feature of that N(P) will check and value the [*u*number] feature of D.

(82)   a.   D[indef, ~~*u*num~~:sing] man[sing]
           b.   D[indef, ~~*u*num~~:pl] men[pl]

When the spellout rules apply, the D with the valued plural features receives a null pronunciation, while the D with singular features receives a pronunciation as the indefinite determiner, *a*. This system means that it is simply impossible to have an example with a bare singular, because there is no spellout for a singular indefinite determiner as a null element.

Our approach interacts with subject-verb agreement in the right way. To see this, take the following contrast:

(83) a.   People like lard.
      b.   *People likes lard

The null D in both of these examples bears valued [pl] features. Although these features have been checked, they can themselves value the ϕ-features on T. Eventually they are pronounced on little v, or on the appropriate auxiliary:

(84)

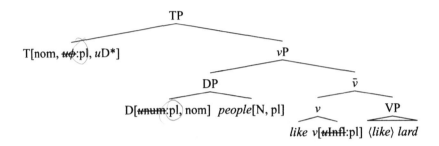

So far, in this chapter, we have established an analysis of nominal phrases which adopts the idea that they are headed by a functional projection categorized as D. This analysis captures the idea that the semantics of Ds is not θ-related, that Ds Merge with a potentially complex constituent, that there is an agreement relation in number between certain Ds and their NP complement, and the complementary distribution of Ds in English. It also provides us with a plausible structural position for Saxon genitives: the specifier of DP.

A final advantage is that our analysis of floating quantifiers is now theoretically consistent. The simplified view that we took in the last chapter was that quantifier phrases which could undergo stranding had the following structure:

(85)

We assumed that the quantifiers were heads, and were left with the problem of why they apparently do not project. The DP approach solves this, since these quantifiers do in fact now project. Our revised structure for these floating quantifiers is as follows:

(86)

What is special about them is that they apparently take a DP complement, rather than an NP complement. This allows them to be stranded when their complement raises to the specifier of TP to satisfy EPP. Of course, this now raises a new problem: this structure does not conform strictly to the Hierarchy of Projections, since we have two D nodes. Clearly there is something special about the syntax of these quantifier phrases, but we will not solve the problem here.

In the remainder of the chapter, we turn to what's going on in the lower reaches of DP: how arguments of N are projected, and how their features are checked.

7.3 Θ-role assignment in DP

In this section we will focus on how arguments of Ns distribute within the DP, trying to tease out similarities with *v*P, and noting any differences. We will focus first on nouns which are transparently related to verbs.

There are many nouns in English which bear semantic relations with DP arguments in the same way as associated verbs do. Take, for example, the verb *analyse*. This is a two-place predicate:

(87) The therapist analysed Morticia.

The related noun *analysis* intuitively assigns the same θ-roles:

(88) The therapist's analysis of Morticia

Whereas in the case of the verbal structure we find a nominative and accusative DP (as evidenced if we swap in pronouns to give *She analysed her*), the arguments in the nominal structure have a different syntax.

The Theme argument is realized as a prepositional phrase, while the Agent appears to have the same syntax as a possessor does—the **Saxon genitive**. When the Agent is a pronoun, it appears in its genitive form (see Chapter 2).

We can compare the case properties of clauses and DPs straightforwardly. Whereas in a clause we find nominative and accusative, in a DP this is impossible, and we find genitive, and an *of*-PP:

(89)   *He analysis her (was flawed)

(90)   His analysis of her (was flawed).

Moreover, it turns out to be the case that there is some unexpected flexibility in the assignment of θ-roles:

(91)   The analysis of the problem was flawed.

(92)   This problem's analysis is made a lot easier when you understand differential equations.

Here we see the Theme argument appearing as a PP (in (91)), but it can also appear as a Saxon genitive ((92)). This kind of flexibility is not observed with Agents:

(93)   Morticia's analysis was the most successful.

(94)   The analysis of Morticia took longer than that of Gomez.

In (94), *Morticia* can only be interpreted as the Theme argument. If there are both an Agent and a Theme in the DP, then the Agent must be a Saxon genitive, and the Theme must be a PP. There are some apparent counterexamples to this generalization, such as (95):

(95)   ?The shooting of the hunters

In this example, it appears that the DP *the hunters* is being interpreted as the Agent. However, closer inspection reveals that the association between this DP and the noun is much looser. If we put this DP in a sentence, we see the following contrast:

(96)   a.   The shooting of the hunters was very loud.
       b.   The shooting of the hunters took a long time.

The (b) example shows that, if the interpretation of *shooting* is really that of an event, then *the hunters* can only be interpreted as a Theme; this sentence is ungrammatical if *the hunters* is interpreted as an Agent. This suggests that what we are seeing in the (a) example is an interpretation where the hunters are associated in some plausible fashion with the shooting: in a sense, the shooting belongs to the hunters, rather than them being its Agent.

We will assume, then, that our generalization stands, and we can summarize it as follows:

(97)

	(Saxon) genitive	PP
Agent	✓	*
Theme	✓	✓

Not all nouns assign θ-roles. For example, simple nouns like *wallet* or *goldfish* have no arguments. As we have already seen, though, they may occur with possessors:

(98)   Morticia's goldfish

(99)   Gomez's wallet

(100)   The goldfish of Morticia's

(101)   The wallet of Gomez's

In none of these examples is the proper name interpreted as Theme or Agent. It is interpreted instead as a possessor.

The last two examples are cases where possession is marked with a prepositional phrase. The nominal in this PP is also marked, with something that looks rather like a Saxon genitive. However, a deeper look tells us that this marking is not exactly the same, since pronouns in this position have a different morphological form from pronouns in Saxon genitives:

(102)   My book

(103)   *A goldfish of my

(104)   A goldfish of mine

We will call this special marking that appears in a possessive *of*-PP the **independent genitive**. The independent genitive is not used to mark Themes, only possessors:

(105)   *The therapist's analysis of Morticia's

What we have, then, are certain nouns which seem to have argument structure and assign θ-roles, while other nouns have no argument structure. For nouns with arguments, these arguments can be realized as a PP headed by *of* when the argument is a Theme, and as Saxon genitive when the argument is an Agent or

Theme. Nouns without arguments may have possessors which are realized as an independent genitive or as a Saxon genitive. It is not possible to have two Saxon genitives both applying to the same noun:

(106)   *Morticia's Gomez's wallet

Finally, it also does not seem to be possible to express both an Agent and a possessor in the same DP. Take a noun like *photograph*, which is semantically capable of having an Agent (the person who took the photograph) and a possessor (the person who now owns the photograph). Since the Agent does not have to be the possessor, and since possessors can appear as *of*-PPs with independent genitive marking, it should be possible to have both:

(107)   Morticia's photograph of Pugsly

(108)   That photograph of Pugsly of Morticia's

(109)   *Gomez's photograph of Pugsley of Morticia's

Example (107) shows that it is possible to have a prenominal Saxon genitive with an Agent interpretation, and (108) shows that it is possible to have a postnominal independent genitive whose interpretation is unambiguously possessive. What does not appear to be possible is to have both together, as in (109). This seems to be a purely syntactic restriction, rather than anything semantic, since it is possible to express the Agent instead as a *by*-PP or the possessor by using an extra modifying adjunct:

(110)   That photograph by Gomez of Pugsley of Morticia's

(111)   Gomez's photograph of Pugsley belonging to Morticia

Let us now try to develop an analysis of the syntactic behaviour of arguments within the DP.

7.4 Little *n* and the low structure of DP

In this section we will provide the beginnings of an analysis of the fact that Agents do not appear as *of*-PPs in nominals. We will do this by extending our treatment of clausal structure to nominal structure. We will argue that, just as verb phrases are contained in a little *v* projection, noun phrases are contained within a little *n*P. This means that the Nominal Hierarchy of Projections looks as follows:

(112)   Nominal Hierarchy of Projections

D) *n*)N.

The main theoretical motivation for this kind of approach is that the generalizations we stated above which governed the appearance of arguments within DP
are very similar to what would be predicted if we were to generalize the UTAH to
nominals. Recall that Agents could not be realized as post-nominal *of*-phrases:

(113)   *The imposition of the government of a fine

(114)   The government's imposition of a fine

This is parallel to the syntax of verb phrases: the Agent cannot occur as a postverbal object. This phenomenon follows from the UTAH, which states that arguments Merged as daughters of VP are interpreted as Themes and that, to have an
Agent interpretation, an argument would have to be Merged as the specifier of *v*.

The UTAH straightforwardly generalizes to the nominal domain. We can say
that arguments which are Merged as daughters of NP are interpreted as Themes,
and that arguments which are Merged as specifiers of a little *n* projection are
interpreted as Agents.

This would give us a structure for the DP which would look as follows:

(115)

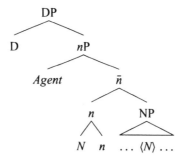

This basic structure gives us a partial explanation of why Agents do not appear
as *of*-PPs. It is for just the same reason that Agents do not appear as objects:
they are in the wrong position to have this interpretation. We will see exactly
how the UTAH, combined with case-checking mechanisms, gives us the right
results in section 7.4.2, but we will leave the explanation at this intuitive level
for the moment.

From what we have just said it appears that there is good motivation to extend the UTAH to the nominal domain. However, we have not yet seen any evidence that such a category as little *n* exists. We turn to this in the next section.

7.4.1 Motivation for little *n*

Just as we argued that Agents in verb phrases are Merged as specifiers of little *v*, we can bring to bear the same kind of evidence, from binding and co-ordination, that Agents in noun phrases are Merged as specifiers of a little *n*.

It is difficult to come up with clear contexts with which to test reflexive binding, but from the contrasts in the following examples, it appears that the Theme c-commands the Goal in DPs, just as it does in *v*Ps. For the following sentences, the context is one where gladiators are slaves whose masters may free them by giving them to themselves:

(116)   The consul's gift of the gladiator to himself.

(117)   *The consul's gift of himself to the gladiator

More obvious evidence comes from co-ordination. We find the same pattern within the NP as we found within the VP:

(118)   Richard's gift [of the helicopter to the hospital] and [of the bus to the school]

This suggests that, just as a VP is selected by a little *v*, an NP is selected by a little *n*, whose function is to introduce an Agent. It is this category that is being co-ordinated in (118). The structure we adopt is, then:

(119)

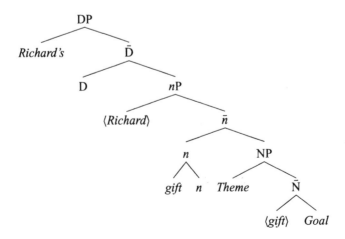

Once again, in the same way as V moves and attaches to *v*, N moves and attaches to *n*. I have also represented the idea that *Richard's* has moved from the specifier of *n* to the specifier of DP, just as the subject moves to the specifier of the TP in a sentence. We will return to this movement process in section 7.4.2.

One final question we need to address is whether *n* is projected in all DPs, or just those with Agents. If we look at the noun *gift*, we can see that it need not have an Agent, and we might think about dealing with this by saying that the projection of little *n* is optional. However, note that the noun still precedes both Theme and Goal arguments. If the structure we proposed above is right, then *gift* must raise to *n* to get the right word order, suggesting that *n* is projected even if there is no Agent.

(120)

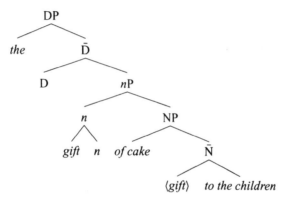

We will assume, then, that just as little *v* is an obligatory projection, but may lack a specifier, little *n* behaves in the same way. This will mean that even a simple noun like *cat* will have the following structure:

(121)

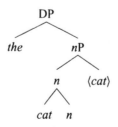

7.4.2 Case checking in DP

We have already met the type of feature that regulates the positions of DPs in sentences. Recall that pronouns are specified for different case features depending on their position:

(122)   He loves him

(123)   *Him loves him

(124)   *His loves him

(125)   His book

(126)   *He book

(127)   *Him book

In (123) and (124), we can see that neither an accusative nor a genitive version of the pronoun can go in subject position (the specifier of TP). This slot is reserved for nominatives. Similarly, only a genitive pronoun can occur in the same slot as a possessor phrase in DP, nominatives and accusatives are barred ((126) and (127)). The case feature on a DP is intrinsically linked to the syntactic position of the DP.

In (122), we find nominative case on the pronoun, rather than accusative or genitive, because the T node checks case on the DP that ends up in its specifier. We can straightforwardly extend this approach to case checking internal to DPs: we find genitive case in a DP rather than nominative because the D head in a DP checks genitive case.

Let us now transfer these ideas to our analysis of Saxon genitives in general. The hypothesis we have developed so far is that arguments of a noun are generated in the lexical projection. The Theme is Merged as the daughter of NP and Agents are Merged as the specifier of *n*. We need to account for the fact that Themes may appear as Saxon genitives or *of*-PPs, while Agents only appear as Saxon genitives.

We can do this using the kind of theoretical tools we have already developed for sentences. We assume that *n* checks a case feature on the *of*-Phrase which we will just represent as [*of*], while the zero determiner we motivated in Section 7.2.5 checks a [gen] feature on the Agent. This gives us the following kind of structure:

(128)

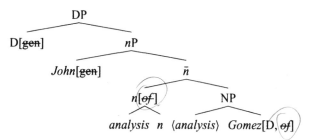

The [*of*] case feature on *n* is weak, and so the *of*-Phrase stays *in situ*. However, there is evidence that the Agent actually moves to the specifier of the DP. Recall that the determiner *every* allowed a Saxon genitive, and that this came before the determiner:

(129)   Evan's every desire

This suggests that the Agent DP raises past the determiner into the specifier of the DP:

(130)   Evan's every ⟨*Evan's*⟩ desire

What is this movement driven by? As usual, we attribute it to the strength of a feature. Now, whereas there was good evidence in the clause that the relevant feature was not case, but rather a special EPP feature, there is no such evidence in the DP. We assume then that the [gen] feature of D (which is optional) is strong, and that movement of the Agent takes place to satisfy the locality requirement imposed by this feature:

(131)

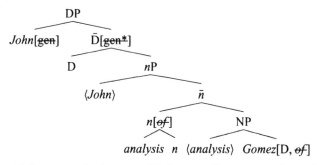

The [gen*] feature on D Agrees with the case feature on John, valuing it. In order to achieve the locality required by the strength of this feature, it projects to the D̄ level, and *John* raises to the specifier of DP.

This tree is then spelled out by special morphological and phonological rules. The ones which are of particular interest to us are those that spell out the case features [gen] and [*of*]. We can state them roughly as follows:

(132)   Pronounce [DP, ~~gen~~] by pronouncing everything within the DP and then *s*.

(133)   Pronounce [DP, ~~of~~] by pronouncing *of* and then everything within the DP.

Since null D values the case feature of the possessor or Agent, this DP has to appear as a genitive:

(134)   The girl's book

(135)   *The girl book

(136)   Her book

(137)   *She book

We can now turn to the fact that Saxon genitives may also be interpreted as Themes. This follows from our earlier claim that little *n* only optionally projects a specifier (that is, its selectional D feature is optional). If the little *n* is of the sort which projects no specifier, then the [gen*] feature on D will match the case feature of a DP generated as the Theme, correctly predicting that the Theme can raise to the specifier of D and be realized as a genitive:

(138)   The enemy's destruction (by the troops)

The derivation for such an example is straightforward and parallels that of an unaccusative. First, *the* bearing an unvalued [case] feature is merged with *enemy*. This DP is then merged with *destruction*, thereby obtaining a Theme θ-role. Since there is no overt Agent in the DP, little *n* is Merged but selects no specifier. The zero determiner is then Merged. The strong [gen*] feature on this determiner matches and values the case feature on the Theme, attracting it into the specifier of the whole DP.

(139)

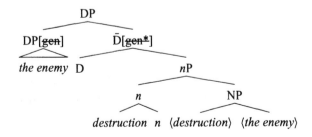

We have now captured some important facts about the syntax of DPs. Our system correctly predicts that the Agent will never appear as an *of*-Phrase. This is because it is Merged after the little *n* which bears the [*of*] case feature. Since the *n* head searches in its complement (its c-command domain) for a matching [*of*] feature, the Agent will never appear as an *of*-Phrase. We therefore correctly rule out examples like the following, with an Agent interpretation for the *of*-Phrase:

(140)   The destruction of the enemy

We also rule out structures like the following, with a prenominal agent and an overt determiner.

(141)

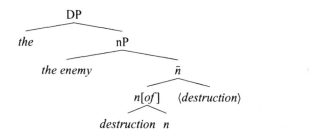

Two things are wrong with this structure: the [*of*] feature on *n* has not been checked, and the Agent has not had its case feature valued.

Notice that we correctly rule in (140) with an interpretation for *the enemy* as Theme. In this case, we Merge *destruction* with the syntactic object *the enemy*. The [*of*] feature on *n* values that on *the enemy*, and the structure is well formed:

(142)

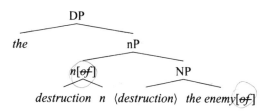

We also capture the fact that a Saxon genitive may have an interpretation as a Theme, in a parallel fashion to the way we captured the fact that certain subjects could be Themes: all of these constructions involve movement of the Theme into a higher position.

7.4.3 Possessors

In this section we briefly discuss the syntax of Possessors. We saw earlier that nouns which have no argument structure may still occur with possessors:

(143)   Jenny's cat

(144)   My penknife.

The surface syntax of possessors is just the same as that of other Saxon genitives: they are in the specifier of the DP, and they have their case value assigned by the D head of DP. However, the Merge position of these categories is far from clear.

If the generalization of the UTAH to the nominal domain is correct, possessors cannot be Merged as daughters of NP, or as specifiers of *n*, since these are positions which are reserved for particular θ-roles. An alternative proposal is to assume that there is an optional functional category, specified as part of the Hierarchy of Nominal Projections, and that Possessors are Merged in the specifier of this category. Such a structure would look as follows:

(145)

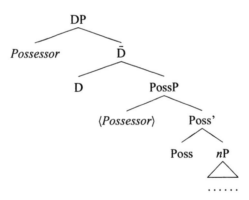

The function of this functional head is to introduce a semantic relationship between the element in its specifier, and the *n*P. Often this relationship is one of possession, but this is not necessary. An example like (146) can have a plethora of interpretations: it could be the book belonging to Anson, the one he's holding, the one that he drew the cover illustration for, etc.

(146)   Anson's book.

We will not motivate this approach to possessors any further. See the Further reading section for further details. We will also ignore the licensing of independent genitives. There is no clear consensus in the literature as to the proper analyses of these constructions.

Let us summarize our final position on the analysis of arguments within DP:

1. The UTAH generalizes to the nominal domain. Agents within DP are generated in the specifier of a little *n* whose complement is NP. The head of NP raises into *n*, just as the head of VP raises into *v*. Little *n* optionally selects a specifier.

2. The genitive-marked DP which fills the specifier of genitive-marked Ds (i.e. *s* and *every*) moves to that position from lower in the structure, driven by the strength of valued genitive case.

3. Possessors are Merged in the specifier of a specialized optional functional head Poss, which establishes an underdetermined semantic relation. The Possessor checks its [case] feature with the [gen] feature of D, and moves to satisfy strength of this feature.

7.5 AP modification in DP

In previous sections, we have concentrated on the functional structure in DP and on the case checking and position of arguments. In this section we will look briefly at adjuncts in DP. We will concentrate on the behaviour of adjectival phrases (APs) as exemplified in the following examples:

(147)   The **complicated** analysis

(148)   A **stunning** photograph of Jenny

(149)   Mary's **striking** resemblance to Sue

In each of these examples the determiner is separated from the head of the noun phrase by an adjective. The adjective itself can be modified by elements like *very*, *extremely*, *quite*, etc., forming an adjectival phrase (AP). We will ignore the structure of AP itself, and concentrate on how APs are merged into DPs:

(150)   The [very complicated] analysis

(151)   An [extremely stunning] photograph of Jenny

(152)   Mary's [quite striking] resemblance to Sue

APs behave semantically as modifiers. They are not assigned θ-roles. Given this, there are two plausible approaches to take, within the framework of assumptions we have been developing: they are adjoined to some projection, or they are in the specifier of a functional (non-θ-related) head. We will pursue the former approach here, maintaining uniformity in our treatment of adjuncts in general. However, see the Further reading section for alternative approaches.

In this section, then, we will briefly explore the first option: that APs are adjoined to projections within the DP. Since the APs in the examples above occur between D and (the final position of) N, it is reasonable to assume that they are adjoined to nP, in the same way as adverbs are adjoined to vP:

(153)

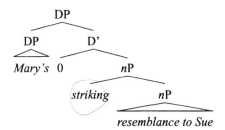

This approach predicts that APs are optional, since the operation Adjoin is not an operation which is triggered by feature-checking requirements, and furthermore, it predicts that APs may recurse, since the output of the adjunction operation is still an nP. Both of these predictions are confirmed:

(154)   Mary's resemblance to Sue

(155)   Ron's sleepy little rat

(156)   Jenny's scraggy extremely demonic cat

APs clearly signal semantic modification of nPs, as do PPs:

(157)   The gryphon in the dungeon howled loudly.

(158)   Ron's sleepy mouse in his pocket sneezed.

It is important to think carefully about the semantic relationship between a noun and a PP which occurs within the noun's DP. If the PP is an argument of the noun, then it must be in complement position. If the PP is not an argument, then it must be adjoined. In (157) and (158) the PP is clearly not an argument, since it simply signals the location of the entity picked out by the noun, so the PP is adjoined to the noun.

We represent the adjunction of PP as adjunction to *n*P, in much the same way as APs are adjoined to *n*P:

(159)

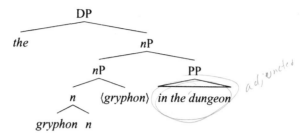

When we have both an AP and a PP adjoined to *n*P, there is usually no syntactic way of knowing which is joined lower. However, since adjunction corresponds semantically to modification, in (160) what is in the dungeon is a dangerous gryphon, while in (161) the thing that is dangerous is the gryphon in the dungeon:

(160)

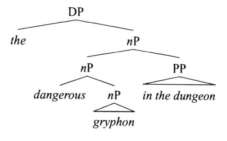

(161)

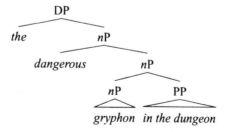

PPs like those just seen differ from cases like the following:

(162)   Mary's resemblance to Sue

(163)   Lucy's disdain for Edmund

(164)   Our discussion of porcupines

In each of these cases, the PP is an argument of the noun. These PPs are complements of N, Merged with N because of N's selectional P-feature:

(165)

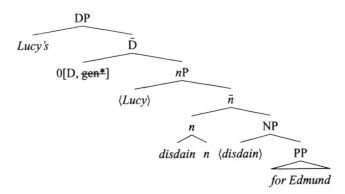

One final thing to watch out for with PPs is that they can be complements and adjuncts to verbs as well as nouns. This means that, when a PP or a series of PPs comes at the end of the sentence, it is important to work out whether they belong to the object or to the verb. Take, for example, a case like the following:

(166)   Ron heard a discussion in the foyer.

Here the PP *in the foyer* is not a semantic argument of *discussion*, and so it cannot be a syntactic complement—it must instead be adjoined somewhere. The question is whether it is adjoined to NP or to VP. In this case the sentence is ambiguous: the discussion itself might be located in the foyer, with Ron listening to it via a keyhole from a classroom, or the discussion might be taking place in a secret chamber, buried beneath the foyer. Ron's hearing of the discussion, however, occurred in the foyer. In the first case the PP is adjoined to NP, since it modifies the noun *discussion*, in the second case it is adjoined to VP, since it modifies the verb *heard*.

7.6 Order and movement in DPs

Before leaving DPs, we should note that the analysis we have developed leads to particular expectations about cross-linguistic variation in DPs. In Chapters 5 and 6, we saw that some languages raised *v* to T (French), while others did not (English and Swedish), and that some languages allow the subject to remain in its base position (Scottish Gaelic), while others require it to raise (English and

French). We encoded these differences via the varying strength properties of features on functional heads.

Our analysis of DP structure in English also depends upon functional heads and their featural properties. The structure of DP looks schematically as follows (abstracting away from possessors):

(167)

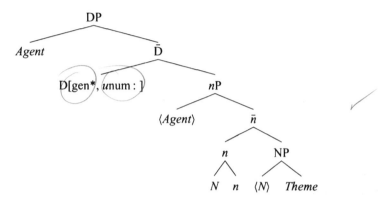

The [gen*] feature of D is strong, and forces movement of the closest DP whose case feature it values (in this case, the Agent, but it could instead have been a Possessor, or a Theme). The [unum:] feature on D encodes the number agreement relationship betweeen D and the noun, and ensures that Ds like *each* combine with a singular noun, while those like *many* with a plural. We encoded this via Agree. This feature is weak in English.

Now, if we vary the strength of these features then we would expect to find languages where [unum] is strong, and [gen] on D is weak. This would predict that the N+n complex would raise to D, and that the Agent would stay *in situ*.

In fact, such languages do exist, and the construction that displays these properties is known traditionally as the construct state. The construct state is found in Semitic languages, and I give examples here from Modern Hebrew:

(168)   harisat   ha-oyev   'et ha-'ir
        destruction the-enemy OM the-city
        "The enemy's destruction of the city"

(169)   tipul   ha-Siltonot   ba-ba'aya
        treatment the-authorities in-the-problem
        "The authorities' treatment of the problem"

In each of these cases, the whole DP is interpreted as though it is definite, even though there seems to be no definite determiner as its head. What we find instead is that the noun head appears before the Agent, and that the Agent appears before the object (OM in (168) stands for **object marker**, a special preposition-like element in Hebrew whose syntactic function seems to be to realize accusative case).

What is most interesting about the construct state is that no determiner is possible:

(170)   *ha-harisat   ha-oyev   'et ha-'ir
        the-destruction the-enemy OM the-city
        "The enemy's destruction of the city"

Furthermore, the order of the Agent and Theme is strict:

(171)   *harisat   'et ha-'ir   ha-oyev
        destruction OM the-city the-enemy
        "The enemy's destruction of the city"

These two properties are immediately accounted for on the analysis suggested above. If the N + n complex raises to D, because [unum:] (or its value) is strong, then the lack of a D in the construct state can be explained by assuming that the N + n complex 'fills' the D position in the structure (or alternatively, that the D bearing [unum*] is null). If [gen] on D is weak, then we explain why the Agent appears after the noun rather than before. Finally, since the UTAH governs where Agents and Themes will be realized, the strict order of the arguments within the DP is predicted. Under this set of proposals, the construct state in Hebrew looks roughly as follows:

(172)

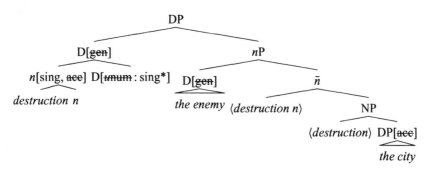

The [acc] feature on little *n* is analogous to the *of*-feature we proposed for English. The [gen] feature of D checks and values the case feature of *the enemy*, but does not trigger it to raise, since [gen] is weak. However, the [unum] feature on D is strong, and triggers movement of little *n* (and everything inside it) to D.

This analysis barely scratches the surface of the complications we see in cross-linguistic variation in DP structure, but it gives some indication of how the framework we are developing leads to expectations about the kinds of variation we might expect. See the Further reading section for more information.

7.7 Summary

In this chapter we have developed the proposal that there is a significant parallelism between the clausal and nominal phrases. We have argued that a number of aspects of the syntax of nominal phrases receive explanations if we adopt the idea that these phrases are headed, not by a noun, but rather by an element of category D.

We proposed that D appeared even in nominal phrases which were apparently missing a determiner, and we developed a theory of null Ds, which captured the selectional properties inside DP, and allowed us to maintain our theory of agreement features.

We also argued that D could be a locus of case checking for arguments inside the DP, much as T is in TP. We proposed that D bears a strong [gen*] feature in English, so that the specifier of certain Ds comes to be filled with a Saxon genitive.

We also argued that the UTAH extended to θ-role assignment within DPs, and proposed that, analogous to little v, DPs contained a little n, whose specifier receives an interpretation as an Agent. Little n is responsible for case checking of any Theme in the DP. The syntax we proposed allowed us to capture generalizations about the realization of arguments within DP, specifically that Agents could not be realized as *of*-PPs, and that Themes and Agents could both be realized as Saxon genitives.

We tentatively suggested that true possessive DPs were generated in the specifier of an optional functional head, which we placed above little nP. Just as D[gen*] enters into an Agree relation with the Agent, and triggers the Agent to move to the specifier of DP, it may instead enter into an Agree relation with a possessor, so that the possessor can end up having the same syntax as a raised Agent or Theme.

In order to explicitly state our analysis of DP structure, we extended the Hierarchy of Projections to cover the nominal domain:

(173)   **Hierarchy of Projections**
  Clausal: T 〉 (Neg) 〉 (Perf) 〉 (Prog) 〉 (Pass) 〉 *v* 〉 V.
  Nominal: D 〉 (Poss) 〉 *n* 〉 N.

We looked briefly at adjectival and prepositional modification in DPs, and proposed that these elements were adjoined to the little *n* projection. We noted that other analyses, which extend the Hierarchy of Projections yet further, are also possible for AP and PP modifiers.

Finally, we showed that our analysis of DPs extends in the expected way to constructions in other languages which look radically different. Once again, the differences reduce to parametric settings in feature strength of heads in the Hierarchy.

In this chapter more than in previous chapters we have left many loose ends: the interactions between possessors and Agents, the syntax of the independent genitive, alternative approaches to modification, and the potential of richer functional structure in the Hierarchy. This has been necessary so that this particular chapter does not grow out of all proportion. You will have a chance to explore some of these topics in the exercises, and I have included relevant references in the Further reading section.

Once again, here are the most important phenomena we met, and the basic features of their explanations:

Phenomenon	Explanation
Complementary distribution of Ds	The Hierarchy of Projections extends to the nominal domain
Selectional relationships between Ds and Ns	Uninterpretable features on D, which are valued by features on N or *n*
The appearance and position of arguments of nouns	Extension of the UTAH to the nominal domain, and case valuing by functional heads
The case of arguments inside DPs	[gen*] on some Ds, and [*of*] on little *n*
AP and PP modification	These elements are *n*P adjuncts
Construct state phenomena	Parametric variation in the strength properties of [gen] and [*u*num]

Exercises

Exercise 1 Gerunds

In English, there is a form of the verb called the **gerund**. This form is specified by suffixing -*ing* to the verb. In this exercise, we will suppose that -*ing* in English is ambiguous between being a little *n* bearing an [*of*] case feature, and a little *v* bearing an [acc] case feature.

Part A

Task 1 Draw a tree, fully specified for case features, for each of the phrases in bold in the following sentences. Note that the phrases in bold have to be DPs, since they are in subject position.

(1)   **The reading of Shakespeare** satisfied me.

(2)   **Reading Shakespeare** satisfied me.

Part B

Task 2 There now follow some data sets. Say for each data set whether it supports the tree you drew above, or whether it is problematic. Say why in each case:

Data set 1

(3)   The constant reading of Shakespeare (satisfied me).

(4)   Constantly reading Shakespeare (satisfied me).

(5)   *The constantly reading Shakespeare (satisfied me)

(6)   *Constant reading Shakespeare (satisfied me)

Data set 2

(7)   The readings of Shakespeare (satisfied me).

(8)   *Readings Shakespeare (satisfied me)

Data set 3

(9)   No reading of Shakespeare (satisfied me).

(10)   *No reading Shakespeare (satisfied me)

(11)   *Not reading of Shakespeare (satisfied me)

(12)   Not reading Shakespeare (satisfied me).

Data set 4

(13)   Every reading of Shakespeare (satisfied me).

(14)   *Every reading Shakespeare (satisfied me)

(15)   Every reading of Shakespeare (satisfied me).

(16)   *Every reading Shakespeare (satisfied me)

Data set 5

(17)   *Having read of Shakespeare (satisfied me)

(18)   Having read Shakespeare (satisfied me).

Note that (17) here is grammatical on a different interpretation. It can mean having read about Shakespeare but it can't mean having actually read Shakespeare's works. The star in the example is indicating that this sentence is ungrammatical under the reading where Shakespeare is the Theme argument of *read*.

Part C

Gerunds can also have subjects. Examples of these appear in the following data set:

Data set 6

(19)   Bill's reading of Shakespeare (satisfied me).

(20)   Bill's reading Shakespeare (satisfied me).

Task 3 Say how you think these subjects are added on to the structures you drew in Part A. Point out anything unexpected that is going on in the trees.

Part D

Task 4 Now look at the following data set. Here you can see that the little *v* version of *-ing* can have a different kind of subject which is accusative. It is possible to capture this difference by positing a null determiner. Say what you think the selectional and case properties of this null determiner are.

Data set 7

(21)   *Bill reading of Shakespeare (satisfied me)

(22)   Bill reading Shakespeare (satisfied me).

Part E

Task 5 The null D approach to these data captures everything we have seen so far. The following data set, however, shows that it is not the last word. Given the data in (23) and (24), explain why the last two examples are problematic.

Data set 8

(23)   *Bill's reading Shakespeare and Maureen's singing Schubert satisfies me

(24)   Bill's reading Shakespeare and Maureen's singing Schubert satisfy me.

(25)   Bill reading Shakespeare and Maureen singing Schubert satisfies me.

(26)   *Bill reading Shakespeare and Maureen singing Schubert satisfy me

Exercise 2 Trees for Ds

Draw trees, fully annotated with case features, for the following DPs:

(1)   Her every wish

(2)   That book's cover

(3)   Each picture of Hermione's aunt's fish

(4)   The sultan's every desire's fulfilment

(5)   That girl's best friend's fluffy moustache

Exercise 3 Diagnostics for P

A good test for telling whether a word is a preposition in English is that the word *right* may be inserted immediately before it:

(1)   I climbed up the tree.

(2)   I climbed right up the tree.

Apply this test in the following examples to the words in bold, which would all be traditionally analysed as prepositions. Can you see anything in common between the prepositions which fail this test? Think carefully about the θ-roles assigned in the sentences:

(3)   I compared Ginger **to** Fred.

(4)   We took the car **to** the town.

(5)   I bought a book **about** Harry.

(6)   We arrived **about** six o'clock.

(7)   They depend **on** Mary.

(8)   They sat **on** Mary.

(9)   I thought **of** the moon.

(10) She took a picture **of** the hippogryph.

Is there anything special about the preposition *of*?

Exercise 4   Adjunct or argument?

For the following examples, state whether the final PP is more likely to be construed with the verb or with the object. If you think it is ambiguous, try to state as clearly as you can what the difference in meaning is:

(1)   They brought the hat to the teacher.

(2)   No one could remove the blood from the wall.

(3)   No one could remove the blood on the wall.

(4)   The flying car hit the tree in the air.

(5)   The elixir was hidden in a hole in the ground.

Exercise 5   More tree drawing

Task 1 Draw trees for the following DPs and sentences. Annotate the trees with bar-levels and phrasal status, but leave out selectional features, case features, etc. You may assume that adjectives are always adjoined lower down than PP adjuncts.

(1)   Our discussion of previous students' failures in exams traumatized every nervous student in the class yesterday.

(2)   The continual implementation of modularization in this University demands constant attention.

(3)   Merlin's remarkable recovery from his hideous disease surprised the evil warlocks' chief curser.

Task 2 Now give a derivation for one of these sentences.

Further reading

Section 7.1

An early discussion of how determiner-like elements enter into the syntax of nominals can be found in Jackendoff (1977). See also Haegeman and Guéron (1999), Ch. 4, for a thorough textbook treatment. A good discussion of definiteness is Lyons (1997), and see Heim (1982) for a thorough theoretical treatment. For the semantics of quantifiers, see any good semantics textbook (Saeed 1997 provides a basic account, and de Swart 1998 and Heim and Kratzer 1998 give more theoretical approaches).

Section 7.2

A full-length discussion of the question of whether determiners are heads can be found in Abney (1987). A more cross-linguistic perspective, focusing on the differences between Germanic and Romance languages is Giorgi and Longobardi (1991). Szabolcsi (1983) provides a full discussion of the Hungarian data mentioned here, which is considerably more complex than what is sketched in the text (see also Szabolcsi 1994). There have been various theoretical extensions of the basic idea that nominal phrases are headed by D: for proper names see especially Longobardi (1994), and for pronouns see Cardinaletti and Starke (1999).

Section 7.3

An early discussion of how θ-role assignment takes place in nominals can be found in Chomsky (1970). For later work see especially Grimshaw (1990). Barker (1991) discusses how possessors are integrated into the semantics of DPs.

Section 7.4

The analysis we adopted in the text is essentially an updating of Abney (1987) with some changes to fit the current state of the theory. A good collection of papers on the issues here is Alexiadou and Wilder (1998).

Section 7.5

The approach we adopted in the text, whereby APs adjoin to *n*P, is an update of a standard Government and Binding approach (see textbooks in GB theory, for example Haegeman 1991). Valois (1991) argues for this approach. The alternative view, that APs are specifiers of functional heads, is argued for by Cinque (1994), among others. See Svenonius (1993) and Alexiadou (2001) for discussion.

Section 7.6

The construct state has received a great deal of attention in the literature on Semitic syntax. See Borer (1999), Ouhalla (1991), Ritter (1991). Constructions very similar to the Semitic construct are also found in Celtic languages: see Duffield (1996) for Irish, and Rouveret (1991) for Welsh.

8

Functional Categories III—CP

In Chapters 5 and 6 we saw that the clause splits roughly into two parts: the lower part has to do with the thematic properties of the predicate (essentially the VP), and is associated with the lexical projection, while the upper part seems to have to do with non-thematic semantic properties such as mood, tense, and aspect. This upper part is associated with functional projections.

In this chapter we will introduce one further clausal layer, which is higher still than T and its associated projections. This layer is also functional in nature, and bears close affinities to the T layer. However, the semantic properties associated with this higher level do not have to do with tense/aspect and other properties of the event picked out by the verb. Rather they have to do with the semantic status of the whole proposition.

8.1 Complementizers

8.1.1 *that*

The evidence for the syntactic presence of this higher layer is actually fairly easy to come by. You may have noticed, whenever we have discussed the embedding of one clause inside another, that many of the examples given had an alternative. So, in addition to (1), we have (2):

(1)   I claimed she was pregnant.

(2)   I claimed that she was pregnant.

The word *that* in these examples optionally occurs at the start of the embedded clause. We can use simple constituency tests to show that this word forms a constituent with the following clause, rather than with the embedding verb.

For example, pseudoclefting shows that *that* forms a constituent with the following TP, rather than with the preceding verb:

(3)   What she thought was that the poison was neutralized.

(4)   *What she thought that was the poison was neutralized

Similarly, movement tests show that it is possible to raise *that* plus its following TP, once again suggesting they are in constituency. Interestingly, it is not possible to strand *that*, leaving it behind by moving the TP on its own. The simple active sentence in (5), for example, can be passivized as in (6). When this happens, note that the *that* is carried along with the rest of the clause to the front of the sentence:

(5)   Everyone claimed that the poison was neutralized.

(6)   ?That the poison was neutralized was claimed by everyone.

(7)   *The poison was neutralized was claimed that by everyone

It is also possible to move *that* plus its TP to the right, across a prepositional phrase:

(8)   It was claimed by everyone that the poison was neutralized.

(9)   *It was claimed that by everyone the poison was neutralized

Verbs like *claim, think, believe, say, decide,* and many more take a clausal complement that may be introduced by the word *that* in English. Words which introduce clauses in this way are called **complementizers**. With some verbs, there is no option: the complementizer is obligatory:

(10)   *Jason whispered the phoenix had escaped

(11)   Jason whispered that the phoenix had escaped.

In other languages, complementizers are obligatory for all clausal complements:

(12)   Thuairt   mi gu bheil i   tinn (Gaelic)
        Say-[PAST] I   that was she ill
        "I said that she was ill."

(13)   *Thuairt   mi bheil i   tinn (Gaelic)
        Say-[PAST] I   was   she ill
        "I said she was ill."

(14) J'ai   dit qu' elle était malade (French)
I-have said that she was ill
"I said that she was ill."

(15) *J'ai   dit elle était malade (French)
I-have said she was ill
"I said she was ill."

The appearance of the word *that* in English in constituency with the embedded clause motivates the idea that it is a syntactic element which merges with TP, but does not tell us anything about the category of this element. An obvious possibility is that the relevant category is D, since, in English, the word *that* also serves as a demonstrative. However, this approach fails for a number of reasons. First, no other demonstrative can occur in this position with the appropriate reading:

(16) *I said this he left

(17) *Jason knew those Medea had cast the spell

This strongly suggests that the word *that* is not a demonstrative in these contexts; secondly, other languages have complementizer elements that are nothing like any element of their demonstrative system. As can be seen from the examples above, in French, the complementizer is *que*. However, the demonstratives are *ce/cela/ça*; similarly, in Gaelic the demonstratives are *seo/sin*, but the complementizer is *gu*. The third argument against treating *that* as a D is that there are other complementizers in English, which look nothing like any part of the determiner system. We will look at these in more detail below.

For these reasons, most linguists analyse the word *that*, and other complementizers, as elements of a new syntactic category, C (for Complementizer). C merges with TP and projects, giving structures like (18):

(18)

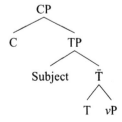

8.1.2 Declaratives and interrogatives

It is clear that C must be a functional rather than a lexical category, as it does not assign a θ-role. The semantic function of complementizers is a complex matter, but intuitively, a complementizer indicates how the hearer should think of the proposition expressed by its clause: the two main possibilities are whether the clause should be thought of as a simple statement of fact, or as a question about the facts. So we find complementizers introducing questions, as well as the cases with simple propositions that we have already met:

(19)   Jason asked **whether** the potion was ready.

(20)   Medea wondered **if** the potion was ready.

We can see that *whether* and *if* are in complementary distribution to *that* in English:

(21)   *Jason asked whether that the potion was ready

(22)   *Medea wondered if that the potion was ready

and that they are in constituency with their following clause:

(23)   What Jason asked was whether the potion was ready.

(24)   *What Jason asked whether was the potion was ready

(25)   ?What Medea wondered was if the potion was ready.

(26)   *What Medea wondered if was the potion was ready

This suggests that *if/whether* are also complementizers. Given their different semantic function, we can distinguish *that* from *whether/if* by means of an interpretable syntactic feature. The common term used for clauses which are questions is **interrogative** while clauses which are non-questions are said to be **declarative**. The status of a clause as interrogative or declarative is its **clause type**.

We will assume, then, a feature [clause-type] whose values are either [Q] (for an interrogative clause) or [Decl] for a declarative. Q is, of course, a mnemonic for question. These features are interpretable on C, and give rise to the different semantics of declaratives and questions.

We can state the c-selectional requirements of predicates which take a clausal complement in the lexical entries for the predicates as follows:

(27)   ask, [V, uC]

(28)   exclaim, [V, uC]

However, we still need to distinguish between these two classes of predicates, since the predicate seems to be able to determine whether its complement is interrogative or declarative:

(29)   *Ron asked that the potion was ready

(30)   *Medea exclaimed if the potion was ready

(Note: this last example is well formed for some speakers on a reading where, whenever the potion was ready, Medea exclaimed. This reading is irrelevant here, and arises from a different syntactic structure, which we will cover in section 8.3 below.)

The question is whether this information should be built into the c-selectional properties of the selecting predicate, or whether it is a simple s-selectional fact.

There is some evidence that the semantic (s-selectional) approach is the correct one. There are verbs like *maintain* which behave just like *exclaim* in rejecting a [Q] complement clause:

(31)   Julie maintained that the barman was sober.

(32)   *Julie maintained if the barman was sober

These verbs, however, also allow DP complements:

(33)   Julie maintained her own ideas over the course of the argument.

Interestingly, these verbs seem to be incapable of combining with a DP whose semantics is that they refer to a question:

(34)   *Julie maintained her own questions over the course of the argument

Since, from a syntactic point of view *her own ideas* and *her own questions* are identical, we need to appeal to a semantic incompatibility to rule out (34). Since we need to appeal to this semantic explanation in other cases, it makes sense to appeal to it to rule out examples like (30) as well.

Given these lexical entries for verbs that select a declarative or interrogative clausal complement, we are led to assume that the cases with an optional *that* are actually cases with a zero complementizer, so that the higher predicate always selects a CP.

(35)

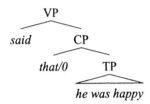

This position naturally leads to another question: do simple matrix sentences contain complementizers? That is, should we assume that a matrix sentence is really a CP rather than a TP?

There is no agreed-upon answer to this question. Some linguists have argued that, in the interests of economy, a simple sentence is just a TP, since there is no evidence for more structure. Other linguists have argued, on the basis of uniformity across clauses, that simple sentences must be CPs, since embedded sentences clearly are.

It is certainly the case that some simple sentences are CPs. We can see this with matrix questions, like the following:

(36)   Had the potion boiled over?

(37)   Did the magic work?

These simple interrogatives (often termed **yes/no questions**, because of their most obvious answers) contrast with their declarative counterparts in an obvious way. The auxiliary appears, not after the subject, but before it. Traditionally, this construction is known as **Subject-Auxiliary Inversion (SAI)**, since the first auxiliary inverts with the subject (we discussed this construction briefly in Chapter 1).

What is the analysis of such structures? If we assume that matrix sentences are CPs, then we have a simple analysis: the collection of features that projects T (i.e., tense) moves into the C position, in much the same way as the highest auxiliary moves into T in modern English and as the verbal cluster moves into T in French (see the discussion in Chapter 5). We will assume that tense adjoins to C, in the same way as we assumed that auxiliaries adjoined to T.

(38)

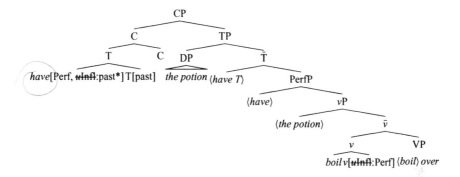

What we have here is a situation where the perfect auxiliary is moved to T, creating an adjunction structure with T. Tense has then raised into C, again creating an adjunction structure. The resulting structure is created by successive steps of head movement.

Movement of the perfect auxiliary to T is triggered by the strength of the valued tense features in *have*, as discussed in Chapter 5. The question that remains is why the complex in T moves to C.

Once again, to motivate movement, we appeal to strength of features. If we assume that T bears an uninterpretable unvalued clause-type feature[*u*clause-type:], then this feature can check with a [Q] feature on matrix C. On the assumption that the clause-type feature on T when valued as Q is strong in English, T will move to C, carrying along everything inside it.

Let's see how this works. At the point in the derivation where Perf has already moved to T, we have the following rough structure:

(39)   [$_{TP}$ Subject Perf+T[*u*clause-type:] ...

When C[Q] is Merged with this TP, it values the clause-type feature of T as strong Q:

(40)   C[Q] [$_{TP}$ Subject Perf+T[*u*clause-type:Q*] ...

Given that Q on T is strong, it raises into a local relation with the feature that it Agrees with, giving (41) as the final structure:

(41)

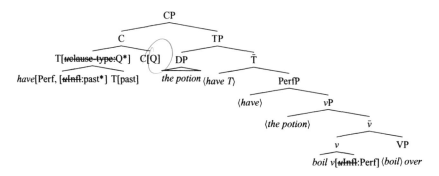

Interestingly, this analysis also predicts the correct occurrence of *do*-support in these sentences. Interrogative C triggers movement of T to C. Once this movement has taken place, T no longer c-commands little *v*. This means that a chain cannot be formed between them, and so the Rule for Pronouncing Tense cannot apply; *do*-support applies as a last resort instead.

(42)   Did the potion boil over?

(43)

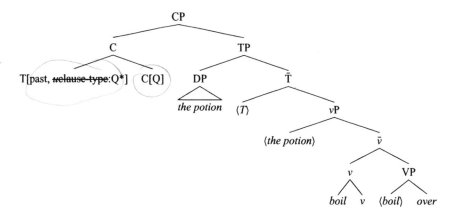

The existence of SAI structures strongly suggests that a CP layer is present in at least matrix yes/no questions.

We will assume further that CP layers are actually present in all matrix sentences, but that, for matrix declaratives, the topmost C position is occupied by a phonologically null complementizer, which values the uninterpretable clause type feature on T as Decl. The difference between Q and Decl is that the latter is weak, and so no movement takes place. The structure of a simple clause is then the following:

(44)   The potion boiled over?

(45)

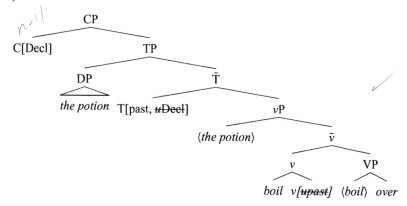

In future structures we'll usually abbreviate clause-type features as follows:

(46)   a.   [clause-type:Q] (interpretable clause-type feature with value Q) abbreviated as [Q]

b.   [*u*clause-type:] (unchecked, unvalued, uninterpretable clause-type feature) abbreviated as [*u*clause-type]

c.   [*u*clause-type:Q*] (checked, uninterpretable clause-type feature valued as strong Q) abbreviated as [Q*].

These abbreviations are analogous to the ones we developed for case. We will usually ignore [Decl] since its syntactic efforts are trivial in English.

8.1.3 Subject clauses

The examples we have seen so far of clauses introduced by complementizers have all been in complement position. We also, however, find clauses in subject positions:

(47)   [That Jason abandoned Medea] stinks!

(48)   [That the golden thread would show Jason his path through the labyrinth] was obvious.

(49)   [That I am here] proves [that I care].

(50)   [That Zeus was so promiscuous] astounded the other gods.

(51)   [That Medea murdered Jason] didn't surprise anyone.

The first two examples here are cases of one-place predicates: *stink* and *be obvious*. Example (49) is a case where a two-place predicate allows both of its arguments to be clausal, while examples (50) and (51) show cases where we have a clausal subject but a non-clausal object.

A natural analysis of these examples is to assume that the clausal subject is in the specifier of TP position, and that it has raised from a VP internal position. So an example like (49) would have the structure in (52):

(52)

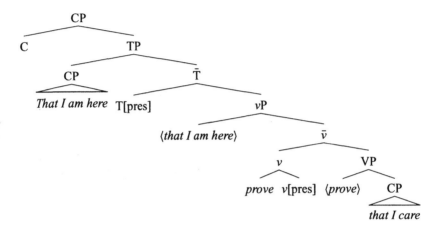

An alternative analysis that has been proposed treats the first clause as being in the specifier of CP, with an empty element of some kind in the subject position. The empty element is the true subject, and the CP is associated with it semantically:

(53)

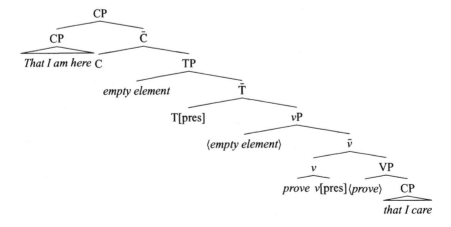

In order not to prejudge the analysis, let us call the CPs we are interested in here **initial CPs.**

The reason that the second analysis for initial CPs has been proposed is that these CPs do not behave like other subjects. For example, they do not appear to undergo Subject Auxiliary Inversion (SAI):

(54)   *Did that Medea killed her children upset Jason?

(55)   *Has that we have arrived back at our starting point proved that the world is round?

Similarly, while it is clearly possible to have a DP subject in an initial CP, it is not possible to have an initial CP in an initial CP:

(56)   [That [the answer] is obvious] upset Hermes.

(57)   *[That [that the world is round] is obvious] upset Hermes

(58)   *[That [whether the world is round] is unknown] bothered Athena

These examples show that 'normal' DP subjects have a different distribution to the initial CPs that interest us, suggesting that they are in different syntactic positions.

Finally, in other languages, it is clear that an initial CP is not in subject position, because a special pronoun form appears. The following example is from Dutch:

(59)   Dat hij kommt, dat is duidelijk
that he comes   that is clear
"That he will come is clear."

The idea, under the second analysis, is that Dutch and English are structurally just the same, but that the English equivalent of *dat* is null (represented here just as *e*):

(60)   That he is coming *e* is clear.

Let us think about how this proposal would actually work. The null pronoun Merges with the bar-level projection of little *v* and then raises to the specifier of TP, checking case and the EPP feature of T. We then Merge C, and then a previously constructed CP. This Merger needs to be triggered by a selectional feature of C, so the matrix C itself has to have a *u*C feature which is projected to C̄ and then checked by the initial CP:

(61)

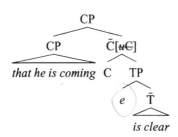

One theoretical advantage that this proposal has is that it allows us to maintain our idea that the EPP feature on T is an uninterpretable [D] feature of T. This feature is satisfied by merging into the thematic subject position the demonstrative pronoun *dat* in Dutch and raising it to the specifier of TP to satisfy the EPP feature. The derivation is just the same for English, except that the pronoun is null. If we were to adopt the alternative analysis, and to put the initial CP in the specifier of TP, we would need to rethink exactly what the EPP feature is, since it would then be able to be satisfied by DP or CP.

Under the null pronoun analysis, we also have a way of encoding the fact that SAI does not occur with initial CPs. Recall that SAI is triggered by C valuing the clause-type feature of T as [uQ^*]. We can block SAI occurring where we have an initial CP by simply stating that the matrix C[uC] that appears in initial CP constructions is incompatible with the Q feature. Since this special C is needed to have an initial CP, initial CPs are incompatible with SAI. Of course, without independent motivation, this is just a way of formalizing our description, rather than providing an explanation. It does, however, at least allow us to capture the correct patterns.

Finally, the proposal makes possible an analysis which predicts why initial CPs can't occur inside other initial CPs. If we look at an initial CP with a DP subject, the subject occurs after the complementizer:

(62)   [That **Jason** arrived] infuriated Medea.

(63)   [Whether **Agamemnon** had triumphed] was unknown.

Under our new analysis of initial CPs, however, they are in the specifier of a null C[uC], and the subject position is filled by an empty element. This explains why we never find an initial CP after a complementizer: initial CPs are themselves actually Merged with the projection of a special complementizer, so we will never find them following *that* or *whether*. However, the proposal makes mysterious the unacceptability of examples like the following:

(64)   *[[That Jason had arrived] C *e* was obvious] C *e* infuriated Medea

If we say that the null C[*u*C] is restricted to matrix-clause positions, then (64) will be ruled out, since there is an occurrence of this null C in an embedded clause. This same restriction will correctly rule out examples like the following:

(65)   *I said that that Jason was jealous annoyed Medea

We have adopted a syntactic approach to the behaviour of initial subjects which assumes that they are introduced by a special null C, which bears a selectional C feature, allowing a CP to merge in its specifier. We adopted this analysis because it allowed us to deal with certain differences between initial CPs and DP subjects by claiming that there was a structural difference between them. An alternative approach would be to adopt the idea that initial CPs really are in the standard structural subject position (the specifier of TP) and to say that their odd syntax is the result of something else.

One of the earliest approaches to initial subjects adopted this second idea. Ross (1967), in his Ph.D. thesis, argued that the odd syntax of initial CPs was due to a general parsing principle which prohibited CPs from being **internal** to other CPs, where a constituent is internal to another constituent just in case it is surrounded by phonological material from that other constituent. He termed this the **Internal S Condition**.

Let us see how this would work: first, we would assume an analysis where initial CPs are in the specifier of TP. If T to C movement takes place, then the initial CP is internal to the matrix CP, since there is phonological material from the matrix CP on both sides of the initial CP:

(66)

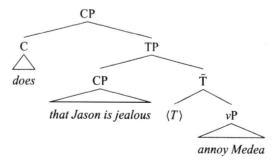

Similarly, if an initial CP is the subject of another initial CP, then clearly it will be internal. On one side it will have the higher CP's complementizer, and on the other, the rest of the sentence:

(67)

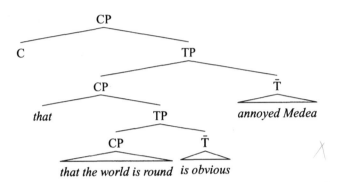

However, there are sentences which seem to fall foul of the Internal S Condition, but which are perfectly well formed:

(68)   Believing [that the world is flat] gives one some solace.

In (68) the matrix CP contains *believing* and *gives one some solace*, which appear on either side of the internal CP. This should be ruled out by the Internal S Condition, but the sentence is, of course, perfectly grammatical.

For this reason, we will adopt the specifier of CP analysis for internal CPs from now on. We should note, though, that this analysis itself has some problems. The most worrying is how to rule out the following:

(69)   *e is obvious

We will return to this problem in section 8.2.8.

8.2 Non-finite CP complementation

In this section we will explore the behaviour of non-finite clausal complements to various kinds of predicates. Before we do this, we will tease out an implication of the ideas we developed about θ-roles in Chapter 4. This idea will be important for our discussion of clausal complementation.

Recall that lexical items are specified with c-selectional features, and that these features are associated with θ-roles in the lexical representation of words. Since all uninterpretable features have to be checked, it follows that all the θ-roles of a particular predicate will be assigned.

In the theory we developed in Chapter 4, this was the only way that something could be interpreted as an argument. The UTAH specified that certain syntactic configurations had certain thematic interpretations. If a DP, say, was not in one of these configurations, then it could not be interpreted as an argument.

This theory made sense of expletive elements, which are not interpreted as arguments, and which are inserted just to satisfy EPP requirements. Expletives are inserted in positions where no θ-role is assigned (the specifier of TP, for instance). In a sentence like (70), all the θ-roles are assigned internal to the vP projected by unaccusative *arrive*:

(70)   There arrived a new actor.

Although these sentences are fairly marginal in English, they are possible. What is impossible is to put a non-expletive DP in the place of the expletive:

(71)   *The doctor arrived a new actor

It follows, then, from our treatment of the relationship between the syntax and the semantics of arguments, that a DP can never be interpreted as an argument unless it has Merged in a position which the UTAH determines as an **argument position**.

A second point about the theory of θ-roles which we need to remember is that a DP is assigned only a single θ-role. An argument receives its θ-role in the position that it is Merged. Once it has a θ-role, it may not move into another position where it will receive a second role. This restriction is what rules out examples like the following:

(72)   *Medea murdered

If a single DP were able to receive two θ-roles, then *Medea* could be Merged as sister to *murder*, thus receiving a Theme interpretation, and then raised to the specifier of little vP, where it would receive an Agent interpretation. However, this is not possible, and we will assume that this is because DPs may occur in only one **argument position** in a derivation.

Let us sum up these ideas as follows:

(73)   a.   A DP may receive only one θ-role.
       b.   A DP must receive a θ-role.

We will use these ideas to develop an analysis of infinitival complementation. The analysis we will develop is only as strong as these generalizations, so that, if it turns out that these generalizations have to be jettisoned, our analysis will have to be reconsidered. See the Further reading section for suggestions for alternative approaches to infinitival complementation that reject these ideas from θ-theory.

8.2.1 PRO and control clauses

We have seen that finite CPs may act as subjects and as complements to verbs. We met examples of non-finite clausal complements in Chapter 5, when we used the distribution of non-finite *to* to motivate TP:

(74)   Medea tried [to poison her children].

(75)   Odysseus planned [to hear the sirens].

Note that the verbs in the embedded clauses are two-place predicates. The Agent of these verbs is interpreted as being referentially dependent for its interpretation on the Agent of the matrix verb; so in (74), Medea, not anyone else, is the person envisaged as poisoning her children. Likewise, in (75), it is Odysseus who is going to hear the sirens.

Note that in neither of these examples is it possible to realize the subject of the lower clause overtly:

(76)   *Medea tried [Medea to poison her children]

(77)   *Medea tried [the nurse to poison her children]

(78)   *Odysseus attempted [Odysseus to hear the sirens]

(79)   *Odysseus attempted [the helmsman to hear the sirens]

Poison is a two-place predicate in (74), assigning an Agent and a Theme θ-role. The Theme θ-role is assigned to *her children*. What receives the Agent θ-role? It can't be *Medea* in the matrix clause, because Medea has a θ-role which it receives from *tried*. This means that, under the assumptions we have developed so far, there must be a null element in (74) which is Merged in the specifier of little v. This null element receives a θ-role from the verb in the non-finite clause. This whole clause then gets a θ-role from the matrix verb. For convenience, we term this null subject PRO. Given our theory so far, PRO is Merged in the specifier of little v (we will address the question of whether PRO moves below):

(80)   Medea tried [to PRO poison her children].

In sentences like (80), PRO is said to be **controlled** by the matrix subject. Clauses with PRO in them are then said to be **Control Clauses**.

PRO may also occur in structures where it is not controlled by another DP, in which case it is arbitrary in its interpretation, a little like the pronoun *one* in formal English:

(81)   PRO to steal hexes from witches is dangerous.

(82)   If one were to steal hexes from witches, then that would be dangerous.

(83)   It is not allowed to PRO perjure oneself.

We will not delve into the question of when PRO gets a controlled interpretation, and when it gets an arbitrary interpretation here, but we will try instead to solve the syntactic question of what PRO's distribution is.

8.2.2 ECM clauses

Control clauses have PRO as their subject, and the control clauses we have seen so far do not allow overt DP subjects. However, there are non-finite complement clauses which allow overt subjects:

(84)   We believed Zeus to be omnipotent.

(85)   No one expected Agamemnon to win.

Each of the matrix verbs in these examples is also a two-place predicate relating an individual to a proposition. We can see this by using finite clauses instead of non-finite ones:

(86)   We believed that Zeus was omnipotent.

(87)   No one expected that Agamemnon would win.

On the assumption that the θ-role assigning properties of these verbs remains constant, this suggests that the structure of these sentences is as follows:

(88)   We believed [Zeus to be omnipotent].

(89)   No one expected [Agamemnon to to win].

If we substitute pronouns for the subjects of these non-finite embedded clauses, we find that they are accusative:

(90)   We believed [him to be omnipotent].

(91)   No one expected [him to to win].

The traditional name for these constructions is **ECM constructions**, where ECM stands for Exceptional Case Marking. This name is really just a leftover from an earlier theory of this phenomenon (previously they were referred to as Raising-to-Object constructions). We shall keep this name, even though the theory we develop of this phenomenon will turn out to involve just the same case-assigning mechanism as is at play in standard verb-object structures.

So in English we have seen so far two different types of non-finite clause: one type disallows overt subjects, and requires PRO. This is what we see with verbs like *try, attempt, endeavour*. The other type allows overt subjects in the non-finite clause, as seen above. In fact, matters turn out to be more complicated because some of the verbs that allow an overt subject prohibit PRO, while others don't:

(92)   *We believed to PRO be omnipotent

(93)   No one expected to PRO win.

The question we are faced with, then, is how to syntactically distinguish the three types of verb we have just met: verbs that take non-finite complements with obligatory PRO (*try, attempt, endeavour*); verbs that take non-finite complements but don't allow a PRO subject in these complements (*believe, consider, think, assume*); and verbs that allow both PRO and overt subjects (*want, expect, prefer*). These verbs clearly fall into different semantic classes, but we'd like to know how their syntactic specification differs. We will attempt to solve this problem by developing the account of case and EPP that we have used so far.

8.2.3 C in non-finite clauses

Given that finite clauses can be headed by complementizers, the natural assumption is that non-finite clauses may be as well, completing the parallel. In fact there is clear evidence that this is the case:

(94)   I intended [for Jenny to be present].

(95)   [For you to do that] would be a mistake.

In (94), we see that we have an overt subject in the non-finite clause (*Jenny*) which is preceded by an element which looks like the preposition *for*.

At first blush, a plausible approach to this sentence would be to treat *for Jenny* as a constituent: a simple PP.

(96)   I intended [for Jenny] [to be present].

This would predict that it should be possible to cleft this PP, or to topicalize it:

(97)   It was for Jenny that I intended to be present.

(98)   For Jenny, I intended to be present.

Notice that these sentences are in fact well formed, but they do not have the meaning we would expect on the basis of our original sentence. In each of these cases Jenny is treated as a **benefactive** argument: someone for whose benefit either the act of intending took place (unlikely, but possible), or the act of being present took place. The most natural interpretation for the person who is present is the subject (*I*), rather than Jenny.

Now, while this is a possible interpretation for our original sentence, it is not the only one. The interpretation we are interested in here is one where Jenny is the person who is present, and what I have intended is that this situation should come about.

This means that our original sentence is actually structurally ambiguous. In one structure, *for Jenny* is a PP which is interpreted as holding a benefactive relation with the verb *intend*. In the other structure, *Jenny* is interpreted as being the subject of the clause.

Further evidence that the *for Jenny* string in (97) is part of the embedded clause, rather than a separate constituent of the matrix clause, can be found by looking at pseudoclefting:

(99)   What I arranged was for Jenny to be present.

(100)   *What I arranged for Jenny was to be present

The example in (100) is ungrammatical on the reading where the arrangement involved Jenny being present, rather than the speaker being present. There is again an alternative reading where (100) is grammatical, but this is irrelevant for our purposes (this is the reading where *Jenny* behaves as a benefactive argument of *arrange*).

We can see, then, that distributionally, *for* in non-finite clauses occurs immediately before the subject of the clause, and forms a constituent with CP. This is exactly parallel to *that* in finite clauses, so we have good reasons to classify *for* as a complementizer.

(101)

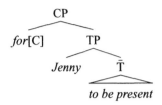

Interestingly, whenever the complementizer *for* appears in a non-finite clause, the clause must have an accusative subject, much like the obligatory ECM verbs we met in the last section. PRO is ruled out:

(102)   Jason intended for him to learn magic.

(103)   *Jason intended for he to learn magic

(104)   *Jason intended for PRO to learn magic

The same observation can be made for this non-finite C in subject clauses:

(105)   *For to do that would be a mistake

It appears that we need a way of letting C determine the case of the subject of the non-finite clause. This is straightforward enough, since we simply extend the mechanism of case checking that we have already developed. Our treatment of case allows a case-checking relation to be established between a higher functional head and the closest DP it c-commands. Assuming that the non-finite T that *for* selects has no case feature at all, then a case-checking relation can be established between *for* and the subject of the clause. To see this, look at the following schematic structure at a point in the derivation where *v* has been Merged:

(106)   *v*[acc] V DP[3, sing, fem, case]

The [acc] feature on *v* will value the [case] feature on the pronominal object:

(107)   *v*[acc] V DP[3, sing, fem, acc]

We then Merge the subject (also a pronominal), followed by T and the complementizer *for*:

(108)   [*CP* for[acc]... T... DP[3, sing, masc, case] *v*[acc] V DP[3, sing, fem, acc]]

Now, just in the same way as v valued the [case] feature of the object, *for* will value the [case] feature of the subject:

(109)   [$_{CP}$ for[~~acc~~]... T... DP[3, sing, masc, ~~acc~~] v[~~acc~~] V DP[3, sing, fem, ~~acc~~]]

This structure will eventually have the following spellout:

(110)   [$_{CP}$ for[~~acc~~]... T... DP[3, sing, masc, ~~acc~~] v[~~acc~~] V DP[3, sing, fem, ~~acc~~]]
　　　　　　for　　　to　him　　　　　　　　　　see　　　her

This means that we get a non-finite clause with two accusatives:

(111)   I arranged [for him to see her].

Notice, though, that the word order generated by the structure in (110) is not right. The non-finite T precedes rather than follows the accusative subject. However, this also follows from our treatment of the syntax of T and how it relates to the subject (see Chapter 6): we adopted the idea that case features on T were divorced from the EPP feature of T, and that it was the EPP feature that drove movement. If non-finite T differs from finite T just in having no case feature, then it is the EPP feature of T in (110) that causes *him* to raise to its specifier, before *for* is Merged deriving the correct order.

(112)   [$_{CP}$ for[~~acc~~] [DP[~~acc~~] T[~~uD*~~]... ⟨him⟩ v[~~acc~~] V DP[~~acc~~]]]
　　　　　　for　　him　　to　　⟨him⟩ see　　her

What this analysis does, then, is capitalize on the distinction we drew between the EPP feature of T and its case feature. Non-finite T lacks a case feature, so the case of the subject in a non-finite clause is determined by something else. However, the word order is still determined by the EPP property of T.

8.2.4 Null case and PRO

We can now return to the phenomenon of control clauses and provide an answer to the following question: what mechanism ensures that control clauses selected by verbs in the *try* class have a PRO in them? The intuition we will pursue here is that, just as case is the feature that regulates the appearance of an accusative DP in *for* clauses, it is case that regulates the appearance of PRO in control clauses.

We therefore extend our case features for English to include, as well as [nom], [acc], and [gen], a new feature. We will call this case feature [null], and its morphological effect is to ensure that the pronoun that it is on is unpronounced (just as the morphological effect of [nom] on [3, sing, masc] is to ensure it is pronounced *he*).

We now propose that a verb like *try* selects a CP headed by a complementizer with this [null] feature. This complementizer is itself not pronounced.

Our assumption leads to the following derivation for a control clause: First the little *v*P is constructed, with a pronoun in its specifier:

(113)   [*v*P pronoun *v*[~~acc~~] V *Object*[~~acc~~]]

Then non-finite T *to* is Merged. T has an EPP feature but no case feature. The EPP feature on T and the D feature of the pronoun in the specifier of little *v*P agree, and the latter raises to the specifier of TP:

(114)   pronoun T[~~uD*~~] ⟨*pronoun*⟩ *v*[~~acc~~] V *Object*[~~acc~~]

Null C is merged, bearing the case feature [null]. This values the case feature on the pronoun as [null]:

(115)   C[~~null~~] pronoun[~~null~~] T[~~uD*~~] ⟨*pronoun*⟩ *v*[~~acc~~] V *Object*[~~acc~~]

The selecting verb *try* is Merged, as is the remainder of the structure. Once this structure goes through the rules of spellout, the pronoun bearing [null] is spelled out as just a null element (or alternatively, it is not spelled out).

(116)   try [C[~~null~~] pronoun[~~null~~] T[~~uD*~~] ⟨*pronoun*⟩ *v*[~~acc~~] V *Object*[~~acc~~]]
        try   PRO   to   ⟨PRO⟩   see   him

Note that we have an EPP-driven movement of the pronominal feature bundle which is eventually spelled out as PRO.

This analysis immediately accounts for the impossibility of examples like the following:

(117)   *Medea tried her to leave

In order to ensure that no DP can occur as the subject of one of these structures, we simply state that the [null] feature is only a feature of pronouns. If we have a full DP Merged as the subject of the non-finite clause, then its case feature will not be checked by the null C:

(118)   *Medea tried 0[null] Jason[case] to leave

This system also captures the fact that non-finite clauses with *for* must have an overt accusative subject. If we Merge in a pronoun, whose case feature is valued by *for*, then it will have an overt spellout as an accusative pronoun. Examples like (119) simply can't be generated, because the case value of any pronominal subject would be [acc] and not [null]:

(119)   *I arranged for PRO to see her

We have now provided a partial answer to the question of the distribution of subjects of non-finite clauses. The answer rests on the idea that T in non-finite clauses actually does not check case. Rather, the case of the subject of an infinitival clause is checked by some other element. In both of the situations we have examined here, that element is the C which selects the non-finite T. The actual position of the subject is determined by the EPP feature on non-finite T, rather than the case feature, just as in our revised analysis of finite clauses.

8.2.5 Cross-clausal case checking and ECM

How do we deal with those cases where there is no overt complementizer but where the embedded subject may be only an overt NP?

(120)   We believed him to be the headmaster.

(121)   I assumed him to be innocent.

(122)   *We believed to be the headmaster

(123)   *I assumed to be innocent

An obvious approach would be to say that the embedding verb selects a complementizer in the same way that *try* does. However, this complementizer has accusative features rather than a [null] case feature:

(124)   believe, [V, *u*C[acc]]

This complementizer will be specified for an [acc] feature, leading to the obligatoriness of an overt embedded subject. The derivation for an ECM clause will then be exactly the same as for a clause headed by *for*, except that the complementizer will be null:

(125)   [CP for[acc] [DP[acc] T[*u*D]... *v*[acc] V   DP]]
              0   him   to   see her

This analysis makes these cases completely parallel to the *for* cases, except that the complementizer is null. Examples where we have a null PRO are ruled out becase the null complementizer selected by *believe* would value any pronominal as [acc], and not [null].

However, as our theory stands, we simply have no way of stating the lexical entry in (124). C-selectional features are simply uninterpretable categorial features with no further structure, just like all other syntactic features in a lexical entry. Syntactic features in a lexical entry may have the properties of strength and (un)interpretability, and they may have a value, but they do not, in our current theory, have any further structure. The proposed lexical entry in (124), however, assumes a complex feature bundle is being selected, contrary to our usual assumption.

We now have to decide if we should allow such complex feature bundles. From a theoretical perspective, it would seem that this would run counter to our drive for theoretical simplicity. It also turns out that there is an alternative analysis which does not require us to change our theory.

This alternative analysis is as follows: the case feature of the embedded subject is checked not by a null complementizer which transmits its feature to T, but rather by the usual case properties of the embedding verbal complex. Notice that ECM verbs may usually take a DP object:

(126)   Anson believed the report.

(127)   Ron expected the sack.

The approach we developed to the case properties of objects in general was that their accusative case was checked by an [acc] feature on little *v*:

(128)

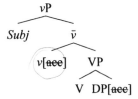

As an alternative to the idea that ECM verbs involve a null C, we could adopt the position that they instead select a non-finite TP. The subject of this TP enters into a case-checking relationship with the little *v* above *believe*, and checks [acc] in that way. This would give us a structure very similar to our normal structure for objects:

(129)

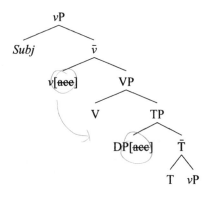

This analysis immediately explains why ECM verbs do not allow PRO:

(130)   *Anson believed PRO to be happy.

Since it is little v that values the case feature of the lower subject, that lower subject can never be PRO. This is because little v bears [acc] rather than [null].

A second argument for adopting the TP analysis for ECM constructions is that control clauses and *for*-clauses behave similarly with respect to pseudoclefting, and they both contrast with ECM clauses:

(131)   What Medea arranged was for her children to be poisoned.

(132)   What Medea attempted was to poison her children.

(133)   *What Medea believed was Jason to be a murderer

This set of data shows that control clauses pattern in the same way as *for* clauses with respect to pseudoclefting, but that it is impossible to pseudocleft an ECM clause. If ECM clauses and control clauses are just exactly the same (that is, they both consist of a null C which checks case on PRO or a DP), then they should pattern in the same way. However, if control clauses are CPs but ECM clauses are TPs, then we can explain the pattern we see by the assumption that it is impossible to pseudocleft a TP. This assumption is backed up by the following data:

(134)   What I said was [$_{CP}$ that we would go].

(135)   *What I said that was [$_{TP}$ we would go]

If we accept these arguments then we have the following distinctions:

(136)

1. Control clauses are headed by a null C which bears [null] case. The [null] feature on C values a [case] feature on a pronominal as [null], thus forcing those verbs which obligatorily select this null C to occur with PRO, rather than with an overt DP.

2. ECM clauses are just TPs, selected by higher verbs. The accusative feature of the higher little v checks an accusative feature on a subject in the ECM clause. PRO is ruled out because any pronoun in this position would have its case feature valued as [acc] rather than as [null].

3. *for* clauses occur with overt accusative subjects because the complementizer *for* is specified with [acc]. PRO is again ruled out because any pronoun in this position would have its case feature valued as [acc] rather than as [null].

This last point might be challenged by data from non-standard dialects of English. In certain dialects of English (those spoken in Belfast and Dundee among other places), we find examples like the following:

(137)   I went to the shop for to get bread.

(138)   They are going home for to see their parents.

However, the element *for* in these dialects seems to be not exactly the same as the complementizer *for* seen in standard English. Unlike the complementizer, the dialectal *for* may appear with verbs which do not usually accept the *for* complementizer. The following sentences are well formed in Belfast English (see the Further reading section at the end of the chapter for sources):

(139)   I tried for to get them.

Moreover, in ECM sentences, these dialects permit *for* but *after* the embedded subject:

(140)   I wanted Jimmy for to come with me.

It seems, then, that the syntactic position of this element is lower down in the clause structure than the position of the standard complementizer. We might analyse it as attached to T in some fashion, and as lacking the accusative case feature associated with the standard English complementizer *for*.

Before we leave this classification, we should note a weakness in our analysis: we need to be able to say that ECM verbs select either a finite CP, or a non-finite TP. As far as s-selection is concerned, this is unproblematic, since CPs and TPs are both propositions. But if we say that ECM verbs have a c-selectional C-feature then we need to ask why they can occur with a TP, and, vice versa, if they have a uT feature, why they can occur with a CP. For our purposes here, we will simply say that this is what is 'exceptional' about these verbs: that they allow either T or C as their c-selectional feature. This stipulation, however, is really just a 'placeholder' for a real analysis.

Note that the crucial theoretical ideas that we used in motivating our analysis of control clauses (and ECM clauses) came from θ-theory. In all of the examples we have been looking at, a θ-role is assigned to the subject of the embedded clause, and the whole embedded clause is assigned a θ-role by the higher predicate. The fact that control clauses are semantically dependent on their embedding clauses (inasmuch as PRO is controlled by a higher argument) arises through a separate semantic process from θ-role assignment. In the next section we turn to a new set of cases where the same θ-theoretic principles suggest a different analysis.

8.2.6 Raising

We now turn to a further type of non-finite clause. This type occurs with certain single-argument verbs, notably *seem* and *appear*, which allow non-finite as well as finite clausal arguments:

(141)   It seems that Agamemnon is a maniac.

(142)   It appears that Hephaestus owns a dragon.

(143)   Agamemnon seems to be a maniac.

(144)   Hephaestus appears to own a dragon.

Examples (141) and (142) have exactly the same thematic roles assigned as (143) and (144), respectively. In both cases the matrix verb is assigning a θ-role to a proposition. In (141) and (142) the proposition assigned the θ-role appears to be a clausal argument of the matrix verb, just as we have seen in all the cases above. In (143) and (144), however, there is no obvious constituent that receives this θ-role. Agamemnon isn't engaged in some act or state of 'seeming'. Rather, the sentence is just interpreted as meaning that the situation of Agamemnon being a maniac seems to be the case.

If we were to ignore this intuition, and to blindly follow the procedure we established above, we might posit a PRO in the subject positions of the non-finite clauses in (143) and (144). After all, they look rather similar on the surface to familiar examples like (145):

(145)   Agamemnon attempted to behave well.

However, this analysis is not motivated by our principles of θ-role assignment, since the argument in the specifier of each matrix clause (*Agamemnon* and *Hephaestus* in (143) and (144) respectively) would not receive a θ-role. This means that the following kinds of structure are ruled out:

(146)   *Agamemnon seems [PRO to be a maniac]

(147)   *Hephaestus appears [PRO to own a dragon]

In (146) and (147), PRO would check a null case feature in the embedded non-finite CP, and would receive the Agent θ-role of the embedded predicate. Since *seem* and *appear* are single-argument verbs, they have only one θ-role to assign, and they assign it to the non-finite clause. This means that *Hephaestus* and *Agamemnon* are not assigned θ-roles. Since these DPs cannot have an expletive interpretation, the structures are ill formed.

What then is the correct analysis of these structures? Clearly something must fill the specifier of the embedded finite T, and in order to capture the generalization that (141) means (143) and (142) means (144), that something must be dependent for its interpretation on the matrix subject. One way of dealing with this, which we have seen already at play elsewhere in the grammar, is to adopt the idea that the subjects in the matrix clauses have got there by movement, from underlying structures where they appear in their θ-positions.

Let's see how we can make this idea more explicit.

We start first from the lexical entry for the verb *seem* (we'll concentrate on this verb, but our remarks will apply equally to *appear*, and other verbs in this class, like *turn out* and *happen*). This verb may take a single finite CP. When it does so, we have the following schematic structure:

(148)   [it [seems [$_{CP}$ that Agamemnon left]]]

Agamemnon receives its θ-role from the verb *leave* (more precisely, by being in the specifier of the little v associated with *leave*). It has its [nom] case checked by the finite T of the embedded clause, and T triggers movement of *Agamemnon* into its specifier to check its EPP feature. The complementizer is then Merged in, followed by the verb *seem*. This verb does not have an Agent, or any other kind of subject θ-role to assign, so we Merge an unaccusative little v. Recall that this was the analysis we adopted for unaccusatives in Chapter 4:

(149)

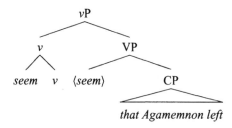

We then merge T[uD, nom], as usual.

There is nothing in the structure at this point with an unchecked [nom] feature. We could raise *Agamemnon* from the embedded clause to check the EPP feature of the matrix T, but we will leave this possibility aside for the moment. We will see in Chapter 10 that such movement is ruled out by independent principles:

(150)   *Agamemnon seemed that left

However, there is another possibility, which is to Merge an expletive element *it* into the specifier of *v*P, checking the [nom] feature on T with the case feature of this expletive, and raising the expletive to the specifier of TP to check the EPP feature of T and derive (149). Since expletives do not receive θ-roles, this is a legitimate operation, and results in the following sentence:

(151)   It seems that Agamemnon left.

This approach derives the simple finite complement structure for *seem*. However, we are also interested in deriving the case where *Agamemnon* is the subject of the matrix clause:

(152)   Agamemnon seems to have left.

We will analyse (152) by adopting the following assumption: verbs like *seem*, as well as being able to Merge with a CP, can also Merge with a TP. In a sense, then, these verbs are very much like ECM verbs in that they have the same exceptional property. Let's see, then, what happens if we choose a non-finite T in the embedded clause.

After we have built the *v*P, we have the following structure (I ignore the perfect auxiliary here for simplicity's sake):

(153)

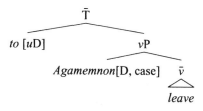

Although *to* can check its EPP feature by attracting *Agamemnon*, it cannot value *Agamemnon*'s case feature, since it lacks a case feature of its own.

However, given that we then Merge in *seem* and the higher finite T, it becomes possible to check the case feature of the matrix T with that of *Agamemnon*:

(154)

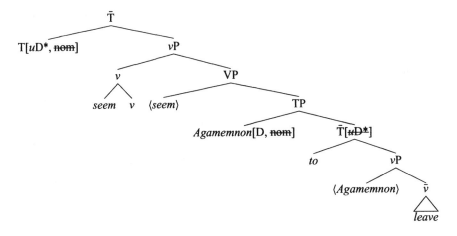

At this point in the derivation, it is also possible to move *Agamemnon* into the specifier of the higher T, since the D feature on *Agamemnon* is interpretable, and therefore has not been deleted when it was used to check the EPP feature of non-finite T. We therefore derive the following structure:

(155)

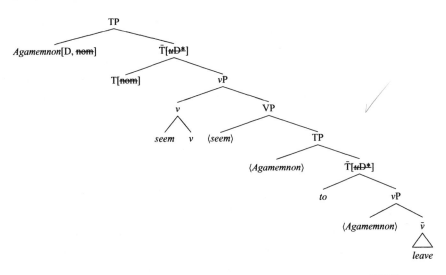

The classical name for this construction is **Subject-to-Subject Raising** (or often just **Raising**), for obvious reasons.

Notice that what we have here are two movements, both essentially of the same type (i.e. both driven by the EPP feature of T), both of the same syntactic element. First, the subject moves from the specifier of little *v* to the specifier of the embedded non-finite T, driven by the EPP feature of this T. Following this, the subject moves from this position to the specifier of the matrix T, again driven by the EPP property of T.

Interlude: Solving a technical problem

It is at this point, however, that our system of case checking faces the technical problem mentioned in Chapter 6, section 6.3.1. We have said that *seem* may select a TP, and we saw that we derived raising constructions rather neatly if that TP was non-finite. Unfortunately, if we choose a finite TP, rather than a non-finite one, then the derivation incorrectly converges, and we make the wrong prediction.

Recall that finite T bears a [nom] feature:

(156)

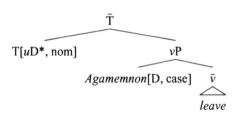

The [nom] feature on finite T can, under the system we have developed so far, Agree with the [case] feature on *Agamemnon* and *Agamemnon* will raise to the specifier of TP. Now, however, this TP can be selected by *seem*. When finite T Merges with the *v*P containing *seem*, its [nom] feature matches with that of *Agamemnon*. Remember that the non-abbreviated versions of these features are as follows:

(157) a. T bears [*u*case:nom].
       b. *Agamemnon* bears [~~*u*case~~:nom].

Although the case feature of *Agamemnon* has been checked, it still Agrees with the case feature of T. Agree requires only that the features match, and we developed an analysis of subject-verb agreement which allowed a higher feature to be checked and valued by a checked lower feature. However, this approach gets us into trouble here, since we should now just be able to check the case features by matching them, and then raise *Agamemnon* satisfying EPP of the higher clause and deriving (158), with *seem* having a finite TP complement:

(158)   *Agamemnon seems [$_{TP}$ ⟨Agamemnon⟩ has left]

There are a number of solutions to this problem. A standard approach in the literature is to say that there's something special about case features, such that, when a case feature has been checked and valued, it deletes immediately. This would mean that, in our derivation above, once *Agamemnon* has checked case with the lower finite T, its case feature disappears and is no longer available to check the case feature of the higher finite T. This will mean that the derivation will crash. This approach does, however, require us to say that case features and other feature have very different syntactic behaviour, which must be stipulated somewhere.

However, another solution is available to us here, which relies on the idea we have independently made use of: that finite T bears an uninterpretable [$u$clause-type:] feature, which receives its value from C. If *seem* selects a finite TP, then the [$u$clause-type:] feature of this T must be checked and valued. However, it can't be checked by its own C, since, by hypothesis there is no such C:

(159)   seem [$_{TP}$ ... T[$u$clause-type:] ...]

The only possibility is that it could be checked by a higher matching feature. There are two candidates for this: the higher T and the higher C. Let's see what happens when we continue the derivation:

(160)   T[$u$clause-type:] ... seem [$_{TP}$ ...T[$u$clause-type:] ...]

At this point, the two features match, but clause type is not a privative feature: it requires a value, and no value is forthcoming. No checking is possible yet. We then continue the derivation:

(161)   C[Decl] T[~~$u$clause-type~~:Decl] ... seem [$_{TP}$ ... T[$u$clause-type:] ...]

Now [Decl] on C has checked and valued [$u$clause-type] on the higher T. Notice by Locality of Feature Matching, it can't check the [$u$clause-type:] feature on the lower T. Also, the valued feature on the matrix T can't check the one on the lower T, since feature-checking operations always have to involve the root projection of the derivation. This latter constraint follows from the Extension Condition discussed in Chapter 4, and repeated here:

(162)   **The Extension Condition**

A syntactic derivation can only be continued by applying operations to the root projection of the tree.

This condition blocks the valued higher T in turn valuing the features of the lower T. This is because the higher T is not in the root projection at this point in the derivation. It then follows that the derivation is correctly predicted to crash.

It follows that the independently needed clause-type feature, which only appears on finite T, interacts with our approach to case features to block a derivation where a subject raises from a finite TP. In fact, this approach blocks a verb like *seem* (or an ECM verb like *believe*) from taking a finite TP complement. Clausal complements must be either CPs, or non-finite TPs.

Back to raising

Raising constructions can be strung together. We find examples like the following:

(163)   Hephaestus appears to have turned out to have left.

(164)   Jason happens to appear to seem to be sick.

In these examples, the intermediate non-finite TPs have EPP features but no specification for case, just as in the examples we have already seen. Schematically, we have the following structure:

(165)   Jason happens ⟨*Jason*⟩ to appear ⟨*Jason*⟩ to seem ⟨*Jason*⟩ to ⟨*Jason*⟩ be sick.

Notice that not all single-argument verbs which take finite clausal complements can behave like raising verbs. So alongside (166), we cannot have (167):

(166)   It stinks that Zeus is omnipotent.

(167)   *Zeus stinks to be omnipotent

The obvious way to deal with this is to assume that such verbs, in contrast to true raising verbs, cannot select a TP.

Before leaving raising verbs it is important to note one final structure in which they participate. As well as allowing *it* expletives when they take a finite clausal complement, raising verbs also allow a *there* expletive when they take a non-finite clausal complement:

(168)   There seemed to be three men in the garden.

(169)   There appears to be a problem with this solution.

The derivation of these sentences is fairly straightforward, although it raises an important point about the behaviour of Merge and Move. Take (168) as an example. We will assume that the verb *be* in these examples is a main verb, and takes a PP complement, and a DP subject. (This is a highly controversial assumption, but since we are not focusing on the behaviour of *be* here, it will serve us for now. Note that this is a slightly more complicated analysis than that assumed in Exercise 2 of Chapter 5.)

(170)   [[$_{DP}$ three men] [be [$_{PP}$ in the garden]]]

We then Merge an unaccusative little *v* which attracts *be*. Then we Merge in *to*:

(171)   to be [[$_{DP}$ three men] [[$_{PP}$ in the garden]]]

At this point, *to* has an EPP feature to be satisfied. We can satisfy this by merging in the expletive *there*. On the assumption that the *there* expletive is distinguished from the *it* expletive by the fact that it does not have a [case] feature, it can Merge directly with the projection of non-finite (caseless) T:

(172)   there to be [[$_{DP}$ three men] [[$_{PP}$ in the garden]]]

We then continue the derivation as above. We Merge in *seem* and its little *v* and finite T.

(173)   T seem there to be [[$_{DP}$ three men] [[$_{PP}$ in the garden]]]

The EPP feature of finite T attracts the expletive *there*, while its case feature values the case feature on *three men*. This derives the correct result:

(174)   There T seem ⟨*there*⟩ to be [[$_{DP[nom]}$ three men] [[$_{PP}$ in the garden]]]

Notice that the checking relation that holds between T and the embedded subject also allows us to capture the fact that the finite verb agrees with the embedded subject (that is, in this sentence we have *seem* rather than *seems*, the verb showing agreement with the plural *three men*). The agreement relation is just checking of ϕ-features between finite T and the embedded subject; the relation is structurally just the same as the case-checking relation.

Although this derivation gives us the right result, it raises a new problem. At the point in the derivation where we are satisfying the EPP feature of the lower (non-finite) T, why do we not raise the subject, giving (175)?

(175)   [$_{DP}$ three men] to be[*e* [[$_{PP}$ in the garden]]]

This is apparently a perfectly legitimate step; nothing we have said so far rules it out. Continuing this derivation gives us, then, the following result:

(176)   *There seem three men to be in the garden

Here we have Merged *there* with the matrix T, satisfying its EPP feature. The [nom] feature of matrix T checks the [nom] feature of the embedded subject *three men*. The EPP feature of the lower T has been satisfied by the raising of *three men*.

We need some way to rule out this derivation. One solution that has been suggested is that the operation Merge is preferred over the operation Move. If we can apply either, then we take the option of Merge.

How does this help us? At the crucial step of the derivation we have the choice of Merging an expletive, or of Moving the embedded subject. If Merge is preferred to Move, only the former is possible, and so the derivation which leads to the ungrammatical outcome in (176) does not occur.

This general economy condition (if there's a choice, take Merge in preference to Move) has a range of subtle effects throughout the grammar which we will not consider here. See the Further reading section.

8.2.7 Object control

Turning now to three-place predicates with clausal arguments, we find examples like the following:

(177)   Jason persuaded Medea to desert her family.

(178)   Agamemnon forced Zeus to leave the school.

Looking at the θ-structure of these examples, it is fairly clear that *persuade* and *force* take three rather than two arguments. This means that the structure of (177) must be (179) rather than (180):

(179)   Jason persuaded [Medea] [to desert her family].

(180)   Jason persuaded [Medea to desert her family].

In (179) *persuade* has the three arguments *Jason*, *Medea*, and *to desert her family*, while in (180) there are only two arguments, *Jason* and *Medea to desert her family*. The structure in (180) is just the same structure that we gave to ECM verbs.

As well as this intuitive idea about θ-role assignment, we can make fairly solid syntactic arguments which show that verbs like *persuade* have a different structure from ECM verbs. The first comes from the behaviour of expletives.

Recall that expletives do not receive a θ-role. This means that they are Merged in a non-θ position, and this Merge is triggered by an EPP feature. The EPP feature appears only on T in English, which means that expletives are restricted to the specifier of TP.

This appears to be the right result. We cannot Merge a *there* expletive as an object:

(181)   *I found there

(182)   *I destroyed there

These sentences are ungrammatical because they require an object. The expletive *there* cannot behave like an object. Contrast this with the following:

(183)   There seems to be a problem.

As we saw in the previous section, we can Merge an expletive in a subject position (or Move it to such a position).

With this in mind, consider now the following difference between ECM verbs and verbs in the *persuade* class:

(184)   I expected there to be a problem.

(185)   *I persuaded there to be a problem

(186)   I believed there to be three books on the subject.

(187)   *I ordered there to be three books on the subject

If the structures for ECM verbs and for *persuade*-class verbs were exactly the same, we would expect there to be no contrast, contrary to fact. However, if the postverbal DP in *persuade* constructions is an object, rather than an embedded subject, the contrasts we have just noticed are predicted by the restrictions on the distribution of expletives.

A second argument comes from the differential behaviour of these classes of verbs when the complement is passivized. If we take an ECM verb, like (188), and then we passivize its complement, giving (189), the resulting interpretation is roughly the same:

(188)   Jason expected the doctor to treat Medea.

(189)   Jason expected Medea to be treated by the doctor.

In both cases the sentences roughly paraphrase each other: Jason has an expectation, and that expectation is that the doctor will treat Medea. Contrast this to what happens with *persuade*-class verbs:

(190)   Jason persuaded the doctor to treat Medea.

(191)   Jason persuaded Medea to be treated by the doctor.

In this case the paraphrase relation breaks down spectacularly: in (190) the doctor is being persuaded, while in (191) it is Medea that is being persuaded. This difference is again explained if the postverbal DP in an ECM construction is a subject, whereas it is an object in *persuade* constructions. This structural difference means that in (191), *Medea* is not really a passivized subject, it is just a normal object. In (190), it is *the doctor* that is the object. Since the two sentences have a different object, we clearly do not expect them to be paraphrases of each other.

Contrast this with the ECM cases. On our assumption that the complement of *expect* is a full clause, passive takes place internal to this clause. This means that *expect* has the same complement in both cases, it's just that one of these is an active sentence, and the other is passive. Since actives and passives are rough paraphrases of each other, we predict the observed paraphrase relations.

These kinds of syntactic arguments back up the idea that the structure of *persuade*-class verbs is different from ECM verbs, and that the DP immediately after the verb is like a true object in the former case, while it is like a subject in the latter case. This pushes us into adopting the following ditransitive analysis for these verbs:

(192)   Jason persuaded [Medea] [to desert her family].

This analysis is further backed up for those verbs in this class that allow a finite CP to appear in place of the non-finite one we have been considering:

(193)   Jason persuaded [Medea] [that she should desert her family].

Given that these verbs are essentially ditransitive, we assume the following kind of structure:

(194)

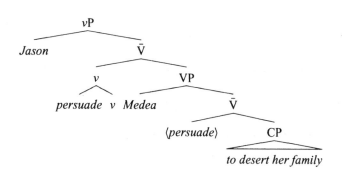

Here *v*P will be the complement of T, and Jason will raise to the specifier of TP to check EPP and case features.

The next question is what the analysis of the embedded CP is, and more particularly, what the status of the subject of this clause is. This question can be answered immediately by reference to the θ-criterion. We know that *desert* is a two-place predicate, so a θ-role has to be assigned to the subject of the embedded clause. The interpretation of this embedded subject is controlled by the matrix object (i.e. *Medea*), since it is Medea that is being interpreted as at least intending to desert her family. Since the DP *Medea* receives a θ-role from *persuade*, and since the θ-criterion prohibits a single DP from receiving more than one θ-role, it follows that *Medea* cannot have moved to its surface position from the embedded subject position. If it had, then it would be receiving θ-roles from the verb in the embedded clause as well as the verb in the matrix clause. It therefore follows that the subject of the embedded clause is PRO, rather than the trace left by raising:

(195)   Jason persuaded Medea [PRO to desert her family].

Given that we have a control clause here, we extend our earlier analysis of control clauses to this case:

(196)

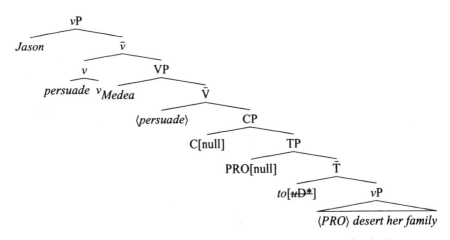

Since it is the object, rather than the subject, that controls the interpretation of PRO, verbs like *persuade* and *force* are said to be object control predicates.

8.2.8 Summary and further implications

This brings to a close our discussion of non-finite CP complementation. We have adopted the basic theoretical position that non-finite T is specified with an EPP feature but not with a case feature. The case of the subject of a non-finite clause is then determined by the complementizer that introduces that clause (a null C[null] or *for*[acc]) or by some element outside the clause (*v*[acc] for ECM clauses and T[nom] for raising clauses).

Notice that we have now developed the theoretical technology to answer the question that we were left with at the end of section 8.1.3. We had proposed that initial CPs were in the specifier of a C head, and that there was a null pronominal in the specifier of TP, as follows:

(197)   [That the world is round] *e* is obvious.

This leads to the question of why we can't simply have the following:

(198)   *e* is obvious.

The answer to this is now clear: the C head that selects for an initial CP bears a [null] case feature.

8.3 Adjunct clauses

We close this chapter with a brief look at adjunct clauses. We have already seen examples of PP and AP adjuncts, which serve to semantically modify an event or entity. We have assumed that, syntactically, these constituents are integrated into the tree via the operation Adjoin, rather than by Merge. Adjoin is not triggered by the need to check features, and it is therefore optional. CPs also may be adjuncts, which serve to semantically modify the proposition expressed by the main clause.

Adjunct CPs fall into two main classes: those that relate the propositions expressed by the two clauses in terms of time, and those that link the clauses via a relation of cause or reason.

Examples of the first class are:

(199)   Before the executioner arrived, Hephaestus had escaped.

(200)   When the executioner arrived, Hephaestus was asleep.

(201)   After the executioner left, Hephaestus wept.

The adjunct clauses here are the ones introduced by the temporal complement-izers *before*, *when*, and *after*. Note that they can be adjoined on either side of the main clause:

(202)   Hephaestus had escaped, before the executioner arrived.

(203)   Hephaestus was asleep, when the executioner arrived.

(204)   Hephaestus wept, after the executioner left.

Note too that they appear between embedding complementizers and the subject:

(205)   Medea thought that, after the executioner had left, Hephaestus would be relieved.

These properties suggest that temporal adjunct clauses adjoin to TP:

(206)

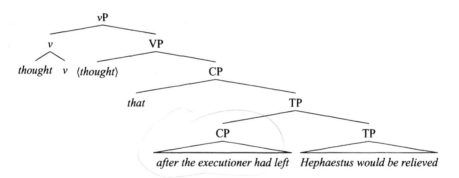

The internal structure of these clauses is fairly straightforward. They are headed by the temporal complementizer, which takes a TP complement:

(207)

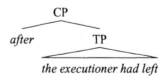

The syntax of cause/reason clausal adjuncts differs little from this. These adjuncts are exemplified by clauses headed by *because*, *since*, and *so that*:

(208)   Medea was happy, because she had got the highest marks.

(209)   Because she had got the highest marks, Medea was happy.

(210)   Jason became invisible, so that he could escape.

(211)   So that he could escape, Jason became invisible.

Once again, these adjuncts attach to TP, on either side. One problem we will not address here is the position of *so* in *so that*. The natural assumption is that it is adjoined to the complementizer *that*, but we will just assume that this apparently two-word phrase is a single syntactic formative.

8.4 Cross-linguistic implications

In this chapter, so far, we have focused on how the C-domain of the clause is implicated in constructing questions (via movement of T to C) and in embedded clause structure. In this section, we will look at a case where the C-domain of the clause is used in Declarative matrix constructions.

The core phenomenon we will focus on is known as **Verb-Second** (usually abreviated as **V2**), and is found in most of the Germanic languages. The phenomenon is known as V2, since the finite verb ends up in the second position in the clause, immediately after the first constituent. Here are some examples from German. I have italicized the first constituent, and put the finite verb in bold face:

(212)   *Ich* **las** schon   letztes Jahr diesen Roman
         I   read already last   year this   book
         "I read this book already last year."

(213)   *Diesen Roman* **las** ich schon   letztes Jahr
         this   book   read I   already last   year
         "I read this book already last year."

(214)   *Schon letztes Jahr* **las** ich diesen Roman
         already last   year read I   this   book
         "I read this book already last year."

As you can see, the basic (θ-related) meaning of the sentence remains the same; there is a difference in meaning between these clauses, but it is related to the way that the information is presented, rather than to differences in argument structure. Roughly, we can say that the first constituent in each of these cases counts as the **topic** of the clause.

More importantly, for our purposes here, we see that some constituent appears in the first position in the sentence, and the verb appears in the second position.

We can adopt the techniques we have already devised to provide a rather elegant analysis of this phenomenon: whereas in English we proposed that when the features of C valued the [uclause-type] feature on T, the Q value was strong but the Decl value was weak, we can say that in German, matrix C, when it values [uclause-type] on T, always provides a strong feature.

Schematically, we have the following, at the point in the derivation where we Merge in a declarative C. It values the [uclause-type] feature as strong Decl (we adopt the usual abbreviations here, so [~~Decl~~*] stands for [~~uclause-type~~:Decl*]:

(215)   C[Decl] Subj T[~~Decl~~*] Adv Obj

Because of this, T (and whatever is in T) raises to C in matrix declarative clauses:

(216)   T[~~Decl~~*]+C [Decl] Subj ⟨T⟩ Adv Obj

However, this is only half the story. We still need to ensure that a constituent appears in the first position. Since this constituent is a topic, we will propose that any constituent can bear a [top] feature, which is eventually interpreted as signalling that that constituent is to be interpreted as a topic. In order to ensure that the topic appears locally to C, we will assume that matrix C in German bears a strong topic feature which needs to be checked: [utop*]

If we take our schematic structure in (216), we have the following possibilities at least, depending on whether the subject, object, or adjunct is the topic:

(217)   Subj[top] T[~~Decl~~*] + C[Decl, ~~utop~~*] ⟨Subj⟩ ⟨T[Decl*]⟩ Adv Obj.

(218)   Obj[top] T[~~Decl~~*] + C[Decl, ~~utop~~*] Subj ⟨T[Decl*]⟩ Adv ⟨Obj⟩.

(219)   Adv[top] T[~~Decl~~*] + C[Decl, ~~utop~~*] Subj ⟨T[Decl*]⟩ ⟨Adv⟩ Obj.

Of course these are exactly the possibilities that we find in the German examples above.

This approach is backed up by what happens in subordinate clauses in German. These clauses are, for most verbs, headed by a normal embedding C, just like English *that*. This embedding C, unlike matrix C, does not trigger V2:

(220)   Er sagte dass ich schon   letztes Jahr diesen Roman **las**
         He said that I   already last   year this   book   read
         "He said that I read this book already last year."

What we see here is that the verb appears to the right of the object in the embedded clause, suggesting that German is really, at bottom, an OV language. In fact, if we put an auxiliary into this sentence, we can see that the VP occurs before T as well:

(221)   Er sagte dass ich schon   letztes Jahr [$_{vP}$ diesen Roman **gelesen**]
        He said that I   already last   year   this   book   read[PAST PARTICIPLE]
                                       habe
                                       have

        "He said that I have read this book already last year."

On the assumption that V raises to T in German, as in French, we can see that if T raises to C in a matrix clause, the finite verb will be in C. Since matrix C bears a [$u$top*] feature, this gives rise to V2.

   This approach makes exactly the right predictions if we look at a matrix clause with an auxiliary verb. Since the auxiliary verb will be in T, and the main verb will be lower in the structure, only the auxiliary should participate in the V2 phenomenon; the main verb should stay *in situ*, which predicts that it will be in its base position, to the right of the object. This is exactly the right prediction:

(222)   *Ich* **habe** schon   letztes Jahr diesen Roman gelesen
        I   have already last   year this   book   read[PAST PARTICIPLE]
        "I have read this book already last year."

Let's see how this will look as a full tree structure. German is an OV language, where objects usually precede verbs, and T precedes its complement. Only C takes a complement to its right:

(223)

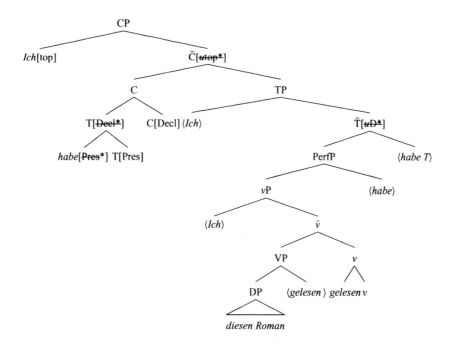

Here the VP, vP, and all the TP-related projections (in this case just PerfP and TP) are taken to be right-headed, with Perf raising to T, which then raises to the left-headed C. The subject *Ich* raises from the specifier of vP to the specifier of TP, to satisfy EPP, and then to the specifier of CP to satisfy the [*u*top*] feature on C.

We have now seen a further parametric pattern: whether the [*u*clause-type] feature on T is valued as strong or weak. If it is valued as strong, then T to C raising will take place, as in English SAI constructions or German V2. Otherwise, T remains *in situ*. We have also proposed that German triggers movement of topics to the specifier of CP. It is not clear whether English also has such an operation. Clearly topics are able to move to an initial position in English, but, unlike in German, it does not have to be the case that something in the sentence must be such a syntactic topic:

(224)   His analysis, I never liked.

(225)   I never liked his analysis.

Example (224) shows that topics in English may appear on the left periphery of the clause, and perhaps in the specifier of CP, but (225) shows that, unlike German, this is not obligatory.

We can capture all these differences as follows:

(226)

	Infl on Aux	Infl on v	EPP on T	Decl on T	[top] on C
English	strong	weak	strong	weak	optional
French	strong	strong	strong	weak	?
Swedish	weak	weak	strong	strong	strong
Scottish Gaelic	strong	strong	weak	weak	weak
German	strong	strong	strong	strong	strong

I have marked Swedish as having strong values for the Decl on T and the [top] on C parameters, since it has the V2 property, although there are many further intricacies here. Scottish Gaelic shows no evidence of T to C movement, and no evidence for syntactic topics in the specifier of CP. French does not have the V2 effect (except, as in English, for questions), and the status of obligatory topicalization, in spoken French at least, is unclear.

As usual, the more parametric options we introduce, the more urgent becomes the question of the status of the missing rows in the table: do these languages exist? If not, is this an accident, or is there a principled reason? Perhaps UG restricts not just principles of syntactic combination, and the architecture of the clause, but also relations between parametric values. These are empirical questions that still await an answer.

8.5 Summary

In this chapter we have examined a second major division of the clause. The first was between the structure of the projections associated with the VP and those associated with the TP. The new division we have introduced splits off the TP and the CP.

We proposed that all clauses contained Cs, which implies that the Hierarchy of Projections should be expanded as follows:

(227)   **Hierarchy of Projection**
        Clausal: C ⟩ T ⟩ (Neg) ⟩ (Perf) ⟩ (Prog) ⟩ (Pass) ⟩ v ⟩ V
        Nominal: D ⟩ (Poss) ⟩ n ⟩ N

We proposed that C is the place where the interpretable-clause-type feature is found. This feature determines whether a CP is interpreted as a question or as a declarative statement. This feature is also responsible for valuing an uninterpretable-clause-type feature on T: when this feature is strong, as in the case of Q in English, then T to C movement takes place, so that the auxiliary inverts over the subject. We abbreviated the clause-type system as follows:

(228)   a.   [clause-type:Q] (interpretable-clause-type feature with value Q) abbreviated as [Q].
        b.   [$u$clause-type:] (unchecked, unvalued uninterpretable-clause-type feature) abbreviated as [$u$clause-type].
        c.   [$u$clause-type:Q*] (checked, uninterpretable-clause-type feature valued as strong Q) abbreviated as [Q*].

We then looked at cases of apparent clausal subjects, and proposed that we should analyse these as involving a null pronominal element in true subject position. The apparent clausal subject is in the specifier of a special CP.

We argued that, just like T and D, C could also be a locus of case checking, and we introduced a new case feature [null] to account for the distribution of different kinds of subjects in embedded non-finite clauses. The net effect of our approach is that in non-finite clauses the subject receives its case from C or from some higher projection, while in finite clauses it has its case checked by finite T.

Finally, we turned to questions of parametric variation, and looked at the role of the C projection in explaining the V2 effect. We then incorporated the parameters responsible for this effect into our table of parametric options.

Once again, here are the most important phenomena we met, and the basics of their explanations:

Phenomenon	Explanation
Subject Auxiliary Inversion (SAI) in yes/no questions	T to C movement driven by uQ* as a value of [$u$clause-type] on T
Subject clauses	In the specifier of C[uC, null]
Control clauses	Headed by a null C[null]
ECM clauses	Selected by Vs that can take a TP, case on subject checked by v[acc]
Raising clauses	Selected by Vs that can take a TP, movement driven by EPP of higher T
V2 phenomena	Parametric variation in the strength properties of Decl value of [$u$clause-type] on T, and [top] on C

Exercises

Exercise 1 **Obligatory** *that*

Part A

Task 1 Classify the following words into two groups: those that introduce their clausal complement optionally with the complementizer *that*, and those that do so obligatorily. Make up an example for each which justifies your classification. Some of the words are ambiguous in their syntactic category, and I have indicated whether you should include both possibilities, or just the verbal case.

> belief; believe; sure; important; indicate; indication; signal (V and N); shout (V only); scribble down; claim (V and N); whisper (V and N); report (V and N); murmur (V and N); fax (V only); email (V only); certain; amazing; posit; exclaim; exclamation.

Part B

Task 2 What generalizations can you draw from your classification? Think about both syntactic and semantic possibilities.

Exercise 2 Negation in interrogatives

Assume the analysis of Subject Auxiliary Inversion given in the chapter. Explain what problems arise for this analysis given the well-formedness of examples like (1) and (2):

(1)   Hasn't the potion worked?

(2)   Didn't the magic work?

Hypothesize a way to get round this problem, and outline an analysis. Explain what you think the strengths and weaknesses of your analysis are. Hint: concentrate on the different behaviour of the two expressions of negation, *n't* and *not*. You might find the following data helpful:

(3)   Has the potion not worked?

(4)   *Has not the potion worked

Exercise 3 Embedded inversion

In some dialects of English, notably many of those spoken in Ireland, we find so-called **embedded inversion**. These are structures where SAI occurs in embedded clauses, selected by an interrogative predicate:

(1)   He asked did I live there.

(2)   I wondered had he left yet.

What do you think is going on here? Draw trees for these sentences under your hypothesis.

Exercise 4 Combining verbal classes

The following sentences involve at least two degrees of embedding. Discuss the derivation of each, saying how the mechanisms for control, ECM, and raising interact.

(1)   Medea tended to appear to be evil.

(2)   Jason persuaded Medea to try to run away.

(3)   Agamemnon expected Clytemnestra to seem to be happy.

(4)   Zeus wanted Hera to persuade Athena to leave.

(5)   For Zeus to appear to be happy would be impossible.

(6)   Hera tried to appear to be happy.

Exercise 5 Trees for prefer

Draw trees for the following three sentences, and then discuss what these structures imply for the lexical entry for *prefer*.

(1)   Jason would prefer for Medea to have cursed Agamemnon.

(2)   Jason would prefer Medea to have cursed Agamemnon.

(3)   Jason would prefer to have cursed Agamemnon.

Exercise 6 Other non-finite clausal complements

Consider the following sentences. Assume that T in each case contains the inflectional affix *-ing*. Try to motivate analyses which maximize the parallelism between these constructions and the non-finite constructions discussed in this chapter:

(1)   Jason refrained from casting the spell.

(2)   Agamemnon stopped Jason casting the spell.

(3)   Agamemnon stopped Jason from casting the spell.

(4)   Jason thought of defending the dragon.

(5)   Medea denied poisoning the phoenix.

Exercise 7 Classifying verbs

Use the tests discussed in the text (expletives, passivization, etc.) to determine whether the following verbs are raising, ECM, subject control, or object control. We are only interested in cases where the verb is followed by an infinitive headed by *to*:

nominate; allege; command; fail; guarantee; judge; happen; convince; choose; demonstrate; pick; remain; know.

Exercise 8 **V2 trees**

Task 1 Draw a tree for the following sentence of German, marking all movements, and indicating the relevant checking relationships (I have altered standard German punctuation conventions here in case this leads to confusion):

(1)   Er sagte daß er gestern   schon   angekommen ist.
      He said that he yesterday already arrived   is
      "He said that he had arrived already yesterday."

Task 2 Now look at the following example, where the complementizer *dass* is missing. This is a case of **embedded V2**. Provide an analysis for it and draw a tree structure embodying your analysis:

(2)   Er sagte gestern   ist er schon   angekommen.
      He said yesterday is he already arrived
      "He said that he had arrived already yesterday."

Exercise 9 **Trees once again!**

This exercise involves putting together everything you have learned in this chapter. Draw tree structures for the following sentences, and annotate each tree with a discussion of the motivation of any phonologically null categories (PRO, trace, null complementizers, etc.):

(1)   Because they hated him, the druids forced Jason to live in a cupboard.

(2)   The students decided that, after they had passed the test, they would take a trip on a magic carpet.

(3)   It appears that the magic potion has fallen into the wrong hands, since the mandrakes don't seem to be growing.

(4)   That Ariadne tended to collapse when she was kissing the minotaur didn't surprise Theseus, because she had always been prone to fits of fainting.

(5)   Athena decided to persuade Agamemnon to forgive Jason, since she was sure that he was not likely to be lenient to him.

(6)   When dining with evil crocodiles, it is advisable to wear armour.

Exercise 10   Locality in binding

Recall that we have developed three generalizations about the distribution of reflexives, pronouns, and R-expressions, which we abbreviated using the concept of Binding (see the Exercises in Chapter 4). Our latest versions of the Reflexive Generalization is repeated here:

(1)   **The Reflexive Generalization**

A reflexive must be bound.

    Recall that for A to bind B, A must c-command B and A, and B must be coreferential.

Part A

Task 1 It turns out that this generalization needs to be further restricted. The following set of data makes this point. For each example, explain how the generalization above is satisfied, and try to characterize the nature of the locality constraint:

(2)   *Anson thought that himself was happy

(3)   *Anson believed Jenny to have hurt himself

(4)   *Anson left before Jenny saw himself

Part B

Task 2 Some linguists have argued that the relation between the reflexive and its antecedent is similar to the feature-checking relation discussed in the text. Feature checking requires c-command, as does Reflexive Binding. Feature checking requires that the features on both elements involved in the operation are the same, and so does binding. Finally, feature checking is constrained so that it only looks at the closest element with matching features. Go through Part A once more, and see if you can use these properties of feature checking to explain the ungrammaticality of the examples, adopting the following working hypothesis:

(5)   **Reflexive Binding**

The ϕ-features of a reflexive must be checked by a higher antecedent.

Task 3 One of the sentences in Part A is problematic for this approach. Say which, and explain why.

Task 4 Explain how the following refinement predicts the correct result:

(6)   Reflexive Binding

The ϕ-features of a reflexive must be checked by a higher antecedent within the same CP.

Part C

Task 5 Go through the derivation for the following examples, and explain why they are ungrammatical, under this set of assumptions:

(7)   Anson believed himself to be handsome.

(8)   Anson tried to shave himself.

(9)   *Jonathan persuaded Kate to lick himself

Further reading

Section 8.1.1
The first exploration of the properties of complementizers is Bresnan (1970). The idea that sentences are projections of C stems from Chomsky (1986*a*), and has been adopted in almost all subsequent work within the general framework we are adopting in this book. See Roberts (1996), Haegeman and Guéron (1999), Ouhalla (1998).

Section 8.1.2
Grimshaw (1979) is a detailed exploration of the different syntactic and semantic selectional properties of various kinds of verbs. See Adger and Quer (2001) for a discussion of how the syntax and semantics of verbs which select [Q] CPs work, and Nakajima (1996) for further detail.

Section 8.1.3
The two analyses we compared in the text are updatings of Ross (1967) and Koster (1978).

Section 8.2
Initial work on the distribution (and interpretation) of PRO stems from Chomsky (1981). For the [null] case approach, see Chomsky and Lasnik (1993) (published also as chapter 1 of Chomsky (1995*b*)). See also Koster (1984), the papers in Lahiri, Larson, Iatridou, and Higginbotham (1992), and for more

recent approaches rejecting the θ-theoretic assumptions in the text, Hornstein (1999) and Manzini and Roussou (2000). The syntax of ECM constructions was extremely important in the development of Generative Grammar; see Postal (1974) for a book-length discussion of different non-finite complementation types. The current approach is a development of Chomsky (1981), which in turn develops ideas from Rouveret and Vergnaud (1980). More recently, various authors have argued that objects in English, just like subjects, raise to the specifier of a functional projection (see, especially, Johnson (1991)). For arguments based on ECM constructions see Lasnik and Saito (1991), and, more recently, Lasnik (2001). Raising constructions also received a great deal of attention in early Generative Grammar (again, see Postal (1974)). The interaction of raising with expletives is considered in detail in Chomsky (1995b), and Chomsky (2000).

Section 8.4

The V2 phenomenon is a traditional concern of descriptive Germanic grammarians. The approach outlined in the text stems from den Besten (1983), but see Travis (1984) and Zwart (1993) for an alternative. The examples in the text are adapted from Roberts (2001) who situates V2 in a general theory of head movement. Roberts and Roussou (2002) is a theoretical account which is close in spirit to what we discussed in the text, although they propose that the requirement that the specifier of CP be filled is due to an EPP feature on C, rather than a feature related to topichood. For the syntactic position of topics, an important reference is Rizzi (1997).

9

Wh-Movement

9.1 Introduction

In the previous chapter we saw that clauses were headed by a functional projection which we labelled C. We saw evidence for C in matrix questions, as well as in embedded clauses. This evidence came from the phenomenon of Subject Auxiliary Inversion (SAI), which we analysed as movement of C to T driven by an strong [Q*] feature which is the value given to an uninterpretable [uclause-type] feature on T. If T bears [Q*], then it moves into a local configuration with C:

(1)   Did Medea poison Jason?

(2)

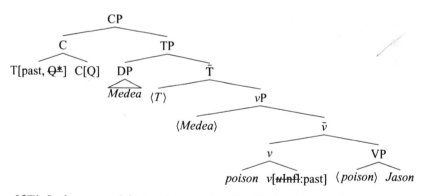

If T's [uclause-type] feature is valued as [Decl], then it is weak, and so T does not move to C. We then just get a simple declarative clause, with the following structure (I abbreviate [~~u~~Infl:past] as [~~past~~]):

(3)

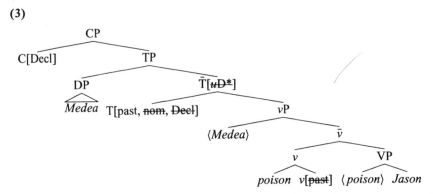

Recall that, by the PTR, *v* bearing checked tense features is not pronounced when the chain between T and *v* is broken, hence we have *poison* rather than *poisoned*.

This gives us evidence for C as a head position, but we might also like to see evidence that C has a specifier. We saw some evidence from the V2 phenomenon found in Germanic that C may project a specifier, but evidence is also closer at hand in English constructions like the following sentence:

(4)   Who did Medea poison?

This kind of sentence is known as a **wh-question**, and has some interesting properties which we will investigate in this chapter and the next.

On the assumption that the tree in (2) provides the right analysis for cases where the auxiliary precedes the subject, we then ask the question what the structural position of *who* in (4) is. On analogy with the structure of TP, *v*P, and DP, we hypothesize that *who* is in the specifier of CP.

(5)

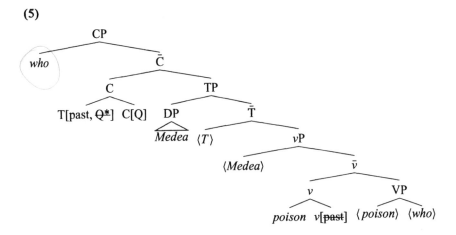

In this tree, we have moved *who* from the complement of V position to the specifier of TP. We will look at the way that this movement operation works in more detail in the remainder of this chapter. At a first approximation, we notice that *who* in (4) is assigned the Theme θ-role by *poison*; the question in (4) is a question about the person who is poisoned. Given the UTAH, this suggests that *who* is initially Merged with *poison* in the usual Theme θ-position and that it subsequently moves to its surface position, as diagrammed in (5).

This analysis predicts that if we take the tree in (5) and embed it under a verb which s-selects a question (giving an embedded question), then *who* will appear immediately between the selecting verb and the complementizer of the embedded clause. This prediction is almost correct, but not quite, as we can see from (6):

(6)   I asked who Medea poisoned.

The sentence in (6) has *no* embedded complementizer. Contrast this with (7):

(7)   I asked if Medea poisoned Jason.

It appears that the embedding complementizer which occurs with wh-movement in standard English is null, unlike the embedding complementizer that appears with simple embedded yes/no questions. That this is the right approach is backed up by dialects like those spoken in Northern Ireland, which allow embedded inversion for yes/no questions:

(8)   I asked did Medea poison Jason.

These dialects also have inversion in embedded wh-questions:

(9)   I asked who did Medea poison.

Since, by hypothesis, the auxiliary is in the C position, the word *who* is sandwiched between the selecting verb and the auxiliary, as expected.

Structurally, then, we assume that an embedded wh-question looks as follows:

(10)

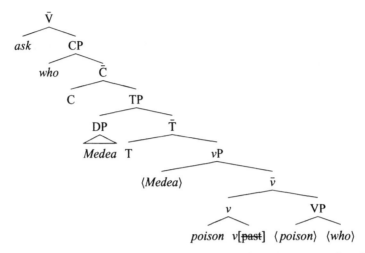

In the remainder of this chapter we will explore the wh-construction further, determining what the properties of the items that undergo this movement are, what motivates this approach, and how we capture the particularities of the construction in our system.

9.2 Elements that undergo wh-movement

In our example of a wh-question, we suggested that a movement operation applies to the word *who*, displacing it from its θ-position so that it ends up in the specifier of CP. This operation does not apply to just any word or phrase in English, but only to a specific subset of words and phrases. Compare, for example, (11) and (12):

(11)   Who did Medea poison?

(12)   *Someone did Medea poison

The expressions to which this movement process applies are called **wh-expressions**, because most of them, in English, begin with the letters *wh*.

(13)   What have you eaten?

(14)   When did you arrive?

(15)   Where are you living?

(16)   Which book are you reading?

(17)   Why are you leaving?

(18)   How are you feeling?

Only the word *how* does not begin with *wh*. Of course, wh-movement does not apply to just any word that begins with *wh*; this movement operation isn't triggered by phonological features, but, just like all of our other cases of Movement, it's triggered by morphosyntactic features:

(19)   *Whales have I seen

(20)   *Whisky do I drink

We therefore set up a morphosyntactic feature [wh] which picks out this class of elements. We will assume that [wh] is simply a privative (that is atomic) feature, which does not participate in feature valuing under Agree.

9.2.1 Wh-expressions

Most of our wh-expressions are simple words: *when, where, who, what,* and so on. These words are just like [wh] versions of the pro-forms: *then, there,* and the third-person pronouns. We treat them, then, as heads bearing the appropriate category feature together with [wh]:

(21)   where [wh, P, locational]

(22)   when [wh, P, temporal]

(23)   who [wh, D, human]

(24)   what [wh, D, non-human]

I have used various interpretable semantic features to distinguish these wh-forms yet further. Syntactically, *where* and *when* consist of the same features. Note that the first three of these expressions are pronominal in nature. They cannot combine with another syntactic object and project a larger wh-phrase:

(25)   *[where place] are you living

(26)   *[when time] will you be there

(27)   *[who guy] did you see

Under the theory we developed in Chapter 4, this means that they are both lexical items, and, simultaneously, phrasal items. They are initially Merged as arguments or adjuncts, and as such, they project no further. They are, at this point of the derivation, phrasal. They then undergo movement as phrases, and so target the specifier rather than the head of CP.

The wh-forms *what* and *which* do allow a complement though. Both can combine with nominal phrases to form a larger wh-DP:

(28)   [Which poem about Achilles] did Homer recite?

(29)   [What kind of actor] is he?

These words, then, seem to be the [wh] counterparts of determiners, or demonstratives:

(30)   Homer recited [the poem about Achilles].

(31)   He is [that kind of actor].

This idea is further backed up by the fact that, in English, these wh-elements are in complementary distribution with Ds:

(32)   *Which the poem did Homer recite

(33)   *What a kind of actor is he

We will therefore treat them as *wh-determiners* which combine with *n*P complements:

(34)

The wh-forms *how* and *why* don't have such clear non-wh pro-form counterparts (although the somewhat archaic *thus* provides a partial parallel), but syntactically they seem to behave in a similar way to *where* and *when*. *How* is also capable of combining with adjectives and adverbs to create larger structures:

(35)   [How fond of Clytemnestra] is Agamemnon?

(36)   [How quickly] did the Greeks take Troy?

We will treat these wh-words as being wh-versions of degree expressions like *very*, and for concreteness, we will assume that these expressions are of a category Deg(ree):

(37)

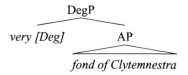

Deg is a functional head which appears above APs and AdvPs, in much the same way that D projects above *n*Ps and T above *v*Ps. This means that we need to state a new Hierarchy of Projections:

(38)   **Hierarchy of Projections**
       Clausal: C 〉 T 〉 (Neg) 〉 (Perf) 〉 (Prog) 〉 (Pass) 〉 *v* 〉 V.
       Nominal: D 〉 (Poss) 〉 *n* 〉 N.
       Adjectival (Deg) 〉 A.

We will not pursue the functional structure dominating adjectival elements any further here. See the Further reading section for references.

With this in place, we can now treat *how* as the wh-version of this Deg head:

(39)

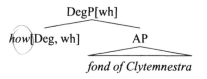

Other languages also display morphological regularities in their wh-words. I give below the wh-words of Zuni, a Native American language of New Mexico, of Kiowa, an unrelated Native American language spoken in Oklahoma, and Classical Hebrew, a Semitic language. None of these languages is related to the Indo-European group to which English belongs, but all display regularities in the construction of their wh-expressions.

(40)

English	who	what	where	when
Zuni	cop	kwap	hop	kyaayip
Kiowa	hà:tèl	hò:ndé	hà:yá	há:oy
Hebrew	mi	mah	'ayin	matay

As you can see, all of the Zuni wh-expressions end in -*p*; all of the Kiowa expressions begin with an *h*, and three of the four Hebrew expressions begin with an *m*. Of course, not all languages display morphological regularities in their wh-expressions (Turkish, for example, does not), however, enough unrelated languages do to suggest that the feature [wh] is morphologically motivated as one of the features that Universal Grammar (UG) makes universally available.

9.2.2 Interpretation of wh-questions

When we turn to the semantics of these expressions, we find that they have a fairly uniform interpretation. It is usually possible to paraphrase wh-questions as though they contain an **interrogative quantifier**. By interrogative quantifier, I mean that the question can usually be paraphrased as "For which x is it the case that...". Here are some examples:

(41)   **Who** ate the cake?

For which x, x a human, is it that case that x did that?

(42)   **When** did you eat the cake?

For which x, x a time, is it the case that you ate the cake at time x?

(43)   **Why** did you eat the cake?

For which x, x a reason, is it the case that you ate the cake for the reason x?

(44)   [**Which** girl] ate the cake?

For which x, x a girl, is it the case that x ate the cake?

(45)   **What** did she eat?

For which x, x a thing, is it the case that she ate x?

(46)   **Where** has he put the cake?

For which x, x a place, is it the case that he put the cake in place x?

(47)   **How** did you eat the cake?

For which x, x a manner of doing something, is it the case that you ate the cake in manner x?

(48)   [**How** quickly] did you eat the cake?

For which x, x a measure of quickness, is it the case that you ate the cake at that measure of quickness?

Recall that in our discussion of the motivations behind positing features we said that the strongest motivation for a feature was when there was some morphological and semantic expression of that feature. This is exactly the situation here: we have a limited class of words, most of which share a morphological peculiarity, and all of which share a semantic commonality. Moreover, this class of words displays the same syntactic behaviour. They all may move to the specifier of CP.

We are justified, then, in setting up the [wh] feature which picks out this class of elements.

9.3 Mechanics of wh-movement

We now turn to how wh-questions are derived syntactically. Under our approach to θ-role assignment, θ-roles are determined by the UTAH which essentially inspects the initial Merge of the DP argument with the verb (or other major category). Take our initial example again:

(49)   Who did Medea poison?

Since in a wh-question like (49), it is the wh-expression that is interpreted as bearing the Theme θ-role, we assume, as discussed above, that this expression was originally Merged with V, and is then displaced to its subject position. The question then arises of what motivates this movement, and why it only occurs with wh-expressions.

9.3.1 Checking wh-features

Recall that, in our analysis of Subject-Auxiliary Inversion, we proposed that the feature [Q] was involved. We argued that English had a complementizer marked with [Q] which caused the sentence to be interpreted as a question. We then proposed that a strong version of Q appeared as the value of a [$u$clause-type] feature on T. When C[Q] values [$u$clause-type] on T as [Q*], T must move into a local configuration with C[Q]. Since T is a head, rather than a phrase, it raises and head-adjoins to C. This gives us the following structure:

(50)

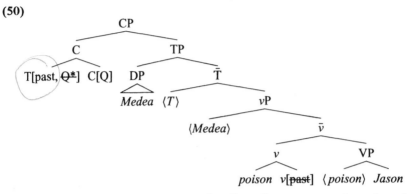

Looking at wh-questions, we see that T to C movement takes place here too, and that the wh-expression moves into the specifier of T. We can implement this by assuming that C[Q] can optionally bear a strong [$u$wh*] feature which checks with a wh-expression it c-commands. Since [$u$wh*] on C is strong, the wh-expression must move into a local configuration with C. Since the wh-expression is a phrase, it moves into the specifier of CP. Roughly, we have:

(51)   [XP[wh] C[Q, ~~$u$wh*~~] ... ⟨XP[wh]⟩

We treat this [$u$wh*] feature as being optional, since in a yes/no question, no wh-expression appears to the left of the inverted auxiliary:

(52)   Did Medea poison Jason?

The existence of these sentences suggests that [$u$wh*] on C[Q] is optional, since there is no wh-expression in this sentence. We will, however, return to whether this is the right analysis below.

To see this proposal in action, consider a stage in a derivation just like that for (52) above, except that the object is a wh-expression, and C bears [$u$wh*]:

(53)

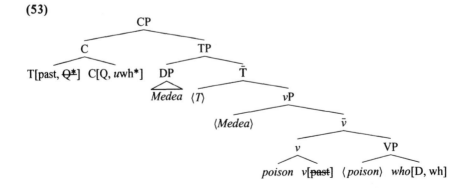

The complementizer C[Q, *u*wh*] checks its [wh] feature with *who*[wh] under c-command (Agree), the strength of this feature forcing surface locality to obtain between C and *who*. Since *who* is phrasal, it moves into the specifier of C:

(54)

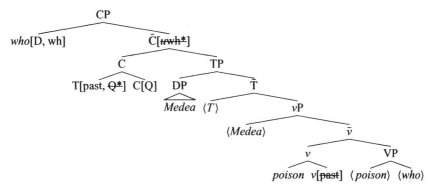

Technically, the locality enforced by the strength of [*u*wh*] is achieved by projecting this feature to the C̄ level, just as the EPP feature is projected to T̄, or the [gen*] feature to D̄. When the wh-expression Merges with C̄, it is in a sisterhood relation with the strong wh-feature.

However, the optionality of the wh-feature on C[Q] which we proposed to deal with the existence of simple yes/no questions actually leads to a serious problem. Let us assume that we decide to take the option not to specify C[Q] with [*u*wh*]. If we do this then, although we correctly predict that an auxiliary can move across a subject to C, we incorrectly predict that the following sentence should also be fine:

(55)   *Did Medea poison who?

This is because *who*, so far, has no special requirement placed on it. It bears an interpretable wh-feature, which does not need to be checked. T to C movement has taken place to satisfy the strength of the strong [Q*] on T. The derivation should converge quite happily.

We could solve this problem by proposing that wh-expressions themselves have a strong feature (perhaps a Q feature) which forces them to move to the specifier of CP. This would give us a structure like (56):

(56)

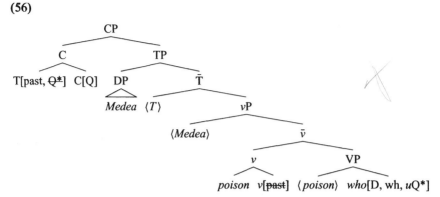

Since, under this particular hypothesis, the [*u*Q*] feature on *who* is strong, then this wh-expression will have to move to ensure that it is in a local configuration with its checker. This approach would allow us to rule out (55), since in that example, the wh-expression *who* stays in its base position.

However, this doesn't seem to be the right way to go. Wh-expressions are perfectly well formed in sentences like the following, where they are apparently in their base positon (such wh-expressions are commonly said to be *in situ*):

(57)   Medea saw who?

(58)   Jason gave the poisoned clothes to who?

These are called **echo-questions**, and they are well formed under a particular intonational contour, and under a particular interpretation where the paraphrase is not 'for which x ...' but rather 'repeat the word which *who* stands for in this sentence'. Echo-questions are usually used to express surprise or amazement, or to simply request that a Part of a sentence should be repeated for clarity. They are not questions in the usual sense of the word, and don't seem to involve the kind of semantics we have been attributing to the feature [Q] on C.

We conclude from this that if there is a C in an echo-question, it does not bear [Q]. If we go down the route of attributing a [*u*Q*] feature to a wh-expression to make it move, then we would have to face the question of why wh-expressions do not seem to need to check this feature in echo-questions.

In addition, English and many other languages allow **multiple wh-questions**, where there is more than one wh-expression in the clause:

(59)   Who poisoned who?

(60)   Who showed what to who?

These can have the typical wh-quantifier interpretation, with rough paraphrases as follows:

(61)   For which pair(s) x and y, did x poison y?

(62)   For which triple(s) x, y, and z, did x show y to z?

These multiple wh-questions clearly have at least one wh-expression *in situ*, so an approach which requires all wh-expressions to move to some position to check a strong feature is problematic.

This discussion leaves us with our initial problem: how do we rule out cases where we have an unmoved wh-expression but where T has moved to C?

(63)   *Did Medea poison who?

Let us summarize where we have got to.

- We have motivated the idea of a wh-feature on the basis of morphological and semantic evidence.

- We can implement wh-movement by assuming that C[Q] can optionally bear a strong [$u$wh*] feature. The presence of this feature means that a phrase bearing an interpretable [wh] will have to move to the specifier of CP.

However:

- We found that our system as it stands has no way of ruling out examples where we have T to C movement but no wh-movement. This is because we have treated the [$u$wh*] feature on C[Q] as optional.

9.3.2 Refining the system

In this section we will tackle the problem we outlined above. This problem clearly stems from the idea that the [$u$wh*] feature on C[Q] is optional. What happens, then, if we make it obligatory?

The obvious problem occurs with yes/no questions. These are questions, and so must have a C[Q], but there appears to be no wh-element, as we saw above:

(64)   Did Medea poison Jason?

If C[Q] always bears [$u$wh*], then how do we explain this?

We can solve this problem by assuming that the obligatory [$u$wh*] feature on C[Q] is satisfied in a yes/no question by a null expression bearing a wh-feature which is Merged directly in the specifier of CP. Following tradition, we will call this expression a **null operator** and notate it as *Op*:

(65)

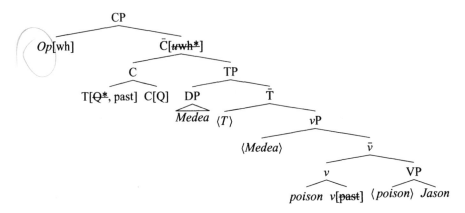

Once we have this idea in place, we can appeal to the preference for Merge over Move that we discussed in the last chapter to explain why (66) is ungrammatical:

(66)   *Did Medea poison who?

Consider again a point in the derivation where T has been raised to C[Q, *u*wh*]. We project the wh-feature to C̄:

(67)

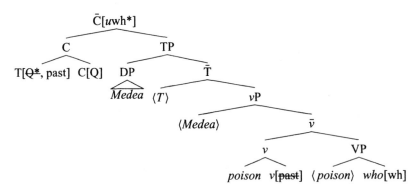

Now, assume that the numeration contains a null operator of the sort we just discussed (if it does not, then clearly the wh-expression *who* will have to raise to satisfy the strength of [*u*wh*]). We now have a choice of operations which will satisfy the strength of the uninterpretable [wh] feature on C: we can raise *who*

or we can Merge the null operator. The preference for Merge over Move forces us to Merge the null operator.

However, the null operator does not have the semantics of an interrogative quantifier. Rather, it simply asks whether the proposition expressed by the sentence is true (in which case the answer is yes) or false (no). We can represent this semantics roughly as follows:

(68)   Is it true or false that p?

Now, recall that for multiple wh-questions, we essentially constructed a complex interrogative quantifier, so that, for example, (69) has the reading in (70):

(69)   Who kissed who?

(70)   For which pair of entities x and y is it the case that x kissed y?

This semantics is triggered when there is more than one wh-expression in the sentence. Now, in the structure we have built up so far for our problematic example, we have two wh-expressions. One is the null operator, and the other is the expression *who*. Schematically, this looks as follows:

(71)   *Op*[wh] . . . *who*[wh]

If we try to apply the same semantic procedure, we find that we can't. Our procedure constructs a complex interrogative quantifier out of two simple ones. But in the case at hand, we don't even have two simple interrogative quantifiers: we have one (*who*) and an operator which gives rise to a yes/no question. Our semantic rule simply can't apply to the structure we have generated, and it is ruled out as perfectly well-formed syntax, but semantic gibberish. The final result is something which the semantic component just can't make any sense of.

The position we have taken, then, crucially appeals to the way that the semantic contribution of the syntactic structures is built up. A wh-expression may check the [*u*wh*] feature in C syntactically. When the semantics comes to interpret the syntactic structure, it treats wh-expressions as wh-quantifiers. However, the null operator in yes/no questions requires a completely different kind of answer to other wh-quantifiers, which will lead to semantic incoherence if they are combined.

This is the position we will take: the [*u*wh*] feature appears obligatorily on C[Q]. This feature is satisfied by movement of a wh-expression into the specifier of CP. In the absence of such a wh-expression, the derivation will have to contain a wh-operator which will give rise to a yes/no question semantics.

9.3.3 Other wh-movements

Before moving on to look at embedded questions and subject questions, we should note that wh-questions can also be formed from objects of prepositions and adjuncts:

(72)   Who did you introduce Athena to?

(73)   Why did you kill Pegasus?

(74)   Where did Perseus see the Gorgon?

Analogously to our discusion of wh-objects, each of these wh-expressions is Merged in its base position and then moved. The object of the preposition is straightforward: it is initially Merged with the preposition, which is itself Merged with a projection of the verb. Later on in the derivation, the wh-expression is moved to the specifier of CP.

(75)

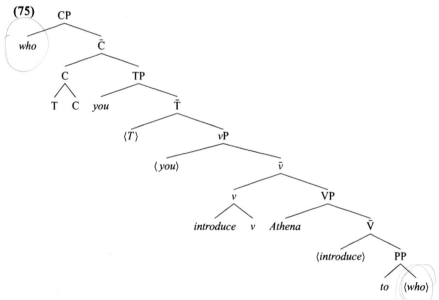

The adjunct cases work in just the same way. We have treated temporal, manner, and causal adjuncts as adjoining to vP:

(76)   Perseus saw the Gorgon in his shield.

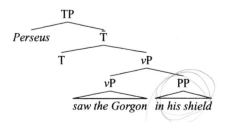

In this case, the PP may be a wh-expression *where* which moves to the specifier of CP:

(77)

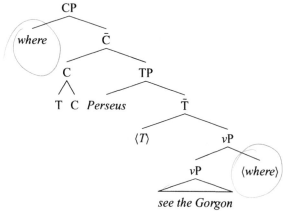

(78)   Where did Perseus see the Gorgon?

9.3.4 Embedded wh-questions

We now turn to wh-questions in embedded contexts. Recall that we saw yes/no questions could be embedded under certain predicates:

(79)   I wondered whether Medea had fled.

(80)   I enquired if we could leave early.

These same predicates allow wh-questions to be embedded under them as well:

(81)   I wondered who Medea had poisoned.

(82)   I enquired when we could leave.

As discussed in section 9.1, these wh-questions involve movement of the wh-expression to the specifier of the embedded CP. This means that the embedded C must be [Q, *u*wh*], given our discussion in the last section.

Notice, however, that in Standard English (and many dialects), no T to C movement takes place in embedded questions:

(83)   *I enquired could we leave early

We can straightforwardly analyse this as arising from the lexical specification of the embedded C, which would have the property that it values the [*u*clause-type] feature of T as just weak [Q] rather than strong Q. Since our analysis of embedded questions and our analysis of wh-questions is syntactically parallel, we correctly predict that we do not find inversion in embedded wh-questions.

(84)   *I wondered who had Medea poisoned

(85)   *I enquired when could we leave

We will return to the possibility of having embedded inversion in the exercise section, when we look at some dialectal variation in embedded wh-question formation.

9.4 Subject wh-questions

We now turn to subject wh-questions, which, in English, raise special problems. Take examples like the following:

(86)   Who has drunk the poison?

(87)   Which goddess might help us?

(88)   Who is sailing to Ithaca?

At first glance, it appears that we can treat these in a parallel fashion to the way that we dealt with object wh-questions. We derive a TP, as usual, with the wh-subject raising from the specifier of vP (or from lower down in the case of unaccusatives) to the specifier of TP. We then Merge in C[Q, $u$wh*], which values [$u$clause-type] on T as strong [Q*] causing T to raise to C, and then *who* to raise to the specifier of CP to check [$u$wh*], giving the following rough structure (I have suppressed irrelevant details in this case):

(89)

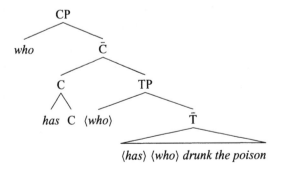

However, it turns out that this approach fails: we run into a problem with examples where there is no auxiliary:

(90)   Who drank the poison?

(91)   Which goddess helped us?

If the derivation we just went through is correct, then these sentences too should involve T to C movement. However, T to C movement where T contains just the T head, with no attached auxiliary, usually triggers *do* support:

(92)   Did you drink the poison?

(93)   Did Athena help us?

This is because movement of T to C breaks the chain between T and *v*. Once the chain is broken, the tense features on T cannot be pronounced on *v*, and therefore *do*-support applies (see Chapter 5, section 5.5).

Since the analysis we have built up in this chapter requires T to C movement in matrix wh-questions, we would predict that *do*-support should apply here too, giving the following examples:

(94)   Who did drink the poison?

(95)   Which goddess did help us?

These sentences are grammatical, but only on a special emphatic interpretation. What is worrying is that there appears to be no way to predict the grammaticality of the examples without *do*-support (examples (90) and (91)), or the ungrammaticality of (94) and (95) without a special interpretation.

The problem that we are faced with here arises because the complementizer which forces wh-movement in matrix clauses also forces T to C movement. The latter movement is forced because C[Q] values the [*u*clause-type] feature on T as strong Q, thereby triggering movement. The solution has to be something to do with the syntactic properties of wh-subjects in particular, since it is only here that the problem arises.

One crucial syntactic property of structural subjects which is not shared by objects and adjuncts is that the subject c-commands T. This opens up for us the possibility that it is actually the subject that checks the [*u*clause-type] feature on T, rather than C. Let us make this move, and see how successful it is:

(96)   [*u*clause-type] on T may have [wh] as a value.

With this hypothesis in mind, now consider a point in a derivation where a wh-subject is still *in situ* but T has been Merged:

(97)

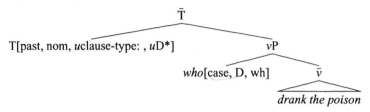

I have explicitly marked that [*u*clause-type] requires a value by placing a colon after it, rather than adopting our usual abbreviation. This is to make the details of the derivation as clear as possible.

We now apply Agree between [past] on T and *u*Infl on *v*, valuing the latter so that the appropriate past tense form of *drink* eventually results. We also apply Agree between [nom] on T and [case] on *who*, valuing the latter, and checking both case features. We also apply Agree between EPP in T and the closest DP (which is *who*). To satisfy the strength property of EPP, we raise *who* to the specifier of TP:

(98)

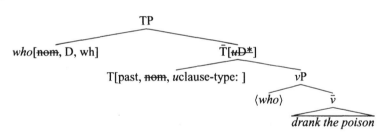

Now the subject DP c-commands T, and this DP bears an interpretable [wh] feature. Given our hypothesis about checking of [*u*clause-type], we then apply Agree between *who* and [*u*clause-type] on T, valuing and checking this feature:

(99)

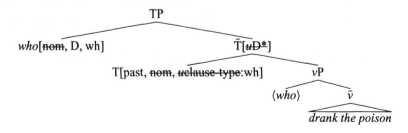

Finally, we Merge in C[Q, *u*wh*], in order to derive the fact that this is a question. The [*u*clause-type] feature on T has been checked and valued, so Agree does not apply between C and T, and no movement of T to C takes place. The wh-subject, however, does raise to the specifier of CP, since Agree applies between it and [*u*wh*] on C:

(100)

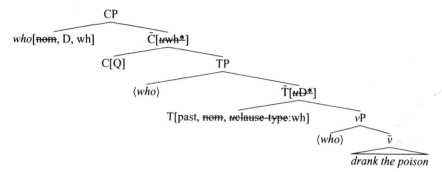

If we look at this final tree, we see that all the relevant features have been checked, and that T has not raised to C as required.

9.5 Long-distance wh-movement

Wh-questions have the interesting property that the wh-movement operation may apply across a clausal boundary:

(101)   Who did Jason think (that) Medea had poisoned?

(102)   What did you say (that) the poet had written?

In each of these examples, the wh-element is assigned its θ-role by the verb in the embedded clause, but its surface position is the matrix specifier of CP.

There are two plausible hypotheses about how these examples are derived. The first idea is that the movement takes place in one step, so that the specifier of the embedded CP is never filled during the derivation. The other alternative is that movement is more local, and that it takes place in two steps: first the wh-expression moves into the specifier of the embedded CP, and then it moves from this position to the specifier of the matrix CP. Schematically we have the two following derivations:

(103)   XP[wh] ... think [$_{CP}$ that ... ⟨XP[wh]⟩].

(104)   XP[wh] ... think [$_{CP}$ ⟨XP[wh]⟩ that ... ⟨XP[wh]⟩].

Simplicity might seem to favour the first derivation, in a number of ways. First, it involves fewer operations, so it is more economical. Secondly, we know that verbs like *think* cannot take wh-question complements, and so it would seem sensible that they should never have such a complement during the course of a derivation. In other words, the existence of (105) would suggest that a configuration like (106) is illicit. Yet (106) is exactly the configuration which appears in a derivation like that sketched in (104):

(105)   *Jason thinks who Medea had poisoned

(106)   ... think [[Wh-XP] ...]

However, there is empirical evidence from various languages which suggests that the derivation involving movement to the intermediate specifier is the correct one. These are languages where these long-distance questions involve a special intermediate complementizer.

One good example of such a language is Scottish Gaelic. In this language the normal embedding complementizer is *gu(n)* (the appearance of the final *n* here is a purely morphophonological fact, and irrelevant to the syntax):

(107)   Bha mi ag ràdh **gun** do bhuail i   e
        Was I asp saying that prt struck she him
        "I was saying that she hit him."

(108)   Tha mi a' smaoineachadh **gu** bheil Iain air a   mhisg
        Am I asp thinking   that is Iain on his drink
        "I think that Iain is drunk."

When we form a wh-question on one of the arguments of the lower clause, we see that the intermediate complementizer changes its form from *gu* to *a* (with a concomittant change in the following verb form):

(109)   Cò bha thu ag ràdh **a** bhuail i
        Who were you asp saying that struck she
        "Who were you saying that she hit?"

(110)   Cò tha thu a' smaoineachadh **a**   tha air a   mhisg
        Who are you asp thinking   that is on his drink
        "Who do you think is drunk?"

On the hypothesis that movement takes place in one single swoop, from the θ-position to the matrix specifier of CP, there seems to be no reason for the change in complementizer. However, if the wh-expression moves into the specifier of the intermediate complementizer, then this gives us a plausible reason for the change. We can say that the intermediate complementizer bears a strong [uwh*] feature, which is checked off by moving the wh-expression into its specifier. The complementizer *gu(n)* does not bear this feature.

Note that this is motivation for the idea that wh-movement, after its initial launch from its Merged position, proceeds from specifier of CP to specifier of CP, and that it cannot skip a specifier of CP. It does not, on its own, derive this restriction. For the moment we will just accept this as a stipulation, to which we will return in the next chapter:

(111) A wh-expression cannot skip a specifier of CP when it moves.

This idea forces us to adopt derivations like the following for long-distance wh-questions:

(112)

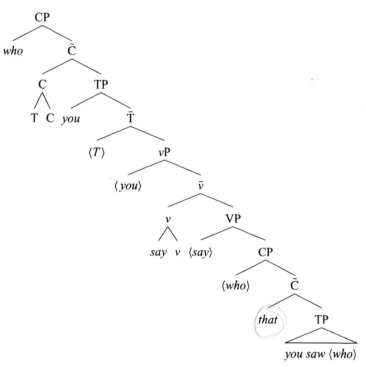

We will return in the next chapter to many more cases which argue for this kind of derivation.

9.6 Wh-*in situ*

We discussed cases of wh-*in situ* earlier on in this chapter. We saw two such cases: echo-questions and multiple wh-questions:

(113)   Medea poisoned who?

(114)   Who poisoned who?

Whereas (113) does not have the semantics of a true question, (114) clearly does. Let us see how it is derived.

Recall that wh-features on a wh-expression are interpretable. It is the strength of the uninterpretable wh-feature on C which causes wh-movement to take place. In an example like (114), we first Merge *who*[acc] with the verb, then having built up the *v*P, we have (115):

(115)

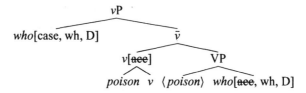

We then Merge T, checking case and attracting the subject which checks the EPP feature. Once the subject has raised, it Agrees with the [*u*clause-type] feature on T, valuing it:

(116)

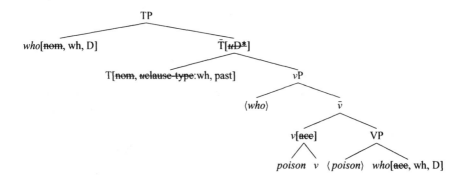

Finally, we Merge in C[Q, *u*wh*], which triggers movement of the wh-phrase in subject position to the specifier of CP, checking off the uninterpretable features on C:

(117)

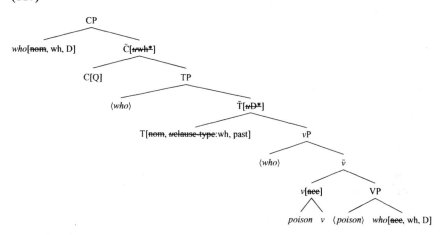

Notice that all the uninterpretable features have been checked in this final syntactic structure to which the semantic rules can then apply. We therefore derive (118), with the rough interpretation in (119):

(118)   Who poisoned who?

(119)   For which pair x and y is it the case that x poisoned y?

9.7 Superiority

Let us now turn to the question of how we rule out a derivation where the wh-object Moves across the subject, deriving (120):

(120)   *[_{CP} Who [_{TP} who poisoned]]

In the derivation for this sentence, we have raised the wh-subject to the specifier of TP, valuing [*u*clause-type] on T, so no T to C movement takes place. We have then raised the object across the subject and Merged it in the specifier of CP, thereby checking the strong [*u*wh*] feature of C[Q].

In fact, our general approach to feature checking already rules (120) out. Remember that a head checks the closest matching feature that it c-commands. In the present case, when C is Merged with the TP, the closest wh-phrase is the one in subject position (this intervenes between C and the wh-object), so it is this one that raises into the specifier of CP. This effect is traditionally known as a superiority effect, since it is the superior (or highest) wh-phrase that moves.

Superiority also surfaces with three-argument verbs. In an example like (121), the Theme c-commands the Goal, according to our analysis from Chapter 4:

(121)   Athena introduced [Medea [to Jason]].

If we replace both the Theme and the Goal by wh-phrases, then we predict that it is the Theme, rather than the Goal, that undergoes wh-movement, since it is closest to the complementizer. This is the correct prediction:

(122)   Who did Athena introduce to whom?

(123)   *Who did Athena introduce who to?

We should note at this point, though, that superiority appears to be a weak phenomenon. If we replace simple wh-words with a more complex expression containing *which*, then both orders of wh-expression are well formed:

(124)   Which poet wrote which ode?

(125)   Which ode did which poet write?

This effect is known as the **D(iscourse)-linking effect**, since it occurs when the wh-determiner ranges over elements which are already established in the discourse. Notice that it is infelicitous to use a wh-phrase headed by *which* unless the discourse has already established the existence of the things that *which* is asking a question about:

(126)   Look at all these books. Which book would you like?

Non-D-linked wh-words, like *who*, are less fussy about what has been mentioned in the previous discourse. It's perfectly fine to open a discourse with a wh-question containing one of these words. Imagine, for example, a context where you have entered a dark room and you hear a noise, it's fine to say (127), and distinctly odd to say (128). (I have used # here to mark that the sentence is pragmatically odd, rather than ungrammatical.)

(127)   Who's there?

(128)   #Which person is there?

We shall not attempt to provide an explanation for the D-linking effect or for the anomalous appearance of SAI in examples like (125) in this book. See the Further reading section for references.

9.8 Cross-linguistic variation in wh-constructions

Our approach to wh-movement relies on the idea that it is motivated by a strong [$u$wh*] feature on C. Given our previous approach to cross-linguistic variation, which ties most variability down to the strength properties of features of functional heads, we predict that there should be languages which have a weak [$u$wh] feature on C[Q]. It would follow that these languages should have wh-*in situ* generally, even in simple wh-questions. There are, in fact, many languages with this property, among them Chinese and Japanese.

Compare the example below from English with its Japanese counterpart:

(129)   What did John buy?

(130)   John-wa   nani-o   kaimasita ka?
        John-TOP what-ACC bought   Q
        "What did John buy?"

Japanese is a head-final language, so the verb occurs to the right of its complement, and the complementizer (*ka*) appears to the right of the inflected verb. The wh-element is accusative, and appears in just the normal position for an accusative object. In other words, it does not undergo wh-movement.

Roughly, we have the following structure:

(131)

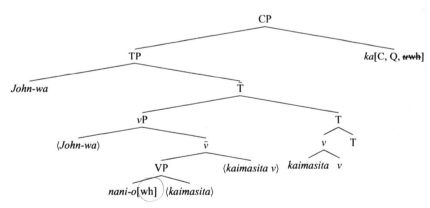

Here the [$u$wh] feature on C[Q] is weak, and so it is checked by being in an Agree relationship with the wh-object, but no movement takes place. Chinese works in the same way.

There are also languages which move all their wh-phrases to some position which is peripheral in the clause. Here is an example from Bulgarian:

(132)   Kogo kakvo e   pital Ivan
         Whom what Aux asked Ivan
         "Who did Ivan ask what?"

This is actually somewhat unexpected under our current assumptions, since once one wh-expression has moved to the specifier of CP, it should check a strong wh-feature there, and the derivation should converge, with all other wh-phrases *in situ*. Clearly something extra is needed to capture such languages. We will not delve into this problem here, but see the Further reading section for references.

We can now enter this parameter into our table, and we find the following set of properties:

(133)

	Tense on Aux	Tense on *v*	EPP on T	Decl on T	[top] on C	wh on C
English	strong	weak	strong	weak	optional	strong
French	strong	strong	strong	weak	?	optional
Swedish	weak	weak	strong	strong	strong	strong
Scottish Gaelic	strong	strong	weak	weak	weak	strong
German	strong	strong	strong	strong	strong	strong
Japanese	strong	strong	strong	weak	weak	weak

Japanese seems to have V to T movement, hence the [strong] specification for the Infl properties of Aux and *v*, although, as with many head-final languages, the jury is somewhat out on this. There is also some evidence that there is a *v*P-external designated subject position in Japanese, hence the [strong] EPP feature. There is no evidence for V2, and so Japanese contrasts with German in specifications for Decl and [top], and since it is wh-*in situ*, it has a weak value for [wh] on C. All of the other languages require the specifier of C in a wh-question to be filled by a wh-phrase, hence their strong features for this parameter, except French, which appears to allow both possibilities.

Of course, as we expand the table in (133), the particular specifications of parameters become more and more controversial, and few of these parameters have been settled decisively. However, the growing typology should give you an idea of how cross-linguistic effects can be dealt with in the Principles and Parameters model we are developing here.

9.9 Summary

In this chapter we have looked at wh-movement, and argued that it was driven by strong wh-features which appear on C. We have argued that simple yes/no questions also involve a wh-expression which is Merged directly in the specifier of CP.

We have not introduced many new aspects of the theoretical system in this chapter, rather we have explored how the system which we set up to deal with the syntax of DP-movement can be extended to wh-movement. By and large, this extension has been successful, with only a single stipulation needed to deal with the lack of T to C movement in subject wh-questions.

Not only do the mechanics of the system work for simple wh-questions, they extend naturally to wh-*in situ* phenomena, both in English and in other languages. One interesting prediction which is at least partially correct is the way that wh-movement works when there is more than one wh-expression in the sentence. We saw that (putting the D-linking phenomenon aside) the system we adopted for feature matching, which was independently motivated for dealing with DP-movement, also captured the superiority effect both in subject-object multiple wh-questions, and in Theme-Goal ones.

We have also introduced the idea that wh-movement, when it is cross clausal, always stops off in the intermediate specifier of CP, if there is one. We will explore the ramifications of this idea, and the motivations behind it, in much more detail in the next chapter.

Finally, we looked very briefly at how wh-constructions vary cross linguistically, as usual concentrating on what predictions varying the strength of features makes. We saw that our system correctly predicted that some languages should have generalized wh-*in situ*. Here are the most important phenomena we met, and the basics of their explanations:

Phenomenon	Explanation
Wh-questions with one wh-word	Movement of wh-phrase to the specifier of CP triggered by [$u$wh*]
Yes/no questions	Null *Op*[wh] Merged in specifier of CP
Subject wh-questions	[$u$clause-type] feature on T can have [wh] as a value, so no T to C movement takes place

Phenomenon	Explanation
Complementizer alternations in Gaelic	Movement takes place from specifier to specifier
Multiple wh-questions	Only one wh-phrase needs to move to specifier of CP
Superiority	Locality condition on Agree applies to wh-feature matching
Wh-*in situ* languages	Weak [*u*wh] feature in C

Exercises

Exercise 1 Wh and binding

Since reflexives can appear in DPs, and be bound, and since DPs can happily wh-move, we expect to find reflexives in moved wh-phrases. This is exactly what we do find:

(1)   Which book about himself did Anson write?

Part A

Task 1 Explain why (1) above is problematic for the rule of reflexive binding developed in the previous chapter, on the assumption that this rule applies to the final syntactic representation.

Task 2 Now assume that the rule applies instead during the derivation, just as Agree usually does. Go through a derivation for (1), and explain what the result of this change is.

Part B

Task 3 Interestingly, binding can give us evidence for the intermediate sites of wh-movement. Consider an example like (2):

(2)   Which book about herself did Jenny say that Anson had written?

For most speakers, (2) is perfectly grammatical. Go through a derivation of (2), showing at which point the reflexive rule has to apply, adopting the analysis we gave in the text where the wh-phrase stops off in the intermediate specifier of CP. Once you have done this, show why a derivation which moved the wh-phrase in one sweep, from its θ-position to the matrix specifier of CP, would predict (2) to be ungrammatical, contrary to fact.

Exercise 2 On categories that undergo wh-movement

Task 1 What do you think the category of the wh-phrase in (1) is, given the other examples? Justify your answer:

(1)   What did he reply?

(2)   He replied that he was happy.

(3)   *He replied his answer

Exercise 3 Relative clauses

In the chapter we looked at wh-movement in questions. We also find wh-movement in relative clauses. Relative clauses are clauses which can be used to modify nouns. We will assume that they are CPs attached at the nP level, just as other adjuncts are:

(1)

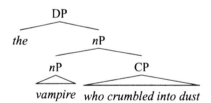

Here are some more examples.

(2)   The book [which Anson lent to Jenny]

(3)   The time [when you left me]

(4)   The place [where we lived for six years]

(5)   The vampire [who Mina loved]

Part A

Task 1 Provide an argument, on the basis of the c-selectional requirements of elements in the sentences above (where possible), that relative clauses which have a wh-word in them involve movement. You will have to make up the relevant sentences.

Part B

Task 2 We will assume that these relative clauses are just like wh-questions, except that their C which heads them bears an interpretable clause-type feature [Rel], rather than [Q]. This is why they are interpreted as relative modifiers rather than as questions. Given this assumption, draw trees for each of the DPs in the examples above, and specify whether [Rel] as a value of [*u*clause-type] on T is weak or strong.

Part C

Task 3 This approach predicts that relative clauses should occur long distance. Is this true? Make up some relevant examples.

Part D

As well as relative clauses with movement of a wh-expression, we also find relative clauses which contain just the complementizer *that*:

(6)   The book [that Anson lent to Jenny]

(7)   The time [that you left me]

(8)   The place [that we lived in for six years]

(9)   The vampire [that crumbled into dust]

Task 4 What problems arise in carrying over the analysis in Part A to these examples? Can you think of any ways around these problems?

Exercise 4 **Negative movement**

Task 1 The following sentences involve movement of a negative phrase. Some of them are only well formed in a rather high register of English. Compare these examples with parallel wh-movement examples, and hypothesize a derivation for each example:

(1)   Never will I do syntax again.

(2)   Nothing like that would I ever eat again.

(3)   Nobody (*did) put up with her.

Task 2 Once you have done this, look at the following example, and explain whether it is problematic for your approach, or whether it follows from it.

(4)   I swore that never again would I drink absinthe.

Exercise 5 **Trees**

Provide tree structures for the following sentences, with a commentary on how the checking of features works.

(1) Why did you say that you were leaving?

(2) I asked who John would introduce to who.

(3) Which book about Ulysses did you say that you would read?

(4) Who did you say that John thought would leave early?

(5) Who has drunk my whisky?

(6) Who seemed to have left first?

(7) Whose poem about Achilles did Homer persuade Jason that he should read?

(8) Who did Gilgamesh believe to have kissed Enkidu?

Exercise 6 **Binding again**

In previous exercises we have developed a number of generalizations about the binding of reflexives and pronouns. The Binding Generalizations we saw in Chapter 4 are repeated here:

(1) a. A reflexive must be bound.
     b. A pronoun cannot be bound.
     c. An R-expression cannot be bound.

We saw in Chapter 8, Exercise 10, that at least the condition on reflexives had to be further restricted, to rule out examples like (2):

(2) *Anson thought that himself was going to the club.

Let us hypothesize that the locality domain that is relevant to binding is the CP, so that the generalizations now read as follows:

(3) a. A reflexive must be bound to an antecedent in the same CP.
     b. A pronoun cannot be bound to an antecedent in the same CP.
     c. An R-expression cannot be bound.

Task 1 Use these new generalizations to discuss the binding possibilities for the pronouns and reflexives in the following sentences.

(4) *Dracula thought that himself was the Prince of Darkness

(5)   Dracula thought that he was the Prince of Darkness.

(6)   Dracula thought himself to be the Prince of Darkness.

(7)   Dracula thought him to be the Prince of Darkness.

(8)   He thought that Dracula was the Prince of Darkness.

Further reading

Section 9.1
The phenomenon of wh-movement received initial extended theoretical attention after the publication of Chomsky (1977), although there were important studies before this date as well (Baker 1970). Chomsky has repeatedly returned to this construction, and related ones (see Chomsky (1981), Chomsky (1982), Chomsky (1986a), and Chomsky and Lasnik (1993), and Chomsky (1995b)). See Emonds (1976) for a broad-ranging discussion of English wh-constructions.

Section 9.3
The approach we adopt here is influenced by Rizzi (1996), and especially by Chomsky (2000), although I have adapted ideas from these papers to fit in with the system we have been developing in the book.

Section 9.4
Subject questions in English have been a perpetual empirical thorn in the analytical side of wh-constructions. See Koopman (1983), Rizzi (1996), and Pesetsky and Torrego (2001) for different approaches.

Section 9.5
Chomsky argued for the idea that wh-movement took place in short steps as early as Chomsky (1973). This argument was made on the basis of unifying some of the locality effects on wh-movement we will talk about in the next chapter, and it wasn't until later that simple morphosyntactic evidence of the sort discussed in this section (and in the next chapter) became available. See May (1979) and Freidin (1978) for some discussion, and, more recently McCloskey (forthcoming) and Adger and Ramchand (2002).

Sections 9.6 and 9.7
The idea of superiority was first discussed by Chomsky (1973). See Pesetsky (1987) for discussion of the notion of D-linking.

Section 9.8

See Huang (1982) for an extended discussion of the syntax of wh-*in situ* languages, and Cheng (1991) and Richards (2001) for more recent theoretical discussion of parametric variation in wh-constructions, and see Rudin (1988) for an in-depth discussion of multiple wh-fronting languages.

10

Locality

10.1 Introduction

In this chapter we explore the behaviour of wh-movement yet further. We will see that, although wh-movement may, in certain circumstances, move a phrase to an apparently unbounded distance away from its launching site, this movement always involves a number of short **local** steps, rather than a single long leap. This idea builds on the observations we made about complementizer alternations in Gaelic in that last chapter. We will introduce the idea that a syntactic derivation takes place in small chunks, called **phases**, and see how this approach forces wh-movement to take place in small steps. We will then explore to what extent the notion of phase can explain some traditional constraints on wh-movement, usually called **island constraints**.

In the last chapter we posed the following question: does wh-movement across an intermediate clausal boundary take place in a single step, or in two (or more) steps? By wh-movement, here, we mean those steps of movement motivated by a strong wh-feature. This question, then, assumes that one of the following two representations is correct:

(1) [$_{CP}$ XP[wh] C[$u$wh*] ... V [$_{CP}$ ⟨XP[wh]⟩ C ... ⟨XP[wh]⟩   **local wh-movement**

(2) [$_{CP}$ XP[wh] C[$u$wh*] ... V [$_{CP}$ C ... ⟨XP[wh]⟩   **long wh-movement**

In (1), two steps of movement take place: the wh-XP first moves from some position inside the sentence (a position which itself could be a derived position such as the specifier of TP) to the specifier of the embedded CP, and then it moves into the specifier of the matrix CP. In (2), in contrast, the wh-XP simply moves from its position in the lower clause to the higher specifier of CP, 'skipping' the potential lower specifier of CP position.

We suggested in the last chapter that (1) was actually the correct approach, and we shall provide further evidence for this in this chapter. The standard terminology for a derivation that proceeds in this way is that it involves **successive cyclic** movement, since it successively cycles up through CPs in the derivation.

10.2 Empirical evidence for local movement

In this section we will look at three arguments which suggest that movement is successive cyclic: (i) the distribution of floating quantifiers in a dialect of English; (ii) the alternating complementizer phenomenon in Scottish Gaelic; (iii) inversion phenomena in Spanish. We will conclude from these arguments that wh-movement does indeed take place in successive cycles.

10.2.1 Floating quantifiers

The first piece of evidence we shall look at comes from a dialectal form of English spoken in West Ulster. In this dialect, the quantifier *all* can be attached to a wh-word as follows:

(3)   What all did you get for Christmas?

(4)   Who all did you meet when you were in Derry?

(5)   Where all did they go for their holidays?

Recall that we saw that some quantifiers could be **stranded** in English, and that we used this as an argument for the idea that subjects were Merged in a VP-internal position (Chapter 6, section 6.2.1). In West Ulster English, the *all* that attaches to a wh-word can also be stranded:

(6)   What did you get all for Xmas?

(7)   Who did you meet all when you were in Derry?

(8)   Where did they go all for their holidays?

This observation is as true of embedded questions as it is of matrix questions:

(9)   I don't remember [what all I said].

(10)   I don't remember [what I said all].

In order to capture this patterning of the data, we assume that the quantifier attaches to the wh-word, and that this constituent is Merged in its θ-position. Just as we saw with movement of subjects, it is possible to raise just the wh-phrase, stranding the quantifier. This means that an example like (6) will be derived with the following structure:

(11)

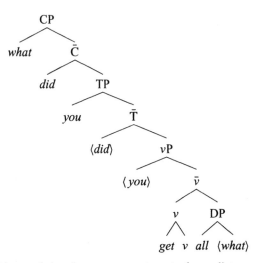

Now, with this much in place, we can turn to long-distance wh-extraction. Just as we expect, we can move the whole wh-phrase, as in (12), or strand the quantifier in its base position as in (13):

(12)   What all did he say [(that) he wanted]?

(13)   What did he say [(that) he wanted all]?

Now, if movement of the wh-phrase first targets the intermediate specifier of CP, then we would expect, all other things being equal, that it might also be possible to strand the quantifier in this intermediate specifier. This is exactly what we find:

(14)   What did he say [all (that) he wanted]?

(15)   Where do you think [all they'll want to visit]?

(16)   What do they claim [all that we did]?

Notice that we correctly predict that the quantifier precedes the complementizer *that*, rather than follows it:

(17)   *What did he say [that all he wanted]?

The basic structure looks as follows:

(18)   [$_{CP}$ *what* . . . [$_{CP}$ ⟨what⟩ all C [$_{TP}$ . . . ⟨what all⟩.

Note that none of these sentences can even be generated if movement takes place in one step, missing out the intermediate position, since there will be no structure built up at any point where *all* is in the intermediate specifier. This means that we have to either abandon our analysis of quantifier stranding, or abandon the claim that movement can take place in one step, skipping intermediate specifiers of CP.

This analysis predicts that the quantifier should also be able to be stranded in the specifier of a non-finite C. This is correct:

(19)   What were you trying all to say?

(20)   What did you mean all for me to do?

Once again, the stranded quantifier is found preceding the non-finite complementizer *for*, as we would expect if wh-movement always stops off in specifiers of CP.

What this argument shows is that we must at least allow wh-movement to take place in successive steps, via specifiers of CP, so that the 'one long swoop' approach cannot be the only approach. The behaviour of stranded quantifiers in West Ulster English does not show that the one long swoop approach is wrong, just that it is, at least, insufficient. The next argument we will look at, however, suggests that derivations with long swoop wh-movements should be ruled out.

10.2.2 Complementizer agreement again

In the last chapter we suggested that a special change in the form of the embedding complementizer that took place in Scottish Gaelic could be traced back to the claim that wh-movement must be successive cyclic. We will now make this argument a little stronger.

First, recall that sentences like the following, which have no wh-movement, have the embedding complementizer *gu(n)*:

(21)   Bha mi ag ràdh **gun** do bhuail i   e
           Was I   asp saying that prt struck she him
           "I was saying that she hit him."

(22)   Tha mi a' smaoineachadh **gu** bheil Iain air a   mhisg
           Am I   asp thinking   that is   Iain on his drink
           "I think that Iain is drunk."

We assume that the feature specification for *gu(n)* is just [C, finite].

Unlike in English, matrix wh-questions in Scottish Gaelic have an overt complementizer, *a*. This complementizer is not pronounced when the wh-word ends in a vowel, but otherwise it is. This can be clearly seen when we examine examples with a full wh-phrase which has undergone wh-movement. The complementizer is marked in bold:

(23)   Cò   an duine **a** tha thu a' pòsadh
       Who the man   C are you asp marrying
       "Which man are you marrying?"

(24)   Cò   a' chaileag **a** tha thu a' pògadh
       Who the girl   C are you asp kissing
       "Which girl are you kissing?"

In order to analyse these sentences, we need to propose that *a* has at least the specification [C, *u*wh*]. This is just like the corresponding English complementizer, except that it lacks a [Q] feature marking that it is to be interpreted as a question. The lack of the [Q] feature is simply because this same complementizer is used in cleft constructions and relatives, neither of which are questions. We put aside here the question of how wh-questions in Gaelic come to be interpreted as questions. Putting all this together, we have a structure for (23) roughly as in (25):

(25)

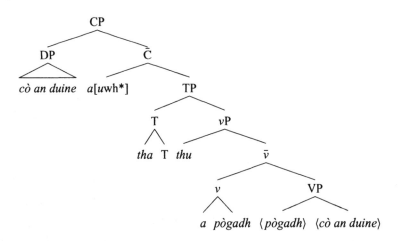

The feature specifications we have motivated for the two complementizers allow us to state the following generalization:

(26)   If the specifier of CP is filled with a wh-phrase, then the complemetizer *a* heads the CP; otherwise, the complementizer *gu* heads the CP.

Armed with this generalization, we now turn to wh-extraction from embedded clauses.

When a constituent from an embedded clause wh-moves into the matrix specifier of CP, then the complementizer *gu*, which would be expected to introduce the embedded clause, does not appear. Instead we find the complementizer *a* (with a concomitant change in the following verb form). The embedded *a* complementizer is marked with bold face:

(27) Cò an duine a bha thu ag ràdh **a** bhuail i
      Who the man   C were you asp saying that struck she
      "Which man were you saying that she hit?"

(28) Cò am bodach a tha thu a' smaoineachadh **a** tha air a mhisg
      Who the old-man that are you asp thinking   that is on his drink
      "Which old man do you think is drunk?"

Our generalization, to the extent that it embodies a correct analysis, immediately tells us that movement to the embedded specifier of CP must have taken place. So far, this is just like the West Ulster case discussed in the previous section. However, the Gaelic data make a stronger point, since the following sentences, where wh-movement has taken place but the complementizer *gu(n)* is used, are ungrammatical.

(29) *Cò an duine a bha thu ag ràdh **gun** do bhuail i
      Who the man   C were you asp saying that prt struck she
      "Which man were you saying that she hit?"

(30) *Cò am bodach a tha thu a' smaoineachadh **gu** bheil air a mhisg
      Who the old-man that are you asp thinking   that is on his drink
      "Which old man do you think is drunk?"

What this shows us is that stopping off in the specifier of the intermediate CP is not just an option, it is obligatory. Without this assumption, there would be no way of explaining why sentences like (29) and (30) are ungrammatical.

Notice that this argument is a little different from the argument based on quantifier floating. The latter is an empirical argument that there is some position available in long-distance wh-questions which provides a stop-off point for the wh-phrase; the West Ulster data do not rule out possible derivations which use the one long swoop movement, they merely show that this cannot be the only kind of derivation. The current argument from complementizer agreement, however, does rule out derivations where wh-movement takes place in one long swoop, since then we would have no way of ruling out the examples where the intermediate complementizer is *gu*.

10.2.3 Successive inversion phenomena

Another argument which works in the same way as the complementizer agreement argument comes from a phenomenon known as **subject inversion**, which can be found in Spanish. Spanish (and Italian) optionally allow the subject to appear after the verb phrase:

(31)   Maria contestó la pregunta
       Maria answered the question
       "Maria answered the question."

(32)   Contestó la pregunta Maria
       Answered the question Maria
       "Maria answered the question."

In wh-questions, this inversion is not optional. It must take place:

(33)   Qué querían esos dos?
       What wanted those two
       "What did those two want?"

(34)   *Qué esos dos querían?
       What those two wanted
       "What did those two want?"

We can then formulate the following generalization:

(35)   When a wh-word is in the specifier of CP, inversion is obligatory; otherwise, it is optional.

We can now use this generalization as a probe as to what happens in long-distance wh-questions. If the generalization is correct, and wh-movement stops off in intermediate specifiers of CP, then we would expect to see inversion in each clause through which the wh-element has been extracted. If, on the other hand, wh-movement takes place in one long swoop, then the intermediate clauses should be unaffected.

The data point in the direction of wh-movement by successive steps through intermediate specifiers of CP. Take first a sentence with multiple embedded clauses:

(36) Juan pensaba que Pedro le   había dicho que la revista había publicado
      Juan thought that Pedra to-him had   said that the journal had   published
      ya   el artículo.
      already the article.
      "Juan thought that Pedro had told him that the journal had published the article already."

In this declarative sentence, the subjects of the embedded clauses are *Pedro* and *la revista*, "the journal". These subjects precede their main verbs (respectively *le había dicho* and *había publicado ya el artículo*). If we wh-extract the most embedded object, *el artículo*, we find that subject inversion takes place in each intermediate clause:

(37) Qué pensaba Juan que le   había dicho Pedro que había publicado la
      What thought Juan that to-him had   said Pedro that had   published the
      revista?
      journal.
      "What did Juan think that Pedro had told him that the journal had published?"

In this example, not only does the subject (*Juan*) follow its verb (*pensaba*) in the main clause, but the embedded subject (*Pedro*) follows its verb (*dicho*) in the intermediate clause and the most embedded subject (*la revista*) also follows its verb. It is ungrammatical to wh-move the most embedded object without subject inversion taking place in each clause:

(38) *Qué pensaba Juan que Pedro le   había dicho que la revista había
      What thought Juan that Pedro to-him had   said that the journal had
      publicado?
      published

If our generalization is correct, then the derivation of (37) must involve a wh-phrase being in each intermediate specifier of CP, or else inversion would not be obligatory. The lack of inversion in (38) leads to ungrammaticality, and this means that a derivation where the wh-movement takes place in one long swoop must not be available.

Note that it is not necessary to know the exact mechanism which leads to subject inversion here. It is enough to see that obligatory subject inversion correlates with a filled specifier of CP, and to extrapolate from this to saying that in other contexts where subject inversion is obligatory, the specifier of CP must be filled.

This argument depends on the solidity of our generalization, and on its comprehensiveness. Of course, it could be true that there are completely independent reasons for the inversion of subjects in embedded clauses like those just discussed. However, no such reasons have so far been forthcoming.

Once again, we are led to the conclusion that wh-movement takes place through the specifiers of CP, and that it is not allowed to skip these specifiers.

10.3 Ensuring successive wh-movement

The last section went through a number of arguments which all pointed in the same direction: long-distance wh-movement does not take place in a single step; rather it takes place in a number of successive steps, each one targeting a specifier of CP. In this section we will try to organize our theory so as to capture this idea, and solve the Economy problem.

10.3.1 Locality in feature matching

Recall that wh-movement is triggered by the strength of an uninterpretable wh-feature on C. If we have a single clause, then this wh-feature can match another wh-feature on a constituent within that clause.

(39) $C[u\text{wh}^*] \ldots XP[\text{wh}]$

However, the arguments we went through in the last section show that the matching operation does not seem to be able to reach into a *lower* clause any further than that clause's specifier. If the matching operation could do this, then it would be difficult to rule out long movement of the wh-expression. If, however, the matching operation can only see as far as the specifier of a lower CP, then, if there is some way of ensuring movement of a wh-expression to that lower specifier, we can force movement to take place in local steps.

Putting this another way, it is as though the complement of any C is invisible to the feature-matching operation, so that the higher F in (40) will never be checked:

(40)   C[uF] ... [_CP_ C [_TP_ ... XP[F] ...

However, if we were to move XP[F] to the specifier of CP, then the feature-matching operation takes place:

(41)   C[u̶F̶] ... [_CP_ XP[F] C [_TP_ ... ⟨XP[F]⟩ ...

Let us state this hypothesis explicitly:

(42)   Feature checking under c-command reaches no further than the specifier of any embedded CP.

However, this idea on its own is not enough to ensure success. Assumption (42) will rule out a derivation which moves a wh-element in a lower clause to a higher one, skipping the intermediate specifier of CP, but it will not, on its own, force anything to move into that intermediate specifier.

We can accomplish this second task by assuming that Scottish Gaelic, and other languages which overtly mark the intermediate position, are actually the languages which are wearing their syntactic feature specifications on their morphological sleeves. Just as we assume that DPs in English bear an abstract case feature (that is, a case feature with no phonological realization), we will assume that English embedding Cs may optionally bear an abstract [uwh*] feature. Unlike in Scottish Gaelic, this extra feature is not morphologically marked.

(43)   Embedded C may optionally bear [uwh*].

We will treat (43) as a principle of UG. As it stands it entails that every language has two (relevant) Cs: one bearing [uwh*], and one not. Some languages may spell out these two Cs differently (as Scottish Gaelic does), and some languages may not (English), but there is always a choice between these two different functional heads.

Putting these two ideas together, we can now force wh-movement to take place. Let us see how.

Imagine that we have built up a CP, which has embedded inside it a wh-XP:

(44)   C ... XP[wh]

If we were to embed this CP under a verb, which itself is (eventually) contained within a CP headed by C[uwh*], then, since feature checking can't see any further than the specifier of the next C down, we will never be able to match the wh-features. This derivation will therefore crash.

However, if we take the option of using the C bearing [*u*wh*] in the embedded clause, then this feature can match with the wh-feature on the XP, and since it is strong, it enforces locality, driving movement of the wh-XP into the specifier of the lower CP:

(45)   XP[wh] C[~~*u*wh*~~] . . . ⟨XP[wh]⟩.

From this position, the wh-XP is accessible for feature matching, and therefore can check the (strong) uninterpretable wh-feature on the higher C. This forces wh-movement to take place in successive steps.

The idea that the feature-matching operation is local is usually generalized from just CPs. We will see in section 10.4 that DPs behave in the same way, and that PPs also seem to do so, at least in certain languages. We call the categories that give rise to this behaviour **phases**, and rephrase our feature-matching generalization as follows:

(46)   Feature matching reaches no further than the specifier of an embedded phase.

We will call this generalization the **Phase Impenetrability Constraint** (PIC).

Chomsky has argued that this notion of phase can be derived from the general structure of derivations, essentially by enforcing derivations to have short memories: they forget about material inside embedded phases. We will not go into this idea in any depth here, but instead explore how the notion of phases can be used to give an account of various restrictions on movement.

10.3.2 Solving an old puzzle

In Chapter 8, section 8.2.6, we looked at raising verbs and noted a puzzle, which we have not yet addressed. The puzzle arose in structures like the following:

(47)

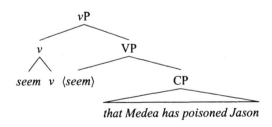

that Medea has poisoned Jason

In this structure we have built a finite clause *that Medea has poisoned Jason* and embedded it under the raising verb *seem*. If we then merge T[uD^*, nom], as usual, we need to check its EPP feature and [nom] case. On the assumption that feature matching can apply between the [nom] feature on T, and that on *Medea*, and that the EPP feature of T and the D feature of *Medea* match, we should be able to raise Medea into the matrix subject position:

(48)   *Medea seemed that has poisoned Jason

However, given the PIC, (48) is immediately ruled out. Since *Medea* is not a wh-phrase, it does not move into the specifier of the lower CP, and so it is never accessible to check the EPP feature of the matrix T. This means that there is no way of deriving (48) from (49):

(49)   [$_{TP}$ T[uD^*] seemed [$_{CP}$ (that) Medea[D, ~~nom~~] has poisoned Jason.

Of course, this now raises a new version of the same problem. We know that wh-phrases do move into the specifier of intermediate CPs, so we now have to ask the question of why the following is ungrammatical:

(50)   *Who seemed (that) had poisoned Jason?

For this sentence, it seems that the following derivation should be possible:

(51)

1. Build TP [$_{TP}$ *who poisoned Jason*].
2. Merge C[$u$wh*] and raise *who* to its specifier giving: [$_{CP}$ *who*[D, wh, ~~nom~~] C[~~$u$wh*~~] . . .].
3. Merge *seem*, *v* and T[uD^*, nom].
4. Match EPP and case features on T and D feature on *who*, raising who to the matrix specifier of TP. This gives:
   [$_{TP}$ who[D, wh,~~nom~~] T[~~uD^*, nom~~] seemed [$_{CP}$ ⟨who⟩ (that) ⟨who⟩ had poisoned Jason.]
5. Merge matrix C, and raise *who* to its specifier.

The only unusual aspect of this derivation is the movement of *who* from the specifier of CP to the specifier of TP. So far, all of the cases of wh-movement we have seen move to the specifier of CP. The traditional term within Generative Grammar for movements which proceed from the specifier of CP to some other kind of position is **improper movement**. We will capture improper movement with the following stipulation; its deeper explanation is a matter for current theoretical debate:

(52)   Improper Movement Restriction
Only wh-features are visible in the specifier of CP.

This condition will rule out the illegitimate step in our derivation, since the EPP feature of T will be unable to match with the D feature of *who* in the specifier of CP. Of course, if *who* stays in the specifier of TP, then it is too far away for feature matching to take place.

The Improper Movement Restriction is mysterious, as it stands. We'd like to be able to derive it from some deeper properties of our theory. However, it will suffice for our purposes here.

10.4 Island phenomena

In this section we will investigate a number of other locality effects that relate to wh-movement. The first effect we will look at involves cases with multiple wh-phrases. We will first recap on our analysis of these, and then look at some of the consequences that the theory we have developed in this chapter has for this analysis.

10.4.1 Wh-islands

In Chapter 9 we examined cases where we had more than one wh-phrase in a sentence. When this happens, the highest wh-phrase raises to the matrix specifier of CP:

(53)   Who C ⟨who⟩ T ... ⟨who⟩ saw what?

We argued that the lower wh-phrase did not move because the feature-matching operation targets the closest wh-phrase, thus ruling out examples like (54) (putting aside D-linking effects):

(54)   *What did who ⟨did⟩ ... ⟨who⟩ see ⟨what⟩?

This same effect appears in embedded clauses:

(55)   I asked who saw what.

(56)   *I asked what who saw?

Now, notice that the system we have developed previously in this chapter makes the prediction that, if some wh-phrase has been moved to the specifier of an embedded C, then it will be impossible to move the more deeply embedded wh-phrase any higher. The relevant configuration looks roughly as follows:

(57)   ... V [$_{CP}$ XP1[wh] ... XP2[wh] ...]

Only XP1 is available to be moved into the matrix specifier of CP. This is for two reasons: first, the matrix C will attract the closest wh-phrase, and second, the embedded wh-phrase (XP2) is not in the specifier of the CP phase. We therefore rule out examples like the following via the PIC:

(58)   *What did you ask who saw ⟨what⟩?

Exactly the same argument holds for examples with ditransitives:

(59)   I asked who Medea gave what?

(60)   *What did you ask who Medea gave ⟨what⟩?

Our system, then, derives the following generalization:

(61)   It is impossible to move a wh-phrase out of a CP with another wh-phrase in its specifier.

This generalization is an old one in the Generative Grammar literature (see the Further reading section) and it is commonly known as the **Wh-Island Constraint**. The terminology is based on the idea that a wh-expression contained in a CP which itself has a wh-expression in its specifier is 'cut off' from the higher clause: it can't get off the island that it is on. The word **island** is a useful descriptive term to describe a constituent which is impervious to wh-movement. Notice that this is not the same as a phase. The term phase is a theoretical term used for constituents which have the property that only their specifier is accessible for feature matching; the word 'island' is just used to describe a constituent which, descriptively, it is impossible to wh-move out of, but it does not, itself, tell us why.

We can see the island effect more strikingly if we use D-linked wh-expressions. With non-D-linked wh-phrases it is often unclear whether the ungrammaticality of the example is due to superiority or to the wh-island effect.

Recall that D-linked wh-expressions escape the superiority effect, so that a low wh-expression can raise over a higher one. This means that both of the following embedded wh-expressions are well formed:

(62)   I asked which king invaded which city.

(63)   I asked which city which king invaded.

The second example shows that it is possible to void superiority, and raise the lower wh-phrase into the embedded specifier. This means that, before the embedded CP is Merged with its selecting verb we have the following structure:

(64)   [$_{CP}$ which city C[$uwh*$] [$_{TP}$ which king invaded ⟨which city⟩]]

This predicts that it should be possible to raise the object wh-phrase further since it is in the specifier of the embedded phase. The following example shows that this prediction appears to be correct:

(65)   ?Which city did you ask which king invaded?

This example is, for most speakers, slightly degraded, but it contrasts dramatically with examples where we try to move the embedded wh-subject:

(66)   *Which king did you ask which city invaded?

This sentence only has the irrelevant (and pragmatically bizarre) interpretation where a city invaded a king. It is completely ungrammatical on the same interpretation as (63). Our theory predicts this, since the embedded subject is not in the specifier of the CP phase. Note that we can't put down the ungrammaticality of (66) to superiority, since the wh-subject DP is D-linked.

Before we leave wh-islands, notice that our theory predicts that the following sentences should be well formed:

(67)   Who did you ask saw what?

(68)   Which king did you wonder invaded which city?

In both of these examples we have raised the embedded subject to the embedded specifier of CP, and from there into the matrix specifier of CP, with no violation of PIC. Again, these examples are a little difficult to parse, but contrast dramatically with the wh-island violations we saw above.

We have seen, then, that a traditional observation about how wh-movement is constrained (the wh-island constraint) can be captured by adopting the PIC.

10.4.2 DP islands

Another set of island phenomena involve DPs.

Consider the following examples:

(69)   I believed [$_{DP}$ the claim [$_{CP}$ that Philip would invade the city of Athens]].

(70)   *Which city do you believe [$_{DP}$ the claim [$_{CP}$ that Philip would invade]]?

In (69), the noun *claim* takes a CP complement. Example (70) shows the result of wh-moving the object of the verb inside that CP complement. The question is why (70) is ungrammatical. Given what we have said so far, it should be possible to move the wh-object into the specifier of the complement CP, and from there, it should be accessible to the Matrix C[$u$wh*].

The following examples are similar:

(71)   Plato listened to [$_{DP}$ Demosthenes' oration [$_{PP}$ about Philip]].

(72)   *Who did Plato listen to [$_{DP}$ Demosthenes' oration [$_{PP}$ about]]?

In this case, there isn't even an embedded CP boundary. Finally, we have the following examples:

(73)   Phaedo was interested in [$_{DP}$ Plato's description [$_{DP[of]}$ of geometry]].

(74)   *What was Phaedo interested in [$_{DP}$ Plato's description [$_{DP[of]}$ of]]?

In each of these three cases we have some XP serving as the argument of a noun: CP, PP, and DP[of], respectively. Each example with wh-movement is far less well formed than we would expect on the basis of the theory we have built up so far. Traditionally, these cases are termed **Complex Noun Phrase Islands**, although the term is a little out of date, since we would usually assume that what we are dealing with here are full DPs rather than NPs.

We can capture this effect by assuming that DPs as well as CPs are phases. This assumption will have the consequence that any wh-expression inside a DP will be inaccessible for Matching with a [$u$wh*] C which is Merged later in the derivation. Recall that, under the PIC, except for its specifier, anything in a phasal category is inaccessible for matching. None of the cases we looked at above involved a wh-expression as the specifier of DP, and so wh-movement is correctly predicted to be impossible in each case.

To see this, take the CP complement case.

(75)   *Which city do you believe [$_{DP}$ the claim [$_{CP}$ that Philip would invade]]?

This sentence would have to be derived by first Merging *which city* with the verb *invade*. We would then build up the remainder of the CP *the claim that Philip would invade which city* and, in order to get the wh-expression to its specifier, we would choose C[*u*wh*]. This would give us the following structure:

(76)   [*CP* which city that[~~*u*wh*~~] [*TP* Philip would invade ⟨which city⟩]]

This CP then Merges with *claim* and the remainder of the DP is built up and Merged with the verb *believe*. Once the rest of the matrix CP has been constructed, a C[Q, *u*wh*, nom] is Merged. This gives us the following structure, after raising of T:

(77)   [*CP* [*do* C[Q, *u*wh*]] you believe [*DP* the claim [*CP* which city that[~~*u*wh*~~] [*TP* Philip would invade ⟨which city⟩]]

At this point in the derivation, it is impossible to match the uninterpretable wh-feature of matrix C with the wh-expression in the specifier of the embedded C. This is because of the assumption that DP is a phase, combined with the PIC.

One might imagine that it might be possible to instantiate a [*u*wh*] feature on D, thus triggering movement of a wh-expression to the specifier of DP. To make this idea more concrete, take our example of wh-movement from a CP complement of a noun:

(78)   *Which city do you believe the claim that Philip would invade?

To derive this we would have to move *which city* from its Merged position to the specifier of the complement CP, and then, once the DP has been built up, to the specifier of the DP. This gives us an intermediate structure something like the following:

(79)   [which city] the claim that Philip would invade.

Even to get as far as this, we have to assume that the determiner *the* is able to host [*u*wh*]. But this seems to be incorrect. We do not find DP-internal wh-movement inside DPs headed by *the*.

(80)   *Which god the statue

(81)   *How fierce the battle

This suggests that the determiner *the*, in English, cannot host [*u*wh*]. The same seems to be true of all the other definite determiners, including the zero determiner that case checks genitive possessors. These all give rise to the island effect:

(82)   *Which poem did you hear Homer's recital of last night?

(83)   *Which poem did you hear those recitals of last night?

What about other determiners than *the*? Take, for example, the singular indefinite determiner:

(84)   Which poem did you go to hear a recital of last night?

(85)   Who did you get an accurate description of?

(86)   Who did you hear an oration about?

In general, it seems that definite DPs are islands, but indefinite ones are not. The question is, why this should be.

There are two prima facie possibilities: (i) phasehood depends on definiteness of D; (ii) indefinite Ds allow a wh-specifier (that is, just like C, they can be optionally specified with a [*u*wh*] feature).

One reason to pursue the second possibility is that we do actually find DP-internal wh-movement, and it appears to be restricted to indefinite DPs:

(87)   A fierce battle $\sim$ How fierce a battle.

(88)   The fierce battle $\sim$ *How fierce the battle.

However, this DP-internal movement does not seem to apply to arguments of nouns:

(89)   An oration about Philip $\sim$ *Who an oration about

We will leave the answer to the question open here, and assume that it is just definite DPs that are phases.

10.4.3 Subject islands

A third kind of island discussed in the literature is the **subject island**. Take the following two sentences which contain the adjective *obvious* which takes a single CP argument:

(90)   That Plato loved Aster was obvious.

(91)   It was obvious that Plato loved Aster.

It is possible to wh-move the object of *love* in (91) but not in (90):

(92)   Who was it obvious that Plato loved?

(93)   *Who was that Plato loved obvious?

This effect also obtains when we have a CP subject of a verb:

(94)   That Plato loved Aster seemed to be known by everyone.

(95)   *Who did that Plato loved seem to be known by everyone

(96)   That Plato loved Aster proved to be his undoing.

(97)   *Who did that Plato loved prove to be his undoing

In general, it is impossible to wh-move the object of a CP subject. In fact, we can make this claim rather more general, since it is impossible to extract anything from a CP subject. The following pairs show extraction of a subject, a prepositional object, and a manner adverbial, respectively:

(98)   a.   That Plato loved Aster was obvious.
       b.   *Who was that loved Aster obvious

(99)   a.   That Plato lived in the city of Athens was well known.
       b.   *Which city was that Plato lived in well known

(100) a.   That Plato loved Aster deeply was obvious.
       b.   *How deeply was that Plato loved Aster obvious

The generalization here is that subject clauses are islands:

(101) **The Sentential Subject Island Constraint**
       Nothing can be moved out of a clausal subject.

Wh-movement from a non-initial CP argument of *seem* is correctly predicted by our system. For example, the sentence in (91) is easily derived by first building up the CP argument, wh-moving *who* to its specifier by opting for C[*u*wh*], and then Merging the result with the adjective *obvious*:

(102)

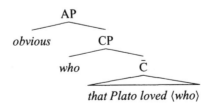

If we were to continue this derivation by Merging in the verb *be* and an expletive in the subject position, then we could extract *who* to the specifier of the matrix CP, giving the well-formed (103):

(103)   Who was it obvious that Plato loved?

Let's now look at the two possible analyses of sentential subjects: they were in the specifier of TP, or they were base adjoined to TP, with a null pronominal in the specifier of TP.

On the former analysis, the subject island facts are mysterious. Let us see how the derivation would continue were we to move the CP argument of *obvious* into the specifier of TP:

(104)   [*TP* [who that Plato loved] was obvious]

It is now possible to Merge C[Q, *u*wh*] with this TP, raising the auxiliary to satisfy the strength of the clause-type value on T. It is then possible to raise *who*, which is in the specifier of the subject CP, and hence is in the specifier of the relevant phase, into the specifier of the matrix CP in order to satisfy the strong wh-feature on C:

(105)

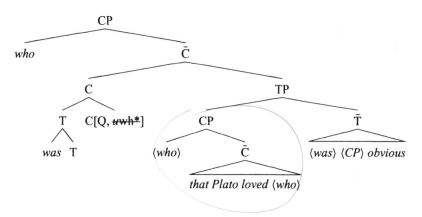

The derivation converges, with all the uninterpretable features checked, yet the sentence is completely ungrammatical.

However, if we adopt our alternative story, we are in a better position. Under this analysis, the clausal subject is in the specifier of a special CP, and the specifier of TP is filled by a null pronominal:

(106)

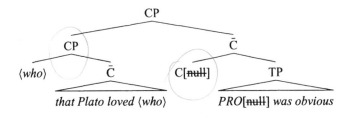

It is impossible to make this into a wh-question as it stands, since the specifier of CP is already filled by the clausal subject. It is also impossible to embed this structure yet further, since the special C involved is only legitimate in matrix clauses.

It seems, then, that we can derive the Sentential Subject Island facts from our independently motivated approach to clausal subjects, surely a good thing.

However, the sentential subject facts are actually part of a more general property of subjects. In fact, it seems to be impossible to extract from subjects in general:

(107)   a.   A programme about Euripides is on Radio 4 tonight.
           b.   *Who is a programme about on Radio 4 tonight?

Remember that it is possible to extract from an indefinite DP, like *a programme about Euripides*. We can see this if we construct this sentence with an expletive in the subject position:

(108)   a.   There is a programme about Euripides on Radio 4 tonight?
           b.   Who is there a programme about on Radio 4 tonight?

What this contrast shows us is that extraction from an element in the specifier of TP is degraded.

One approach to this problem has been to appeal to the fact that subjects are not in surface positions where they are *selected* or *assigned a θ-role* by their head. The specifier of TP is a non-θ position, unlike the specifier of *v*P, or the complement position.

With the distinction between θ and non-θ positions in mind, we can then state the following constraint:

(109)   The specifier of a phase is only visible to feature matching if the phase is in a position where it is selected by a θ-assigning head.

Let us see how this constraint on feature matching will work. First, take a simple sentence where wh-movement is legitimate:

(110)   Who is it obvious that Plato loves?

This sentence is generated by first constructing the embedded CP and wh-moving the wh-expression *who* to its specifier. This CP then Merges with the adjective *obvious* which assigns a θ-role to it. We then build the remainder of the sentence, and since the embedded CP is in a position where it is selected by a θ-assigning head, its specifier is visible, allowing wh-movement of *who* to take place.

(111)

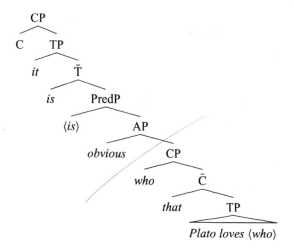

Now consider a point in the derivation where, instead of Merging an expletive *it*, we move the embedded CP into the specifier of TP.

(112)

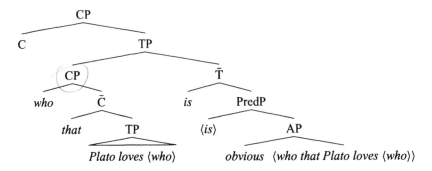

Now this CP is not in a position where it is selected by a θ-assigning head, since T does not assign a θ-role. This means that the specifier of the phase is not visible for feature matching, and the derivation crashes, since the wh-feature of the matrix C cannot be checked. The same approach will predict ungrammaticality of extraction from a normal DP subject in the specifier of TP, correctly deriving the contrast we noted above:

(113)   a.   A description of Aristotle is in the book.
         b.   *Who is a description of in the book?

(114)   a.   There is a description of Aristotle in the book.
         b.   Who is there a description of in the book?

Of course, if the approach to clausal subjects which assumed that they were in the specifier of a special CP is correct, then extraction from this CP is now ruled out by both the condition on phases being in θ-positions, and the special syntax of these constructions. What we have here is some **redundancy** in our theory, since completely different theoretical principles rule out the same structures. Redundancy in a theory is obviously not ideal, since we want theories to be minimal, in the way discussed in Chapter 1. However, we will live with it here.

Our theory now contains three different constraints pertaining to locality of wh-movement:

(115)

    1. Feature matching reaches no further than the specifier of an embedded phase (PIC).

2. The specifier of a phase is only visible to feature matching if the phase is in a position where it is selected by a θ-assigning head.

3. Only wh-features are visible in the specifier of CP (Improper Movement).

10.4.4 Adjunct islands

The final case of island phenomena that we will look at is **Adjunct Islands**. We already met various CPs which appear in adjunct positions in Section 8.3. Here are examples of temporal, causal, and conditional clausal adjuncts:

(116)   Hephaestus had run away, before the executioner murdered Hera.

(117)   Hephaestus had run away, because the executioner murdered Hera.

(118)   Hephaestus would run away, if the executioner murdered Hera.

Note that, in each case, it is impossible to wh-move anything out of the adjunct clause, showing that these are islands.

(119)   *Who had Hephaestus run away, before the executioner murdered ⟨Hera⟩?

(120)   *Who had Hephaestus run away, because the executioner murdered ⟨Hera⟩?

(121)   *Who would Hephaestus run away, if the executioner murdered ⟨Hera⟩?

Our theory, as it stands, already predicts the ungrammaticality of these examples, since adjuncts are never in a position where they are θ-marked by a selecting head. This means that, even if the complementizers which introduce these clauses can have an optional [$u$wh*] specification, any wh-phrase in their specifiers will be invisible to the matrix C.

10.5 Summary

In this final chapter, we have looked at how the wh-movement operation is constrained beyond the usual intervention effect on Agree. We first motivated the idea that wh-movement took place successive cyclically, using data from dialectal English, Scottish Gaelic, and Spanish. What these data showed was that wh-movement was **forced** to proceed from the specifier of one CP to the specifier of another.

We captured this theoretically with two ideas: Agree sees no further than the specifier of the next lowest CP, and Cs optionally may bear a strong [*u*wh*] feature:

(122)   Feature checking under c-command reaches no further than the specifier of any embedded CP.

(123)   Embedded C may optionally bear [*u*wh*].

We assumed that these are invariant principles of UG.

This approach allowed us to solve a problem that we had left open in Chapter 8, which is how to rule out raising of the subject of a finite CP into a higher clause containing a raising verb. We proposed that this was ruled out by (122), but saw how this then raised a new problem: how to rule out a lower wh-expression raising into the subject of a raising verb. We appealed to a general principle of improper movement to rule this out:

(124)   **Improper Movement Restriction**
         Only wh-features are visible in the specifier of CP.

Finally, we turned to other cases where wh-movement was illegitimate, and argued that these could be captured by generalizing the idea that feature matching could see no further than the specifier of an embedded CP. We introduced the notion of phase, and argued that feature matching could see no further than the specifier of an embedded phase. We called this principle the Phase Impenetrability Constraint (PIC):

(125)   **Phase Impenetrability Constraint**
         Feature checking under c-command reaches no further than the specifier of any embedded phase.

This allowed us to unify two island constraints, capturing why it is impossible to wh-move out of wh-islands or out of certain DPs. We extended this approach to subjects and adjunct islands by further requiring that a phase had to be in a θ-position for it to be accessible to feature Matching:

(126)   A phase must be in a θ-position if its specifier is to be accessible for feature matching.

We have captured the various facts as follows:

Phenomenon	Explanation
The successive cyclicity of wh-movement	PIC and optional [$u$wh*] on C
DP islands and wh-islands	PIC
Subject islands and adjunct islands	Phases must be in a θ-position for Agree

It's fairly obvious that the theory we have developed in this chapter is much more embryonic than those in previous parts of the book. We have essentially stipulated the results we have achieved here, rather than constructing the system so that the results fall out from more abstract properties. Ideally, we would like the architecture of our theory to give us the results that we have stipulated via the PIC, the Improper Movement Constraint, and the condition that phases must be in θ-positions for their specifiers to be accessible for feature matching. However, we have at least motivated the PIC via arguments for successive cyclicity, and then found that it independently gave the right results for wh-islands and (some) DP-islands.

Aside from these theoretical considerations, we have only scratched the surface of the incredibly complex question of the empirical base of island effects (how much is due to parsing, and how much to syntax), and, unlike in previous chapters, we have not even touched on the subtle and intriguing variation that we find in island constraints cross-linguistically. Clearly, there's a lot of work still to do.

Exercises

Exercise 1 Long-distance wh-movement

Provide tree structures for the following sentences, showing all steps of movement:

(1) Who asked which statue which tourist had taken a photo of?

(2) Who did you persuade to go?

(3) Who did you attempt to force Jason to kill?

(4) Which poisonous plant is it certain that we will find in Amazonia?

(5) Who seems to be certain to leave first?

Exercise 2 **Islands**

Explain why each of the following examples is ungrammatical, making reference to phases where relevant.

(1) *Who did a statue of surprise Medea?

(2) *Which temple did Athena contemplate the reason that her devotees had built?

(3) *Who did you believe that to kiss seemed wrong?

(4) *Who was for Medea to poison awful?

(5) *Where did you disappear before you hid the gold?

Exercise 3 **Topicalization**

We have mentioned a movement operation called **topicalization** in our discussion of constituency tests. This exercise is about whether topicalization has the same kinds of properties as wh-movement. A simple case of topicalization looks as follows:

(1) Medea, Jason poisoned.

Assume that topicalization is driven by a feature [top], and that [$u$top*] may be optionally instantiated on C.

Task 1 Construct four sentences to show whether topicalization is subject to the wh-island constraint.

Task 2 Construct four sentences to show whether topicalization is subject to the DP-island constraint. Ensure that you check whether the definite/indefinite contrast discussed in the text appears.

Task 3 Construct four sentences to show whether topicalization is subject to the subject-island constraint.

Task 4 Construct four sentences to show whether topicalization is subject to the adjunct-island constraint.

Task 5 Given that (2) is ungrammatical, reformulate the Improper Movement Restriction so that it captures topicalization too:

(2)   *Medea seems (that) has poisoned Jason.

Exercise 4 Tough movement

English has a construction traditionally termed **tough-movement**. Some examples are given below:

(1)   a.   It is tough to teach syntax.
      b.   Syntax is tough to teach.

(2)   a.   It is easy to slay the Gorgon.
      b.   The Gorgon is easy to slay.

The adjectives *tough* and *easy* seem to assign just one θ-role to a clausal argument, as can be seen from the (a) examples. However, it is possible to apparently move an argument inside that selected clause to the matrix specifier of TP, as in the (b) examples.

   Just like wh-movement, tough-movement seems to be able to operate over unbounded distances:

(3)   Syntax is easy to pretend that you can teach.

Task 1 Provide five other adjectives that work in the same way as *tough*.

Task 2 Interestingly, tough-movement appears to be subject to island constraints, as (4) shows for a DP island. Provide examples which show that tough-movement is subject to the other island constraints. Make sure that you check the judgements with native speakers.

(4)   *The Gorgon is easy to believe the claim that Perseus slew.

Task 3 Given that tough-movement both is able to take place long distance and is subject to island constraints, it must, under the theory we have developed, be movement that proceeds from the specifier of one CP to the specifier of another. Given this, explain why it seems to violate the improper movement restriction, and provide a derivation for a simple case of tough movement.

Exercise 5 **Light verb constructions**

Task 1 The following examples appear to be problematic for our claim that DPs are phases. Explain why.

(1) a. We made the claim that Perseus killed the Gorgon.
     b. Who did you make the claim that Perseus killed?

(2) a. I had the strangest feeling that I knew you.
     b. Who did you have the strangest feeling that you knew?

(3) a. I have every hope that you will defeat him.
     b. Who do you have every hope that you will defeat?

The nouns that behave in this way seem to have a semantic commonality with simple verbal constructions:

(4) We claimed that Perseus had killed the Gorgon.

(5) I felt that I knew you.

(6) I hoped that you would defeat him.

Task 2 Make up other examples, and try to see if this generalization holds.

Exercise 6 **Comparative deletion**

The following sentences display what is known as **comparative deletion**.

(1) Mary is faster than John is.

(2) Medea poisoned more children than Jason did.

Task 1 Provide examples which show that comparative deletion can take place long distance (that is, over an indefinite number of clausal boundaries).

Task 2 Show that comparative deletion is subject to island effects.

Task 3 Sketch an analysis for comparative deletion.

Exercise 7 **So-XP movement**

Task 1 What do you think is going on in sentences like the following:

(1) So quickly did the vampire move, that we barely saw him.

Task 2 Show that this movement is can be long distance.

Task 3 Show that it obeys island constraints.

Task 4 Sketch an analysis for So-XP movement.

Exercise 8 Co-ordination

Task 1 Provide examples to test whether co-ordinate structures, such as (1), are islands.

(1)   Willow said that she'd kiss Tara and kick Xander.

Is there any way to extend our approach to islands to these structures?

Task 2 Is the following sentence problematic for how you categorized co-ordinate structures in Part A?

(2)   Who did Maria say that she'd kiss and kick?

Exercise 9 Clefts

Do clefts obey the island constraints?

Exercise 10 Relativization

As well as involving wh-movement, relative clauses can be constructed with no apparent wh-phrase:

(1)   The poem that Homer wrote.

(2)   The shield that saved Achilles' life.

(3)   The book that I said that I'd never read.

Now, since PIC constrains feature matching, and since it is movement which allows the relevant features to be carried up the tree, it follows that if these relatives are sensitive to islands, then they will involve movement.

Task 1 Show that relativization of this sort is sensitive to island conditions.

Task 2 Assume that the θ-role of the 'gap' in the relative clause is assigned to a caseless null pronoun bearing a [Rel] feature (essentially, a sort of null operator). Provide a derivation for the relative clauses above.

Exercise 11 French ECM

French does not allow ECM of the English type:

(1)   *Je crois   Georges être   le meilleur
       I   believe George to-be the best

But it does allow PRO in these clauses:

(2)   Je crois   PRO être le meilleur
       I   believe PRO to-be the best
       "I believe myself to be the best."

Task 1 Recall the analysis we proposed for English ECM. Can you posit a single difference which will explain the contrast between the two languages? (Hint: think of the selectional properties of *believe* proposed to capture ECM in English.)
    The following sentence is fine in French:

(3)   Qui crois-tu   être le meilleur
       Who think-you to be the best
       "Who do you believe to be the best?"

Task 2 Explain why this is unexpected.

Task 3 Now construct a derivation for (3) and try to explain why (3) is well formed.

Further reading

Section 10.2

The idea that wh-movement is local stems from Chomsky (1973) and the extension of this analysis to other constructions is taken up in Chomsky (1977). The data from West Ulster English are from McCloskey (2000). For a discussion of complementizer alternation effects in Irish, see McCloskey (1990) and McCloskey (forthcoming), and for more on Scottish Gaelic see Adger and Ramchand (2002). The Spanish inversion facts are discussed by Torrego (1984) among others.

Section 10.3

The proposal that successive cyclicity is forced by the interaction between PIC and optional features on C is developed in Chomsky (2000) and Chomsky

(2001*b*). For improper movement, see the (admitttedly technical) discussion in Chomsky (1981), pp. 200 ff.

Section 10.4

The classic reference for island effects is Ross (1967). For more up-to-date approaches to dealing with locality effects in wh-movement see Chomsky (1986*a*), Rizzi (1990), Cinque (1990), Manzini (1992). The last of these has an excellent first chapter outlining various approaches to the problem of the locality of wh-movement.

Bibliography

ABNEY, S. P., 1987, 'The English noun phrase in its sentential aspect', Ph.D. thesis. MIT, Cambridge, MA.

ADGER, DAVID, and QUER, JOSEP, 2001, 'The syntax and semantics of Unselected Embedded Questions', *Language* 77: 107–33.

ADGER, DAVID, and RAMCHAND, GILLIAN, 2002, 'Phases and interpretability'. In K. Megerdoomain and L. A. Bar-el, eds, *Proceedings of the West Coast Conference on Formal Linguistics (WCCFL) 20*, 1–14. Somerville, MA: Cascadilla Press.

ALEXIADOU, ARTEMIS, 1997, *Adverb Placement. A Case Study in Antisymmetric Syntax.* Amsterdam: Benjamins.

ALEXIADOU, ARTEMIS, 2001, 'Adjective syntax and noun raising: Word order asymmetries in the DP as a result of adjective distributions', *Studia Linguistica* 55: 217–48.

ALEXIADOU, ARTEMIS, and WILDER, CHRIS, eds, 1998, *Possessors, Predicates and Movement in the DP*. Amsterdam: Benjamins.

ANDERSON, STEPHEN, 1992, *A-morphous Morphology*. Cambridge: Cambridge University Press.

ATKINSON, MARTIN, 1992, *Children's Syntax*. Oxford: Blackwell.

BACH, EMMON, 1964, *Syntactic Theory*. Lanham, MD: University Press of America.

BAKER, L. CARL, 1970, 'Notes on the description of English questions: the role of an abstract question morpheme', *Foundations of Language* 6: 197–219.

BAKER, L. CARL, 1981, 'Auxiliary-adverb word order', *Linguistic Inquiry* 12: 309–15.

BAKER, MARK, 1988, *Incorporation: a Theory of Grammatical Function Changing*. Chicago: University of Chicago Press.

BAKER, MARK, 1996, 'On the structural position of Themes and Goals'. In Johan Rooryck and Laurie Zaring, eds, *Phrase Structure and the Lexicon*, 7–34. Dordrecht: Kluwer.

BAKER, MARK, JOHNSON, KYLE, AND ROBERTS, IAN, 1989, 'Passive arguments raised', *Linguistic Inquiry* 20: 219–51.

BARKER, CHRIS, 1991, 'Possessive descriptions', Ph.D. thesis. UCSC.

BARSS, ANDREW, and LASNIK, HOWARD, 1986, 'A note on anaphora and double objects', *Linguistic Inquiry* 17: 347–54.

BELLETTI, ADRIANA, 1988, 'The case of unaccusatives', *Linguistic Inquiry* 19: 1–33.

BESTEN, HANS DEN, 1983, 'On the interaction of root transformations and lexical deletive rules'. In Werner Abraham, ed., *On the Formal Syntax of the Westgermania*, 47–131. Amsterdam: John Benjamins.

BLOOMFIELD, LEONARD, 1933, *Language*. New York: Holt.

BOAS, FRANTZ, 1911, *Handbook of American Indian Languages*. Washington: US Government Printing Office.

BOBALJIK, JONATHAN, 1998, 'Floating quantifiers: Handle with care', *GLOT International* 3.

BOBALJIK, JONATHAN, and JONAS, DIANE, 1996, 'Subjects positions and the roles of TP', *Linguistic Inquiry* 27: 195–236.

BORER, HAGIT, 1999, 'Deconstructing the construct'. In Kyle Johnson and Ian Roberts, eds, *Beyond Principles and Parameters*. Dordrecht: Kluwer.

BORER, HAGIT, 2002, 'The exoskeletal trilogy', manuscript. University of Southern California, CA.

BORER, HAGIT, and GRODZINSKY, YOSEF, 1986, 'Syntactic cliticization and lexical cliticization: The case of Hebrew dative clitics'. In Hagit Borer, ed., *The Syntax of Pronominal Clitics*. San Diego: Academic Press.

BRESNAN, JOAN, 1970, 'On complementizers: toward a syntactic theory of complement types', *Foundations of Language* 6: 297–321.

BRESNAN, JOAN, 2001, *Lexical-Functional Syntax*. Oxford: Blackwell.

BROWN, R., 1973, *A First Language: the Early Stages*. Cambridge, MA: Harvard University Press.

BURZIO, LUIGI, 1986, *Italian Syntax. A Government-Binding Approach*. Hingham, MA: Kluwer.

CARDINALETTI, ANNA, and STARKE, MICHAL, 1999, 'The typology of structural deficiency: a case study of the three grammatical classes'. In Henk van Riemsdijk, ed., *Clitics in the Languages of Europe*, 145–233. Berlin: Mouton de Gruyter.

CHENG, LISA LAI-SHEN, 1991, 'On the typology of wh-questions', Ph.D. thesis. MIT, Cambridge, MA.

CHOMSKY, NOAM, 1957, *Syntactic Structures*. The Hague: Mouton.

CHOMSKY, NOAM, 1965, *Aspects of the Theory of Syntax*. Cambridge, MA: MIT Press.

CHOMSKY, NOAM, 1970, 'Remarks on nominalization'. In R. A. Jacobs and P. S. Rosenbaum, eds, *Readings in English Transformational Grammar*. Waltham, MA: Ginn-Blaisdell.

CHOMSKY, NOAM, 1973, 'Conditions on transformations'. In Stephen Anderson and Paul Kiparsky, eds, *A Festschrift for Morris Halle*. New York: Holt, Rinehart, and Winston.

CHOMSKY, NOAM, 1977, 'On *wh*-movement'. In P. Culicover, T. Wasow, and A. Akmajian, eds, *Formal Syntax*, 71–132. New York: Academic Press.

CHOMSKY, NOAM, 1980, 'On binding', *Linguistic Inquiry* 11: 1–46.

CHOMSKY, NOAM, 1981, *Lectures on Government and Binding*. Dordrecht: Foris.

CHOMSKY, NOAM, 1982, *Some Concepts and Consequences of the Theory of Government and Binding*. Cambridge, MA: MIT Press.

CHOMSKY, NOAM, 1986a, *Barriers*. Cambridge, MA: MIT Press.

CHOMSKY, NOAM, 1986b, *Knowledge of Language*. New York: Praeger Publications.

CHOMSKY, NOAM, 1993, 'A minimalist program for linguistic theory'. In Kenneth Hale and Samuel Keyser, eds, *The View from Building 20*, 1–52, Cambridge, MA: MIT Press.

CHOMSKY, NOAM, 1995*a*, 'Language and nature', *Mind* 104: 1–61.

CHOMSKY, NOAM, 1995*b*, *The Minimalist Program*. Cambridge, MA: MIT Press.

CHOMSKY, NOAM, 2000, 'Minimalist inquiries: the framework'. In R. Martin, D. Michaels, and Juan Uriagereka, eds, *Step by Step: Essays on Minimalist syntax in honour of Howard Lasnik*, 89–115. Cambridge, MA: MIT Press.

CHOMSKY, NOAM, 2001*a*, 'Beyond explanatory adequacy', manuscript. MIT, Cambridge, MA.

CHOMSKY, NOAM, 2001*b*, 'Derivation by phase'. In Michael Kenstowicz, ed., *Ken Hale: a Life in Language*, 1–52. Cambridge, MA: MIT Press.

CHOMSKY, NOAM, and HALLE, MORRIS, 1968, *The Sound Pattern of English*. New York: Harper & Row.

CHOMSKY, NOAM, and LASNIK, HOWARD, 1993, 'The theory of principles and parameters'. In J. Jacobs, A. von Stechow, W. Sternefeld, and T. Vennemann, eds, *Syntax: an International Handbook of Contemporary Research*, 506–69. Berlin: de Gruyter.

CINQUE, GUGLIELMO, 1990, *Types of Ā-dependencies*. Cambridge, MA: MIT Press.

CINQUE, GUGLIELMO, 1994, 'On the evidence for partial N-movement in the Romance DP', in G. Cinque *et al.*, eds, *Paths towards Universal Grammer*, 85–110. Washington, DC: Georgetown University Press.

CINQUE, GUGLIELMO, 1996, 'The Antisymmetric programme: Theoretical and typological implications', *Journal of Linguistics* 32: 447–64.

CINQUE, GUGLIELMO, 1999, *The Syntax of Adverbs*. Oxford: Oxford University Press.

COMRIE, BERNARD, 1976, *Aspect*. Cambridge: Cambridge University Press.

COMRIE, BERNARD, 1985, *Tense*. Cambridge: Cambridge University Press.

CORBETT, GREVILLE, 1991, *Gender*. Cambridge: Cambridge University Press.

CORBETT, GREVILLE, 2000, *Number*. Cambridge: Cambridge University Press.

CORBETT, GREVILLE, FRASER, N., and McGLASHAN, S., 1993, *Heads in Grammatical Theory*. Cambridge: Cambridge University Press.

COSTA, JOAO, 1996, 'Adverb positioning and V-movement in English', *Studia Linguistica* 50: 22–34.

CRAIN, STEPHEN, and LILLO-MARTIN, DIANE, 1999, *An Introduction to Linguistic Theory and Language Acquisition*. Oxford: Blackwell.

CRAIN, STEPHEN, and NAKAYAMA, M., 1987, 'Structure dependence in grammar formation', *Language* 63: 522–43.

CRUSE, ALAN, 2000, *Meaning in Language*. Oxford: Oxford University Press.

DALRYMPLE, MARY, and KAPLAN, RONALD, 2000, 'Feature indeterminacy and feature resolution', *Language* 76: 759–98.

DE SWART, HENRIETTE, 1998, *Introduction to Natural Language Semantics*. Stanford: CSLI.

DE VILLIERS, J., and DE VILLIERS, P., 1985, 'The acquisition of English'. In Dan Sobin, ed., *The Crosslinguistic Study of Language Acquisition (Vol. 1)*, 27–139, Hillsdale, NJ: Lawrence Erlbaum Associates.

DOUGHERTY, R., 1970, 'A grammar of coordinate conjoined structures', *Language* 46: 850–98.

DOWTY, DAVID, 1991, 'Thematic proto-roles and argument selection', *Language* 67: 547–619.

DUFFIELD, NIGEL, 1996, 'On structural invariance and lexical diversity in VSO languages: Arguments from Irish noun phrases'. In Ian Roberts and Robert Borsley, eds, *The Syntax of the Celtic Languages*, 314–40. Cambridge: Cambridge University Press.

EMONDS, JOE, 1976, *A Transformational Approach to English Syntax: Root, Structure-Preserving and Local Transformation*. New York: Academic Press.

EMONDS, JOE, 1978, 'The verbal complex V'–V in French', *Linguistic Inquiry* 9: 151–75.

FEYNMAN, RICHARD, 1965, *The Character of Physical Law*. Cambridge, MA: MIT Press.

FILLMORE, C., 1968, 'The case for case'. In C. Bach and R. Harms, eds, *Universals in Linguistic Theory*, 1–81. New York: Holt, Rhinehart and Winston.

FRAZIER, LYNN, 1987, 'Sentence processing: a tutorial review'. In M. Coltheart, ed., *Attention and Performance XII: The Psychology of Reading*, 559–86. London: Lawrence Earlbaum.

FREIDIN, ROBERT, 1975, 'The analysis of passives', *Language* 51: 384–405.

FREIDIN, ROBERT, 1978, 'Cyclicity and the theory of grammar', *Linguistic Inquiry* 9: 519–49.

FREIDIN, ROBERT, and VERGNAUD, JEAN-ROGER, 2001, 'Exquisite connections: some remarks on the evolution of linguistic theory', *Lingua* 111: 639–67.

GESCHWIND, N., 1974, *Selected Papers on Language and the Brain*. Dordrecht: Reidel.

GIORGI, ALESSANDRA, and LONGOBARDI, GIUSEPPE, 1991, *The Syntax of Noun Phrases. Configuration, Parameters, and Empty Categories*. Cambridge: Cambridge University Press.

GOPNIK, MYRA, and CRAGO, M., 1991, 'Familial aggregation of a developmental language disorder'. *Cognition* 39: 1–50.

GOPNIK, MYRA, DALALAKIS, JENNY, FUKUDA, SUZY, AND FUKUDA, SHINJI, 1997, 'Familial language impairment'. In Myra Gopnik, ed., *The Inheritance and Innateness of Grammars*, 111–40. New York: Oxford University Press.

GREENBERG, JOSEPH H., 1966, *Language Universals, with Special Reference to Feature Hierarchies*. The Hague: Mouton.

GRIMSHAW, JANE, 1979, 'Complement selection and the lexicon', *Linguistic Inquiry* 10: 279–326.

GRIMSHAW, JANE, 1981, 'Form, function and the language acquisition device'. In Charles L. Baker and John McCarthy, eds, *The Logical Problem of Language Acquisition*. Cambridge, MA: MIT Press.

GRIMSHAW, JANE, 1990, *Argument Structure*. Cambridge, MA: MIT Press.

GRODZINSKY, Y., 1990, *Theoretical Perspectives on Language Deficits*. Cambridge, MA: MIT Press.

GRUBER, J., 1965, 'Studies in lexical relations', Ph.D. thesis. MIT.

GUILFOYLE, EITHNE, HUNG, HENRIETTA, and TRAVIS, LISA, 1992, 'Spec of IP and spec of VP: Two subjects in Austronesian languages', *Natural Language and Linguistic Theory* 10: 375–414.

HAEGEMAN, LILIANE, 1991, *Introduction to Government and Binding Theory*. Oxford: Blackwell.

HAEGEMAN, LILIANE, 1997, 'Elements of grammar'. In *Elements of Grammar: Handbook of Generative Syntax*. Dordrecht: Kluwer Academic Publishers.

HAEGEMAN, LILIANE, and GUÉRON, JACQUELINE, 1999, *English Grammar*. Oxford: Blackwell.

HALLE, MORRIS, and MARANTZ, ALEC, 1993, 'Distributed morphology and the pieces of inflection'. In Ken Hale and Samuel Jay Keyser, eds, *The View from Building 20*, 111–76. Cambridge, MA: MIT Press.

HARLEY, HEIDI, and RITTER, ELIZABETH, 2001, 'Meaning in morphology: Motivating a feature-geometric analysis of person and number', University of Arizona. **www.arizona.edu/~ling/hh/PDFs/Papers.html**.

HARRIS, ZELLIG, 1951, *Methods in Structural Linguistics*. Chicago: University of Chicago Press.

HEIM, IRENE, 1982, 'The semantics of definite and indefinite noun phrases', Ph.D. thesis. University of Massachusetts at Amherst.

HEIM, IRENE, and KRATZER, ANGELIKA, 1998, *Semantics in Generative Grammar*. Oxford: Blackwell.

HORNSTEIN, NORBERT, 1999, 'Movement and control', *Linguistic Inquiry* 30: 69–96.

HORNSTEIN, NORBERT, and LIGHTFOOT, DAVID, 1981, *Explanation in Linguistics*. London: Longman.

HUANG, JAMES, 1982, 'Logical relations in Chinese and the theory of grammar', Ph.D. thesis. MIT, Cambridge, MA.

IATRIDOU, SABINE, 1990, 'About AgrP', *Linguistic Inquiry* 21: 551–77.

JACKENDOFF, RAY, 1977, $\overline{X}$-*Syntax*. Cambridge, MA: MIT Press.

JACKENDOFF, RAY, 1987, 'The status of thematic relations in linguistic theory', *Linguistic Inquiry* 18: 369–411.

JACKENDOFF, RAY, 1990, 'On Larson's treatment of the double object construction', *Linguistic Inquiry* 21: 427–55.

JAEGGLI, OSVALDO, 1986, 'Passive', *Linguistic Inquiry* 17: 587–633.

JENKINS, LYLE, 2000, *Biolinguistics: Exploring the Biology of Language*. Cambridge: Cambridge University Press.

JOHNSON, KYLE, 1991, 'Object positions', *Natural Language and Linguistic Theory* 9: 577–636.

KAYNE, RICHARD, 1984, *Connectedness and Binary Branching*. Dordrecht: Foris.

KAYNE, RICHARD, 1994, *The Antisymmetry of Syntax*. Cambridge, MA: MIT Press.

KAYNE, RICHARD, 2000, *Parameters and Universals*. Oxford: Oxford University Press.

KEMPSON, RUTH, 1977, *Semantic Theory*. Cambridge: Cambridge University Press.

KOIZUMI, MASATOSHI, 1993, 'Object agreement phrases and the split VP hypothesis', *MIT Working Papers in Linguistics* 18: 99–148.

KOOPMAN, HILDA, 1983, 'ECP effects in main clauses', *Linguistic Inquiry* 14: 346–50.

KOOPMAN, HILDA, 1984, *The Syntax of Verbs. From Verb Movement Rules in the Kru Languages to Universal Grammar*. Studies in Generative Grammar 15. Dordrecht: Foris.

KOOPMAN, HILDA, and SPORTICHE, DOMINIQUE, 1991, 'The position of subjects', *Lingua* 85: 211–85.

KOSTER, JAN, 1978, 'Why subject sentences don't exist'. In S. Jay Keyser, ed., *Recent Transformational Studies on European Languages*, 53–64. Cambridge, MA: MIT Press.

KOSTER, JAN, 1984, 'On binding and control', *Linguistic Inquiry* 5: 417–59.

KRATZER, ANGELIKA, 1996, 'Severing the external argument from its verb'. In Johan Rooryck and Laurie Zaring, eds, *Phrase Structure and the Lexicons*, 109–38. Dordrecht: Kluwer.

LAI, CECILIA S. L., FISHER, SIMON E., HURST, JANE A., VARGHA-KHADEM, FARANEH, and MONACO, ANTHONY P., 2001, 'A forkhead domain gene is mutated in a severe speech and language disorder', *Nature* 413: 519–23.

LARSON, RICHARD, 1987, 'On the double object construction', *Linguistic Inquiry* 19: 33–91.

LARSON, RICHARD, 1990, 'Double objects revisited: a reply to Jackendoff', *Linguistic Inquiry* 21: 589–632.

LARSON, RICHARD, LAHIRI, UTPAL, IATRIDOU, SABINE, and HIGGINBOTHAM, JAMES, 1992, *Control and Grammar*. Dordrecht: Kluwer.

LASNIK, HOWARD, 1992, 'Case and expletives: Notes towards a parametric account', *Linguistic Inquiry* 23: 381–405.

LASNIK, HOWARD, 1995, 'Verbal morphology: *Syntactic Structures* meets the Minimalist Program'. In H. Campos and P. Kempchinsky, eds, *Evolution and Revolution in Linguistic Theory*, 251–75. Georgetown, DC: Georgetown University Press.

LASNIK, HOWARD, 2000, *Syntactic Structures Revisited*. Cambridge, MA: MIT Press.

LASNIK, HOWARD, 2001, 'Subjects, objects and the EPP'. In William Davies and Stanley Dubinsky, eds, *Objects and other Subjects*, 103–21. Dordrecht: Kluwer.

LASNIK, HOWARD, and SAITO, MAMORU, 1991, 'On the subject of infinitives'. In L. Dobrin *et al.*, ed., *Paper from the 27th Meeting of the Chicago Linguistics Society*, 324–43.

LEGATE, JULIE, and YANG, CHARLES, 2002, 'Empirical re-assessment of stimulus poverty arguments', *The Linguistic Review* 19: 151–62.

LEMMON, E., 1966, 'Sentences, statements and propositions'. In B. Willliams and A. Montefiore, eds, *British Analytical Philosophy*, 87–107. London: Routledge and Kegan Paul.

LEVIN, BETH, and RAPPAPORT-HOVAV, MALKA, 1995, *Unaccusativity: At the Syntax-Lexical Semantics Interface*. Cambridge, MA: MIT Press.

LONGOBARDI, GIUSEPPE, 1994, 'Proper names and the theory of N-movement in syntax and logical form', *Linguistic Inquiry* 25: 609–65.

LYONS, CHRIS, 1997, *Definiteness*. Cambridge: Cambridge University Press.

LYONS, JOHN, 1968, *Theoretical Linguistics*. Cambridge: Cambridge University Press.

LYONS, JOHN, 1977, *Semantics*. Cambridge: Cambridge University Press.

MANZINI, RITA, 1992, *Locality: a Theory and its Consequences*. Cambridge, MA: MIT Press.

MANZINI, RITA, and ROUSSOU, ANNA, 2000, 'A Minimalist theory of A-movement and control', *Lingua* 110: 409–47.

MARCUS, G. F., 1993, 'Negative evidence in language acquisition', *Cognition* 46: 53–85.

MATTHEWS, PETER, 1974, *Morphology*. Cambridge: Cambridge University Press.

MAY, ROBERT, 1979, 'Must COMP to COMP movement be stipulated?', *Linguistic Inquiry* 10: 719–25.

MCCLOSKEY, JAMES, 1990, 'Resumptive pronouns, A-bar binding and levels of representation in Irish'. In Randal Hendrick, ed., *The Syntax of the Modern Celtic Languages: Syntax and Semantics 23*. New York: Academic Press.

McCloskey, James, 1991, 'Clause Structure, ellipsis and proper government in Irish', *Lingua* 85: 259–302.

MCCLOSKEY, JAMES, 1996, 'On the scope of verb movement in Irish', *Natural Language and Linguistic Theory* 14: 47–104.

MCCLOSKEY, JAMES, 1997, 'Subjecthood and subject positions'. In Liliane Haegeman, ed., *Elements of Grammar: Handbook of Generative Syntax*, 197–235. Dordrecht: Kluwer Academic Publishers.

MCCLOSKEY, JAMES, 2000, 'Quantifier float and *wh*-movement in an Irish English', *Linguistic Inquiry* 31: 57–84.

MCCLOSKEY, JAMES, forthcoming, 'Resumption, successive cyclicity, and the locality of operations'. In *Prospects for Derivational Explanation*, Oxford.

MILSARK, GARRY, 1974, 'Existential sentences in English', Ph.D. thesis. MIT, Cambridge, MA.

MUYSKEN, PIETER, AND VAN RIEMSDIJK, HENK, 1986, *Features and Projections*. Dordrecht: Foris.

NAKAJIMA, HEIZO, 1996, 'Complementizer selection', *Linguistic Review* 13: 143–64.

OUHALLA, JAMAL, 1991, *Functional Categories and Parametric Variation*. London: Routledge.

OUHALLA, JAMAL, 1998, *Introduction to Transformational Grammar*. London: Arnold.

PAOLI, SANDRA, 1997, 'Agreement: a relational property or a functional projection? Evidence from past participle agreement in Friulian', Master's thesis. University of York.

PERLMUTTER, DAVID, 1978, 'Impersonal passives and the unaccusative hypothesis'. In *Proceedings of the Fifth Meeting of the Berkeley Linguistics Society*, UC Berkeley.

PESETSKY, DAVID, 1987, '*Wh*-in-situ: Movement and unselective binding'. In Eric Reuland and Alice ter Meulen, eds, *The Representation of (In)Definiteness*, 98–129. Cambridge, MA: MIT Press.

PESETSKY, DAVID, 1995, *Zero Syntax: Experiencers and Cascades*. Cambridge, MA: MIT Press.

PESETSKY, DAVID, and TORREGO, ESTHER, 2001, 'T to C movement: causes and consequences'. In Michael Kenstowicz, ed., *Ken Hale: a Life in Language*, 355–426. Cambridge, MA: MIT Press.

PINKER, STEVEN, 1984, *Language Learnability and Language Development*. Cambridge, MA: Harvard University Press.

PINKER, STEVEN, 1994, *The Language Instinct*. London: Penguin.

POLLARD, CARL, and SAG, IVAN, 1994, *Head Driven Phrase Structure Grammar*. Stanford: CSLI.

POLLOCK, JEAN-YVES, 1989, 'Verb movement, Universal Grammar and the structure of IP', *Linguistic Inquiry* 20: 365–424.

POSTAL, PAUL, 1974, *On Raising*. Cambridge, MA: MIT Press.

POSTAL, PAUL, 1986, *Studies of Passive Clauses*. Albany, NY: SUNY Press.

RACKOWSKI, ANDREA, and TRAVIS, LISA, 2000, 'V-initial languages: X or XP movement and adverbial placement'. In Andrew Carnie and Eithne Guilfoyle, eds, *The Syntax of Verb Initial Languages*, 117–41. New York: Oxford University Press.

RADFORD, ANDREW, 1981, *Transformational Syntax*. Cambridge: Cambridge University Press.

REINHART, TANYA, 1976, 'The syntactic domain of anaphora', Ph.D. thesis. MIT, Cambridge, MA.

REULAND, ERIC, and TER MEULEN, ALICE, eds, 1987, *The Representation of (In)Definiteness*. Cambridge, MA: MIT Press.

RICHARDS, NORVIN, 2001, *Movement in Language: Interactions and Architectures*. Oxford: Oxford University Press.

RITTER, ELIZABETH, 1991, 'Two functional categories in noun phrases: evidence from modern Hebrew'. In Susan Rothstein, ed., *Syntax and Semantics 26*, 37–62. New York: Academic Press.

RITTER, ELIZABETH, 1993, 'Where's gender', *Linguistic Inquiry* 24: 795–803.

RIVERO, MARIA-LOUISA, 1992, 'Adverb incorporation and the syntax of adverbs in Modern Greek', *Linguistics and Philosophy* 15: 289–331.

RIZZI, LUIGI, 1990, *Relativized Minimality*. Cambridge, MA: MIT Press.

RIZZI, LUIGI, 1996, 'Residual verb second and the wh-criterion'. In Adriana Belletti and Luigi Rizzi, eds, *Parameters and Functional Heads*. New York: Oxford University Press.

RIZZI, LUIGI, 1997, 'The fine structure of the left periphery'. In Liliane Haegeman, ed., *Elements of Grammar: Handbook of Generative Syntax*. Dordrecht: Kluwer.

ROBERTS, IAN, 1985, 'Agreement parameters and the development of English auxiliaries', *Natural Language and Linguistic Theory* 3: 21–58.

ROBERTS, IAN, 1996, *Comparative Syntax*. London: Arnold.

ROBERTS, IAN, 2001, 'Head movement'. In Mark Baltin and Chris Collins, eds, *The Handbook of Contemporary Syntactic Theory*, 113–47. Oxford: Blackwells.

ROBERTS, IAN, and ROUSSOU, ANNA, 2002. 'The Extended Projection Principle as a condition on the Tense dependency'. In Peter Svenonius, ed., *Subjects, Expletives and the EPP*, 125–55. Oxford: Oxford University Press.

ROSS, JOHN ROBERT, 1967, 'Constraints on variables in syntax', Ph.D. thesis. MIT, Cambridge, MA.

ROUVERET, ALAIN, 1991, 'Functional categories and agreement', *Linguistic Review* 8: 353–87.

ROUVERET, ALAIN, and VERGNAUD, JEAN-ROGER, 1980, 'Specifying reference to the subject: French causatives and conditions on representations', *Linguistic Inquiry* 11: 97–202.

RUDIN, CATHERINE, 1988, 'On multiple questions and multiple wh-fronting', *Natural Language and Linguistic Theory* 6: 445–501.

SAEED, JOHN, 1997, *Semantics*. Oxford: Blackwell.

SAFIR, KEN, 1985, *Syntactic Chains*. Cambridge: Cambridge University Press.

SAFIR, KEN, 1987, 'What explains the Definiteness Effect'. In Eric Reuland and Alice ter Meulen, eds, *The Representation of (In)Definiteness*. Cambridge, MA: MIT Press.

SHIEBER, STUART, 1986, *An Introduction to Unification-Based Approaches to Grammar*. Stanford: CSLI.

SPENCER, ANDREW, and ZWICKY, ARNOLD, 1998, *The Handbook of Morphology*. Oxford: Blackwell.

SPORTICHE, DOMINIQUE, 1988, 'A theory of floating quantifiers and its corollaries for constituent structure', *Linguistic Inquiry* 19: 425–49.

STOWELL, TIM, 1981, 'Origins of phrase structure', Ph.D. thesis. MIT, Cambridge, MA.

STROIK, THOMAS, 1990, 'Adverbs as V sisters', *Linguistic Inquiry* 21: 654–61.

SVENONIUS, PETER, 1993, 'The structural location of attributive adjectives'. In Donka Farkas E. Duncan and P. Spaelti, eds, *Proceedings of WCCFL 12*, 438–54.

SZABOLCSI, ANNA, 1983, 'The possessor that ran away from home', *Linguistic Review* 3: 89–102.

SZABOLCSI, ANNA, 1994, 'The noun phrase'. In Franz Kiefer and Katalin Kiss, eds, *The Syntactic Structure of Hungarian*, 179–274. San Diego: Academic Press.

TALLERMAN, MAGGIE, 1999, *Understanding Syntax*. London: Arnold.

TOMBLIN, J. BRUCE, and BUCKWALTER, P., 1998, 'Heritability of poor language achievement among twins', *Journal of Speech, Language and Hearing Research* 41: 188–99.

TORREGO, ESTHER, 1984, 'On inversion in Spanish and some of its effects', *Linguistic Inquiry* 15: 103–30.

TRAVIS, LISA, 1984, 'Parameters and effects of word order variation', Ph.D. thesis. MIT, Cambridge, MA.

TRAVIS, LISA, 1988, 'The syntax of adverbs'. In Denise Fekete and Zofia Laubitz, eds, *McGill Working Papers in Linguistics/Cahiers linguistiques de McGill*, 280–310.

VALOIS, DANIEL, 1991, 'Internal syntax of DP', Ph.D. thesis. UCLA.

VIKNER, STEN, 1995, *Verb Movement and Expletive Subjects in the Germanic Languages*. New York: Oxford University Press.

WELLS, R., 1947, 'Immediate constituent analysis', *Language* 23: 81–117.

WILKINS, WENDY, 1988, *Syntax and Semantics 21: Thematic Relations*. New York: Academic Press.

ZAENEN, ANNIE, MALING, JOAN, and THRÁINSSON, HOSKULDUR, 1985, 'Case and grammatical functions: the Icelandic passive', *Natural Language and Linguistic Theory* 3: 441–83.

ZWART, JAN WOUTER, 1993, 'Dutch syntax. A minimalist approach', Ph.D. thesis. Rijksuniversiteit Groningen.

Index

Printed and bound by CPI Group (UK) Ltd, Croydon, CR0 4YY